STARTING YOUR CAREER AS A
GRAPHIC
DESIGNER

STARTING YOUR CAREER AS A GRAPHIC DESIGNER

MICHAEL FLEISHMAN

ALLWORTH PRESS
NEW YORK

Allworth Press books may be purchased in bulk at special discounts for sales promotion, corporate gifts, fund-raising, or educational purposes. Special editions can also be created to specifications. For details, contact the Special Sales Department, Allworth Press, 307 West 36th Street, 11th Floor, New York, NY 10018 or info@skyhorsepublishing.com.

15 14 13 12 11   5 4 3 2 1

Published by Allworth Press, an imprint of Skyhorse Publishing, Inc.
307 West 36th Street, 11th Floor, New York, NY 10018.

Allworth Press® is a registered trademark of Skyhorse Publishing, Inc.®, a Delaware corporation.

www.allworth.com

Cover and interior design by Michael Fleishman

Chapter title illustrations Copyright © 2014 Michael Fleishman

LIBRARY OF CONGRESS CATALOGING-IN-PUBLICATION DATA IS AVAILABLE ON FILE.

ISBN: 978-1-62153-398-6

Ebook ISBN: 978-1-62153-412-9

Printed in the United States of America

It's been one helluva year. Gimme da pie first.

TABLE OF CONTENTS

ACKNOWLEDGMENTS

First and above all: to my wife, Joanne Caputo. Next, to my sons, Cooper and Max, plus the two floor managers, Tilly and Simon. Words may fail me here, but my heart does not, because family is what counts—especially when you absolutely, positively have to get your book written overnight.

From here, a big thank-you to all the good folks who added their unique insights, wisdom, and seasoned commentary—your invaluable input was far more than appreciated. Some contributors were generously there from *go, team, go*: Ken Bullock, Kristine Putt, and Kelly White. Julie Buschur, Lara Kisielewska, Antonio Rodrigues, Ellen Shapiro, and Vickie Vandeventer. Ty Cooper, Rigie Fernandez, Mega, and Allan Wood. All yinz guys from Pittsburgh—hey, Kennywood's open. A shout out to Deborah Budd, Gerald D. Vinci, and Rebecca Hemstad; Ilise Benun, Neal Pemberton, Maria Piscopo, and Brad Reed; Alison Miyauchi, Al Wasco, and C.J. Yeh; Roger Starnes and Joy Ring (badda bing!). A chunky note of gratitude goes out to: Jane Baker, Ed Davis, Cathy Essinger, Norton Gusky, Elizabeth Lutz, and Jamie Sharp—where were you wonderful editors all my literary life?

To my esteemed colleagues, valued counselors, and dear friends (particularly Ellen and Ven Adkins, Phyllis and Ron Schmidt, Doc Pete, Neil Silvert, and Tom Verdon, Nancy Lee Cooper and Maureen Dawn): I am deeply indebted to you for your comic timing, gracious help, solid guidance, and unstinting support.

Finally, my great thanks to Thornwell May and Tad Crawford, along with all the crew at Allworth and Skyhorse (and to all the folks who contributed to the first edition of this book).

◫ INTRODUCTION

There have been incredible changes in the profession since this book first appeared as two separate volumes for another publisher. Fire up the Wayback Machine, Mr. Peabody, to see just when those titles were combined to create the grand update as then offered by Allworth Press.

And since that second go-round, there has been an epic interaction of art and technology, plus a radical morphing of communications and marketing through the rise of social media. This has resulted in modern (and extraordinary) delivery systems squarely slamming the globe into your backyard. The thud of that shock wave has forever rocked both design and illustration and, not coincidentally, rolled that second incarnation back to the future of two volumes again.

Starting Your Career as a Graphic Designer and its sister volume, *Starting Your Career as an Illustrator*, address the common challenges facing those who want to move up, out, or on. You might be a beginner—long on talent but short on experience—or perhaps you're a burgeoning professional just getting out of school. You could be on staff and interested in branching off, or you simply want to explore a new arena.

Wherever you are on the continuum, I wanted to keep this updated volume as realistic and honest as the original, but now even more pertinent and absolutely up to date. Toward that goal, I adapted (and folded in) some particularly relevant content from my book *How to Grow as an Illustrator*.

There has been a gale storm of changes as previously mentioned, but to paraphrase Ward Schumaker from an earlier interview, those who gracefully lean into those winds will do quite well. Schumaker, whose work has appeared in numerous publications worldwide, remarked that there is no such thing as thinking locally, and I agree, now more than ever. The technology that has made this possible was only hinted at in the very first editions of this work. It is simply business as usual now and continues to evolve.

Throughout the years, some lessons remain constant. Of course, what you know is key. Great chops construct the shark tank of talent you must demonstrate every day, on every job. It still matters who you know—in any business climate, military-grade networking is important. As Schumaker says, "We must use each other to compare techniques, talk business and finances, to join in solidarity, we must be there for our colleagues."

Another insight, as master marketer Roger Brucker will tell you: diversify, diversify, diversify. To paraphrase Elwood Smith, changes in the industry have opened the gates to other venues and fresh disciplines that mark whole new opportunities for creative growth. Award-winning and internationally respected, Smith says, "The Muse is guiding me into areas I never dreamed of. I am inspired to move into other areas of creative activity that I've been meaning to investigate (but previously too busy to do)."

This *Starting Your Career* . . . is still liberally salted and generously stacked with studio-smart tips plus nuts-and-bolts information from designers up and down the ladder. It answers some basic questions including:

- ◪ How to find jobs and analyze what market is right for you
- ◪ Ways to stay ahead of the competition and pick up new business
- ◪ How to get noticed
- ◪ How to network and get referrals

—and much more.

The new *Starting Your Career* . . . presents a positive yet practical look at biz, process, and product. And this update, like the earlier editions of the book, offers the same well-rounded, personal perspective from men and women who've been there (and seen that, and done that, too). Hopefully, it's obvious; but if not, all contributors quoted in this book without an introduction are either designers or illustrators, unless otherwise noted in the text.

So hey, enough schmoozing already—let's get started. Forward!

SECTION I
STARTING OUT

CHAPTER 1

SO YOU WANT TO BE A DESIGNER?

A beginner should have an image in mind of what he or she would like to be in ten years, and then never waver from that.

—Fred Carlson

Be realistic; not too dogmatic; set goals and benchmarks, but stay flexible in your approach.

—Allan Wood

BY DEFINITION

A graphic designer orchestrates type and visuals to communicate, sell, provoke a response, inform, or educate a mass audience. Bob Bingenheimer defines it this way: "Graphic designers are professionals trained in communications problem-solving through the use of typography, symbols, and images; they are schooled in information technologies. Design means organization, and arose out of the need for an interface between aesthetics and the industrial age. The modern designer develops communications materials based on knowledge of the afore-mentioned typography, images, symbols, as manipulated through those information technologies."

Type and image are still the core of graphic design no matter how we look at it, but this is merely the top of something more than the flat promise of a traditional "good read." Designers today provide the push and play of interactive information and animated content for eager readers, hungry for more (or at the very least, different) than the static page—or image—may offer.

For some, the preceding definition may be too dry and clinical—a some-what uninspiring way of describing something far more shimmery. For many, a designer's very mission transcends standard, textbook interpretations. Allan Wood smiles here and quotes that prodigious designer, Willy Wonka, (who, in the movie *Willy Wonka & the Chocolate Factory* quotes from Arthur O'Shaughnessy's famous poem, "Ode": "We are the music–makers / And we are the dreamers of dreams.")

"Designers," says Wood, "facilitate a creative process and collaborate with our clients to help manifest their ideals. We engage and communicate with our client's audience through visual language. In essence, we create cultural arti-facts—no different from ancient Greek or Egyptian artifacts (the only differ-ence is that our focus is not religion, but consumerism).

"Our work at its most basic level," Wood says, "reflects the cultural views of the times. At its height, design reflects and creates—and at times, challenges—the cultural ideals of the times."

Design, either by definition or through perspiration, should be both prag-matic and inspiring, for as Mr. Wonka also says, "There is no life I know to compare with pure imagination."

INTENDED MEANING

You might never have thought you'd grow up to be a "designer." Perhaps your teachers and high school guidance counselors—maybe even your parents—told you that "you can't make a living in art."

Phillip Wilson is here to tell you—well, he'll tell you from his home in Pittsburgh, Pennsylvania—that this simply is not true. "The Design business is a business like any other business," he says, "and good people will make a good

DOING IT ALL

As this book is the sister volume to the forthcoming *Starting Your Career as an Illustrator*, let's address a topical question: is your perspective that of a designer or an illustrator?

"The great thing about being a designer," says Brian Fencl, "is that you don't have to choose what you want to be—illustrator, photographer, designer, etc.—you can set up a business where you do all of it."

And one of the key ingredients in becoming a do-it-all designer is being a problem solver and a divergent thinker (what Fencl labels as "creative intelligence"). "You need to be a life long learner," he says, "the technology is so fluid, sometimes the right answer to a design problem is via techniques or media you haven't mastered (yet).

"When these foundations are learned at a deep level, you have creative people prepared to work, contribute, adapt, and innovate."

Although he can surely speak of his own illustration skills, Jason Petefish has hired his share of illustrators to work for him on projects in the past. He's quick to confess that he's not what he calls a "bona fide 'arty-type' illustrator" and assesses that there are totally separate skill sets involved.

Petefish specifies that both design and illustration fall under the general topic of "visual communication," but says, "The illustrator is not necessarily a 'designer,' and on a design gig, it may be the designer who hires the illustrator." He's not saying that illustrators are subordinate to designers. Hardly—they're more like copilots on the same bombing run.

"Many excellent illustrators hold their own very well without being hired by a designer or creative director," he says. They are skilled in both design and illustration.

"If you, the designer, wears the 'make-the-client-happy' business hat," he says, "you might certainly oversee a project's illustration. 'Good' visual design subjectively means tasteful skills and the marketplace will be the ultimate purifying arbiter of quality (or lack of)—especially the higher up you go."

"You know, the head of an in-house design department—we'll call them Fizzy Cola (FizzCo for short)—once told me that it doesn't matter how much good packaging design costs," Petefish says. "$100 . . . $150 . . . $200 an hour—it didn't matter. FizzCo would pay it—if, of course, they 'approved' the initial design contract, which was based initially on a mature designer's portfolio. And that, obviously, was based on excellence as determined by their incredibly high design standards." Here, Petefish smiles and adds, "In other words, prove you've been working in the field successfully."

So Petefish has been in business long enough to understand how illustrators and designers get hired, which he insists is remarkably simple and actually more arbitrary than scientific. "It's a combination of: (1) who you know, (2) who you can 'get to,' (3) the need of the person doing the hiring, and (4) what they want," he says frankly.

living at it. But you must be prepared and know your craft inside and out. You have to take it seriously as a career and not 'play' at it half-heartedly.

"You have to want it more than anything else. It has to be as important and as necessary to you as the air you breathe," Wilson says. "You have to be dedicated and disciplined. As to your work ethic—putting in whatever hours it takes to do a job and do it professionally; to do every job on time and with the utmost attention to the requirements, quality, and detail. . . . There will be no room for slop."

Rigie Fernandez never thought he would be a designer. As a kid raised in the Philippines, all he wanted to do was draw from (and dream up characters for) Filipino comic books. Artists like Levi and Joey Celerio (huge comic illustrators at that time in his homeland) inspired him to pursue his passion for drawing.

His father motivated and helped Fernandez to follow his muse. This eventually led to Fernandez obtaining a degree in Fine Arts. So why become a designer? "It fuels the same passions I had when I was younger," he considers, "to create all the things that I imagine and share it with the world.

"Labels—'freelancer,' 'independent'—are not important to me," Fernandez says, pausing to consider. "But it's important to clients. Why? Even though freelancing is not new, there are still clients who prefer to give their projects to a company instead of 'freelance' designers. This is why freelance designers must work on their personal branding, establish their credibility, and improve their client-handling and communication skills."

Working under today's model, designers like Fernandez will tell you that you should be a jack-of-all-trades and master of something. Not everyone will be able to "do it all." But being knowledgeable in certain areas of expertise will definitely help and offer a distinct advantage. "Strive to become an authority in a certain field," Fernandez says, "be it print, web, or video. Know a thing or two in the other fields. Gone are the days where a designer is only doing print."

Play it smart. Networking and collaboration are perfectly acceptable if some part of a project is not your specialty. Collaborate with developers on the back end development if you have to; cozy up to project managers to supervise an assignment (allowing you to focus on what you really excel at—design).

"You need to be up-to-date with the latest trends," Fernandez says, "but the task becomes easier when you collaborate; and these days you don't even need to be in the same location physically."

POS/NEG

Some decisions often come down to simply looking at life's two-column ledger: the left is labeled "plus," with the tag "minus" on the right. The vocation of design is a demanding job. You're going to hustle. You'll work extended hours, and the buzzword here is "more." More hours, yes, but theoretically you can do a wider

FOLKS JUST LIKE YOU (LIFE IN THE TRENCHES)

FLOW WITH IT

Stephen Michael King lives in a mud brick house on an island off the coast of Australia, and has, in his words, designed, illustrated, and written a whole bunch of books. About seventy-two was his count when this was composed.

King will tell you that this prolific career has been based on trusting his intuition and following his heart. "Not too many business principles have purposely entered my life," he says, "but I'm reliable, always meet a deadline, and aim for a personal creative truth in all my characters and designs."

He's a self-professed "go with the flow" kind of guy, who has a happy track record of keeping big publishers rather pleased—his repeat customers seek him out for his hand skills and that old-world view of putting something beautiful out into the world for people to find. "This joyfully naive concept means that I've lived a life where I can accept fallow periods, similar to a farmer at the mercy of good and bad seasons," King says. But he also celebrates that he's had a bumper crop for some fifteen years now. "The seasons have been kind to me," he says, "I've been booked out roughly two years in advance on all jobs."

King told me that he considers promoting himself more, but I fear there wouldn't be enough work hours in his day to handle the resulting volume. And all this derived off minimal marketing from a wee, coastal Pacific isle. King also realizes that a full-scale program may very well distract him from his true passion: writing, illustrating, and designing.

variety of better (read "more creative") assignments (or at least do more of the type of work you want to do) with the potential to earn more money in the process. More. More. More.

Freedom, at last, or freedom, at least. Basically there's no time clock to punch, and it's your schedule. Providing you meet your deadlines and make your meetings, you decide when you go to work, where, and for how long. No toiling "nine-to-five," unless you want it that way (or unless your client asks you to come in and work on their turf during their prescribed workday).

The flipside to this is that the steady paycheck may be history. Your money could come in dribbles or drabs, spurts, bursts, (or hopefully, and better yet) torrents. You will finally understand the true meaning of the terms "accounts receivable" and "accounts payable." Boys and girls: can you say "cash flow"? What you knew as professional security at your full-time position is not applicable here, as the business of freelance or independent design can be a bit of an emotional and fiscal roller coaster ride. Jobs may not be steady; you may skip a meal or two. You certainly won't land every exciting assignment you pursue, and odds are you'll have to take some mundane jobs simply to pay the bills. (Join the club.)

"As a designer," says Allan Wood, "it's important to look at your 'mundane jobs' as your bread and butter. Not only are they an opportunity to further explore and refine your business and design skills, they help sustain cash flow which in turn establishes a strong foundation to pursue what you really want in a calm and calculated manner."

You must tap into great reserves of self-discipline; if you don't, you won't be working this time next year. Say a fond goodbye to that grumpy manager staring over your shoulder. Look in the mirror and meet a tough new employer. And that salesman's gig your dad was always telling you about? Congratulations, you got the job. Marketing and self-promotion will become very important to you. Like it or not, we should emphasize right now that this is a business. However, the worlds of art and commerce can be quite compatible—how else are there so many successful designers out there?

FREELANCE OR INDEPENDENT?

Gee whiz, should you call yourself a freelance or an independent designer? Oy, what's the rub here?

Writing in *HOW* magazine, Ilise Benun asks if that term *freelancer* is a bit of a dirty word. And, frankly, you may well question the perceived gulf between the "independent" and "freelance" protocols as more attitude than reality. But given that your clients' perceptions and mindset are beyond your control, let's gauge the apparent differences.

Benun cites a few somewhat arbitrary criteria (nothing is written in stone, of course, and you will certainly find exceptions to any system or rule). In general, freelancers charge by the hour, while independents price per project (plus rates differ; independents charge more). On that clock, the tasks may vary: freelancers handle creative and production protocols; independents deal with concept and strategy (and do it earlier in the design process). A freelancer has minimal contact with actual clients while the independent works directly. There's the notion that the less creative freelancer takes overflow work and acts as more of a wrist—simply a production assistant with little (maybe no) artistic or tactical say on a gig.

Beyond the fact that the term *freelance* may be too nonspecific and vague, one shouldn't lose much sleep over that tag. Yes, labels often carry the heavy lifting of self-perception (which obviously may influence your business presentation), so you owe it to yourself to describe whatever you say you do as what feels right to you. The true debate here is how you conduct yourself professionally, how you run your practice, and how you interact with clients (from clear paperwork to straight pricing structures to critical customer service).

You might think this is a no-brainer, and I really see it as more a matter of outside observations coloring your own mindfulness. But do consider that the undertones of the root words "free" or "independent" may factor into a problem for your potential clients. For instance, if Jan Customer's definition infers "cheap" or "unskilled," "hobbyist," "desperate," or "transitory," it won't bode well for your job prospects. Or if the client assumes "fancy or expensive," "out of our league," or "contrary and dogmatic," equally negative connotations will hold sway.

Maybe, as Benun suggests, it's a simple matter of rephrasing (mix and match at will): "I am self-employed/an independent contractor/entrepreneur; a communications expert/visual problem solver/graphics guru/design consultant; I run a graphic design shop/work solo/own a studio/maintain a firm that offers design solutions and more."

Hey, semantics to the rescue again.

ON THE JOB OR ON-CALL?

Defined simply, both freelancers and independents are self-employed subcontractors who market their design by the job to several buyers. That's very short and sounds just as sweet.

But in the real world beyond the dictionary, you will be the office manager, secretarial pool, sales staff, marketing department, maintenance, and mailroom rolled into one. The ever-growing stack labeled IMPORTANT THINGS THAT MUST BE DONE RIGHT Now lies immediately under the bowling ball, cleaver, and cream pie you'll swear you're juggling as a one-person shop.

Common to both freelancers and independents (in fact, their primary motivation) is a dedicated passion for their chosen vocation. It's more than a mere job; it's a calling. Call yourself an entrepreneur with an independent spirit, a sense of adventure, and your own bold vision of success.

Come April 15, you'll benefit from the same tax breaks any small business enjoys. And, as with small business owners, there is a certain pride one gets from calling one's own shots. A freelance business is the vehicle to exercise your particular talents on demand.

Like a classic Western movie, it's not so complicated. That new job is essentially just somebody telling you to "draw, pardner." And before you slap the leather of your briefcase, you will face off as a hired gun (and yep, maybe not the top gun). But you go to the Okay Corral (get it?) loaded up with a silver bullet: the power to say no thank you at any time. Yes—any time; you always have the choice to say no, always. The code of the West, of course, dictates that you clarify, document, and agree to (in writing, of course) a job before consenting to the task.

WHO DA MAN?

So, ultimately, are you really your own boss? Understand that somebody is only contracting for your services, not buying your soul. So, sure, you will be signing off on the workflow (and work environment) as well as the hours. And yes, you must consent to who is calling the shots. Being in charge of your career is not about always being in charge. If that is the critical rub, to consistently jockey for the power seat, you'll have to earn it through experience and expertise.

And in many respects, you may consider yourself the master facilitator and supreme collaborator. "My skills and knowledge are utilized by my clients for their benefit," says Allan Wood. "I facilitate a creative process for my clients and collaborate with them in manifesting their ideas, ideals, and vision for their business, organization, product, or event."

Wood realized that in the cosmic scheme of things, it's the client who will use the finished design, not him. He came to understand that designers work with an incredible variety of clients, and as he puts it, "It was naive to think we come with all the answers."

Here's a simple what-if scenario Wood throws at you to challenge your critical thinking: "Imagine you have two new clients. Both want a brand identity created. Both are from the same industry. Obviously, you can't provide them with the same logo; how do you resolve this?"

ON STAFF

So, will a staff position be more helpful at first? Working on staff always provides invaluable training and experience. A staff job is a perfect atmosphere to hone your skills and perfect your craft, and I strongly suggest it. Likewise, you'll need an economic cushion when initiating any independent venture, so a staff job is a sensible first step.

Where better to learn and grow, to discover who you are and where your direction lies? However, development is directly proportionate to a nurturing and challenging environment. You must interview with your eyes open, a big nod to the present, but a savvy look to the future.

A staff position can be the perfect place to meet and make contacts (but not beg, borrow, or steal clients). However, a staff job won't necessarily teach you about the business end of things. Unless you interact with those contractors interfacing with your company, you may have no idea about how these independents actually operate. If you're a staffer and wish to prepare for freelancing, work yourself into assignments that involve freelancers—and don't balk at added responsibilities; seek them out.

You can gain valuable negotiating skills by sitting on the other side of the table as the art buyer. Relating to clients takes on a new perspective when *you* are the client. By guiding a job to fruition, you'll balance brainstorm and budget;

A LITTLE FRONTLINE SELF-ASSESSMENT

You're thinking about striking out on your own. Right off the bat, you will want to do an initial self-reflection. We will dive into this much deeper in the next chapter, but for now, let's mull it over just a bit, shall we? Consider this a wee pop quiz.

Be honest and objective about who you are, what you can do, and how well you do it. This won't necessarily prevent headaches, heartbreak, or disasters, but it will give you a strong foundation to weather the storm. You'll begin by examining your communication skills, marketing acuity, and knack for self-promotion. And by the way, your sales history (and salesmanship), your experience, and your network are factors here as well. Let's not forget your entrepreneurial savvy, either.

You should look at how—and if—you stand out from the pack. At the same time, your ability to lead will play an important role here. Business acumen, background, and motivation all must strike the right chord here, too.

Your technical prowess is obviously critical. Along with this, examine your organizational skills, drive, and determination to round out this rudimentary exercise.

guide the bright idea into actual screen-ready art, wrangling the technology while dealing with critical service providers to achieve desired results on the page or a monitor. Keeping that aesthetic dream from becoming a production or logistics nightmare garners you much needed technical expertise and practical information and will definitely work to your advantage when you venture out. It's a smart choice, if you're inclined to go this route.

CHAIN GANG, SLAVE MINE, AND SWEATSHOP

Many people actually believe that, because you work from home, you're not really working. As your business takes off, you'll be working alone, without the feedback and camaraderie of coworkers, weathering the peaks and valleys minus the support system of an office or staff. Outside your door, the competition is awesome—in numbers and ability. But you're up to the challenge, right? Your new boss thinks so.

As I mentioned earlier, good organization skills will be crucial. While it is the art that'll be your bread and butter, realize early that an artist's beret is only one hat you'll be wearing. Remember the smiling faces of your coworkers? All those people, doing all those things. Working all day. Getting it all done. Those are all your responsibilities now.

Design must be your love—something enjoyed with all your heart; something you need to do, something you would do purely for yourself without pay.

FOLKS JUST LIKE YOU (LIFE IN THE TRENCHES)

THE GREAT ESCAPE

Brian Allen worked for a well-known yearbook company for seven years, but realized early on that he really wanted to be independent. He put together what he calls his two-year escape plan and determined specific goals for this pre-launch.

Step 1. Allen's strategy was to slowly establish a client base and gain some experience on the side. "I spent about ten hours a week," he says, "evenings and weekends, working on freelance projects and building my portfolio." He found clients mostly through job-posting sites (such as www.Guru.com) but paused in our conversation as he considered the ethics of the whole job-bidding enterprise.

"I thankfully have enough clients and a solid reputation now that I don't need to depend on these sites," he says. "However, when first starting out, I think they were a great way to get a lot of practice and meet a lot of clients quickly. Some of my favorite clients currently were ones that I met through Guru.com. It's important for any freelancer to be aware, though, that there are risks doing business this way. The work is likely to be underpaid, and the clients usually tend to be less experienced." For more on this topic, check out chapter 3.

Step 2. After Allen put together a stronger portfolio and accrued critical experience, he then created a portfolio website. At the same point, to prepare financially, he stashed an additional five month's pay into personal savings, thus giving him some cushion if, as Allen aptly phrases it, "things didn't take off right away. I also spent a lot of time calculating our family's expenses, as well as projected business expenses, and compared that with possible earnings (based on what I was making in freelance currently, assuming that I could work 70 percent more once I quit my day job). I first had to see if the prices I was charging would add up to what it takes to support my family." Reader, this is exceptionally wise advice, and for more on sound financial planning, see chapters 5 and 6.

Step 3. Allen next made a list of the equipment, hardware, and software he would need to freelance full time and purchased this stuff intermittently over the two years. So, shortly before making the leap, he tied up all the loose ends: "I talked to my insurance agent about business insurance," he says, "registered my business name, took as many pens and stationery from old work as I possibly could, and then made the jump."

And by the time Allen vaulted over that hurdle as a freelance enterprise, he was already earning that 70 percent of what he would need to sustain his family full time. He had a desk full of projects, all the requisite hardware and necessary software, with all essential mechanisms already tested and in place.

Presto! Bravo! For continued strategies here, head over to chapter 6, "Setting Up Shop."

When you come right down to it, how many folks can say they truly love their work? Well, you can—and that's the biggest plus of all.

Let's introduce you to some of the concerns you'll deal with here. This is just to kick off the conversation. We'll examine these issues (and more) in depth in later chapters.

SELLING IT

Perhaps you dread the thought of selling your work, let alone "being in business." And Bunky, maybe you question if you're suited temperamentally to freelancing or working independently?

Some artists feel that marketing their work is akin to putting their children up for sale. But realize that you're only selling your skills, not your soul. And then recognize that someone is paying you to produce images for a purpose.

Next, know that you are a real person selling your services as a problem solver. And if you remember that you are selling usage of the art rather than the product itself, this anxiety is easily suppressed.

HUSTLE AND BUSTLE

Your time schedule will hardly be regular, and you're a slave to other people's deadlines. There will be moments so quiet you can hear a pen drip, and hectic periods when twenty-four-hour days are not enough—hustling is all relative for the freelancer.

Happiness and security? It's my experience that happiness and security in freelancing are achieved by hustling. Perhaps we have given this word a bad connotation. Hustling, as I define it, is nothing more than honest, hard effort. It is aggressively and energetically plying your trade; an assertive attitude combined with a robust work ethic and a good product.

Here, Phillip Wilson thinks it's important to start out by getting some experience with an agency or studio before going freelance. "It's just a smart career move," he says. "Learn the ropes from experienced pros before taking the plunge of going solo; it will save you from making a lot of unnecessary mistakes when you're on your own."

With regard to such snafus, there's as much security in this business as in any other profession, but, as Wilson cautions, "There are never any guarantees. If you're really good at it and build up a good client base, the work usually is fairly steady. You can certainly get laid off or fired from any job, but if you're freelance, you're not going to fire yourself!"

STANDS OUT A MILE

At some point, the question about style will insidiously creep into the conversation. In a real sense, knowledge and aptitude, business acumen, energy and perseverance, and—yeah, sure—style, are joined at the hip of your decision to be a designer.

TEN COMMANDMENTS OF FREELANCING

Call it your Declaration of Independence or look at it as rules of the road and, when you read through this inventory, regard these guiding principles as written in stone.

1. Thou shalt learn when to say no. If you don't like the suggestion, work it out amicably. Learn the art of compromise. Be flexible, versatile, and cooperative. Compromise need not be capitulation; it leaves both parties feeling that they work well as a team. However, accept the fact that there are actually some art directors who just won't meet you halfway. These folks are not worth the headaches or heartaches. At this point, you just need to safely get out of Dodge with some style and grace.

2. Thou shalt be polite, persistent, productive, and positive. Always communicate in a professional manner. Follow directions. Listen to your clients and respect their vision. Educate your clients. Don't be a Prima Donna.

3. Thou shalt strive to constantly increase your skill level and expertise. Grow and learn; get it better than the day before.

4. Thou shalt relax and have confidence in yourself. Nobody's shooting at you, and you're not doing brain surgery on your mom. Believe in yourself and others will, too.

5. Thou shalt make it a point to have fun. Love your profession. Remember this when you are putting in the long hours. Do what you want, work where and when you want, and work with nice people only.

6. Thou shalt have a personal life. Never feel guilty about making (and taking) time for yourself and loved ones—it's important.

7. Thou shalt always be honest and ethical. Never promise something you can't deliver; and remember—you are selling a product, not your soul.

8. Thou shalt be a good businessperson. With stars in our eyes, we key on those first four letters in the word *freelancer*. The financial (and physical) costs of running and maintaining your business will quickly educate you as to the realities behind the lofty conceptions. Be an informed freelancer: protect your rights by keeping abreast of the ethical standards, laws, and tax reforms. Stay current with pricing guidelines. Learn effective negotiation skills. Maintain excellent records. Don't start a project without a plan with the appropriate paperwork in place.

9. Thou shalt not take rejection personally.

10. Thou shalt never miss a deadline. Be late with a job and chances are that particular art director will never call you again.

Victor Melamed is a designer, illustrator, and cartoonist, as well as a teacher at Moscow's Higher School of Art and Design (that's Moscow, Russia, by the way). As Melamed will tell you, "Finding a personal style has really nothing to do with finding your audience. And the client relationship is actually only a minor part of creative success."

Think about it: clients—looking for a particular style—expect a certain predictability, but frequently the stylist of a "preferred look" and the guy who gets the commission are two different people. More importantly, "predictable" as an adjective in front of the title "artist" can severely limit you, ultimately blocking your creative and professional growth. So, says Melamed, "Moving through new styles, or even working in several, does not stifle (or ruin) your career. You're in control here . . . what work—style, technique, approach, whatever—and how much of it do you want a client to see?"

One's individuality may not surface on your first attempts. Nor can you wait for it to descend upon you from the heavens. "The only thing to do is work," Melamed says with conviction, "and consciously search for new, interesting possibilities outside of one's safety zone. And style? As that venerable philosopher, Ol' Blue Eyes, sang about it: you've either got it or you haven't got it . . . [and] if you got it, it stands out a mile."

Melamed points out that the critical questions to really ask are: who are you . . . what makes you who you are? What experience brought you to this creative place? What pushes you forward? What interests you? What do you want to talk about . . . what do you have to say to your audience (literally and figuratively)? And who is your audience—men, women; adults, children; students, intellectuals; truck drivers, football fans?

And finally, there's this big one: what is, as Melamed labels it, your USP (unique selling point)? What do you offer that your colleagues don't, and is this what the audience wants to see? If your USP is attached to a very narrow focus—for instance, portraits of tigers—or a small access point—collage portraits of tigers—your USP may be a hard sell, indeed.

THE GAME PLAN

Kristine Putt will tell you that your career should be about growth . . . your development—as a person; as a designer (and not necessarily in that order). To grow, you must seek criticism, not praise. "Praise will only tell you that you've arrived," Putt says. "Criticism points to where you can improve. Understand that graphic design solves your client's communication problem. So we must strive to improve our ability to resolve those difficulties with every new project and each new client. The only way we can get better is by seeking criticism."

To do so, you must stretch and step out of your comfort zone. Be willing to take on those projects that provoke the very bowel-clenching fear that screams

"But I've never done anything like this before. . . . I have absolutely no clue how to even begin!"

Putt insists you jump on this suggestion and take the gig on anyway. She points out that you will figure it out. "And if you have trouble," she says, "there is no better support system than your community of colleagues . . . help is usually only a tweet away."

Such chutzpah also means you should never simply be a "yes" designer. Always be more than willing to say no. For example, Putt refuses to do any design that is either religiously or politically related. She's also walked away from mature-audience-only projects. "Step back from subjects that drag you down, unless of course you really enjoy that specific subject," she says. "And of course, you scrupulously refuse assignments that can damage your credibility or professional image."

Being a focused designer means expanding your horizons. Putt asserts that you can't be a designer twenty-four-seven. "Have other hobbies and interests, or you'll fade fast," she says. "Plus you'll run out of interesting conversation starters in mixed company. Not everyone knows what a 'lasso tool' is. You don't want to be the boring geek at family reunions. Have something other than 'design talk' to contribute."

The play here, according to Putt, is to keep yourself continually stimulated. Sure, you'll land those fascinating, interesting, and ultra-artistic gigs that give you a reason to live (in the studio, at least). But you may not be able to avoid dry, boring, and repetitive assignments that could lead to burnout and possible creative despair. You don't want to wind up hating your clients, despising your work, even dreading stepping into your office in the morning—even if it's just immediately down the hall from the john.

This is a very dangerous place for any designer to be in (the creative funk, not off the john and up the hall). You do know that not every project is nomination-worthy, and you probably appreciate that no amount of remuneration will truly fill such hollows. To prevent this from happening, Putt suggests you make it a point to design personal creative projects. "Even if no one sees them," she says, "even if you're not going to sell them. Design creatively to keep your creative juices flowing, or you'll quickly find that you've lost interest in what you once loved to do."

Working on personal creative projects primes the pump of continued learning and improvement—fuels growth—but only if you stay on top of what keeps it real and fresh. For instance, Google has an eighty-to-twenty policy in place. You do 80 percent for the company and 20 percent for yourself. Often, according to Google, it's the 20 percent time that produces the most innovative solutions for the company.

"The world changes constantly," Putt says. "We need to keep up or we'll fall behind very quickly. Pay attention to what's current and continue to evolve or your style of design will be dumped long before your shelf date.

"Don't be that guy—doing this your whole life, but technically, still stalled back in the day; stylistically stuck on fonts and layout obviously inappropriate by today's standards, glaringly wrong for today's markets."

RIGHT ON POINT

(PROFESSIONAL VIEWPOINTS IN 50 WORDS OR LESS)

What do we want to get out of our business? Some of us need to make a big splash for some dumb reason, so I think we must remind ourselves that we got into this business to have a little fun—it can be an extremely fun filled business.

—Mike Quon

Designing my own brand identity was probably the most difficult yet rewarding job I have done. I was the worst possible client you could imagine.

—Allan Wood

40+
ARTIST'S
EXHIBITING

Save Our Gulf Coalition
2013
Art Exhibition
Official opening:
Friday 24 May
6 pm
23 May – 9 June | Arts Centre Port Noarlunga

© Allan Wood 2013

Work out what you're passionate about. If you enjoy what you're doing, then not only will you perform better day to day, but your work will improve as well.

—Anthony Hortin

There is a stage in a designer's career where the need to design will not be enough. The drive to create something new, own what you do, and establish a name—not only as a designer but as an entrepreneur—will win out.

—Rigie Fernandez

During a class at the School of Visual Arts in NYC, instructor Milton Glaser told us, "Always give your best effort, no matter who it is for." I've never forgotten that.

—Jason Petefish

I wanted to control my destiny. Coupled with that was the strong urge to rise or fall on my own merits. If I failed it would be because of me, not because of someone else. If I were successful, it would be because of my own efforts.

—Tom Nicholson

Running my own business; the "thrill of the hunt"; a satisfaction from complex problem solving; feeling comfortable wearing a wide variety of hats; the downright fear of not being able to support my family—this has given me my second wind (third, fourth . . . and thirteenth winds too).

—Nick Gaskins

CHAPTER 2

EDUCATION

Art is a continuous learning process and it never stops. I've been working professionally for forty-five years now and I feel I'm still learning every day.

–Phillip Wilson

AN EDUCATION

It's like solving a puzzle; design is always about communication (and a commissioned design must be about *immediate* communication). Style and technique are only the underpinnings to the creative event. Fundamentals are inextricably linked to all this. Brainstorming and conceptualizing cohabit in that place where vision wells up and materializes, then (hopefully) blossoms. Your education is the first step; where the artist in you revs the engine, before you gun the motor on the streets and wind it out as a professional.

But this only examines a big picture in a wide frame. Any day in the professional life can teach us *something*. Every assignment—whatever the size and scope—offers some kind of a learning opportunity . . . if we're open to it. Does every day represent a major test or pop quiz? We could make that statement, but I prefer to say that every day—and any day—aboveground is a good opportunity to push forward.

A graphic design education can provide you a euphoric exploration of a visually active idea—that technique and imagination paired with interpretation and the quest for insight and meaning are killer means to make a statement—*your* statement. Making that point effectively can also be big *fun*.

There is a real excitement in problem solving—articulately distilling ideas with minimal, effective language, enticing the audience and maintaining viewer interest; not giving away too much, but saying just enough. Handing off inspiration to concept, the segue from composition into technique, juggling representation with exposition . . . even the most straightforward answers can involve exhaustive process and perception.

CULTURE SHOCK

We cover different educational options in this chapter, and in chapter 21 art director and designer, Mark Hannon, expands on that dialogue to create a simple chart to help you determine which would be a good fit for your situation. Flip to this chapter of charts, forms, and templates to check out his easy pros and cons format offering a great "at-a-glance" comparison.

And while we're hangin' at the water cooler, Hannon has some interesting comments about art school. "It is not a given that artists are misfits within the microcosm of their high schools," Hannon reminisces, "but that was the case with me. In art school I found myself in the company of many other misfits from their own high schools. It was the first time I felt a sense of community within a school setting.

"Many first-year art students come to art school having been the best artist in their high school and were used to all the fawning and admiration that came with it. Once at art school, they are now in the company of the other best artists from their high schools. It can be a shock to some students when they meet other young people whose skills and ability far outpace their own. Things can change in four years', time though."

GOING UP . . .

The 800-pound—or perhaps the (on average) $35,000 per year—elephant in the room is the simple fact that a college education will not be cheap. The cost of post-secondary schooling can be a huge factor in determining where you attend—or if you even *go* to—art school, of course. While there are cost-effective alternatives (community colleges, for instance), we're not going to ignore or gloss over a very real fiscal fact of life.

However, I'm also going to take the high road in our discussion about academics. While financially it may be easier said—actually, written, in this case—than done for you, I'm going to work from another bona fide reality: that your design education is the ground-floor professional investment you make, laying the infrastructure of dedication and commitment to your career.

. . . ONLY UP

Costs aside, from there, what you do with this education—and where you go with that—is up to you. You choose to build from that foundation or spurn any ostensible restrictions and move in a different direction. You decide to pace yourself (or not).

You can push the limits, expand boundaries, play by (or toy with) the rules, but ultimately one relevant question remains: "What did we learn here?" Remember, on his way to turning on the light bulb, Thomas Edison regarded each failed experiment as simply what not to do again. Career-wise, if you learn only that one lesson, I think your education has been worthwhile.

And that's the essence of an education, is it not? You *hopefully* learn to: honestly evaluate your choices; objectively consider what doors to open or close; examine the possibilities fairly; soberly consider your actions, then actually (and hopefully, happily) live with the results.

LEARNING THE ROPES

Many elements factor into a "successful" career. Sure, there's *luck* involved—I wouldn't curse good fortune (especially as it translates into job opportunities).

- *Location* may enter into the equation. Where you do business can be a factor, not to mention being in the right place at the right time (more luck).
- *Attitude*—either positive or negative—may be part of the mix. Who you know can make a difference.
- *Perseverance* comes into play.
- *Energy and stamina* are crucial in both the long and short terms.
- *Business acumen.* If you are into sales (and after all, you are *selling* your design) this makes, well, just plain sense.
- *Aptitude* certainly comes into play. Talent—the natural ability to do something well—must be a prerequisite. Are there individuals who make it with minimal gifts? You'll find them in every endeavor. But if quality is critical, I'll go with chops and panache every time.
- *Age and experience* also factor in. Consider the fabled joys and benefits here: arguably, expertise and efficiency for starters. But this may be outweighed by the ostensible advantages of *youth* (here, you fill in the blanks; to me, this is fairly open-ended and somewhat relative).

As mentioned above, luck may be a small factor where job opportunities are concerned, but not when we're discussing ability. To compete in this field—at any age—an art education is essential.

SCHOOL RULES

Formalities! Do you really *need* art *school?* And by extension, do you actually need a degree? For my money, to compete in this field, some sort of art education is essential. You must learn the basics, understand the tools, and master the necessary skills to play the game well. Unless your name is Wyeth or Tintoretto, the best place I have found to do all this—if not in the shortest, then perhaps the most efficient, time possible—is art school. Yes, those aforementioned dead white guys are painters, but you certainly get my point, by, uh, design.

Tom Garrett is a design professor at the Minneapolis College of Art and Design. "It's true that some designers, somewhere, do not have formal training," says Garrett, "but I think that the majority of students gain tremendous knowledge through a college program."

"I wouldn't be where I am today if it wasn't for my education at Parsons," PJ Loughran adds. "Art school gives you a chance to focus and develop your craft in a way that (usually) can't be done once you're out in the real world and financially independent."

BRICK VERSUS CLICK

Now, let's do a slight spin on that original question . . . is the *physical* art school necessary? In our current day and age with the Internet, the MOOC (Massive Open Online Course) is a relatively recent, hot innovation in distance education.

Is it possible to be a "home schooled" designer? What kind of design education is earned going this route? (And how "good" are the designers earning their stripes here?)

In Kelly White's opinion, choosing the right school provides a critical foundation you won't find elsewhere. According to White, the degree is not the key. Whether you attend community college and/or simply shoot for a certificate, she feels design or art school is important and will give you a huge advantage over simply learning on your own (via YouTube or the like).

"Here you learn to give and get; to respond to creative criticism is incredibly helpful in so many ways. This provides huge lessons that extend way beyond simply adding up 'likes' to your Deviant Art posts. You'll figure out how to accept alternative ideas, but also learn to know when to stick to your guns; how to explain why you did what you did—what really works and what actually doesn't.

"You also get a chance to step out on a limb and experiment (so later you won't be jeopardizing a client's time or money). And maybe most important— you get the opportunity to ask questions . . . lots and lots of questions."

ART SMARTS

I agree with White; and if you're not too cool for school, you might then ask if a two-year commercial art school is better than a four-year art program at a university?

The answer depends on your needs, sensibilities, and attitudes; your goals, personal schedule, and timetable.

A two-year commercial program may be career-focused and technical (if not accelerated). The four-year university curriculum will be rounded and diverse (if not more intensive). It really depends on *your* needs . . . the choice of an eclectic university process versus a concentrated commercial approach must be an individual one.

SMART ARTS

As both a seasoned professional and master teacher, Garrett offers pertinent comments when asked to discuss this angle of art education. He believes that the difference between a four-year program versus two-year vocational training is that the emphasis is placed on learning new ways of problem solving. "In a rigorous four-year program, the student gains a whole range of skills," he says. "Students have the time to grow and develop multiple professional solutions to one assignment. Students learn how to verbally communicate their ideas and gain an understanding of the professional world with exposure to the best business practices and ethics."

Garrett also feels that a longer program enables the student to be aware of history and its context with other disciplines (for instance: illustration, fine arts, fashion, and architecture). The outcome often means that students are not just mimicking the latest styles and trends. Instead, they are learning ways of being more innovative. "This approach," Garrett says, "also prepares them for changes in the field down the road in regards to technology, the economy, and artistic growth."

TEACH ME

Both younger and older designers benefit from education (research and networking, too, but more on that later). Your design education should be—no, make that a *must* be—a lifelong, career-defining journey of personal discovery and professional exploration, regardless of setting. And don't think for a minute that you'll ever corner the market on "lots you don't know." Wow, what a great first-world problem to have.

There are myriad fine (even fun) solutions to address this situation—welcome and embrace the challenge. The modern "global university" can actually be where you make it and how you find it. We live in a wonderful time of fresh (and readily available) academic opportunities—across town, just up the block, or right down the hall and online. Learning situations—and great mentors, teachers, and advisors—are anywhere and everywhere you are (and can be anyone).

What haven't changed—and never will—are the solid, traditional basics of work efficiency: smart time management, determined motivation, serious hard work, obvious design skills, and savvy business chops. Throw in some applied energy and the willingness to explore, learn, and grow. Be aware of the now; stay current with tools, toys, and trends. All the aforementioned requirements know no age bias.

"Q" VERSUS "Q"

At the same time, consider a recurrent hot button (at least, with regard to general education and certainly when discussing academics on the internet): the old debate about *quantity versus quality*. The ultimately long-winded discourse on education and scholarship you'd be participating in—especially when you consider learning online—has always been a pretty chunky time suck (rather like the Internet itself).

The question, as I have heard it, rather comes down to this: is it better to function "a mile deep and an inch wide" or just the opposite at "a mile wide and an inch deep"?

What's better for *you*? Do you prefer a survey-type strategy—the "mile wide/inch deep" hypothesis—that adopts a broad action plan addressing the subject at large (AKA an introduction)? Or does a narrower, in-depth focus that examines a topic (perhaps as a specialization) fit your bill. That's going a "mile deep/inch wide." And indeed, your first design decision may be whether to go to a physical art school at all.

A DESIGN EDUCATION: AN OVERVIEW

According to Fred Carlson, you have many academic alternatives. Carlson shares this expert and succinct overview of the options for this chapter:

- A student may earn a certificate, an associates, a bachelor's, master's, or even a doctorate degree.

- The BA (bachelor of arts), BFA (bachelor of fine arts), and BS (bachelor of science) degrees are granted at four-year colleges and universities. The design training available at two- and three-year professional schools results in a certificate or associate degree in design.

- Large public colleges and universities offer a broad curriculum. Smaller colleges, institutes, and online schools present more specialized experiences (and may concentrate on a particular industry).

- "If you want an education that encourages interaction with a variety of people and subjects in addition to graphic design, plus a range of degrees from the bachelor's level to the doctorate level," says Carlson, "the university experience is probably best. If you prefer more intensive, studio-centered graphic design instruction (and theory), as well as advanced courses targeted to particular markets, a four-year design-focused school with a graphic design specialization is better for you."

- Community colleges typically offer shorter programs—two-year degrees in the form of associate degrees or certification—that tack towards a vocational focus. These credits and degrees offer entry-level opportunities or serve as transfer credits to a four-year school.

- Tech-oriented career programs emphasize computer competence, computer-aided design, and software skills. A vocational, technical education is planned to teach you exactly what you need to know to get a job in a small segment of the graphic design field (including programs in the applied graphic arts, printing industries, and computer graphics).

- Graphic design workshops, trade conventions, and special graphic design training offer brief, intensive training in a desired subject or skill set. These special programs bring adults together to educate and congregate, renew and update horizons in particular graphic arts trade segments.

- Those entering the job market will develop a portfolio, and novice designers can usually expect a two- to three-year period of apprenticeship in their jobs. A bachelor's degree (typically accomplished in four years) is required for most entry-level design positions; graduates of a two-year program normally qualify as assistants to designers. A candidate with a master's degree (usually, a two-year program) often holds an advantage on the job hunt.

DIY

Is it possible to be a self-taught designer? "Definitely," says Gerald D. Vinci. But D. Vinci cautions that most self-taught designers focus on acquiring skills and not about what it means to be an *effective* designer. D. Vinci points to the myriad resources out there allowing the casual designer to expend minimal energy and still achieve a professionally polished, competent piece—prebuilt web templates, stock clip art, stock photos, free Photoshop effects, etc. "There are thousands of forums out there that will tell you how to do just about anything," D. Vinci smiles. "But the issue with this is that instead of learning how to do it yourself, you are just adopting someone else's knowledge, design technique, or coding, what have you."

And such web designers who construct websites often lean toward pre-built website systems (such as WordPress or Joomla.) "These pre-built content management systems take a lot of the skill of web design and development out of your hands," D. Vinci says.

"Anyone looking at the bigger picture can see the major problem with this scenario. What happens when—and it will happen—the website starts malfunctioning or throwing back error codes? If you rely on pre-built systems to produce work for others, there is going to be a point where you will need to troubleshoot issues. Without the background knowledge of how to build things yourself or how to design from scratch, you are missing that key component to being a true professional."

D. Vinci is not saying that all self-taught designers are lazy, cheap, and cutting corners. Cutting corners is not necessarily a bad thing, but here D. Vinci cites the age-old adage, "Work Smarter, Not Harder."

"There are times where finding more efficient ways to do things only makes sense," he states, "but self-taught designers who do not offer the 'total package' of background and service may lack the genuine professionalism a more educated designer can deliver."

D. Vinci and other seasoned professionals know that time and experience typically shake out such inconsistencies. They understand that cutting necessary corners is impractical and your business ultimately will suffer for it. And here, he offers another old saw to ponder: "With age comes wisdom," he asks you to consider. "We can hope, anyway."

CARRY ON

So I'll repeat myself a bit, it's not that much of a conundrum. For me, push doesn't even come to shove, regardless of where you weigh in—I will tell you to go to *school*—get an art education, somewhere, somehow. That chat may begin with the very idea of a formal curriculum; but it will then heat up even further when you consider the idea of a *continued* education: going on to earn a graduate degree—an MA or MFA; a DMBA or dual degree (MFA with, say, a DMBA).

This is another topic of much debate and valuable consideration. Some argue that a master's degree is a mere piece of paper and simply just the path to a teaching gig. They will point out that the caliber of your work experience, backed by the quality of your portfolio, are the only true industry standards.

Without squabbling over the value of that little piece of hard won paper (earned either as an undergrad or graduate), you may want to look into alternatives: online programs and/or the so-called specialty—or portfolio—schools (for instance, The Art Department; Miami Ad School; Creative Circus; VCU Brandcenter; Brainco; and the Chicago Portfolio School).

THE LONG HAUL

Learning is a lifelong process. "Education as an artist is so important," says Scott Bakal, picking up this thread. "Some people disagree, but I feel being in an academic environment with your peers and learning new, contemporary (as well as classic) techniques and styles will only help you grow.

"Even if this doesn't improve your style, you'll gain *knowledge* (which is just as important). Knowing what is happening around you in the field and what has happened in the past will help you make better decisions as your career progresses forward."

This is not just idle chatter for Bakal, who after eleven years in the field, decided to enroll in a masters program. "I felt I needed a psychological and creative kick in the ass," he confesses. "I put myself around other creatives and working professionals to feel that competition and get that sense of group self-exploration again. I wanted to explore new ideas and see how others in the industry were operating."

But he stipulates that you need not be going back for another degree. "I would, however, always recommend a continuing education class," Bakal says. "At the very least, a basics class where you are surrounded by other artists."

MAXED OUT

June Edwards teaches design at Pennsylvania's Slippery Rock University. Edwards tells us that there are many ways you can maximize the benefits—and shelf life—of your undergraduate education:

- Adding a minor to broaden your skills is smart: your advisor will help you select one that enhances your course of study.
- Attend as many exhibits, workshops, seminars, lectures, and forums as you can.
- Enter your work into competitions and exhibitions.
- Become active in a club or organization related to your interests.

- ◘ Many art/design departments organize trips to museums, exhibits, and conferences each semester. During spring break, there may be trips abroad associated with specific classes.
- ◘ Universities often have affiliations with art/design schools in other countries. You may be able to spend an exciting semester studying abroad.
- ◘ School-sponsored activities are enriching, fun, and also cost-effective; the activity fee you pay each semester subsidizes many of them. After graduation, you will probably pay a lot more for similar activities and travel.
- ◘ Your active participation in extra-curricular activities will demonstrate that you are eager to learn and it may help you land an entry-level design position when you graduate.
- ◘ Keep information about each event/activity you attend, and add these items to your résumé. "It is much easier to update your résumé each semester than to try to remember four years of exhibitions, conferences, workshops, etc., as you prepare for graduation and your job search," advises Edwards. A note here: you should adjust your résumé for each job application. Some workshops you attend will be emphasized for one position, and other activities might be more important for other job applications.
- ◘ Visit the career service department at your school early and become familiar with all they can offer. They hold job fairs and will help you explore careers and employers. You can get help composing your résumé, and when you are close to graduation, they will help you sharpen your interview skills.

Most graphic design job listings ask for three years of experience—recent graduates usually have far less than that. Look for opportunities to produce publications and presentations for clients while you are in school, but keep in mind that everyone had to begin somewhere. "A strong portfolio, excellent references, and a history of enriching experiences while in undergraduate school might help compensate for less actual job experience than is asked for," Edwards says.

A REAL EDUCATION

Ken Bullock has an interesting take on the advantages of your design education. Sure, a good design program will teach you the basics. A solid design curriculum *should* provide the (creative and technical) tools you fall back on during production: the brainstorming and conceptualizing; color theory; a foundation in the usual hand skills plus layout, typography, and presentation. The notable school or program (known for producing those top notch designers) cited on your résumé can wedge your foot in the door. Although, as Bullock reminds us, "Your portfolio will generally do a better job here.

"But at the risk of sounding either cynical or silly, the degree only lets you honestly say that *you have a degree*, providing you an edge compared to your competition with no degree (or without a similar pedigree)."

And here is where Bullock really makes his point: "Generally when you graduate from design school, your portfolio is filled with design school samples and projects. After all, you just graduated right?" And then, as Bullock points out, the thing you will hear a lot of will be, "*Have you done any real work?*"

Most employers want to see that you have actually done some graphic design—the "real work" Bullock flags—for authentic clients. They want to be able to judge you/your work based on field conditions. They know that most design school projects aren't as demanding or deadline driven as an agency or design firm assigning genuine projects.

"Get some freelance under your belt before you graduate," Bullock recommends. "This will complement your portfolio and make you a better candidate when you hit the market looking for a job. Critically consider what to put into your portfolio for both school and freelance work. If you have any doubts, leave it out. Even a bona fide assignment that is not seriously strong enough to go into your portfolio should not make the cut."

HIRE ED

June Edwards recommends that students seek out graphic design opportunities on campus. "Many colleges and universities have part-time and work/study programs that offer experience in specialized fields," she says.

According to Edwards, the best opportunity for graphic design experience would be with the university Public Relations Department, but other departments on campus might also be looking for design work to advertise their services or to promote upcoming events. Some departments or service areas you might check into are the library, technology, recreation/fitness, health/medical, bookstore, dining services, and the counseling center.

"Most universities have a Print Services Department," Edwards says. "Those folks are usually swamped with work and often have one or two employment positions for students. The campus newspaper is usually a student-run production; involvement with that (or any of the many newsletters produced by various departments) would look good on your résumé. A 'before' and 'after' example of a publication you redesigned might be an excellent way to demonstrate your skills."

"Regarding the type of degree . . . an associate, bachelor's, or master's . . . most designers working in the industry have either an associate or a bachelor's degree," Bullock says. "I am sure there are designers out there with masters', but I would argue that they are in the minority. Most job postings list a bachelor's degree; but if your portfolio is really good and you've worked a few jobs, they will sometimes overlook the associate degree.

"Generally, smaller shops and privately owned companies are more willing to accept someone with an associate degree than the larger firms and corporations (who often use the degree to screen people out). All of that considered, I have been in graphic design for more than seventeen years. I have worked for small and large Fortune 500 companies (both as in-house and as an independent) and have done quite well with my associate degree."

SUCCESS!

I believe, as does Edwards (who sparked this dialogue), that education is a two-way street. You must show up—you *participate*. Your willing contribution is essential. Edwards's manifesto declares that the student has a responsibility to consciously *engage* in the process. The professor will recognize the quality of that engagement and can make the presentation more meaningful and relevant.

When appropriate, students must *inquire:* ask questions and add your thoughts or ideas. Students must be prepared for each class session and participate in discussions. "All creative exercises—including lectures, discussions, assignments—demand individual, creative problem solving," says Edwards. "Not all aspects will be nailed down or completely defined by your professor. It is up to you to come up with unique, appropriate solutions—your personal interpretations and responses to discussions and assignments are vital."

Long term, the techniques students use to make the most out of each class can be applied to a work situation in the future: cultivating positive student/professor relationships in school can help you understand how to develop positive relationships with art directors. Fully participating in discussions and critiques in school will help you collaborate effectively with colleagues.

CHAIN CHAIN CHAIN

Another life skill you cultivate in school is problem solving. "Sometimes you will encounter a persistent problem in a class even though you work hard and try your best," Edwards says from experience.

"Begin by defining specifically what the difficulty is and whether others are having the same problem. Could the problem be a result of a misunderstanding on your part? Make an appointment with your professor as soon as possible: explain the situation clearly and work together to find a resolution. If the problem persists, you should consult with your advisor to find out whom you should speak with next."

Understand that real problems do not just go away; you must solve them or make a sacrifice. In school, the little burnt offering will be your grade and apparent knowledge of the subject.

"This is an unacceptable outcome given the cost of an education these days," says Edwards. "Be a team player though, and always go up the chain of command. You will find that solving the problems you encounter in school will be similar to solving problems at work."

LEARNING CURVE

"Art school, for me, was just great," Lori Osiecki will tell you. "It gave me the opportunity to experiment and connect with other creative people. At art school, I learned how to pull it all together so that I could actually support myself doing something I enjoy. It doesn't get any better than that."

But during her last months at school, Osiecki utilized her student status to earn some practical, real-world credits. She scheduled interviews with design firms, advertising agencies, and magazines—any art director who would be willing to spend fifteen minutes with her every Friday she had free.

"I told them that I was not asking for work," Osiecki says, "just some *advice*; that I really valued what they had to offer in terms of direction, criticism— anything. I wanted to shape my portfolio. I wanted to be able to find a job. I did not want to do something else to support my art habit."

Osiecki found that these art directors were incredibly generous with their time. And she listened to what they had to say. "I reworked my book so that I felt good about it," she says. "I became less nervous about the interview process. And luckily for me, I landed my first job within two months of graduating.

"It was a fine job and a wonderful experience," Osiecki says. "I had the good fortune of meeting and working with some of the best artists in the country. I still keep in touch with many of the people I met. Creative bonding—there's nothing like it."

LEARNING IN PRACTICE

Yes, you can get the (art) job done even if you are knee deep into another job. Even if that job is not particularly "arty" and even if that job may be a non- or low-paying gig. And, yes, there *is* such a thing as a practical education (directly or indirectly espoused by the pros above).

Certainly, some artists are not cut out for a "traditional" art education. However, life always offers alternatives (one way or another). As Jenny Kostecki-Shaw says, "Life experience is in itself a good art education.

"Ben Shahn advised us to not disregard *anything*," Kostecki-Shaw says. "If you can't go to school or can 'only' get a job in an auto factory then *do that*. If your head and heart are open to all possibilities, it's not 'just work.' Observe, feel, touch, believe, and think—all this can come out in your art."

You can mix and match your options to maximize opportunities, and all of these choices work together as valid means to an end. "There are unique alternatives," Ulana Zahajkewycz says, "enabling you to gain knowledge and skills through your own research."

Let's take a look at a few.

SELF-MADE MAN

Of course, one question will always be right in front of you: if you are making these particular choices, *do you truly know yourself?* Only you know if you can flourish with or without instruction. Knowing yourself is key.

"Being self-taught still encompasses teaching," says Zahajkewycz. "It also involves drive, discipline, the thirst for knowledge, a self-created structure. Few individuals have this sort of urge to succeed.

"And a good teacher pushes you forward, providing critical feedback you cannot get while working on your own," Zahajkewycz points out. School also gives you a sense of community and networking—eyes, ears, and minds that can help set your work free (if you're not interested in what an instructor says, feedback from your peers may be a better fit for your psyche).

"That is not to say that you can't find all of this on your own, in the outside world—you most certainly can," Zahajkewycz says. "If you have a fierce, independent streak (and some serious gumption), then perhaps the school of life *can* be your instructor. Some amazing artists have never gone to school. It's up the individual to find the right fit *for you*."

INTERNSHIPS

Do internships help? Yes, they can. Of course, internships aren't for everyone. Most likely, this will be your first real taste of that particular work experience; and it may not be a paying situation. Also an internship doesn't guarantee you will be hired by the employer at the end of the gig.

Saying that, if you're willing to invest your time and energy in potentially marvelous professional training, an internship can be priceless—just the catalyst to change the course of your life and career. But for the internship to be a smart beginning move for you, it has to be available and practical for your situation (not to mention, affordable).

APPRENTICESHIPS

You might choose to apprentice under working professionals, without the structure of classes or an institution. Here, you learn the foundations of business, as well as mechanical chops; history and fundamentals, all on a one-to-one basis. Zahajkewycz worked with just such an important mentor for roughly five years and found the experience absolutely invaluable.

ABOUT INTERNS

The United States Department of Labor guidelines—labeled as "The Test For Unpaid Interns"—determine an internship by the criteria below. Note that employers calling people "interns" who don't meet these guidelines are liable for significant penalties (including withholding that should have been collected). The information below comes directly from the Department of Labor website.

1. The internship, even though it includes actual operation of the facilities of the employer, is similar to training that would be given in an educational environment
2. The internship experience is for the benefit of the intern
3. The intern does not displace regular employees, but works under close supervision of existing staff
4. The employer that provides the training derives no immediate advantage from the activities of the intern; and on occasion its operations may actually be impeded
5. The intern is not necessarily entitled to a job at the conclusion of the internship; and
6. The employer and the intern understand that the intern is not entitled to wages for the time spent in the internship.

"Seeing the day-to-day operations of his business was an immeasurable help to me," she says. "Observing how a veteran ran his shop is the type of experience I wish all students everywhere could get. Later, at a subsequent teaching position, there was an emphasis on internships, so this became a reality for my students."

ON THE JOB TRAINING

There's a lot to be said for on-the-job training. For many, this combination of drive, hard work, and basic chops is *the* best art school (even *after* two to four years of actual art school).

"I look back at myself and think I was a pretty strong art student," says Doug Klauba. "But by the time I got out of school, I realized I had *so much more* to learn and I needed a little further direction. But I also saw that I really needed to take this direction from *myself.*"

"Your work ethic—your focus—is vital," says Benton Mahan. "You improve, get better. *Motivation is more important than talent.* If you are motivated, you will figure out what you can do with the talent you have."

A BUSINESS EDUCATION

It's simple: if you're in business, you need a business education. Kinda *duh* or *meh*, huh? Maybe we're talking formal schooling. Perhaps it's dedicated reading at the library backed by extensive online research. You could take a few classes at the local community college and network like nobody's business (except it's your *business*).

Wherever you learn it, sound business acumen, good marketing strategies, and a solid financial plan form a critical trifecta. That is, if you want to stay in business, of course. Not "just making it," mind you, but thriving—seriously churning up some water. We should hope for nothing less, right?

In upcoming chapters, we'll assess how much money you'll need, how to realistically plan to earn that, plus where and how to get the needed capital. We'll also look at how to create a working budget to maintain a cash flow to keep your enterprise in the black (for instance: 1. estimating how much you think you'll earn to ascertain if you can make ends meet, and 2. comparing costs and income to see if your business plan is viable). That's all ahead in upcoming chapters 5 through 7, so hang in there and read on.

On a related topic, let's note the pertinent national trend of art schools offering design-focused business programs culminating in an MBA degree or certificate. California College of the Arts, MICA (Maryland Institute College of Art), and Kendall College of Art and Design are just three that will pop up in your research here.

FOLKS JUST LIKE YOU (LIFE IN THE TRENCHES)

GROUND FLOOR OPPORTUNITY

Born in Brazil and earning a degree in fine arts, Antonio Rodrigues will proudly discuss his body of work boasting traditional techniques. But his art (and the related design he did) was very personal. In his words, he hadn't reached an appropriate audience.

Rodrigues earned a decent living at his (Brazilian) government job. But with long, demanding days forcing short, catch-up nights, his creative work was ultimately cubbyholed into hobby status. "I eventually got fed up," Rodrigues says. "Every day was the same thing. I had a stable job. I lived in a nice flat. But something was missing."

Then he did a gutsy thing: he let all that go and started anew in London, England. Rodrigues didn't own a work permit (meaning he couldn't hold a formal job or even sell his stuff). At some point, friends pointed out how much they enjoyed the business cards, CD and DVD covers, posters, as well as character illustration they saw in his portfolio. "I took their advice," says Rodrigues, "and kicked off my new business direction."

He says with candor that he was incredibly new to the game. "London was a great place to learn the craft, as the whole city inspires you visually," he says. "Incredible design events and seemingly uncountable museums and galleries. And, of course, just as I was starting to put it all in gear, it was already time to move from London to Havana, Cuba."

But Rodrigues was determined to stay on track with his master plan; he made the time to keep learning. His fine arts background made it a somewhat easier start. He was already familiar with general hardware and software but knew nothing about Photoshop, Illustrator, or InDesign. "And I was well enough aware that these applications are the critical key," he says. "I had to learn how to integrate my vision with my customer's and how to get inside the client's head, translating a visual into the message they want to pass on."

From Havana, it was back and forth to London; then to Washington, DC, and New York City and back to Brazil. He researched up a storm, became well read, and networked like a demon. But it should be said that grassroots design, while certainly a romantic notion, isn't universally appreciated. His portfolio was met with rejection. "I remember vividly my first interview with an art director in London who, after seeing a few pages of my printed portfolio, told me to look elsewhere—there was no place in the market for 'people like me.' Harsh, mean, somewhat unfair . . . but also true," Rodrigues says honestly.

For Rodrigues, quitting was out of the question. He decided to scrutinize his book and work hard to make that portfolio more professional and marketable. In early 2012, clients started to pop up, exposure in print and online was coming slowly but surely. As of this writing, Rodrigues's goal is to maintain a small studio with a fair list of good clients and eventually grow a team. He shoots for varied styles and techniques and a consistent, fresh approach to every project.

RIGHT ON POINT
(PROFESSIONAL VIEWPOINTS IN 50 WORDS OR LESS)

I read somewhere that when you attend art school, you do not just learn, you become. And while there is only so much you can truly learn in school, don't be a fool and pass up the opportunity for a formal design education.

—Gerald D.Vinci

A passion for [learning] design is what makes me continue along my path.

—Cyndia Lee

As a student, I didn't envision where I'd be now. You can come out of it with a real career.

—Charlene Smith

Anyone can open YouTube or subscribe to a website offering design tutorial videos, and/or read books on the subject. They're all great options. But these resources are just better when complementing an actual classroom setting.

—Kelly White

WE'RE ALL IN

the SOCHE ED conference
February 14, 2014

© Bing Design 2014

Before I went to art school, I was convinced I knew everything I needed to know. But from my first day, I knew I had found my niche. [Art school] didn't affect my imagination, it just gave me the tools to bring my ideas to fruition.

—Erin Brady Worsham

Art School for me was just great. I learned how to pull it all together so that I could actually support myself doing something I enjoy. It doesn't get any better than that.

—Lori Osiecki

© Kelly White 2014

CHAPTER 3

OPPORTUNITIES

I am not just a designer—I am involved in much more.

—Mike Quon

WHAT IS A DESIGNER?

We attempt to adequately answer that question in chapter 1, but it's an appropriate lead-in for this chapter as well. In their excellent book *Becoming a Graphic Designer*, Steven Heller and Linda Fernandes assert that the first proper question to ask is not "How do I become a graphic designer?" but "What is graphic design?"

Back in chapter 1, we asserted that type and image are still very much at the top and/or bottom of any definition of graphic design. But these days, this is merely the proverbial tip of that legendary iceberg and, well, *the tipping point*. The tipping point is that moment—the threshold—of change.

I highly recommend you read Malcom Gladwell's superb book *The Tipping Point*. As Gladwell himself puts it, "It's a book about change. In particular, it's a book that presents a new way of understanding . . . change." And to me, graphic design is all about the threshold of visual change—in concept and manner—as well as fresh understanding beyond an historically fixed image or static page.

In a field that positively pops with diversity (not to mention characters of wild and wide temperament), the prototypical "modern designer" now must be somewhat of a chameleon—a professional shape shifter, managing a career, taking frequent and unpredictable turns as markets spring up to keep pace with technology, which morphs skills in surprising directions mirroring a culture and society evolving with its very mechanics. There, I said it in one sentence.

Maybe the constant is that personalities are ageless—historians have long cited similar versions of this conventional wisdom that remain immune to the vagaries of time. If you're a "designer," you enjoy the challenge and revel in the task. You're a force that burns bright and hot (but not out). You're flexible and versatile; professional (as in reliable/dependable/on time/available).

You team up graciously—collaborating as you must—but roll independently, when you must. You're the leader when you get the shot. You stay easy when it gets hard. Train tough. Reach a little higher and wider. You practice. You practice patience. You can zig and zag—adapt to learn (and vice versa); focus . . . communicate. Discuss. Think. Consider. You work hard to be open and mindful while you strive to be open minded, understanding, and empathetic.

WHAT DOES IT TAKE TO BE A DESIGNER?

Kelly White will tell you it takes thick skin. "Get used to people telling you (in no uncertain terms) that the project you just spent hours (or possibly days) on just isn't good enough. Or isn't what they wanted—even though you gave them *exactly* what they asked for."

But White will also tell you that you can't take it personally. "A true professional lets her client know she cares about this project and conveys a confidence in the job she's doing," she says. Also important: the presence to explain what's needed (and why), or why *this* works when *that* does not.

It's about dedication to and joy in what you do, through slow times as well as through chaos and crunch time (with no weekends off, no free time; no overtime pay either). "The thing is," White says, smiling, "if you love your work, your job, and design . . . it's *all* worth it."

Phillip Wilson tells us that a good designer must be well rounded, and must have, at least, a passing interest in just about everything. "One thing I've learned in this business," Wilson says, "is that you never know what you'll be asked to do. Widen your scope. I believe the more you know, the more opportunities you'll have to get work."

SHOULD YOU DO IT ALL . . .

But we may throw up a wee red flag here. "I have a concern," says Matt McElligott, "that we imply that graphic design is something easily added to an illustrator's skill set (or vice versa). We also might not put enough emphasis on the idea that each endeavor—successful graphic design and triumphant illustration—requires a separate and equally robust amount of training."

You're a well-rounded designer, and illustration may be part of your tremendous skill set. Being a jack-of-all-trades, if you can cut it, would be to your distinct advantage in the beginning, when you may have to do everything to make a living. But as your business takes off, you'll probably—and eventually—concentrate on what you do best.

If you are an illustrator and a designer, you can promote yourself as such, or simply market your illustration to some companies and design work to others. It will be easier—and smarter—to do this on a local level. Granted, it is good for an illustrator to have as much understanding of design as possible, but if you're serious about doing both, you may find it more convenient to market and advertise yourself as a designer.

As part of the team, an illustrator will do only one end of a job—the illustrations, obviously—but a designer may wear many hats on a project (including snagging the juiciest illustrations). The designer controls the creative flow, while an illustrator may not enjoy the same perks.

Of course, along with any perks come added responsibilities. Jobs can become so design-intensive you may not do any drawing for days or weeks at a time. If you want to be an illustrator, this will present real problems, so seriously consider how you're going to sell yourself.

. . . AND SHOULD YOU DO IT RIGHT NOW?

Right out of the gate, should a novice designer freelance (or go independent) immediately out of school? For White, the answer depends on the person and his or her ability. "It can take a while before you make any money," she says, "so in financial terms, if you have a solid support system that enables your freelance enterprise to get up and running, you're off to a good start."

White recommends that you master industry standard (and client friendly) technology, of course. She advises that designers must stay up to date on current trends—including hardware and software—following blogs and listening to podcasts, plus joining groups (LinkedIn or other sites; Twitter, Facebook, Google+, etc.). "Learn all you can about the business side and design side of freelancing," she says.

But beyond these obvious (and perhaps obviously technical) basics, you must simply project an absolute commitment to succeed, a positive attitude and, as she puts it, "[the] sheer initiative to make almost anything possible."

For new freelancers or folks thinking about becoming small business owners, White makes a solid point: "The social media marketing I just mentioned is a big question when starting out," she says. "How to do it, which sites to use, how much time to spend on all this.

"I also believe it is *extremely* important for small businesses and freelancers," she tells you, "to build a following and a *community* that supports their endeavors and creates more trade for them in the long run."

Yes, White flags social media marketing, but in a related thread, she wisely points out that deciding on and finding your target audience (in other words, for whom you want to create designs) is critical. "Whether it be for non-profits, churches, large companies, or whomever," she says, "doping out your target market ranks right up there with learning to manage your time, tying into (then staying on top of) new trends, and monitoring the pulse of what is going on in the industry."

STARTING YOUR CAREER

"I worry that, at this writing, the novel topic of kick-starting your career will be very askew," Ken Bullock says. What the Texas-based designer wants to emphasize is that your career path is paved partially by what you want to do and where you are—both geographically and economically. Larger cities—like Bullock's Houston—may offer both freelance and full-time opportunities. A more economically depressed location presents different challenges.

"You might have to work for someone doing something you don't want to do while you build your portfolio with freelance work," he says. "You might have to take a lesser paying job and make what you can of it until things get better. Take advantage of every opportunity. Fight for a cause and support it with pro bono work—you never know where it might lead. This helps them and yourself."

Let's specifically address some career specifics and look at the choices you may make. Each can make significant differences in your career outcome. Each, of course, comes with unique advantages and disadvantages and each makes individual demands on you. Let's list several options and compare them, shall we?

And for a more visual take on all this, go to chapter 21, "Forms, Charts, and Templates" and check out Bullock's informative table on this topic.

GETTING WORK AND WINNING NEW CLIENTS

Bullock thinks something funny is going on here. "It's a bit of a muddle," he says with a laugh. "In my experience, when you are starting out, getting work is kind of like asking the bank to give you credit. If you don't already have credit, they won't give you any."

Clients want to see work you have done, before *they* will give you a gig, and they really want to see work you've done that relates to their field (or for their competition). You may very likely hear: "Yo—if you haven't done any work in our industry, how do we know you can do this for us?" Credibility and viability—at least in the eyes of a potential client—is usually established via actual (or perceived) experience.

"At a point in my career, people's ears started to perk up because of who I worked *for* and not so much because of my skills (the actual reason I landed these clients)," says Bullock. "My talent earned me a stellar reputation at certain big name companies and my freelance stock soared. I was now very credible as a designer."

Bullock calls this the "he/she actually worked *there*" effect. In a portfolio review, you could replace that "there" with any large reputable company—cue drum roll—and the other party will invariably respond with "Wow . . . *you* worked *there*!" Cymbal crash. They then follow up with: "If you're good enough to be hired by these guys, you can definitely help us!" Rim shot.

At that juncture, your business network opens up exponentially as well. People move on and up to other positions; you stay in touch and—*voila*—inside contacts all over the place. "This network creates invaluable entree into companies for freelance or full-time employment," Bullock says. "Let's face it, when it comes to hiring a contractor or an employee, folks like to hire people they know and like. This has been my largest source of new work."

LET'S PUT ON A PLAY: INVENTORS AND ENTREPRENEURS

What is an entrepreneur exactly? According to Merriam-Webster, an entrepreneur is "one who organizes, manages, and assumes the risks of a business or enterprise." So you come up with a hot idea. And it immediately dawns on you that you need some bucks to make it fly. There is the term *bootstrapping*—which Webster's dictionary says is "to promote or develop by initiative and effort with little or no assistance." Such a self-initiating or self-sustaining process *could* be labeled as entrepreneurial. But you still need the money, honey.

So you hit up one of dem darn venture capitalists or so-called angel investors, even your rich Uncle Eddie from Boca. And how's this workin' for ya? Sheesh . . . nobody enjoys potentially losing money, huh?

Finding the necessary capital could just mean little more than a stroll to the bank (mosey on over to chapter 5, please). But in any event, you, my budding entrepreneur, decide to jump all the requisite hoops. So let's see what those hoops might be. Here's the seven-point plan.

1. Can you pitch your killer concept succinctly in thirty seconds? I don't mean in a tizzy or heated rush. I said *succinctly*—concisely. Better, you can even map it out on the back of a business card in that stomach-dropping elevator ride down to the bar—you're that good.

2. When you have more than thirty seconds, you should be able to demonstrate that you understand who your customers are *and* have thoroughly doped out the competition. You know both, inside and out (in your head and to your intended patron's satisfaction), and can assure you know who benefits, what you're dealing with, who and what you are up against.

    You can fully explain—and easily, too—your client base to anybody. Along those lines, you're prepared to spell out why you shine brighter than the next guy, and why those customers will gladly and quickly open up their wallets to snap up your product or tap into your service.

3. Props and Samples sell. A good Show and Tell is always effective—you learned that at the middle school science fair; the concept hasn't changed—and can help convince whomever that *you* can pull *this* off. *You.*

    Boldly present the compelling value of what you are selling with style, gusto, and panache. Saying all that: humility, sincerity, combined with smarts and rationality, can be very persuasive.

4. You must be able to back it up with a realistic business plan and understandable numbers. Reinforce *that* with a solid Plan B. Foresight equals wisdom. Baby steps are more than smart. This will be most helpful when you target, and then ask for, a clearly defined, reasonable sum of money. Clearly explain how and why you're going to spend that money. Yep, how and why, but also who, what, when, and where. This is for your own purposes as well as for your future benefactor's needs.

5. Break down any corporate sponsors, professional fans, and personal benefactors who have bought into (and/or believe in) the dream. If someone else is on board—particularly corporate someones of note—you will reduce any perceived risk, which can make it easier for somebody to climb on the train.

6. Do dress for success. Exude appropriate confidence. Act like you don't actually need the money (sort of like whistling down a dark alley, or

akin to dancing like nobody's watching). And in light of all this, have I mentioned that humility sells?

7. Regard each pitch like it's the warm-up session for the next; play it like it's perpetual spring training—keep pitching; keep improving your pitch.

THE MORE THE MERRIER?

As is the case with all savvy marketing strategies, astute future entrepreneurs will understand the sale of the product itself. They've done the homework and essential research. They know there's an actual market to eventually sell product to. Obvious preparation and product quality should be a no-brainer, but these hooks aren't always a given. The advantage of a demonstrated track record—either the seller's and/or other products—is certainly a plus.

These days, fundraising can be pushed as a special initiative, promoted as a special event, or touted as a unique experience. To explore this aspect of financial support, you could also look into some current, hot business models: crowdfunding and crowdsourcing.

FACING THE CROWD

Crowdfunding is when a bunch of folks—a "crowd" of investors—finance a project, usually with small (or smaller) chunks of capital. These contributions are somewhat like *stocks* (but are not actual *shares*)—donations that have a face value and ultimately will net you a return in some way. So, a ten-dollar donation garners you eternal thanks and/or gives you a warm, fuzzy on your insides; that hundred-dollar donation will eventually get you a titanium this or that.

When evaluating this funding scenario, you should consider the success stories alongside the tales of disappointment. You won't miss the after-burn of lost potential or the bright glow of triumph that only "full speed ahead" can spark. As of this writing, the crowdfunding platform is arguably best exemplified by sites like Kickstarter and IndieGoGo.

The accounts of wildly successful initiatives *can* be found. Accounts of whopper campaigns generating serious capital (and fervent interest in a future product) are out there. But, truth be told, like the California Gold Rush in the mid-1800s, this is not necessarily the norm. And in the same breath, reports of meager returns (as well as downright futile, dismal efforts) *do* exist. Of course, the sad tales are not a bona fide benchmark of a botched system either.

THE SOURCE

The term *crowdsourcing* is a mash up of "crowd" and "outsourcing." The term is attributed to writer Jeff Howe in a June 2006 *Wired* magazine article, "The Rise of Crowdsourcing." Crowdsourcing is inducing folks to contribute to your project via *their* brainstorms or concepts, info or advice, labor or product, testing (and, hopefully, subsequent results), and so forth.

Let's discuss this by quoting Thomas Edison again: "Genius is 1 percent inspiration, 99 percent perspiration." Thanks, Tom. Many designers and clients are finding value in this, what the *New York Times* has labeled the "new generation of online service marketplaces." For instance, here's the pitch on the 99 designs website (and I quote): "We connect passionate designers from around the globe with customers seeking quality, affordable design services."

That sounds promising (if not downright energizing), right? But for a vocal constituency of disgruntled designers, crowdsourcing competitions demean makers and lower the value of product and services. Some will tell you that such competitions sound the death knell for the industry at large and decry these contests as a scam, existing solely to steal ideas from embattled creatives (if not a diabolical form of thoroughly modern slave labor).

Crowdsourcing, as a term, is relatively current. But the underpinnings of spec work here obviously cannot be denied—you are competing for work with no guarantees of getting paid for it. For a lot of clients—alternately labeled naive and/or exploitive—it may be the first rung on the design ladder. For many novice designers—in turn tagged as naive and/or exploited—it could be their initial steps into the design world.

Here, Rick Antolic rolls his eyes. "Aaaargh ... Contests," he scoffs with derision. "Don't get me started."

NO COMPETITION

Why the righteous anger? I say we get Antolic started, indeed. But we should first discuss design competitions that are a largely undisputed testament to your capabilities and your credibility. These contests are almost always judged by designers who have gained recognition for their own design expertise and won such competitions themselves. In addition to recognition from your peers, competition awards attest to the high quality of your work and can ultimately justify a high level of compensation for your talent and ability. These awards also look great on the wall of your reception area. They are your "credentials"—easily recognizable as such to anyone who walks into your office and has not yet been exposed to the wonderful samples of your work you are about to show them.

There are competitions sponsored by national magazines (for instance, *How*, *Print*, and *CA*) that publish highly revered annuals showcasing the best of the best. Other prestigious national competitions include the CLIO Awards as well as the Society of Publication Designers and the New York Art Directors Club's annual contests. You'll also find a wealth of local opportunities through professional organizations (like your local Art Director's Club, Editor's Association, etc.). You're probably already aware of many of them; you know which ones offer the most prestige in your area.

If you enter a competition and find you have a winner, get some mileage out of this piece by entering it in another competition. If it walked away with a gold award at your local art director's club competition, send it off to a national competition.

And don't forget the peripheral publicity that comes with such awards. When you win an award, let your clients know about it—especially the client for whom you did the award-winning work. You'll want to notify that client personally if this piece has won some recognition. She or he may want to promote the award within the company and industry or your community, giving you additional exposure. If you've produced work for a client whose trade has its own competition for design excellence, check if your client plans to enter anything you've done for him in his industry's competition. Let the client know that you value the quality of the work you did together and would appreciate notification of any industry awards that this piece may garner.

And by all means, "toot your own horn" in a professional manner with a press release to your other clients, local news media, national design magazines, and trade publications (if you feel the prestige of this award is worthy of national recognition).

NO CONTEST

Let's say we find out that WidgeCo—who can more than afford to pay a fair price for certain work—puts that project out there, to anyone, in the form of a contest. And wow; the winner will have her work printed on new mugs, seen all across the country! Big whoop . . . for as Antolic observes, "If you have the money for national distribution, you have the budget to pay for the design." Also to the point, WidgeCo, the very model of a successful big business, has enough money to hire a few artists to come up with a deck of designs, and select the cream out of that crop.

"But instead," Antolic says, "they invite Joe Public to submit a design to a 'contest.' The company pays *bubkis* (zero, nada, nothing) for the influx of ideas they receive, and the 'winner' might get a monetary compensation that is a mere fraction of what the designer should have been legitimately paid for that work."

Antolic then poses some righteously legitimate questions: What other industry will do work for a big business and not get paid, because they want to be a part of a contest? "Would a plumber do that?" he asks, "An architect? An engineer? A doctor? [Righteous expletive deleted.] Not even someone versed in early eighteenth-century romantic poetry and prose would agree to write a classical haiku for a big business *for free, through a contest.*"

Antolic's philosophy is pretty simple. If somebody wants him to design something, he gets paid for it. "I charge fairly," he qualifies, "and I'm almost always willing to work with whatever kind of budget the client has. But I expect to be paid. My 'free time' is not 'free' time if I'm working; that might accurately be identified as 'overtime' and I charge accordingly.

"When I'm not getting paid to design, then I'm attending to other needs, responsibilities, interests, or sleep. Other than the sleep part, I can't attend to those other things without money. If you are asking for my talents and skills, you are asking me because it is of value for you currently. And my needs, responsibilities, and interests have a value to me. Hey—I'm sure we can work something out."

Let's play devil's advocate. It's not a huge stretch to view the contests as an abundant stock of cheap—or to be polite, affordable—design. Likewise, it's no quantum leap to look at these competitions as a ready resource for leads or contacts, maybe even a smart way to build your portfolio (if you need to) or a new model of client-creative interaction.

You can't—or shouldn't—avoid the heated debate over ethics and legalities. Let's just say that, as of this writing, crowdsourcing as a prolific marketing tool (in various incarnations) seems here for the duration. It's certainly a "for better or worse" playbook—the general model may not be universally loved (for good reason) but has been globally embraced with some gusto (for obvious purposes).

Perhaps we simply must fall back on the old adage: you get what you pay for. There is also this appropriate pair of expressions: "keep your eyes open" and "swim or die." In our age of the Internet, opportunities abound to heed all of the above.

WORK VERSUS LABOR

If you do a little homework, you will discover that many tech startup companies are founded by people who have various design backgrounds. Chad Hurley of YouTube fame comes to mind, right off the bat.

But even if you are not of the mad scientist or obsessed inventor ilk, it may be even more critical to try to make an individual *statement* online. I'm of the opinion that the most powerful statement you can make is through your *work*—the quality of, as well as the sweat equity invested. But wait—are we really talking about your *creative labor?*

Writing on the excellent 99U website, Jocelyn K. Glei quotes Lewis Hyde (from his classic book *The Gift: Creativity and the Artist in the Modern World)* to make a neat and clear distinction between *work* and *creative labor.*

"*Work* is what we do by the hour," Hyde clarified. "It begins and, if possible, we do it for money. Welding car bodies . . . washing dishes, computing taxes . . . these are [examples of] *work*. *Labor,* on the other hand, sets its own pace. We may get paid for it, but it's harder to quantify . . . writing a poem, raising a child . . . resolving a neurosis, invention in all forms—these are *labors.*

"Work is an *intended activity* that is accomplished through the will," Hyde continued. "Labor has its own schedule . . . there is no technology, no time-saving device that can alter the rhythms of creative labor. When the worth of labor is expressed [as an] exchange value . . . creativity is automatically devalued every time there is an advance in the technology of work."

By the way, 99U (as an organization) works to help creative professionals dropkick idea generation into idea execution. It takes its name from—hello again, Tom—Thomas Alva Edison's famous quote, "Genius is 1 percent inspiration, 99 percent perspiration." Creative labor lightbulb moment, indeed.

FINDING THE RIGHT MARKETS

How do you analyze what market is right for you? Initially, the job is easy enough: you must keep your eyes wide open. First, consider and understand what you like to do best. Then go online.

As we're going to be sitting some more, get off your butt and scoot over to the local library—yes, we're going to actually move and check out real reference you can physically hold in your hands and study . . . What a concept!

Follow this up with a trip to the bookstore. Find a newsstand, too, if these still exist in your town. Go to the movies (and pay attention to the posters, displays, and ads); watch TV (including the commercials). Your immediate task is to vigorously look around you . . . at anything and everything; *study it all.*

AT A GLANCE

This is serious browsing, but should also be a big hoot. See who's doing what and how they're doing it. Research who's putting it out there (and what *it*, in all its glory, *is*). As Rhonda Libbey tells us, "Figuring out what kind of design you want to do, and creating a portfolio that suits that market best, means a little detective work."

And it's elementary, my dear Watson—we're researching who's designing and what's being designed. The idea is to evaluate *your* work in light of what *you* see as the marketplace's current needs and trends—what resonates with you? Do keep your eyes open (and do take some notes, Holmes).

"Find out who commissions design work—as well as photography and illustration—for those areas," Libbey says, picking up the thread. "Sometimes it is an art director, editor, or publisher, film director, or author. Find out what they like, who is currently designing (plus shooting and illustrating for them). Most importantly, find out how they solicit new talent."

Chances are, according to Libbey, that the most desirable clients are approached by many creatives every day, and these folks will follow a specific protocol to review new material. "Perhaps they seldom scout for new talent at all," she points out.

For example, a well-known comic book company may require you to attend a particular comic book convention and sign up to meet one of their reps in person. Some of these companies will adhere to a very strict "no unsolicited submissions" policy.

"The good news," says Libbey, "is that most companies in the business of commissioning art and design know that they will always need to have a dialogue with new talent, and all of them try to make it easy to find their submission guidelines. Usually it can be found somewhere on their websites."

LOCATION, LOCATION, LOCATION

Do freelancers who live in big cities really have a better chance at success than those who live in small towns? Theoretically, it should be easier to market your services on the spot, as opposed to marketing from a remote location. On the surface of it, small town freelancers wanting to market in the big city reasonably would meet challenges of time and distance their metropolitan brothers and sisters don't face.

Regardless of location, your shot at success will not be the proverbial "piece of cake," and not too many years ago, the answer to the question would have been a resounding yes. But it can be done. It's being done. How? We live in a brave new world—the global village of instant communication and light-speed response.

Any "yes" answer to the big question above must be qualified by many factors: the Internet; state-of-the-art computer production tools plus digital delivery and cloud storage; today's telephone technology, phone answering systems and services; express mail couriers (local, national, and international), too.

This modern mixtape of technology gives an out-of-town freelancer all the tools to effectively set up shop in any city, just about anywhere in the world. Success can be elusive *wherever* you operate. Living in New York City, considered the hub of the industry, doesn't guarantee a cushy career. It's a bit like peeling the layers of an onion and defining what qualifies you as "a success" is relative and rather subjective.

The busy freelancer getting, oh, forty dollars to sixty dollars an hour may be tickled to earn this money, until he talks to a designer making, say, $70,000+ a year (all numbers stated for convenience only). That fellow discovers a colleague who casually drops the bomb that she earned even more while working fewer assignments. The hot ticket designer she met at that conference who netted even more than *that* (and with a month's vacation in Bali, to boot) awes this woman. She vows that she, too, will be "just as successful."

Your stats may vary, but you get the picture. Your chances for success may be better by living in the big city. Without a doubt, there is more work in the right New York City block than in all of my village of Yellow Springs, Ohio. But the relaxed quality of life in *this* friendly, sublimely tranquil haven cannot be found anywhere in (any) metropolis or in Gotham City. It's a trade-off artists living and working here have made without a second thought.

LOCAL VERSUS NATIONAL

What are the best markets for a beginner to try? You shouldn't limit yourself to local clients, but I always advise starting locally and small, but with an eye on the national (yes, even international) markets and the "big time." Learn to conduct business at home, and then use this training to branch out beyond your own turf.

The timetable to climb the ladder is up to you—again, success may be subjective as well as elusive. Modern communications, coupled with digital technology, makes it just as easy to get a job around the world as it is across town, there are good markets waiting for you—literally right down the street.

Local businesses, with needs ranging from advertising or promotional material to signage and stationery, are excellent markets for the beginner. Let's brainstorm a bit.

- The public television station may need you to energize the mail campaign for its upcoming fund drive.
- That local city magazine is putting together a special event issue and needs a hand.
- The university could use a sharp designer to pump life into its website; your neighborhood library, too. And, hey, the library would jump at the chance to design their outdated newsletter.
- How about that busy advertising agency across town? Could they use some help? Call them.
- The corner deli is looking for a new graphic identity.
- Your dentist, interested in stationery and letterheads, also needs a catchy check-up reminder.
- An insurance company wants to soften payment notices and complement other mailed material (and their in-house magazine could stand a serious visual overhaul).

It's easy to see that good assignments are where you find them. Keeping that in mind, I'd look to your own backyard for those first jobs. With this invaluable experience, moving to larger markets will be that much easier.

NEW KID IN TOWN

If you're new in town, getting started again locally or expanding your horizons regionally means that marketing and promotion is the name of the game right now.

Advertise! Of course, update your website (as well as business card and forms). Place an ad in the local newspaper; consider an announcement on your cable channel's community calendar or a late, late night television spot (when ad rates are dirt cheap). Spread the word around. Organize that mailing program. Tell your new neighbors. Join the local art organizations and schmooze. Stuff mailboxes, send emails, or stick flyers on windshields. Check in with the Better Business Bureau and at the Chamber of Commerce; maybe members can refer you to potential clients who need your work. Make cold calls. The idea is to tell one and all (not just the business community) who you are, what you do, and where to find your services.

At some point, it's a relatively short hop to go regional; but initially, establish a home base—professionally and personally. The markets aren't going away; they'll be there when you're comfortably settled and in a position to solicit their business.

TALK IS KINDA CHEAP

Mega, a designer/illustrator actually (and currently) living in Bali, spent six years as an editorial art director (specifically for magazines), so the French native can speak with some authority about working from that side of the drawing table. Based on that experience, he wants to offer what I call five wee pearls of wisdom he says he wished someone gave him when he was a student.

"The first one," he says, laughing, "may seem weird, coming from a guy offering advice, but here it is: just shut up and work. Talkers are not doers." One thing that frustrated Mega in art school was that his teachers used to encourage students to *verbalize* their projects. "But you don't necessarily need to do this," he insists. "I disagree . . . Actions speak louder than words."

As a student, Mega was typically laboring with low or no funds. For a while, he worked in a burger joint to buy a ticket to New York City and pound the pavement. "I went to all the offices of people I wanted to meet—certain record labels, skateboard companies, headquarters of select brands. I would just knock on doors, pretending to be a journalist looking to interview the different players of the New York (so-called) 'underground scene.' And it worked."

His enthusiasm opened doors for him and even established lasting friendships. Back home, he got busy. "I worked and worked a lot. I produced a book called *NYC Rules!*, a fairly ambitious graphic design project about the Big Apple's alternative scenes. Then I would just go to all the magazine offices—with no appointment, mind you—and simply present what I did and give them a copy. (Everybody likes free stuff.) Result: all the important media talked up my project and soon I was hired as the art director of a French publication. This was the beginning of my career in the industry." By the way, folks at his old school are still talking about this bit of guerrilla marketing. As the man said, talkers are not doers. Actions speak louder than words.

But true to his ideals, Mega says this to cap off the discussion: "First and foremost, last but not least—stop listening to me. Form your own opinions, go back to your work, and be awesome."

THE HERE. THE NOW.

Mega will tell you that it's all about the here and now. Yes, you might be too busy, a bit scared, somewhat unsure about what you are actually doing. Or perhaps you're too exhausted because of your day job. You could be just plain sick, even depressed. "But whatever," he emphasizes, "You do what you do because you love art, and you make art because this is your passion . . . so really, you have no excuse. Don't wait. Do. Now. Life is too short to watch any TV. Stop smoking weed, stop procrastinating, stop complaining. Practice. Art is about commitment. It all depends on you. Better to put any available time and your energy into your work, instead of losing a job for the wrong reasons."

When he was working as an art director for magazines, Mega was in charge of every visual aspect of the publication. It was his charge to find illustrators or photographers to complement the articles supplied by his editor. "The problem was," he remembers, "most people don't respect a deadline, and I had to wait on these slowpokes to finish my layout. I quickly realized that if you want something done, you'd better do it yourself." So Mega began replacing late visuals with his own illustrations. Eventually, he started to get noticed purely as an illustrator and other magazines began ordering his artwork.

TIME WILL TELL

Is it a no-brainer to advise you to simply be confident? Mega really started from basically nothing (as he puts it). "Nobody in my family is sensitive to art," he tells us, "I come from a poor background. I had no help (and really, in life, nobody will help you anyway)." He was a garbage collector, cleaned airport toilets, and carried luggage. He worked the door at a nightclub. He even worked as Santa Claus in a clothing shop.

Let me point out that these were full-time gigs. Any money earned bought food and paid the rent. All this, of course, so he could have a place to work on his design, late at night, when he came back from, well, work. Art is nothing if not about perseverance. "The day you can afford to quit your day job," he says, "you just utilize this invaluable extra time to work more and more on your passion. People who spend an hour here and there working on their art cannot compete with you anymore. The labels 'good' or 'bad' don't matter, there is no good and bad. There is only dedication. So fail away . . . get better, stay true to yourself, that's the best way to succeed."

OPPORTUNITY KNOCKS?

Mega's professional journey kicked off with minor gigs in, as he says, "small and boring cities in the south of France. Nothing happening; a general lack of interest for the arts; no great exhibitions, no cool artists." But he ultimately realized that it was better to pull off what he wanted to do, head to where he needed to go, check out what he hoped to see, instead of simply complaining about not having those opportunities.

He can begin new projects (and do what he likes). And what he likes is "everything that is around me," he says, "in my head and in my heart." His latest project, *Longing to Be Knotted Together*, took him about five months to complete, working eight to ten hours a day, seven days a week. "No time for parties, no more girlfriend," he says with a sigh. "Just pure dedication—and a generous slice of craziness I guess." Of course, he then had to figure out the perfect production values—the paper, inks, and screen-printing process, etc., to suit his vision. At that point, he started looking for galleries to show this sweet stuff. "The process was long and painful," he says. "But you don't wait for things to happen. You are the one who can create your opportunities."

By the time you read this, he will have embarked on an exhibition tour that took him to Australia (Melbourne, Sydney, Adelaide), Jakarta, Singapore, Kuala Lumpur, Berlin, back to his native France (Marseille and Paris), and more. "So there's nothing happening in your town?" he asks with a sly and ostensibly sympathetic grin. "Ahh, too bad . . . by drawing or designing what you wish to see; by creating the events you hope to experience; by writing, illustrating, and designing the books you care to read—you can meet all your goals (but of course, you gotta stick to it)."

FOOL OF YOURSELF

Your ego is a great marketing tool; ego is what marketing is all about. But, as Mega reminds you, your ego has no place in real life. "Injecting your giant ego into the work never produces anything of quality," he says. "I can't emphasize this enough: be nice in your real life. Be kind to the people around you (but humbly discount any help you offer). Stay equally humble in your business relationships. The day you need something . . . those folks who benefited by your kindness will line up to return the favor. And, hey, maybe even buy some design."

WORKING WITH NEW BUSINESSES

Freelancers just starting out may look at new businesses as kindred spirits, but some words of caution here: be careful when taking an assignment with a new business, as new businesses frequently fail and don't pay. Do your homework prior to working for any company, regardless of track record. Chances are very good that a pioneering enterprise or established organization will treat you right, but reputation—or bright promise, for that matter—is no guarantee that this firm will be a dream client.

The best offense is always a strong defense. Thoroughly research their website. Write explicit and detailed emails when a job is being proposed and/or then discussed. Take good notes over the phone (if you're a terrible note taker, record—certainly with notification and hopefully with permission—the conversation). Ask incisive questions at every meeting with any opportunity. Be prepared to discuss your rates, terms, and needs, and evaluate how the client's needs compare with yours. It's best to clarify and communicate right at (and from) the start.

NETWORKING

The one thing everybody has (and almost always loves to give away) is advice. Yes, it's okay to seek advice, never shy away or sniff your nose at formal or informal information gathering.

Networking is a low-key, direct means of communication that pays handsome dividends because there is much to learn from other freelancers. Your colleagues are veritable storehouses of information; references and referrals; help, solace, and counsel.

Hobnob. Compare notes. Commiserate. After all, you share the same basic experience, rather identical trials and tribulations. Almost invariably, most contacts enjoy talking shop and are easy to find. Start with the Internet, of course, and the ever-proliferating number of meetups, websites, chat boards, news and discussion groups.

Obviously, check out your local art and design community resources, as well. Do an Internet search for graphic artists in your town or city. Any traditionalists out there? You could start with the local Yellow Pages under "Artists" (commercial and fine arts) or "Graphic Designers."

Does anyone not know how to network? Regardless of method or scope, the formula is simple: introduce yourself; make friendly conversation while asking pertinent questions; acquire other names and numbers; and repeat the process. Then just keep in touch.

The first commandment of networking? "Thou shalt never stop." As Brian Fencl says, "Action creates more action and that leads to opportunity."

WHAT GOES 'ROUND . . .

Invaluable help, stimulating ideas, compelling information, new colleagues, and fresh contacts await. Mary Grace Eubank says, "I'm a firm believer in 'what goes around, comes around.' Keep track of whom you contact and be aware of how they can help you." *And how you can help them.* Eubank made it clear that you should not feel guilty about using connections. Keep in mind that most of your contacts will be receptive and helpful—you must act the same.

And don't network *only* with other designers. If a knowledgeable source is willing and available, cultivate it; network with illustrators, editors, art and design directors, copywriters, or the production coordinator (even when you're not involved with a job). Approach the sales manager, too. If you really want some insider information, talk to any secretary, assistant, or clerk. It's medieval to believe that you're the center of the design universe when so much is accomplished through the collective process. Most folks are flattered to be considered experts. If you have specific questions, why not go right to a particular source?

It should also be said that you could encounter the dark side of networking. Some folks simply lack, shall we say, mature interpersonal skills (read any juicy tweets, lately?). Some people are just plain busy, perhaps too busy, to talk at length—too short in fuse, reason, or self-control.

I've also found that, while just about everybody is willing to contribute a certain amount of information regarding business chops, many are unwilling to share the mechanics behind an innovative technique or unique approach. This is justified and perfectly legitimate; it's not to their advantage to simply give the farm away.

And while most of your contacts will be happy to chat, or will politely decline, you'll inevitably run into those who virtually accuse you of trying to steal state secrets. Remember that stress and competition and drive can create surprising attitudes. Credit that person for her interesting perspective, thank him for his fascinating advice, and say good-bye. Move on.

PRO BONO

Volunteering or donating your time and services can be an effective means of generating publicity (or simply doing a good turn). The trade-off you make with the group commissioning the art is your skill in exchange for a credit on a final product.

Thus, you are doing the job based on a higher calling or as business or marketing strategy (nothing wrong with that). You usually have the chance— or you should make that a caveat—to do your own thing, so you gain a potential showcase.

While the concept of *pro bono* is not universally loved, you shouldn't dismiss pro bono as a simple giveaway or write it off as merely paying your dues. Far from it. If you establish ground rules, define limits, and clarify expectations, *pro bono* could be a healthy investment of your available time, energy, and spirit.

Local arts and theater groups will frequently offer talented designers opportunities for high exposure through posters and other promotional vehicles. There's nothing like seeing your work all over town. Other possibilities for pro bono work include charity fundraisers (walkathons, road races, charity balls). The people who run these events and volunteer their services are often the movers and shakers in your community. They're frequently high-profile types in a good position to circulate your name. And they may be possible sources of future business.

Another advantage to pro bono work is the caliber of the support services—and again, usually—at your disposal. Frequently, top-quality printers and color service bureaus will donate their services for a charitable event, allowing you to familiarize them with your capabilities. You'll also have a chance to use services and goods that budget-conscious clients may not have afforded you.

And don't forget you may donate your time to the firms offering support services in exchange for collaboration on a promotional piece. (Always ask for a credit for your contribution and get an agreement that they won't change your design or illustration without your permission.)

PURPOSE

In the best of all worlds, volunteering your time and/or your art services (pro bono work) to good causes would certainly be only a win/win situation. But, as this is reality, and as we've discussed, the concept of *pro bono* is not universally loved. Let's discuss this a bit, shall we?

Some may see pro bono as merely freebies, but we'll try to look at the big picture from all the angles. As a volunteer, you'll gain confidence at the drawing board doing actual assignments. You'll have creative freedom without any pressures to cut the best deal, and you can design according to your vision. You will learn about deadlines and working with a client.

You acquire a printed piece for your portfolio, work experience for your résumé, and achieve name recognition. You get profitable leads, make new contacts, and establish a reputation as someone willing to go the extra mile. In addition, volunteers have the happy and satisfying experience of completing a job well done for a worthwhile purpose.

PRINCIPLE

You'll find established artists donating their services, so you shouldn't dismiss volunteering as a simple giveaway or write it off as merely paying your dues. Far from it, it could likely be a healthy investment of time, energy, and spirit for any artist, regardless of stature.

But this is not everybody's opinion. "I'm not against pro bono work, *in principle*," Rick Antolic states right upfront, "but I always advise my people to be very, very cautious about who gets work from you for free. You will never stop being asked to do work gratis, so don't ever be known as the go-to guy for freebies. You'll never be able to command higher prices with that kind of reputation (or should I say, 'exposure')."

So when is it okay to work for free? Antolic has a "Rule of Threes" when it comes to accepting pro bono:

1. The assignment is something you'd *love* to do in the first place.
2. You can do the job exactly to your liking, and that end product can strengthen your portfolio.
3. Do pro bono only if you know that the client truly cannot pay.

"Often times, a client can pay, but they will first try to get it for free," Antolic cautions. "Don't fall for that."

REFERRALS

If you do your best work, meet your deadlines, and are dependable, the referrals will take care of themselves.

Referrals come in two varieties: as leads and as references. To get a reference, you'll need a few jobs under your belt first. These referrals usually are the result of a rewarding and positive performance. The client likes your work and passes the word on: "This is the person to see to get the assignment done right; call her."

Leads often accompany references. The satisfied client above not only refers you to one compatriot, she also supplies you the name and address of yet another businessperson needing your services. A graphic designer gives you a hot tip that the design studio across town is looking for someone of your caliber right away. (You send an email or make the phone call, mention your contact, and gently nudge towards a next step.) You call the art director on your last job and network a little: "Do you know anybody who knows anybody who needs anybody?" (This art director, more than happy to help, gives you a list of five new contacts; it's now up to you.)

RIGHT ON POINT

(PROFESSIONAL VIEWPOINTS IN 50 WORDS OR LESS)

The sweetest source of new work comes from old work—through existing work for existing clients. Do superior work and that client will more likely hire you again, talk you up to a colleague or friend, and refer them to you to do the same.

—Ken Bullock

Every day has the potential to be exciting and rewarding. The opportunity of a lifetime could be waiting for you in the next email or phone call.

—Randy Glasbergen

It's not what you know, it's who you know? It's what you know and who you know— the "what" being much more important than the "who." And "doing your best" is really about trying to do a little better than your best—reaching to exceed your grasp.

—Shaun Tan

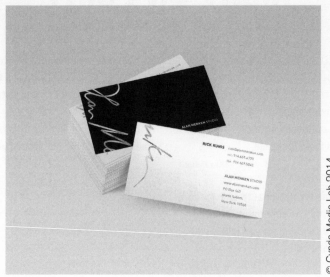

The talent will either be there or not already. You must be incredibly dedicated and focused; it all comes down to "work hard" and then "work harder." You evaluate the rewards honestly and decide whether to stick with it or not.

—Fred Carlson

Designers are no longer just visual artists. Design goes way beyond just logos, typefaces, and brochures. A designer today must become a strategist who can envision designs that are technically feasible, financially viable, and visually engaging.

—C. J. Yeh

CHAPTER 4

OFF ON THE RIGHT FOOT

There is no right way to do the wrong thing.

—Roger Brucker

DRESS FOR SUCCESS

What *do* you need to succeed in your own design business? It's a good question, and one we will explore in depth in this chapter.

For clarity's sake, let's define the basic term *design studio*. A design studio is an entity with a definite name and identity. Something as straightforward as "Sue Jones, Freelancer" would qualify, as well as the more esoteric "Chicken Soup Graphics." These business concerns would be owned by graphic designers who work primarily out of their own place of business (at home or in the studio) and who do not work primarily in someone else's studio, agency, or "graphic design department." The primary business would be total design, from concept to completion, rather than single aspects of production.

Regardless of the moniker, you are engaged in running a design studio—an endeavor fraught with many complexities. To make a go of it, you'll need to be a qualified professional and businessperson.

THE CHASE IS ON

Shaun Tan feels that it's critical to pursue personally challenging work, and says that small jobs can be as significant as high-profile gigs expressly for that reason. Tan estimates his most significant achievements may very well be modest works created in his parents' garage during his early twenties, work which remains unexhibited and unpublished, of no commercial concern or public dimension.

"A good artist," he says, "is an eternal student, and even when most confident, never feels like a master. They forever potter in their backyard spaces, exploring their craft with modest integrity. That's how unusual and original work emerges, not by chasing markets or fashionable movements, or wanting to be conventionally successful."

But, as Tan would be among the first to tell you, for a commercial artist, chasing markets is obviously an essential economic pursuit—the necessary parallel play of a creative practice. However, there's no express roadmap or explicit directions to get where "there" may be, only a multitude of working destinations: adult, young adult, and children's publishing; advertising, editorial, and genre; film (and film design) plus animation; theater; fine arts; games; and other forms not yet invented. Most visual artists—if flexible, versatile, and open-minded—can cross over borderlines, especially in a digital, multimedia environment.

"All commercial work is collaborative," Tan says, "thus, communication is crucial, even in our [somewhat] introverted profession. You need to be able to talk, write about, and create in a clear and explanatory way. You help others understand your ideas, especially when concepts are not immediately visible, and especially to non-artists and certain folk who are, for all practical purposes, aesthetically blind. Empathy and patience almost always win the day here, even in tough situations."

Tan's body of work tips the iceberg of titanic vision and tremendous accomplishment, yet he modestly advises you to stay open to discussion, revision, and compromise *while still maintaining your own artistic integrity*. "These are not necessarily incompatible, as so many people often believe," he comments. "It is worth noting that clients may be right about things as often as artists are. Most problems and rejections result from creative cross-purposes rather than actual disagreements. It's important to understand each others' philosophies and criteria."

THE RIGHT STUFF

If you bought this book, you have more than a vague curiosity about going out on your own. That's a good sign right there. How do you find out if you have the right stuff?

Well, you won't be required to break the sound barrier every workday, but answer these initial queries and then consider the evaluation questions posed under this chapter's later section, "Do You Have What It Takes?" For your best results, respond truthfully and appropriately.

WHAT ARE YOU GETTING OUT OF THIS?

What are you getting out of this? Why are you doing it? Question your motives and answer honestly. You can make a nice hunk of change freelancing, but you could also win the lottery before you create the next *Family Guy*. If you want to freelance just for some easy "big bucks," you're in for a rude surprise. And do you have the special skills that translate into that moneymaking opportunity? Your business exists only to profitably practice your craft. Without talent, even a superbly structured framework won't take you very far.

ARE YOU SELF-DISCIPLINED?

Do you have the drive and ambition to turn that skill into a success? Talent without drive and motivation does not generate income. A dream without desire cannot be fulfilled. Freelancing should be what you *have* to do—for your soul and your checkbook.

It's easy to be excited about getting the Nike account. The great assignments spark an energy that feeds itself. But behind the glitter of those "important" jobs lies your everyday world. As a freelancer, you must diligently face the small daily drudgeries with the same aplomb you show those "bigger" responsibilities. A poor attitude will cripple your workday. Lackadaisical habits will get you into trouble very quickly.

Throw this into the mix: there will be mundane tasks and tiresome chores, and your commitment lies here as well. You may be bored by those simple jobs that cover the rent, but you must have the determination to see them through, to make sure they're done right. You should attend to all the "little" tasks with a healthy, positive spirit. There may come a day when you pick and choose only the select commissions while delegating lesser responsibilities to your assistants. Until then, can you do grunt work and think in the long term?

HOW'S YOUR BUSINESS ACUMEN?

"Good design is good business." You've heard this quote, I'm sure. It's an oldie, but still absolutely relevant and excruciatingly true (maybe now more than ever). If you have little or no sense of how to run a business, it is time to learn. On-the-job training will teach you the hard way; better to read, research, and study before you become the one-minute manager.

How's your bankbook? In times of low pay, slow pay, or (heaven forbid) no pay, can you—should you—support yourself and your business with personal savings? Realistically, how long should you do this if your business is new, not up to speed, or in a lull?

My accountant tells me to have a reserve of at least three months in the bank just in case, but everyone's situation is slightly different; your safety net might be a year or six months. The numbers will vary, but a hard fact of economics remains constant: can you launch and sustain your business if you're not generating income?

ARE YOU DECISIVE?

As the Lord High Everything, you'll be making all of many decisions and taking responsibility for the consequences. Remember, you are the boss. And hey, boss, does taking a risk scare you? If you can't even chance a response, you've answered the question already. Without being cute, freelancing is risky business. After all, it is your time, your energy, and your money being poured into this venture. Professionally, no one else goes down the tubes with you if you fail; personally, you and your family have much to lose.

CAN YOU TOLERATE A FAIR AMOUNT OF REJECTION?

Unfortunately, this is a fact of life for every freelancer up and down the ladder. You will get rejected for many reasons, those misjudgments regarding your abilities probably being the least of your worries. In simplistic terms, the creative director looks at your work and says, "Can I sell my product with this art? Will I make my point by using this illustration?" If the answer is no, your work will be rejected.

When all is said and done, it is the portfolio that counts. Remember that rejection is the downside of an isolated opinion, a particular preference. It's not the gospel. I won't kid you, rejection hurts. But if you have faith in yourself and your ability, it will never kill. Create an inner strength from your substantial talent and draw from it. Rejection is simply part and parcel of freelancing. Can you take it?

The decision that lands you any assignment usually comes down to this question: who's the best and brightest (read the more utilitarian, *appropriate*) designer meeting this job's particular needs?

CAN YOU LAY IT ON THE LINE?

Outside your studio, it's not a controlled experiment. You may well ask how much luck figures into the equation. I'm one of those who believe that luck is that moment when preparation meets opportunity. You minimize the gamble with sweat and organization, but there are no guarantees and lots of variables. You have to be willing to wager a bet to reap the reward.

Serendipity—being in the right place at the right time—is your good fortune, but beyond your control. It's nothing to brood over, nothing you can fine tune. Knowing somebody within the organization can help, but doesn't always. Your politics don't often enter into the scenario (unless your politics are synonymous with your work).

It's not that they won't like your tie—unless you give new meaning to bad grooming or dress like you just lost a bet. You shouldn't lose work because of casual (but tasteful) attire. Assuming you haven't provoked an international incident or insulted anyone's beloved mother, you won't lose an assignment because "they hate you" (always for some vague, undetermined reason).

At some point, an artist's personality can certainly influence the art buyer's decision, and that winning smile is to your definite benefit. Obviously the two parties must interact so personalities can't be avoided. However, if you don't have the style and skills the task requires, you won't get an assignment on pure congeniality.

Attitude and reputation will be factored into the equation, too. Art directors are looking for skilled individuals who can deliver the goods on time. Your samples may sizzle and glow, but if you're an argumentative prima donna who can't meet a deadline, you're not a viable commodity. Be down to earth, be yourself. Be dependable; be on time; be flexible. No matter how small the assignment or business, always do your best job.

CAN YOU THRIVE ON COMPETITION?

They are out there. They're good. They're waiting for you. While this may sound like the promo to a bad slasher flick, it's really not hype or horror. The small army of your skilled peers is tremendously talented, hard working, and organized. In general, I've found the competition to be a rather loose and friendly fraternity. We do play the same game, in the same ballpark. But your comrades-at-arms won't all act like your bosom buddies nor is that a requirement in their job description.

Competition in free enterprise is the American way. Use it as your motivation and you'll have an edge. Have a keen and healthy esteem for your competition. Respect their work and keep your eyes open: know what your associates are doing by researching the trade magazines, creative directories, and annuals. Don't be a rubber stamp of the hot new style, but do know what's current. A key to real success is to offer something that's original and fresh—something the buyer can't get just anywhere, from just anybody. And as Matt McElligott says, "It's vitally important to be true to yourself." Combine this with good service and strengthen it all with determination and forethought, and your competition will not be so scary after all.

And speaking of competition, how do you feel about selling yourself? Aside from your artistic responsibilities, this is a salesperson's job. It's a fairly simple situation (at least on paper): you must bring in the work to sustain the business that satisfies your creative impulse.

HOW DO YOU HANDLE STRESS?

Keep the following buzzwords in mind when pondering the considerable tensions of freelancing: grace under pressure . . . flexibility . . . rolling with the punches . . . shooting from the hip . . . adaptability . . . creativity . . . thinking on your feet. Hey, I'll stop.

If you rattle like nuts in a jar when the pressure builds, you're going to be in trouble. The landlord is banging on your studio door; you are certain there'll be a horse's head in your bed the next morning if you don't pay the rent. A once generous deadline screams at you from the calendar while that simple watercolor wash becomes a life-or-death situation. Panicky?

DO YOU MIND WORKING ALONE?

Hopefully, you have a stunning relationship with the only one who may be sharing your work space—you. Art school is a pleasant memory now—the halls buzzing with kindred spirits spilling into the comfortably familiar studios, a common ground, awaiting the arrival of teachers and students with a singular purpose and shared excitement. That glorious phase of your life's education is over.

At first you'll laugh, as if at a dumb joke, but you'll discover that it's really true: you'll need to get out and practice those "real world" skills. Life away from the studio, with friends and acquaintances who make actual conversation (and not necessarily shop talk) helps balance the isolation. Outside interests temper the hours spent hunched over the drawing table keeping your own company. Seek activities and nurture a support system outside the studio. You may very well be your own best friend, but don't go it alone.

HOW ARE YOUR ENERGY AND STAMINA?

You do understand that you're going to be working hard, right? You will hustle to the left and bustle to the right. You will, at times, pause for a breath and then sidestep to *manic* in the middle. Your time schedule will hardly be regular; you'll be a slave to other people's deadlines. Sure, there will be moments so quiet you can hear a pen drip, countered by hectic periods when twenty-four-hour days are not enough. "Hustling," as we said earlier, is all relative for the freelancer

MAKING THE BREAK

Initially, it may be wiser for you to freelance as a sideline with outside employment (full or part time) smoothing the rough financial edges. It's no crime to build toward independence rather then leaping romantically, albeit imprudently, into the fray.

And there's no federal law prohibiting you from doing outside projects while working on staff. As long as there are no conflicts of interest with house accounts and your freelancing doesn't interfere with your staff work, there shouldn't be any problem.

But obviously, first discuss it with your boss. Perhaps there's a house rule that staff may not freelance. When you signed your contract, you agreed to abide by company regulations, so honor those terms. Don't believe a discreet, covert operation will remain your little secret for long. The artistic community is smaller then you might think; I guarantee that it'll catch up to you.

It's been said (and I firmly believe) that it's better to look for a new position while you still have your old job. It makes a lot of sense, and only you can decide when (and if) you're ready to make a complete break.

If freelancing is okay with your employer, test the water first. *Don't* leave on impulse or in anger. Instead, take a few "casual" assignments and, hopefully, if you can, maintain at least one substantial account. Over a period of time, get a taste of the freelance life. When you're mentally prepared, with your financial safety net in place, simply hold your nose and jump.

See chapter 7 and our sidebar with Brian Allen.

"SALE" ON

Some artists feel that marketing their work is akin to putting their children up for sale. But first recognize that someone is paying you to produce images for a purpose. Next, know that you are selling yourself as a problem solver first and as a person second. And if you remember that you are selling usage of the art rather than the product itself, this anxiety is easily suppressed. Here, Mary Grace Eubank cautions you to "realize that you're selling your work, not your soul. Read books on self-projection and confidence building. Possibly attend motivational seminars on sales techniques. Work with a rep and stay in the background until you can develop a more positive persona."

If you dread the thought of selling your work, but feel you're best suited temperamentally to freelancing, Ben Mahan says you are not alone: "It's just something that you have to do. Most artists can really sell themselves better than anyone else, and you *must* get out and sell yourself a bit. If you don't like dealing one-to-one, work the phones and/or through the mail and email. However, ultimately, you'll need that personal contact, so make the connection."

DO I HAVE WHAT IT TAKES?

The beginning of your career—before you invest your time, energy, and capital—is the best time to objectively assess your design and business skills, (plus personal qualities).

I assure you, this is not as silly as it may sound at first reading. During a crisis, bad year, or crunch time, too many designers question their abilities—or worse yet, realize they can't quite cut it—and throw in the towel.

Ask yourself if you have what it takes to go into business for yourself. Answer this question by breaking it down into parts. Evaluate your . . .

EXPERIENCE

Be honest about who you are, what you can do, and how well you do it. This won't necessarily prevent headaches, heartbreak, or disasters, but it will give you a strong foundation to weather the storm. Begin with this self-evaluation:

1. Design is communication. Are you an effective communicator?
2. Can you market your work and promote yourself?
3. Can you personally sell your vision to the client while translating that client's needs into dynamic materials?
4. One goes to a specialist for something special—not pedestrian or cookie-cutter graphics, but for striking, thought-provoking, quality work. Are you a designer capable of leading the band rather than jumping on the bandwagon?
5. Do you understand (and not fear or loathe) the world of business and finance?
6. Experience makes a difference. Do you have enough? There is an advantage to starting up with some experience versus diving in right out of school. There is foresight in building business gradually as a moonlighter while working full time for someone else. (Some designers get freelance work from their employer's overload or turndowns.)
7. Why are you going into business for yourself? You shouldn't be doing it if you are motivated entirely by ego.
8. Following up here: don't go into business for yourself if you're after fame, fortune, or respect.

9. Continuing that thread (and, definitely last but not least), don't do it out of anger.
10. Finally, is your primary motivation to make money (or more money)? Honest, pay-for-fair work is nothing to be ashamed of. Making enough to buy groceries, make your rent, and pay the bills are solid reasons to strike out on your own.

SKILLS

Knowing that you have the chops to do a job (and do it well) should be a given. You will need to be able to take a project from conceptualization to completion, bring in and supervise support personnel and services, and make sure that all aspects of a project are done right. Your portfolio should reflect this by showing a variety of printed samples.

If you have worked for two or more years in a graphic design studio, advertising agency, or even publishing house, chances are that you've had some experience managing projects through all phases of production. You've probably had experience dealing with vendors, suppliers, and freelancers and have acquired a lot of the know-how necessary to run your own studio. Chances are, especially if this was a small studio, you've been aware of, if not directly involved in, the firm's day-to-day operations.

To determine if you have the design and production skills necessary for going into business on your own, see if you agree with the following statements. Be honest with yourself. If you're lacking in any area, you can always work to develop additional skills or bring on a partner to supplement your abilities.

1. I can render a concept and present it to a client through thumbnails, roughs, or comps.
2. I know how to prepare print-ready design for a printer, color house, or service bureau.
3. I can come up with dynamite visual concepts on my own.
4. I can design just as well or better than my competition.
5. I have good organizational abilities. I can juggle several projects at once and keep track of progress on them all.
6. I can convince clients that my work can help in meeting their business objectives.
7. I am quick and efficient in executing most design and production-related tasks.
8. I know enough about production and printing to know when my client's request is not feasible to produce.
9. I know when (and how) to suggest more cost-effective solutions to achieve a client's end goal.

10. When necessary, I can design for the audience my client is trying to reach rather than just executing my own style (perhaps I even know how to identify my client's target audience).

BUSINESS SKILLS

You will need to practice salesmanship, basic accounting, and business procedures—the kinds of things many college graduates know, but designers are less prepared for. To determine if you have the business and management aptitude necessary for going out on your own, see if you agree with the next statements. Again, if you're lacking in any area, you can always work to develop these skills. There are many courses and books on business management and marketing basics.

1. I have good communication skills. I am familiar with business etiquette and procedures when making written and verbal contact.
2. I can set reasonable goals and follow through on them.
3. I am able to get along with just about anybody and can motivate others to help me with projects I am involved in.
4. I can sell an idea to a client.
5. I make decisions quickly.
6. I don't procrastinate. I work steadily instead of waiting until a few days before a project deadline.
7. I can see and understand the whole picture. I don't concentrate on one thing, while ignoring other aspects of a situation.
8. I have good organizational abilities. I can handle several projects at once and keep track of progress on each.
9. I can juggle the projects at hand while cultivating new business.
10. I know when to turn down work (and I know my reasons why).
11. I can keep clients informed of the job's status and any glitches as they arise.
12. I can keep track of escalating costs and inform clients when a project might exceed the budget before it actually does.
13. I can work with disorganized clients.
14. I can explain the design process to clients and teach them to be better clients, thus helping them to be more time- and cost-efficient.

ENTREPRENEURIAL SAVVY

You will also have to develop strong personal skills. Juggling finance, design, and production is one thing, but you will also need to subjectively appraise your individual strengths and weaknesses. Take stock of your grit, determination, and discipline. To determine how you stack up, see if you agree with the statements below (and be honest, you know yourself best):

1. I am confident in my design abilities. If my work is not appreciated, I can shrug it off and apply myself with confidence to other projects.
2. I am a self-starter. Nobody has to tell me to get going.
3. I am highly motivated. I can keep working on a project for as long as I need to complete it on time.
4. I can concentrate on the task at hand. I'm not easily distracted from what needs to be done.
5. I am persistent. Once I know what I want, or make up my mind to do something, almost nothing can stop me.
6. I am in excellent health.
7. I have a lot of stamina and energy.
8. I can put the needs of my business above my own personal needs when required.
9. I can put the needs of my employees above my own needs when required.
10. I can ask for help when I need more information or feel overwhelmed.

TALLY IT UP

Only you know the outcome of the above evaluations. And because you'll need these abilities to make the business work, you didn't kid yourself, right?

Tally the number of yes and no answers and see how they stack up against your potential for success. All the answers raise issues that are important to maintaining a business. If you answered no to only one item in each of the above sections, chances are good that you can go it alone without any help. But if you answered no to more than three questions or statements total (or more than one in any single category), you may be taking on more than you can handle by yourself. Unless you feel you can cultivate these qualities on your own, consider finding a partner (or rep) to help in the weak areas.

IS THE OPPORTUNITY TO SUCCEED THERE?

You will need to evaluate your potential market. Is there a niche out there that you think you can fill? While it's not best to have all your eggs in one basket, it is good to have at least one major client to rely on—do you already have this client lined up? Do you have some idea of the kind of work you will be doing and the compensation you can expect?

Let's determine the size of your potential market. What type of work do you think you will be doing, and who do you think will buy it? How many clients are out there? You need to get a realistic picture of what you do best and what you think you could be doing to get business. To help guide you in this process, ask yourself the following questions:

1. What do you really like to do? What kind of design makes you happy? Are there any types of design that you dread or in which your skills are not up to par?
2. What's your idea of a dream job, and what would you do gratis (just to have that type of work or client)?
3. What's your design history—what were your biggest triumphs? What were your most successful projects? What were your near near-misses? What were your biggest flops?
4. Who is your competition? Think about your peers and analyze their work. How many other designers are out there doing the same thing you want to do for the same kinds of clients? Realistically assess if you're able to provide better design or better service than your competition. You don't want to spend valuable time where there's little chance of gaining any business. Be a tough (but objective) critic. Who blows you out of the water? Who is the cream of the crop? Be mindful of what the competition is doing and honestly evaluate yourself.
5. Are you in a position to fill a void the competition is not filling?
6. What's your current reputation? What do clients and vendors believe you have going for you? On the street, what might people hear about you and think of you and your works?
7. What work have clients seen? Where has your work been seen?

As nebulous as it all may be, determining where you stand may make the difference between getting a job offer and getting a "Try again next time, bud." You don't want to waste your time marketing stellar design capabilities to your local mechanic. However, if you have very little experience, you'll want to think twice about trying to sell your services to the biggest corporations in town—you may not get beyond the receptionist. Until you've proven yourself, you're better off working as a freelancer with the design firms these corporations are currently employing.

WHERE ARE YOUR POTENTIAL CLIENTS?

After you've taken stock of what you want to do and where you stand relative to others doing similar work, you'll have a better idea of where to direct your marketing efforts. But you also need to ask yourself some more specific questions about your design and production capabilities. What aspects of a job do you do best? Are innovative design concepts your forte, or is meeting impossible deadlines your strongest capability?

Likewise, if there's a particular area of design that you're strongest in, you need to think about what kind of clients are in greatest need of that skill. If you're good at logo and identity work, you're better off looking into the private sector, particularly new businesses. If you're best at print advertising, you're obviously going to be knocking on the doors of all the local agencies.

Consider related areas to expand into as well. If you're a great book jacket designer, expanding into book and brochure design may not make as much sense as considering poster design—essentially a blown-up version of what you're already doing. But if you've been doing brochures, annual reports, and booklets, then magazine and book design would be a natural spin-off.

What's your design style? Is it flamboyant or is it better suited to an attorney's office? Is your work likely to look dated in a few years or does it boast a classic feel? Do you have a diversified style, adapting the look of your work to suit the project at hand? The look of your work, and how well you can adapt it to the client's vision, has a great deal to do with where your work can best be marketed. For example, your local fitness center isn't likely to be sold on portfolio samples with a decidedly sweet slant.

RESEARCH, RESEARCH, AND MORE RESEARCH

Explore websites and blogs; head to the library and bookstore; study products, portfolios, and places. Attend industry conferences. Pore through creative directories and competition annuals. *Kibitz* with your friends to see what services other designers (and design firms) market—network. Window-shop downtown. Walk through the yellow pages.

Really look at who's out there doing what jobs, and who is offering these plum assignments to whom. In your estimation, who makes the Designer A-List (and why)? Where is design expertise needed?

Take note of any client info provided by your sources—particularly those designers whose work you admire, any companies (and their wares) you like. Now evaluate—which clients and which assignments are in sync with your standards and particular design vision?

YOUR CURRENT CLIENTS

If you're currently employed but moonlighting freelance jobs, you have existing clients you can probably bank on to some extent. Get a realistic picture of how much you can count on these clients in the future. Be frank—let them know you're considering going into business for yourself and want to know if they will continue to provide you with work.

Any client you have been working with under your current employer can potentially be one of *your* clients, as long as you don't rob your employer of his existing business with this client. Can you perform a service for this client that your employer doesn't want to perform? Is this client looking to expand its business into an area in which your employer doesn't want to be involved?

Let's say your employer specializes in designing annual reports and doesn't want to be bothered with the company newsletter a client is contemplating; there's no reason you shouldn't have the opportunity to do this. Ongoing projects like newsletters can be the mainstays for a new design studio.

Check it out by gently probing for spin-offs from the projects you are currently involved in. If you have a good relationship with a client who likes your work, go for it. Of course, as Lara Kisielewska says, "Check with your boss first, not only to be ethical and fair to your employer, but also in case the client mentions something to your design firm."

LOVE WHAT YOU DO . . .

Once you get an idea of how to make money, it's also important to be sure that this is the type of work you really want to do and will find fulfilling. Finding your niche involves finding something that you can do well and make a living at, too. To stick with it through both lean and green times means you must truly love your work.

If you're cranking out low-end schlock for the bucks when what really turns you on is coming up with higher profile, innovative concepts, you won't be happy for long. You need to take care of your heart's desire as well as your livelihood if your business is going to thrive over the long haul. Look for the kind of clients who are willing to give you projects that will be personally fulfilling as well as the ones that provide easy cash.

. . . AND STAY WITH IT

Renowned jeweler and educator J. Fred Woell had this take on the idea: "It's kind of a long pull," he said in a 2001 interview with Donna Gold for the Smithsonian's *Archives of American Art*. "Be persistent . . . stick to it. Look ahead. There's a Zen comment—I don't know what they call these things in their philosophy—'Go slow, reach fast.' You just keep working at it, and then suddenly it happens. You keep trying to be keep consistent with what you believe . . . and you get there."

BRAND ME

"It's funny," says Kristine Putt with a smile. "Designers can brand all day long for clients, but it's actually very challenging to brand yourself, especially in a creative field." Putt goes on to explain that, while most designers are trained to produce design, to execute someone's vision (be it a client's or an art director's), there's a disconnect between designing for art's sake and designing for communication.

"Many designers wishing a smooth transition from corporate to freelance eventually learn this," Putt says. "But they struggle to define their own identity. This goes much deeper than visual aesthetics." Let's say there are forty thousand designers graduating from art school every year. The competition is fierce and growing more so every day. As a new freelance designer, Putt asks, how do you stand apart from the crowd?

"A designer who has successfully reached the level of creative director (while employed in the corporate environment) will probably have a good understanding of what I'm referring to," Putt says. "But most junior or mid-level designers have absolutely no clue what brand positioning is, why it's important, or how to achieve it. They just don't grasp the concept."

Why so? According to Putt, junior or mid-level designers are under the false impression that their designs will sell themselves. But it simply doesn't work that way.

WALK THE WALK

To really get off on the right foot, Putt will tell you, sooner than later, you must think like a business *owner* and not a designer. If you freelance because you think that design (with a Big "D") is all you'll be doing, you'll be sadly mistaken. "When you're a freelancer," Putt says, "you only design about 10 percent of the time. The rest of the time you are a business owner. And that requires switching gears. A lot."

As such, it's smart to establish your brand. A valuable brand represents the promise of quality, credibility, and experience. This is what Rigie Fernandez and Ken Bullock refer to earlier in the book as your expertise (and service) as a commodity. Essentially, your brand is your visual identity; in other words, it is you. Your brand displays your image and your passion; it embodies the best combination of emotion and devotion through smart problem solving and high standards.

To establish yourself as a stand-up brand in today's stand-out design field, Putt says, you must establish yourself as a business first: network, call and talk to people (*gasp!*), invoice efficiently, chart accounts accurately (and do the books right), be your own IT department . . . the list goes on. She's saying that to maintain the brand, you have to maintain the bedrock of your business.

"I know far too many great designers who fail as business owners," she says with a sigh. "Design is 'glamorous,' but entrepreneurship is *hard*. Design is 'fun,' but being a business owner requires *focus*." Realistically, being your own boss—and living the brand—will not be for everyone. Going into freelance requires a certain expectation—what Putt labels as the "I knew the job was dangerous when I took it" approach.

RIGHT ON POINT

(PROFESSIONAL VIEWPOINTS IN 50 WORDS OR LESS)

The most important qualification of a good designer is to be aware of the world around you. Pull from the world; absorb that world, visually—this gives you your tools.

—Rick Antolic

You can't have a business without the desire, without the soul. But this spirit [must be] supported financially. You have to have the heart and the head. The most important thing about running a successful creative business is that balance.

—Kim Youngblood

I believe going into business for yourself is the only way to go. And there is no substitute for experience. Art is a continuous learning process and it never stops.

—Phillip Wilson

You don't just master things and you're done; you have to continually learn and expand your skills or you will be left in the dust.

—Nadine Gilden

This is a business; no matter how artsy-shmartsy. It's called "commercial art" and it's a real name for something.

—Elwood Smith

Use what I call the four D's of design: discover, design, develop, and deliver. Designers like to think that we are "different" or "above the rules"; but believe me—I speak from experience—some rules are good.

—Ken Bullock

© Oxycyte2014. Oxycyte mark is property of its owner.

I had a boss who said to me, "Your problem is that you expect everyone to think like you do." She taught me a big lesson in one sentence.

—Kristine Putt

© Ken Bullock 2014

CHAPTER 5

FINANCES

A lot of younger creatives seem confused or concerned; often they are not interested in planning or preparing budgets, but I found the business end of things to be rather creative—I was always somewhat attracted to that process, too.

—Jilly Simons

GET IT DOWN

What's your business plan for the next five years? Mapping out where you want your business to go is just plain smart. Organizing an action strategy to meet that goal—on a daily, monthly, and yearly basis—is only wise.

This written manifesto can be on the back of a business card, or the size of *War and Peace*, but do it. A business plan is the personal, professional, and financial yardstick that gives you a place to start, helps you focus, and fosters growth.

It's a rather straightforward proposition: understand your objectives, know your mission, state your goals, *take action*; revise accordingly.

So . . . what do you *really* want and why?

IT'S ABOUT THE BUCKS

It's dangerous to start out under-financed, yet you don't want to spend too much money at first. In this chapter, we'll assess how much money you will need, how much you can realistically plan to earn, where and how to get the needed capital, and how to manage it. You'll also find out how to create a working budget to maintain a cash flow that will keep your business in the black.

This critical chapter—as well as other keystone business sections in chapters 4, 6, and 7—was written with the gracious consultation and incredibly generous contributions of Lara Kisielewska.

Ms. Kisielewska is a past president of the NY Chapter of the Graphic Artists Guild (2000–2004) *and* the NYC Chapter of the National Association of Women Business Owners (2004–2005). She founded Optimum Design & Consulting in 1992, was National Guild Secretary from 2006–2012, and is currently National Guild Vice President.

You can get this good stuff online as a free ebook. Kisielewska also offers this extraordinary wealth of information in webinars and workshops presented through the Graphic Artists Guild, among other venues. (Please note: you can sign up for that copy of Kisielewska's booklet, *How to Start Your Very Own Communication Design Business!*, on the home page of the Graphic Artists Guild website: www.graphicartistsguild.org.) Look for more from Kisielewska in the chapters listed above.

ACCOUNTING FOR THAT

Right off the top, I'm going to emphatically advocate that, while you keep this book handy, you should also put this text down for a spell and seek an accountant's or financial planner's advice. If you're just starting out, or are in your early years of doing business, you should hire (or at the very least, consult) an accountant.

A good accountant can be the lynchpin of your business. He or she can review your situation and tell you if you need a lawyer and them make recommendations and referrals. An accountant can apprise you of government regulations and requirements, set up your bookkeeping system, and be your financial advisor and tax consultant/preparer.

Find a person you can rely on year-round—don't be tempted to hire a moonlighter around tax time. You'll need to find someone who is well qualified and whom you can trust, because ultimately you will be responsible for any of this individual's mistakes. You may think you will save some money by going to "Taxes 'R' Us" for your tax return, but it may cost you much more in IRS penalties when you find out what Ronald MacCountant didn't understand about tax law. As a designer with a new business, I'd go to a public accountant, an enrolled agent, or a CPA specializing in accounting and tax preparation for graphics professionals and/or small businesses.

As Tom Nicholson says, "Your accountant is probably the centerpiece of it all. An accountant can refer you to most of the other professionals. A designer can do his own bookkeeping, but you don't want to deal with tax situations on your own. For that reason alone, an accountant is a mainstay of your operation."

You, of course, want to work with an artist-savvy accountant or financial planner. Consult with your local arts council or ask your local Graphic Artists Guild chapter for a referral. Do your research and start interviewing.

WHY NOT DO IT YOURSELF?

So, you bought a green eyeshade and you're going to do your own tax return. Here are four well-chosen words: I'd advise against it. I can make it even simpler: *don't.* Personal tax preparation is elaborate enough. Due to your start-up situation, you could make some mistakes; there may be some advantages, requirements of which you might not be aware. Besides, you're a designer, not an accountant. Maybe you can do the job, but you really don't have the knowledge, experience, and expertise to do the job right (this is akin to having your CPA handle your design jobs). And finally, how much creative work will you accomplish away from the board, and what's your time worth?

So, how do you choose an accountant? You'll want to find an accountant or firm with small business experience. Obviously, if you can, find someone who's familiar with designers and illustrators. It's best to get referrals from others in your situation, others who have income comparable to yours.

You'll find four basic levels of experience and confirmation when you shop around: Accountant, Enrolled Agent, Public Accountant, and Certified Public Accountant (the highest degree of professional accreditation).

Consider at least three to four possible candidates. Talk to both accounting firms and sole practitioners. When you interview accountants, evaluate each by considering your mutual rapport, their communication skills, knowledge, and expertise, plus, of course, fees.

THE YEARN TO EARN

Your next step in your financial plan is to estimate how much you think you'll earn. Let's begin by making this general statement: you have a pool of potential clients with a certain amount of business to give you. Think about the demands of these customers and how you can fulfill those needs in order to get a realistic picture of (a) what kind of services you can offer this clientele and (b) how much service you can provide.

Based on the soul searching you did earlier in this book, you should now have some idea of what work you could be doing, which skills you should be marketing, and where your services can best be applied. You'll need to have a practical estimate of how much business you can expect and where it will come from.

Start by thinking how you can build on any existing business. Let's assume that one of your prospective clients is starting up a business and that you're going to be developing a logo for him. Certainly there's the potential for developing other business and promotional materials, as well. Are there other potential clients out there for whom you could be doing similar work? Do you stand a decent chance of building on this business through referrals? Is there a good possibility you could be doing a substantial amount of logo or identity work? If this is the case, make a list. Project how many logo jobs you think will come to you in a given year.

At a cost of $1,500 per logo (an average charge and simple conjecture for the sake of argument—your mileage may vary), what does this come to annually? Figure, from there, how much of this business will spin off into collateral work for each of your logo clients and attach a monetary value to all of it.

Do the same for any other type of work you think you will be doing. Figure out how much business in this area you can realistically rope in, as well as what you are *capable* of doing in a year. Think in terms of projects, on an annual basis, and after you have made a list and totaled it, divide this figure by twelve to get an idea of what your monthly gross profit will be (shoot high or low.)

CAN YOU MAKE ENDS MEET?

But soon this exercise should morph into a serious effort to educate yourself and hash out your master plan of global domination (I'm only half-joking here). You will need to realistically compare costs with income to see if your business plan is viable. Remember that a lowball or highball scheme built around inaccuracies won't get you very far in actual practice, so make sure your eventual projections reflect real-world facts and figures.

IN IT FOR THE MONEY

Take a salary for yourself. Include not only your salary, but also all appropriate payroll taxes in your expense list (employee payroll taxes are different from self-employed taxes, so definitely consult your accountant here). "I can't overemphasize the importance of taking a regular salary," says Kisielewska. "Don't just dip into your business account whenever you need to pay your personal bills; you'll never have a clear handle on the profitability of your business if you don't include your salary. Even pay yourself during the lean months. Write that check anyway—just put it in a drawer until you have the funds to deposit it."

Bone-up! Research the numbers by talking to both buyers and sellers of graphic design. Compare notes with your professional friends; brainstorm with family. Google it. Hit the library and bookstore to study pertinent texts.

Now create a hypothetical budget. A budget is *important*. It's absolutely vital that you have a handle on expenses and income—and it's best to have it on paper. Otherwise, you'll have no idea how you're doing financially (and why) or where your money is going.

IT HAPPENS EVERY MONTH

Get a handle on just what it will cost you to be in business by figuring out how much money you will need. Said very simply: look at your annual costs and divide by twelve (or four, of course, for quarterly expenses) to get the average monthly amount due.

Let's elaborate. First, what are your start-up expenses? Start with all those one-time expenses involved in beginning the business (licenses and permits; decorating and remodeling; new exterior signage and interior fixtures, plus installation for both; utility and phone deposits; the newspaper ad announcing your opening day bash).

Add to these your fixed expenses—rent, utilities, loan payments, parking, and your salary (more on this in a moment). Now mix in variable operating expenses (as in the phone bill) plus so-called hidden costs (life and liability insurance policies) and occasional legal and accounting expenses.

Don't forget any purchases made occasionally (for instance, that case of widgets will last you about twelve months ... take the cost of the pack and divide it by twelve to come up with the monthly cost for this item) and ongoing costs (advertising and promotion).

Don't space out on operating cash. Do this with all your service charges, equipment, and supply costs, and you should have a pretty good idea of what your monthly expenses will be.

A couple of notes to wrap up: don't declare copywriting, photography, printing, illustration (if you're a designer), or design (if you're an illustrator) in your monthly tally. These job expenses should be billed to the client for each job they are purchased for. Any services utilized for your personal promotion should, of course, be considered operating costs and factored into the equation.

FITS THE BILL

Now, estimate your billable hours. Remember, much of your time will be devoted to the more "mundane" (but critically important non-creative) activities like marketing and paying bills, invoicing and correspondence, travel, etc. How many hours a day can you *actually* bill?

Multiply that number by twenty-three (the number of working days in an average month) to get your billable hours per month. Dividing your true billable hours per month should give you your billable rate (or at least the minimum rate you must realistically charge to break even).

You may have to work more hours than you'd like to bill at a comfortable rate. Or you'll have to target specific clients who can actually afford those rates. "Unless you are very lucky," says Kisielewska, "you will probably have to make choices between time and money. Or you will commit to working more hours initially to get the business off the ground, (then look to hire an assistant to help with the workload once it's feasible). Congratulations, you've just completed your monthly budget."

To make your financial projections, Kisielewska instructs you to create a spreadsheet that lists costs down the left-hand side, and the next three years across the top. Fill out your Year One column with the *annual* version of the monthly budget you just created (in other words, multiply monthly figures for each expense by twelve).

Now copy and paste this info for your Year Two. Next, examine each of your costs individually and estimate which ones will increase in the second year of your business. "Will you need to spend more on salary because you're planning on hiring a part-time assistant in your second year?" asks Kisielewska. "If so, then alter that line item in your spreadsheet and annotate it with a footnote of explanation. Do you anticipate increasing marketing in Year Two? Assign a higher dollar amount, and then explain why in a footnote." You do this with each expense, collecting footnotes that are called your *assumptions*; repeating the process with Year Two to obtain projections for Year Three (and generally, three years of projections are considered standard).

A FORMULA FOR SUCCESS

Here's a formula you can use to calculate your break-even point. It's simple math, really, even for me, and I'm quite the pinhead mathematician. Let's assume that your expenses add up to $2,000 per month. You know that every week you have to bill $500 worth of design fees to break even (or $2,000 every month). The break-even point is what you have to bring in for your business to survive. If you want to end up with a $12,000 *profit* at the end of the year, figure on billing $3,000 every month, or $750 every week.

You can take this formula a step further and figure out your billable rate as well. If you can manage twenty-five billable hours out of every week (it's reasonable to assume that that you can squeeze five billable hours of work out of every workday) you will need to bill your time at $30 per hour to cover expenses and achieve your goal of a $12,000 profit at the end of the year.

Of course, all of this figuring is done on an average basis. It's impractical to assume that you will bill $750 on a regular basis. More than likely, you won't bill a cent during some weeks, and then you will bill a number of projects within a given week to make up for the previous week's slack. This is why it makes more sense to figure out what your income will be on an annual basis and then divide this figure by twelve to balance this against your monthly expenses.

What you are doing here is estimating your growth and assigning a rate of growth—let's say, 10 percent per year, for example—to your income projections. "Hopefully, after plugging in all of the numbers you will end up with more revenue than expenses in Year Two," says Kisielewska. "But if not, just go back and readjust your assumptions and/or your projected rate of growth until you do. Just make sure your anticipated growth rate is believable."

The bottom half of the start-up worksheet (see the "Forms" subsection in chapter 21) can be adapted to fit your needs and give you an accurate picture of what it will cost to get your firm off the ground.

THE BUSINESS PLAN

Kisielewska tells us that the most important reason for having a business plan (also known as a financial plan) is that it is the very first step you can take down the path toward defining yourself as a small business owner rather than just a freelancer. "It forces you to think things through," she says, "to answer tough questions *at the outset*, which will help you better position yourself in the marketplace." So before you invest any time into creating your corporate identity, a business plan should always come before starting that business.

"This is *always* necessary," Kisielewska says, "even if you're a one-man (or woman) band." She will point out to you that one may revel in a romantic concept of a utopian art world, free of everyday mundane realities, but actual providers of capital and services want to know that you have a solid plan for building and managing your business. Potential partners and advisers, too, for that matter, will feel more comfortable coming aboard behind that well-thought-out plan. Finally, consider that banks often require them if there is a need for outside financing.

Many tools are available to help you write your business plan: books, software, even people you can hire to write it for you. A good resource for sample business plans (and marketing plans) is www.bplans.com. Kisielewska strongly advises you follow some sort of guide, rather than winging it on your own.

THE JOY OF SIX

Typical business plans usually include the following six sections:

1. *The Executive Summary.* This defines who you are, what you do, and why you exist. How is your studio different from all the other design firms out there? You should have a succinct *mission statement* defining the purpose of the business, backed up by what's called a *positioning statement*, just as concise, defining the selling points of your business and why you are unique in your field. Keep this section to one page; it's a snapshot of your business and can also function as your sales pitch.

2. *Company Strategy.* This section covers how you are going to get your business to where you want it to be—your qualifications and credentials to get it there—and speaks to the credentials of your management team. A management team can be comprised of business associates and advisors: your accountant, lawyer, banker, and insurance agent. Kisielewska emphasizes that you need these people right from the start. "Even if *you* don't think so," she states unequivocally.

This posse of support will be industry experts and other business owners whom you should meet with (about every six months) to pick their brains. "Don't hesitate to discuss your problems and challenges," Kisielewska says. "You'll get invaluable feedback and suggestions from them. Treat them to a dinner meeting in exchange for their time. Don't be afraid to ask these advisors a lot of questions—that's why they're there. A good mentor early on would have prevented me from significant heartache."

3. *Product/Service.* "What are you going to sell, and who will you be you selling it to?" asks Kisielewska. In this section, be specific about what you are going to design. Are you a logo specialist? Do you like editorial design, creating posters or websites? Is product packaging your thing?

"Know what you are really good at," Kisielewska says. "Although you may be capable of doing 'all of the above,' there are surely some areas in which you truly excel. Identify them. Focus on these services."

Why? Most successful companies develop "niche" markets, defined by a company's size, the type of company, or a particular design focus (let's say, annual reports). So, for instance, if you develop campaigns for twelve law firms that adroitly target their needs, you may just earn a reputation as *the* go-to designer for legal marketing materials. "Learn an industry," says Kisielewska. "Educate yourself on this market needs and then think of creative ways to fill their needs and wants."

One of Kisielewska's designer pals—call her Ms. Rand—specialized in websites for nonprofits. As Kisielewska says, "She was adding bells and whistles to one such site and discovered that her client needed faster computers to view the site properly. Rand knew a colleague who was updating his own equipment and arranged for this gentleman to donate the equipment to Rand's not-for-profit client. This sparked an idea. For a broker's fee, the enterprising Ms. Rand would offer another line of services: helping her not-for-profit clients obtain used equipment."

Although this might be a light stretch for certain readers, it's a shining example of how a brilliant (as in creative) idea could generate sparkling, new revenue streams for a bright go-getter like you. Diversifying income sources can help you survive the lean years, so brainstorm ancillary services you can propose that would extend your operations. For example, don't merely deliver that logo; offer branding guidelines. Why just set the copy or layout the images, when you can provide copywriting and/or retouching services? Suggest that you take the market research off the client's hands as the appropriate (and smart) method to support your design work. So what else ya got?

4. *The Competition.* Analyze your market and your competition. Because— guess what—there are a slew of other people out there doing what you do. Find out *how many* and *who* they are. Kisielewska advises you to do a scouting report. This is no cloak-and-dagger *Mission Impossible* scenario. You simply want to learn about their customer service and pricing. However, as Kisielewska points out, you may want to get your James Bond on just a tad.

To begin, you need to check out copies of a competitor's marketing materials. "Believe it or not," Kisielewska says, smiling, "the best way to do this is either to pretend you're a student doing research for a class project, or act like you're a potential client.

"Ask five other design firms for an estimate on the same set of specs, and see what you can learn," says Kisielewska. "How do they treat potential clients? How quickly do they turn around a quote? How high or low is their pricing? How detail-oriented is their estimate? What was the customer experience itself like?"

We should point out that you're not doing this to steal state secrets or sensitive, classified documents, 007. Kisielewska is not advocating that you lift proprietary information (or mimic style, copy technique, loot concepts, or otherwise). You won't suffer double secret probation, nor should you be racked with guilt when you do your fieldwork. If you are uncomfortable taking the covert route, by all means, *don't*. Call and offer full disclosure; you certainly can simply ask (for any and everything) upfront.

Either way, you want to use this information only to figure out how you can do better. Then, on your business plan, restate your unique selling proposition in more detail—what makes you different from your competition?

5. *Sales and Promotion.* Create a marketing plan for your company. This section of the business plan outlines your marketing strategy in more detail and should include specific implementation steps, target goals, a timetable, and a budget. There are many books, websites, coaches, and seminars on marketing, including events offered by groups like the Graphic Artists Guild, American Marketing Association, and AIGA, the professional association for design.

"With an eye on figuring out your cash projections," Kisielewska says, "start thinking about how you are going to get business and how long it is going to take you. At least 10 percent of your time should be spent marketing. Otherwise you'll get distracted by meeting client deadlines or taken by surprise when your current project ends and there is no new project ready to start."

Remember that each new contact is a marketing opportunity, a chance to develop what we know as the "thirty-second elevator pitch." (You'll remember this concept from chapter 3.) This should summarize what your company does and why it is unique in one or two sentences—roughly the length of time available to pitch your business to someone you meet on the elevator (before the door opens to your floor).

The elevator pitch is designed to pique interest and spur others to ask questions that might generate potential leads. "It's important to realize that word of mouth alone cannot sustain your business in the early years," Kisielewska says. "Business is not going to magically fall into your lap. You are going to have to actually market to make things happen."

6. *Financial Considerations.* Kisielewska cites numerous documents that you must submit along with the narrative of your business plan. This includes a profit and loss statement (P&L), cash flow projections, tax returns from prior years, an accounts payable list (AP), an accounts receivable list (AR), a list of assets, and a monthly budget. Heavy volumes have been written on this stuff alone, and it is always best to work with your accountant, but let's touch on some basics for now. Not one to shy away from a challenge, let's walk through a monthly budget with cash flow projections—which Kisielewska says is oft considered the most difficult financial statement to create.

GETTING THE MONEY YOU NEED

Kisielewska smiles when she states that financing your business is even more important than your logo. With your business plan and financials doped out, proper funding should now be a priority. Your cash flow projections can estimate what you'd need in order to maintain operations for three to six months, if you didn't have a single client, before you even open the doors. Even if you must borrow the money from Granny, have these operating expenses in the bank. Says Kisielewska, "Drumming up new business while providing excellent service to your clients is hard enough without also needing to worry about keeping the lights on due to slow-paying clients or jobs that take six months to finish (and bill)."

So, with this safety net, let's get a loan, eh? It may sound crazy, but as Kisielewska points out, the best time to actually seek money is when you *have* money. Most loans need to be collateralized by existing assets (CDs, pension plans, *gulp*, your home) on a one-to-one ratio. If you go for a $25,000 loan, you'll need to have at least $25,000 worth of collateral (likely more). There are always exceptions, such as an SBA loan (more on that later), but primarily we'll investigate a traditional bank loan.

A LOAN AGAINST THE WORLD

If you're like most people considering possible cash sources, you thought first about borrowing from the bank. Yes, a bank loan is certainly a possibility, but the chances, at best, may be slim. To explain why, we'll detail the process of getting a bank loan, exploring what's involved in proving the viability of your business and establishing your credit and credibility (convincing the bank to lend you money through profit and loss statements, your net worth as you start up the business, etc.). We'll look at some other possibilities for obtaining capital, too.

SMALL FRIES

First off, you'll probably have better luck pursuing a loan from a small bank. And let's be frank, up front, right now. When you ask for a loan from any bank of any size, the first question this institution may ask you is, "Why did you quit your full-time job?" Sit down—here are some other facts of life when it comes to banks and loan acquisition.

Banks look upon a freelancer as a rather unstable commodity and are well aware that new businesses frequently fail. Lenders are hesitant—especially in today's economy—to lend any money to a service business because, frankly, there's nothing they can touch should the business go belly-up. You won't be able to use your fledgling design studio as collateral for that same reason.

If it's a non-secured loan, a bank will be unwilling to "give" you money unless you can bring other assets to the table: a car; *gulp*—your house (a second

THE FIVE C'S OF CREDIT

When scrutinizing your loan application, Banker Drysdale reviews the following:

1. *Character.* Who are you, are you reliable, and do you pay your bills on time? Do you know what you're talking about when it comes to your business (as in, can you speak intelligently about your business plan? And you did your business plan before you strolled into the bank, right?). "The best way to make this work for you," says Kisielewska, "is to get to know a decision-maker in the application approval process who will go to bat for you. Develop a relationship with a loan officer and build a collaborative process. If the person you are dealing with doesn't believe in you, find someone else who does."

2. *Cash Flow.* Lenders look at historical and projected cash flow to make sure you will have enough money to keep the business going and still make your loan payments.

3. *Collateral.* If the business does not offer sufficient collateral, the bank will look to personal assets (*gulp*, your home).

4. *Capitalization.* The basic resources of the business, including owner's equity and fixed assets.

5. *Conditions.* Outside factors such as government regulations, industry trends, and economic predictions. Kisielewska speaks from experience here when she pushes this basic mantra: "Know your industry!"

home mortgage); a working spouse (as cosigner); the birthright to your next-born child (only kidding, I think).

If you can get a bank loan, you will have to personally guarantee it (even that vaunted corporation status may not exclude you). You may also face sky-high interest rates and/or unfavorable terms.

What all this means is that your chances of obtaining a loan as a freelancer or new, small, independent business owner drop automatically. But don't totally eliminate the possibility of obtaining a bank loan at some point in the future after your business is established.

Accountants Todd Williams and Kevin Horner advise you to keep your money in your company. "This looks good when applying for a bank loan," Horner says. "After three to four years of retaining profits (and keeping salary low, if possible) you can obtain a loan easier to expand business and salary."

TAKE SOME CREDIT

"The most important thing I tell my new business clients," says accountant Julie Buscher, "is to protect their credit rating at all cost; it will always be their most important asset."

You might want to keep tabs on your credit rating by sending for a credit report from agencies such as Equifax, Experian (the former TRW), and Trans Union. You can find these services online. Even if you have a perfect credit record, incorrect information can sometimes end up in your credit file, so you may want to get a credit report before applying for a loan to ensure that you won't be turned down. Refusals become part of your credit history and several refusals will look bad in your credit report. If you are ever turned down for a loan, make sure you get the name of the credit bureau your lender used. The lender is required by law to make this information available to you, and the credit company is legally obligated to tell you over the phone, free of charge, what is in your credit report.

While we're at it, we should discuss Dun & Bradstreet (D&B), too. Dun & Bradstreet is the Experian/Equifax of the business world. These guys establish a credit report on your business, *regardless of whether you seek them out*, so as Kisielewska advises you, "You might as well contact them and make sure that they're reporting accurate information about your company to the outside world (www.dnb.com)."

When you open up a credit report with them, D&B assigns you a unique DUNS tracking number, after which they establish your credit report and assign you a credit ranking. By the way, the DUNS number and D&B credit ranking can also be requested when applying for credit at banks or with larger vendors.

And finally, do you know what an Employer Identification Number (EIN) is? Commonly referred to as a Federal Tax Identification Number, this is a nine-digit number that the IRS assigns to business entities. It is your business's social security number, and it is required on all legal, tax-related, and financial paperwork. "Getting an EIN takes about five minutes and is free," Kisielewska says, "so there is absolutely no reason to use your own social security number for your business—especially in these days of identity theft when you'd rather not have that number on every form you need to fill out." Simply call 1-800-829-4933 to obtain your EIN.

"EINs can also be obtained immediately and still for free at www.irs.gov as well," accountant Julie Buschur chimes in. She's correct. While the Internet EIN application is a customer fave, you can also obtain your free EIN by fax, through the mails, and over the phone, toll free. (Call the Business & Specialty Tax Line at 1-800-829-4933 for immediate, if not downright instantaneous, service.) Remember that it is still important to get advice from a professional here though, as you want to make sure you answer the questions correctly.

HOT POTATO

Somewhere down the road, your great reputation will be well earned through quality work. You will have cultivated a cozy rapport with your banker and built a solid credit history with a positive net worth. You'll hold substantial security, and, of course, the studio will be turning business away. You may then have a good chance at getting that loan. But even then, it's no sure thing (and you'll probably still have to personally guarantee the debt).

What can you expect when you apply for a loan? Lenders will use certain criteria to determine if you're a good risk. Let's say you have one golden minute to state your case. What would a lender want to know in sixty seconds? She'll ask five basic (but oh, so big) questions. If this sounds suspiciously like our Five Cs above, it should; we're still riffing off that:

1. What is the service or product you're trying to sell?
2. What's your experience and track record?
3. Who are you and what's your credit history?
4. What is your ability to repay the loan?
5. What is my security or collateral for the loan?

The first two questions are the icebreakers. But questions 3, 4, and 5 (representing character, capacity (or capitalization), and collateral) are the nutcrackers, which are the ones the loan officer really cares about. If you have a checkered past with a dubious credit history, that's bad character. If you don't look like you have a good way to repay the debt, that's poor capacity. If you can't bring enough security to cover it, that's inadequate collateral. You're not going to get the loan if you rate poorly in these categories—it's that simple.

BEYOND THE BANK: OTHER LOAN OPTIONS

We can conservatively estimate that it's going to take six to twelve months (or more) of working capital for a start-up business to survive. This is without spending a dollar generated by that business (and don't forget—you'll need living expenses, too). Not to be redundant, but what are those sources of funds? We discussed the bank as the likely place to start and developing a relationship with a banker as you start growing your studio. But we also cautioned that if you're fresh off the bus with no experience, savings, or equity, your chances are marginal. Here's our little top ten list of alternatives:

1. Personal reserves. You could tap into or borrow against your savings; sell off certain assets (stocks, bonds, your other Maserati); take out a home equity loan; or borrow against your life insurance policy.
2. Borrow money from family and friends. Remember: *this is still a business loan, to be repaid in a timely manner.* Writing up a formal document is a prudent plan here.

3. Credit unions.

4. Get a partner and pool resources. Some designers swear by their partners; some swear at them (we'll discuss partners later in this chapter).

5. How about a grant? In my experience (if a grant is a possibility), work with your local arts council as your fiscal agent (they'll take a small percentage, of course).

6. Kisielewska also suggests you put your outstanding invoices from regular clients to work for you. "Pursue *factoring*," she proposes, "selling your accounts receivable for immediate cash less a percentage fee—for instance, with a firm such as Prestige Capital (www.prestigecapital.com)."

7. A small business administration loan—many banks offer loans backed by the SBA, and if you qualify, this might be just the ticket. Write for official SBA guidelines or locate a bank that does this type of loan. In addition to backing loans, the SBA provides a wealth of business start-up information on its website: www.sba.gov.

8. Obtain a line of credit—set up specifically to help if and when you need it. "You only have to pay interest on the portion that you use," says Kisielewska "And if you can swing it, this arrangement is very advantageous when dealing with immediate and unpredictable expenses. In addition, a line of credit remains interest-free when you're not dipping into it."

9. Commercial finance or credit companies—your junk mail is already seeded with mailers from such places. *But be careful.* If you want or need the money badly enough, go ahead, but go in with your eyes open.

10. Credit cards. Literally, a last resort, if there ever was one; but being thorough, you should at least examine this tempting option, square and fair. In a nutshell, this type of financing will be convenient, but exceedingly inadvisable because of extremely high interest rates and invariably ball-busting fine print. If you must, think of your credit cards for short-term financing only. Note: you can build a credit history with credit cards, but be aware that if you ever obtain a bad rating, this can mean big trouble for establishing credit with vendors or when looking for a loan.

DON'T GIVE UP

At this juncture, we must vocalize a sober, but necessary confirmation. The road to landing a loan is rough, even for established designers who've been around the block a few times. With a start-up, it just might be an impossible dream. If you're still employed and want to start your own business, you might apply for a loan while you still have a job and start your business as a moonlighter.

A bank may look at your day job as the capacity to repay a loan. Freelance on the side and grow your business as you simultaneously grow your bank account. Eventually use this reliability, experience, track record, and equity to show a bank you're a good risk.

Although a loan may be out of reach *initially*, look ahead. It bears repeating: form a relationship with your bank as you shape your business and career. While a bank loan might be hard to get at first, it may be a different story once you've established credit and built a good reputation and a solid business.

Accountant Grant Perks asks us to consider these old axioms: banks will lend you money when you need it least; borrow before you need it; banks like to lend money to people who don't really need it (to avoid undue risk). And remember these last words from accountant Gary Teach: "Once you line your ducks in a row, and *if* you succeed in collaring the loan, make sure you obtain the right amount of money the first time. Getting a loan is no picnic, but going *back* to the well will be hard labor indeed."

Know the Score

Sponsored by the SBA, SCORE stands for the Service Corps of Retired Executives. It's a volunteer organization of men and women who counsel small businesses at start-up and offer business education programs. It can be a great clearinghouse of information from local professionals. As these folks have been there, they know and can help a small business through the rough spots. And guess what—their services are free. There are SCORE offices throughout the country, and you can find the one nearest you at www.score.org.

Kisielewska points us in the direction of your local Small Business Development Centers (SBDC). Like SCORE, and also funded by the SBA, a Small Business Development Center will offer free managerial and technical assistance to small businesses. "Located primarily within college campuses," says Kisielewska, "SBDCs combine MBA-qualified consultants with a wealth of governmental programs and services. SBDCs are particularly adept at helping clients seek out and apply for non-traditional funding options (meaning that you need access to capital but don't qualify for traditional bank loans). Check them out at www.sba.gov/content/small-business-development-centers-sbdcs."

MEANINGFUL RELATIONSHIPS

To wrap it up, I'm going to wield an old saw that may be long in the tooth, but is appropriately rather long in the truth, too: *it's all in who you know.* Yes, you will hear me (or others) say elsewhere in this book that the truly killer combination is

ESTABLISHING CREDIT WITH VENDORS

You will want to establish credit with your suppliers (aka vendors). The best way to do this is simple, short, and sweet: *pay up and pay on time*. Develop rapport and a great track record. Keep those bills paid and pay them quickly.

If you're trying to get credit with such providers, many vendors will ask you to fill out a credit form. This form asks where you do your banking and usually requires references (two or three vendors you've used in the past). Once they've checked your references—and you check out—they will extend credit (another great reason to pay your bills on time).

who you know *and* what you know. And I'm not doing a 180 on that. But in this instance (for financial and legal purposes), as Kisielewska wisely puts it, "Carefully set up your business relationships at the outset, and you will be rewarded by years of good advice down the road." So, who to call? Call your:

- ▶ *Accountant.* Invaluable for recommending legal ways to distribute your income to lighten your tax load, and in many ways, as Kisielewska says, "The single most important business relationship you will have. Find one who doesn't charge you to call with questions between visits," she says, "so you are free to utilize their expertise whenever needed."

  Consult the Professional Association of Small Business Accountants (www.smallbizaccountants.com). This organization can provide a wealth of resources, from their small business toolkit to recommending a local accountant from their database. Interview several candidates and ask copious questions; request (and call these) referrals, just as if you were hiring an employee.

- ▶ *Lawyer.* Don't wait until you're "in trouble." Securing an attorney's learned and wise counsel *before* you structure your business decisions can go a long way toward business security. Look for a lawyer specializing in small business law. The Graphic Artists Guild has a lawyer referral resource for members. Another resource is the American Bar Association (www.abanet.org). Legal Shield (www.legalshield.com) and Legal Zoom (www.legalzoom.com) are interesting, lower-cost alternatives. A great source of legal self-help can be found at Wise Counsel Press (www.wisecounselpress.com).

- ▶ *Banker.* Perhaps not so critical at the outset, a good relationship with your banker is akin to preventive medicine (or insurance for your financial future).

RAISE THE BAR: FINDING A LAWYER

How does one find a lawyer? This is not rocket science—finding a rocket scientist is for another book—and it's pretty much common sense or, at least, easy research and legwork. Perhaps the best way—if not the predominant method—is to simply ask family, friends, and work colleagues (including your boss) if they know of, have worked with, or have been represented by a lawyer. It's not such a long shot that one of your circle contains an attorney who can handle your situation. But even if the recommended lawyer does not necessarily have the chops or savvy required, I'd still take the contact info, regardless. Lawyers know other lawyers. Chances are good that your buddy Frank's step-brother Max's legal eagle will know someone who does.

There are legal directories you can find at local public libraries. Legal referral services and legal information helplines abound—online and via the telephone.

Other reasonable (potential) sources of information? In no particular pecking order: your kid's teacher or teacher's union rep; charitable organizations you've donated to; folks at your church or synagogue (or officiants and other leaders of religious affiliations); civic groups and community organizations; your local or state Chamber of Commerce; your local arts council. How about your banker, doctor, insurance agent, or accountant?

▣ *Insurance agent.* "The right broker can help you negotiate the arcane world of insurance," says Kisielewska. "You may be well aware of the need for life and health insurance, but do you know the difference between property and casualty insurance? It is easy to make incorrect assumptions about which types of business insurance are required versus suggested. A broker can advise on what types of insurance are needed by your small business, and can also help find you the best coverage for your budget."

▣

RIGHT ON POINT
(PROFESSIONAL VIEWPOINTS IN 50 WORDS OR LESS)

My biggest mistake was not having clients before I started. It took a while to find them, and even longer to learn how to keep the pipeline full. I borrowed so much to keep the business afloat while I figured it all out that I spent years afterward getting out of debt.

—Lara Kisielewska

The whole reason for my being in communications was because I liked the idea of being paid for what I did. The economics fascinated me.

—Kim Youngblood

A course in business management and marketing prepares you for the practicalities of running a business. It gives you valuable insight into the client's mindset, objectives and priorities, plus empowers you to put design into a business context.

—Allan Wood

I very consciously set certain business goals for myself, the first of which was simply to survive for one year and still be on my feet, independent and serving clients.

—*Tom Nicholson*

© Optimum Design & Consulting 2014

Construction consultants

MERRITT CONSTRUCTION SERVICES, INC.

Financial planning services

Starting out, my goal was to do high visibility projects, and to do the best work I could, no matter what I was charging.

—Rick Tharp (deceased)

My business developed slowly. Accommodating my clients and providing the service promised was my goal. Satisfied clients recommend you to others and this will help your business flourish. Happily, I still work with a number of my original clients.

—MaryAnn Nichols

Goals and success are tightly entwined. Be patient because there are many, many things out of our control. The business is difficult enough and working behind the curve (financially) makes it near impossible.

—Brian Fencl

CHAPTER 6

SETTING UP SHOP

I created an environment I enjoy working in.

—Jilly Simons

If you've always worked for someone else or are just getting out of school, you've probably never had to think about what equipment and supplies a studio requires. One of the joys of having your own studio is that now you can have exactly what you want—if you can afford it.

Before you run out and rent fancy office space and buy expensive furniture and equipment, you should determine what you really need and why. Your first decision should be choosing where you want to work—at home or in a studio away from home—and what you must have to get your job done, including a computer system and peripherals. Figure out these big, but key investments, and then start planning for your own opening day in the space that's right for you.

But always consider that, as Alison Miyauchi says, "A professional working environment, whether in an office, shared space, or at home, can have a huge impact on how you work and the quality of your design. Creating a great work space helps ensure that you are functioning at your best."

OFFICE SPACE

You need a place to work. In theory, that can be anywhere you can get the work done. But in practice, your studio space must provide a professional atmosphere, especially for meeting clients. It must be an affordable place where you can concentrate and have enough room to do the job well.

Whether you find the ideal office, or you simply know your home is just perfect, look at your potential studio and ask some critical questions:

- Are the space and facilities really right for your purposes?
- How's the storage?
- What is the state of the plumbing, sanitary facilities?
- How will you handle cleanup and waste removal?
- Do you have plenty of daylight, interior lighting, and wiring?
- Is there parking?
- What's the traffic like around your location?
- Is the studio easily accessible by standard modes of transportation?
- Is there adequate security?

You may want to consider a studio that, as real estate agents euphemistically (optimistically?) would say, "needs some work." These workspaces, due to neglect or location, are in sub-par condition. If your future office is the proverbial "handyman's special," evaluate how much time, energy, and resources will be spent to get the place to suit your needs and—I must emphasize—*safely up to code* (to avoid potential liability issues should clients or guests injure themselves on the premises). If your goal is to quickly get your business up to speed, I would discourage you from taking this route. There is only so much of you to go around, and I believe your energies should be directed toward becoming a freelance designer, not Joe Contractor.

You may want to look into leasing or owning a condo, renting part of an office suite, or sharing space with another designer or a photographer (or an even larger group). There are benefits in mutual space: a common receptionist and conference room, sharing large equipment, splitting expenses and over-head, and there's valuable camaraderie, in-house feedback, and a ready-made support system.

A business incubator just may work out for your particular situation. Here, single-room offices are rented out to a variety of one- and two-person companies, who don't know each other. Everybody shares a receptionist, conference room, and photocopier, but you don't have to find (or know) your office mates first.

PRACTICALITIES

Many designers feel they must have a fancy address to succeed, but that is simply not true. Although a ritzy-sounding address may attract certain clients, a pres-tigious address is not synonymous with premier design. However, working in a clean, safe neighborhood will obviously help your credibility. You certainly don't want to set up shop in the heart of the high-crime district or in the middle of a heavily polluted industrial zone.

Your studio's location must also be practical. Consider proximity and access to clients, vendors, and suppliers (and be sure your studio is within range of those suppliers who deliver). You want to be close enough to your clients so you can easily visit them and vice versa. You should be able to pick up supplies or drop off a job without having to drive long distances.

DECIDE WHERE YOU WILL WORK

Your dream office (or studio) space will be determined by many factors—only one of which will be personal preference. The first hurdle will probably be capital (money, honey).

Obviously, if you can't afford the basics—all necessary hardware and soft-ware, appropriate furniture, vital supplies and materials—*and* pay the rent or lease (let alone a mortgage), I wouldn't pull the trigger on ritzy office space. The second consideration will be based on your clientele and market. Perhaps your customers' specific industries will determine where you meet these folks, but here the question "My place or yours?" pops into mind.

WORKING AT HOME

Some designers caution against a home studio, citing the major distractions of house, family, and neighborhood. Throw in the potential client attitude of "anyone working out of the house is not a true professional," and you have a potentially big red flag.

But a good proportion of the creatives I interviewed for this book began their businesses working out of their apartments or houses. And those I interviewed who still have home studios wouldn't have it any other way.

There are, of course, ways around most challenges if working at home is important to you. Don't try to set up a studio in the center of a bustling household. You must have privacy in which to work and a way to protect jobs in progress. You need a door you can close on the design world as well as on the living room. To appear your most professional, you can always meet clients at their offices (they'll probably love you for that). Or, have a separate door to the studio portion of your home. Or perhaps you can simply explain, "I hope you don't mind, but the studio's at the house. Be prepared for a warm, fuzzy, and thrilling experience. . . no extra charge." And, as Bullock brought up, there are corporate office centers that rent out meeting parlors.

And on the subject of setting up that home studio, Bullock has some suggestions here, too. First, consider common areas—living room, bathroom, kitchen, foyer, etc.—from a client's perspective. Without a bona fide lobby, a client must come into and navigate to your home office to discuss work or review their project. You want any personal rooms, multitasking as professional spaces, to be clean, uncluttered, inoffensive, and appropriate—nothing to turn off a client or give the wrong impression. "We are in the imaging business after all," says Bullock. "I'm not saying it needs to be sterile like a hospital. Some of the best home studios are hardly squeaky clean but still very business appropriate. We are designers, after all, and we have some latitude—feel free to paint that wall Pantone 286 or display your funky mask collection. Show off some of your own work—and print it out big; mount it to your wall. Definitely display your passion, your image, your brand."

NOT DOGGING IT

Says Nadine Gilden, "The comment I most often get from people when I tell them I work from my home is 'How do you focus?' And then they often protest that they wouldn't be able to concentrate at home and keep to a schedule."

If this is your problem, Gilden has two tips:

1. Create a dedicated office area. Even if you don't target a specific room as your designated office, carve out an area that will be your office *and only your office.*

2. **Establish a routine.** Get up, get dressed, and "Only work in your pajamas when you are sick," Gilden says with a laugh. "Make sure your clients know you are running a regular business with regular office hours." Just a note here: as Vicki Vandeventer reminds you, make sure your friends understand that, too.

Gilden has never minded working alone, but she has also managed her schedule for fourteen years via, shall we say, a pet solution: her dog! "I have to get up and walk the dog," Gilden tells us, "so that becomes the official start to the work day. Her dinner time becomes the end of the shift."

Of course, there are days when she needs to work "after hours," but Gilden still remains "on the clock." These appointed office hours must be free of distractions like phone calls and emails. When it is busy, she avoids taking calls and answering emails—especially if she must work on the weekend. "Avoid this communication if you can help it," she cautions. "Once a client knows they can reach you on the weekend, they will do so repeatedly. Use the time to work without regular workday distractions."

On general communications, Gilden says that it's now much easier to connect with others through social media. "If I need some human contact, I sign on to Twitter and chat for a bit. Here's my water cooler—I talk about books, movies, TV, industry related things, really anything. It's the perfect way to balance working alone."

"It's important to realize," she adds, "that you are going to have periods where you are extremely busy and times when you can practically hear the crickets. You may work weekends and put in long days, and when it's slow, you may not work much at all. When it is slow, use that time to learn new things. Try fresh methods and replenish your creative spirit."

Let's look at the pros and cons of working at home. I am an optimist; we will think positively first.

Ahhh, home sweet office! Really? On the positive side, you won't have to pay for office space, and you won't have extra utility and phone line costs. A home office is tax deductible. For example, a one-room studio in a five-room house garners you, about, a 20 percent deduction off mortgage and utility costs. (see sidebar). You can take care of personal business: home chores and responsibilities. You can save on childcare. You don't have to get dressed up each day. It makes it easier to schedule work to suit your convenience. You're on the spot to take care of those personal emergencies that always pop up in the middle of your workday. You save time and gas money by not commuting from home to work.

Conversely, you can't leave the office behind. Family and friends can interrupt a lot and housework and the aforementioned family responsibilities can distract you. You'll appear less professional. You can spend too much time goofing off—hey, just a few minutes of Facebook can't hurt, right? Let's see what you're doing thirty minutes later. Your workspace may be inconvenient. Your work interferes with your personal life and your personal life interferes with your work.

Finally, consider other core issues when evaluating the home studio. Does your home provide adequate space (and wiring) for your equipment? Can you maintain regular office hours at the house? Will you be able to deter interruptions?

DEDUCTIVE REASONING

One perk of working out of your home is that you can take tax credit. To determine your home-office or studio tax deduction, first calculate the square footage of your office, and then divide that figure into the total square footage of your home. Thus, if your studio takes up 20 percent of your home, in square footage, you can deduct 20 percent of housing costs and expenses (which may include rent or mortgage, mortgage interest, insurance, utilities, repairs, depreciation, and more). The guidelines are extensive (read, complicated) and tests of this deduction seem fairly fluid to me, so it's definitely best to consult your tax preparer (or advisor, if you do your own taxes). Also check out the IRS Publication 587, *Business Use of Your Home*, and hunker down for a long read.

"This is a very popular option with many clients," says accountant Julie Buschur, "especially early on when there may not be a lot of extra money for rent and the like."

However, Buschur always cautions her clients when it comes to the home-office deduction. She educates that it is fine, of course, to deduct direct expenses such as computers, furniture, and office supplies, but when it comes to indirect expenses (like home-mortgage interest, real estate taxes, non business insurance), she advises you to tread carefully.

"First of all," she points out, "the IRS looks at these home-office deductions quite often. So it must be a *dedicated* space, not a corner of a bedroom or a room shared with any other non-business use.

"And while most do not depreciate a portion of their home," Buschur continues, "the IRS regs say that depreciation is 'allowed or allowable.' So even if the taxpayer does not take this deduction, the IRS deems it taken; thus it is possible that the taxpayer could actually have a gain on the sale of their personal residence (because now part of their home is considered business property)."

Buschur's advice here is to be very careful and consult a tax professional before taking this deduction. "One positive thing with the home-office deduction," she adds, "is that mileage from the home office to your client is not considered commuting, so it can be deducted as business mileage."

WORKING AWAY FROM HOME

Now let's evaluate the pros and cons of working away from home. Certainly, you have a fixed center of business and communications that provides a professional atmosphere (for you, any staff, and your clients). Your environment is conducive to work (and reasonably free from the disturbances of personal or family obligations). You project a more professional image. Your work and personal lives are separate. You have better accessibility to vendors and delivery service with a location in a commercially zoned area.

But working away from home is more expensive—you're paying rent twice and shelling out extra bucks for utilities and furniture. If you're at this stage of your life, you may need childcare; you may miss your kids and the interaction with your spouse. You may not be able to dress as casually or comfortably as you prefer. Your workspace may not be in your desired location of choice. Time will be spent commuting between your home and studio. You may not have as much flexibility to work when the mood strikes you or at odd hours.

VIRTUALLY AN OFFICE

"Those clients with expansive offices generally engage designers (or design firms) with a team of their own people," Ken Bullock reminds you. "The team will usually have a decision maker—someone from marketing and probably a technical, content expert of some sort. Generally speaking they will want you to come to them." Conversely, smaller clients (who either don't have large office space or must commute some distance to work) may want to meet in your nice, hopefully centrally located office.

"I think the best option for most designers starting out is the new trend toward *virtual offices*," Bullock opines. "Find a decent office space, maybe with a conference room (often shared, usually cheaper); spend a little money on a phone service (so your phone *always* gets answered. This is like have a secretary and not having to pay for one). The benefits here are that a virtual space is less expensive and a more flexible option for professionals starting out with a modest budget."

Remember that the virtual office can still require significant capital to start and maintain. This can be tough when cash flow is an issue (and only you know the state of your finances to accurately qualify all that). "For those designers," Bullock chimes in, "I would look at sharing office space with another small business owner or creating a space in your home studio."

SIMPLY MOBILE

My son, Cooper Fleishman (an office road warrior, if there ever was one), can probably tell you more about modern technology, but a very simple office solution that should not be overlooked—and one I was actually reminded of by

Ellie Jabbour, a designer just kicking off a great career—is a basic laptop, anywhere, anytime!

"This is fine for people who may not have the money upfront or the space in their apartments for a full desk set up, monitor, what have you," Jabbour says. "In fact, working from the desk, coffee shop, and couch allows for more inspiration and flexibility than a traditional office or even a co-working space.

"The scenario of a co-working space so someone can answer the phone and take messages for you seems obsolete to me, honestly. I rarely talk to clients on the phone, as most communication takes place through email. When we do talk on the phone, a cell phone is acceptable and practically expected."

THE "LEASE" YOU CAN DO

You found this great loft north of Rialto, just off Maxwell Street—very close to Tilly's Art Supply. Absolutely right for an office. Good light, lots of space; that rug really tied the room together, did it not? The landlord smiles and says, "Just sign on the dotted line, Ms. Designer; don't worry about all that stuff on the other page. Pay no attention to that little paragraph set in tiny type. Oh, that clause? It's nothing, nothing at all."

Hold on. Study your entire lease very carefully. Remember that the lease was prepared for the landlord, so it's written with his needs and not yours in mind. A lease is, however, subject to negotiation.

Even though this office is to die for, show the lease to your lawyer before you sign. Examine the lease together. Be sure you truly understand the terms. Can these terms somehow change during the course of your lease? Can the landlord legally cancel your lease—how and why? Can you legally break the lease—how, when, and why? Here's a checklist of points you should be aware of in addition to the monthly rent.

- What is the length of the lease (shorter is better)?
- When and how may the deposit be forfeited?
- Are there restrictions on how you may use the space?
- What are the zoning requirements?
- Is there an option to continue or renew the lease?
- What is the cost for continuing or renewing the lease?
- Can you sublet or assign lease?
- Who is responsible for cleaning and repairs?
- Who is responsible for what utilities?
- Who is responsible for maintenance?
- Does the landlord have the right to move tenants?
- How are disputes handled?

HEY, I'M ON THE PHONE!

Whether you are leasing space, buying an office building, or configuring a home office, modern technology and current phone services have made global communication far more accessible than ever before. Way back in the day, fax machines and express mail couriers revolutionized the size and scope of the marketplace. Today's state of the art gizmos working an exploding Internet have kindled revolutionary digital information and communication (and delivery) systems. As a result, small shops, modest studios, and cottage industries have transformed into general, viable international concerns.

WHOSE LINE IS IT ANYWAY?

What previously was a small but key concern—the business phone versus home phone dilemma—is easily resolved these days. We'll address that shortly, but first some color commentary.

Used to be, B C (before computers), the number of telephone lines needed to maintain business communications (and that all-important professional atmosphere) was a real issue. Obviously, your three-year-old shouldn't be answering your business phone, or *the* phone, if you had only one line, during business hours.

But could you afford two (or more) lines? Factor in another prehistoric conflict of interest to this conundrum—juggling a home and office communications system (telephony and Internet connections)—and communications at the cave could get positively pre-hysterical.

But A D (after digital), the difficult juggle—physical or metaphysical—of a home system on the same line as your business systems is a thing of the past.

A GOOD CALL

You cannot make or take business calls if you (or anyone else) is on that line in the middle of a personal call. If that business line is also your personal cell phone, this can present other complications as well.

Consider separating church and state—installing a business phone number that is not your cell phone (or at least not your personal cell phone). Family members (or your buds) should definitely not have carte blanche access to your business line and only essential calls from key clients should come to your personal cell phone. Think about it—separate phone lines make perfect sense here.

And of course, you never want to take a chance on missing an important call. Busy signals are not quite a thing of the past, but voice mail (voice messaging) or the good ol' answering machine can field calls when you're not around or unable to answer.

Modern phone options, cable modems, and caller ID systems also mean it's never been easier to screen calls these days.

KIBITZ AND BITS

As Brad Reed reminds us, "Almost nobody is saddled with dial-up anymore. Cable modems are almost always faster than DSL and are generally available wherever DSL is available—but even DSL can handle simultaneous voice and data."

As Reed says, DSL (a *digital subscriber line*—or *loop*—providing a connection using a *digital signal line*) permits you to multitask your phone connection—to surf the net and kibitz on the phone simultaneously. The digital line needs certain ingredients to work, and older homes may not have the correct phone set up. This will require the DSL installer to bring in a digital line, which, of course, can add to the total cost.

The DSL line provides a dedicated high-speed connection (whereas a cable modem is a shared connection) and, for a business, a DSL line may be a smart idea.

But in our current age of cell phones and Internet telephony—VoIP (voice over Internet Protocol)—DSL (and cable modems) just may be relegated to the status of a snazzy old hat. Also, Reed says, "we should talk about services such as Google Voice, which gives you a 'dedicated' line that rings into wherever you like and can provide services such as voice-to-text message translation."

ALL FAXED UP

Do people still fax? Some folks have not sent a fax for years. Are you still faxing? As of this writing, traditional fax and newfangled digital technologies do not play all that well together. You may want to consider two phone lines if you fax frequently, dedicating one line exclusively to your fax.

And you don't necessarily need two analog phone lines to accommodate a fax. Good fax machines will be able to decipher between a fax and a voice message and route a signal to the proper destination—voice messages to the telephone, fax signals to the fax—and a call waiting option (as part of your phone service) seals the deal.

Let's not forget that even with all our Star Wars–grade gadgetry and Star Trek–worthy communications systems, faxing is still a viable business mainstay. Internet faxing services—electronic faxing, or e-faxing—are provided by many vendors (yes, you send and receive faxes by email or via the Web).

COMPUTERS, "BUY" AND LARGE

You will certainly buy your computer system for a graphics solution, but it will quickly become a business lifesaver as well. Easy to learn, yet a most challenging and interesting work device, your Macintosh or PC provides a happy marriage of work flow and utility, which is extremely satisfying.

I love my Mac, but remember, digital is not the only game in town, and I wouldn't advise selling your soul at the crossroads for technology. This sentiment is coming from a guy who regards the computer as a gift from the creative gods, but the comment is really neither confusing nor blasphemous.

How so? My Macintosh can never replace the rush I get from the juicy flow of watercolors (or the scratch of a fine pen) on toothy paper. While making art on a computer is a serious hoot—much fun *and* imminently challenging, the elegant and efficient Mac is simply a high-powered, fine-tuned instrument that—like all my high-quality analog toys—sweetly complements and supplements my toolbox.

BLINGWARE

Lara Kisielewska will tell you that acquiring the right equipment, that spanky new, top-of-the-line computer you definitely *need* to buy—just for work, right?— is one of the most exciting aspects of starting a business.

"Well," she says, "if you can afford it, sure. But why not start out in a more modest way and keep that capital for a cash-flow glitch? Trust me, someday you'll be glad that you did."

Derek Kimball sees her point. "For an independent designer to offer versatility, quality work, and a streamlined client experience, an investment into the proper tools is a must," he tells us.

And he agrees with Kisielewska—these tools are not cheap. "A fast computer can run into the thousands," he says, "and good, commercial typefaces can cost hundreds. Let's not forget about software, printers, scanners, drawing tablets, cameras, professional monitor calibration devices, pantone swatch books, office supplies, external hard drives or online storage backup, etc."

However, he also wants you to consider that the upside to all this is that you are investing in yourself and the future of your business. "While the growth process of any new venture is usually slow and organic," Kimball says, "the ultimate reward (if enough hard work is invested) is your success as a self-employed designer. Just don't expect it to be easy."

MVP

Your computer is invaluable and indispensable. A fast, powerful, and versatile creative tool, computers also streamline the business end of your design— it's safe to say that you'll buy a Mac or PC (and related devices) for tracking expenses and time; communications and research; billing, record keeping, and project storage.

But Kisielewska's earlier, wise advice is on the mark. A needs assessment can be very helpful in determining just what equipment to purchase. Consider what you want the system to do, your available resources (both skill and money), and the timeframe available for making the decision and implementing your system.

Yes, timing is important. But waiting for the "latest and greatest" may prevent you from ever getting started. We call for your prudence, but also caution against being a digital wannabe. If you truly and seriously really *need* the stuff, don't make excuses—jump in.

"Think about what you'll be using your computer for, and what your employees will be using them for as well," says Kisielewska, who makes the case that if your work is primarily in, for example, InDesign, and you rarely use multiple applications, you might not need as much RAM as you drool over. "And if your office manager is only working in MS Word and Excel, chances are he won't need a multi-processor machine. Be sensible about what you need versus what you want."

Let's establish some background about which system can contribute what to your creativity and business. We'll also discuss what to look for and what to ask when window-shopping and then buying (or leasing) a computer. First though, a word of caution: as mentioned above, computer technology roars by the consumer like a rocket. Roger Brucker comments that the velocity of computer technology is on an eighteen-month cycle. "As speed and storage go up," he says, "price goes down." Prices as well as hardware and software will most certainly have changed between the time of this writing and the time you read this. Use this info only as a shopping aid, not as a definitive buying guide.

TRADING UP

Kisielewska says it never hurts to comparison shop and tells us to hunt for bargains at vendors like www.buy.com; www.amazon.com; www.dealcatcher.com; and www.pricegrabber.com. She also recommends purchasing used or refurbished equipment—the Apple Store always offers refurbished tech. As of this writing, sites like eBay; Craig's List; Mac of All Trades (www.macofalltrades.com); CPUsed (www.cpused.com); and Pre-Owned Electronics (www.pre-ownedelectronics.com) are all places to check out previously owned paraphernalia. Of course, do look into warranties and warranty periods on such purchases.

Perhaps you earn a discount from a local Big Box store (or from Apple or another maker) as an educator, Graphic Artists Guild member, or through the BBB, for instance. Maybe you qualify for a trade-in program with the local computer repair shop.

BUYING A COMPUTER: THE BOTTOM LINE

If you have the first edition of this book, you will find a fairly elaborate computer buying worksheet; but I'm tossing it for this edition. Why? Brad Reed boils it down for us quite succinctly: "My input on the computer buying sheet is that nobody buys a computer that way," he says. "It should really start with a needs analysis. What applications do you need to run? How many hours a day will you be working on the computer? Who do you need to interact with and how? Is portability a factor? Etcetera. Then you find the system or systems that best satisfy the needs. And sometimes you have to go with the intangibles—which system suits your aesthetic? Where is your comfort zone?"

THE PATH OF "LEASE" RESISTANCE

Another option is to lease your equipment, especially if you need to simultaneously purchase multiple desktops, a server, and printers (which can add up to quite an expensive proposition). "Some leases allow you to upgrade every few years so that you're always able to use the latest equipment without constant significant capital outlay," says Kisielewska.

Should you lease your equipment instead of buying outright? That depends on your financial and tax situation. There are advantages and disadvantages to leasing. Leasing may give you lower monthly payments over a longer period of time than an outright purchase. You can buy your machine at the end of the lease (terms will vary), renew the lease, or tradeup to newer and better equipment. Understand, however, that because you may have to pay top dollar for a system, this can be a more expensive way to go.

But many dealers include a service contract and access to some technical support as part of your lease (not all do, so be sure to read your lease carefully). Otherwise, you'll be responsible for repairs. The cost of your lease is tax-deductible annually, which may be a better deal for you than taking the depreciation allowance from an outright purchase. If your accountant suggests leasing as an option, check it out.

Look into Apple's financing program or lease third-party equipment from companies such as Rent-A-Computer (www.rentacomputer.com). You could secure equipment financing from companies like Fidelity Capital (www.fidelitycapitalonline.com). Computer leasing terms can be negotiable, so compare vendors for the best deals and watch for hidden costs (for instance, end of term computer disposal fees).

"Regardless of where you lease from," Kisielewska advises, "Apple's website is handy for educating yourself on various commercial lease options. Apple compares the Fair Market Value lease, the 10% Purchase Option, and the $1 Purchase Option, each of which is best suited for a specific mix of technology strategies and tax advantages (www.apple.com/ financing/business.html)."

WHY DID YOU BUY THAT?

I was going to say that a computer doesn't *inspire* creativity, but that doesn't exactly ring right. The computer is only a tool and, as such, doesn't generate the design (no more than a hammer left to its own inanimate self builds the house or a guitar displayed on its stand writes a hit tune).

But certain tools generate a creative *spark* within the craftsman attuned to that instrument. Spiritually, mentally, physically, for whatever reason—be it look and feel; heft and grip; lilt and tilt; the sound, sight, and even smell of it—something connects between head and heart, and that *thing* in *those* hands makes something of beauty, worth, and merit.

The computer is one of *those* "things." However, as Reed puts it, "In terms of expressing the human condition, technology has always been the means, art the ends." You don't need to be the fastest chip on the motherboard to see how right this is, of course. Digital corrections and client changes are faster and cheaper. Designers can see how "real" type, copy, and visuals look on the page instantly, and explore multiple variations in less time. Indeed, at least theoretically, working digitally enables you to get more done and faster—you cut down studio hours and production costs while reducing paperwork and streamlining procedures. All of this helps you keep up with or get ahead of your competition.

But why did you embrace the technology and buy what you did? At the bottom of it, be it pencil or pixel, the answer that rises to the top should have something to do with *you* making art—and only *you* do that.

CHIPS OFF THE OL' BLOCK

Editorially, I won't beat the drum for either the Macintosh or PC/compatibles. But, if we talk shop, what's better professionally? Is it simply a matter of right brain versus left brain? Will the Mac actually be faster and easier to use than a PC? What's really the cheaper and/or more powerful system? It depends on how you're most comfortable working and what you want to do.

Just for the moment, we'll enjoy the luxury of speaking in digital generalizations. The designers interviewed for this book predominately employ a Macintosh as a creative, production, and business tool. The debate about which system is the best is pointless and never-ending; all those experts out there have their own agendas and no lack of opinions (and seldom mutually agree on anything).

Truth is, over time, the Mac and the PC have moved closer to each other. Excellent graphics, word processing, and business-related software titles are available for both operating systems. The distinctions are blurring. It all comes down to an accurate, realistic evaluation of your situation, preferences, time-frame for growth, and available funds.

My advice here is that you thoroughly investigate a variety of systems. Today's Macs and PCs offer truly breathtaking speed, awesome power, and amazing grace. As you grow into your business (and skills), moving up into the rarified digital atmosphere has never been easier or more affordable.

FACE-OFF: MAC OR PC?

Nadine Gilden takes the pragmatic approach and tells us she works in both platforms, but adds, "I dread when I have to use my PC. Just starting the machine up takes twice as long."

But she knows it ultimately comes down to a personal choice. And for Gilden, Macs have a built-in support resource—the convenience and reliability of Applecare and/or going to the Apple store. You deal with a slightly higher purchasing structure, but figuring out who to go to and where to get help with her PC has been a bit of a runaround, and for a busy designer who needs dependable tools, that's a critical consideration.

Ken Bullock says he's a little atypical of most designers and other arty-types in the field. "I am a PC/Windows based designer/developer, and for several reasons," he tells us.

When he originally started out (back in the early 1990s), Bullock was very much a Mac guy. But a few years into his career, he delved into multimedia. "A lot of the early tools at the time—while available on both platforms—were being designed and developed for PC users, not Macs," he points out. "Compatibility was a major issue. Thus, as a multimedia developer, testing was easier and faster. So I decided to go to the dark side and become a PC user—and have been for the past twelve-plus years."

However, as Bullock will be the first to admit, these days the game has changed, and regardless of all the fussin' and fightin', he says, "PCs and Macs are equal. There is nothing a PC can do that a Mac can't. Plus these days, Macs will run Windows." And comparing apples to Apples (maybe apples to oranges is a better analogy), Bullock points out that the software works basically the same as well as the final result. "The differences are personal," he says.

Of course, any software you use is directly related to the type of stuff you are designing. Regardless of what hardware you decide to go with, Bullock's only real advice would be to buy in accordance with what you are doing and what you want your computer to do.

"If you are doing web design, you don't need to have esoteric hardware to bang this out. It'll be a waste of money. You don't really need a Ferrari just to drive to the grocery store.

"Print work (brochures, etc.)? You still don't need the Ferrari," Bullock maintains, "but you may want to think Lexus or Acura. But if you are going to get into multimedia—video, 3D-modeling, or animation—now you will probably want the Ferrari."

These are all metaphors for some basic facts of any computing purchase: bottom-end computers will leave the starting flag already old and slow when you buy it. The lower the model (of *any* brand) you buy, the sooner you will need to replace it. "Spend a bit more money to extend the practical shelf life of your machine," Bullock says. "Planned obsolescence? Sure. And accept that eventually you will *have* to buy new hardware to keep up with the advance of the software . . . and on and on the wheel turns."

A final note: you may want to consider extended warranties or insurance for your machine. These "protect yourself" offers cost a little extra, but in the long run may justify the added expense. Is it a "no-brainer" or "done deal"? Hardly. Not quite sure whether to take these warranties? Well, join the big club. My personal experience is that the extended warranties on my computers (it's called AppleCare for the Mac) have been exceedingly well worth it. I've not taken an extended warranty on the peripherals—printers, external hard drives, scanners, etc.—and seldom needed one.

Of course, that's just one user's learning curve, and this is not product endorsement—savvy shopping and careful evaluation (and some luck, too) will always play into smart purchasing and shelf life.

PRACTICALLY FUNCTIONAL

Perhaps it is best to be functionally practical. What type of files will you need to exchange with your clients and vendors; what types of media? Even more importantly, what "stuff" does your service bureaus and printers use?

"Service bureaus and printers significantly prefer Macs over PCs," says Kisielewska. "The Mac has been around in the design world that much longer—much more development in font management and color matching has taken place for the Mac. Service bureaus can rip Mac files much easier, faster, and with far fewer glitches."

I must agree, but zealots for either system can escalate the debate to DEFCON 3. So, of course, there's always the universal fine print here: your results may vary (and you may just have to be a switch hitter). Do *your* homework, and someday next week we'll compare notes over a triple mocha latte over easy, covered and smothered.

Robert Zimmerman will tell you this interesting story: "I'll never forget the first time I walked into the offices of *PC World* magazine. I expected, literally, to see a world of PCs, I suppose. What I found was a world of Macs—not one PC to be seen in the entire art department. It dawned on me then that the industry standard for graphics of any kind was Macintosh."

And at that time, Zimmerman never worked with an art director that wasn't running the Mac OS and he doubted he ever would. We'd have to check if his prediction held up, but you might win the bet if you put some money on that.

SOFTWARE AND TEAR

No matter how fancy the computer system, the most powerful machine remains humbled without the right software. As an artist and businessperson, you will need a variety of applications to effectively run your complete studio: design and illustration software, word processing, and email software for correspondence; a database for file keeping; accounting and/or bookkeeping programs; plus organizational software for your office management.

When it comes to graphics software, it's a real buyer's market—creatives can pick and choose from many possible options. But we don't need to go into any real detail about design software. If you're starting a design business, you already know all that, right? But if you are new to the game, somehow, suffice it to say you'll find a variety of entry-level, mid-range, and high-end applications (determined by a combination of price, degree of difficulty, and features). No matter where you are on the learning curve, you should be able find software to meet your needs.

However, what does the small design studio need in terms of *business* software? As mentioned earlier, electronic spreadsheets, databases, communications software, and accounting packages can help the artist manage an efficient and organized business. Look into integrated (all-in-one) packages or bundled software that combines the basic business applications—text, spreadsheet, database, and telecommunications. As of this writing, some software to evaluate would be Apple's iWork suite (comprising Pages, Numbers, and Keynote), and Microsoft Office.

Specialized programs or general-purpose applications designed to handle most of your business chores can be found right on the shelf. With a bit of research, you can get great performance and good value. If you can't get to the store, you need go no further than the current computer magazines or shop on the web. Window-shop a few issues and websites, read the reviews, or call the mail order houses for recommendations.

Also at this writing, there is a rush of designers moving their data into the "cloud" and taking advantage of services like Google Drive (and Google Play),

Skydrive, and iCloud. Cloud storage of documents and notes, art and photos, and, of course, music, can be synched across all your devices.

"You should also consider Software as a Service options (SaaS)," Reed says. Indeed, Microsoft is moving to a subscription service for its Office products, as is Adobe with the core Design applications. Google Drive provides both online storage and basic word processing and spreadsheets for free. "And don't forget to evaluate Quickbooks," Reed says, "however, cloud accounting solutions such as FreshBooks can help with time tracking and invoicing."

Remember, even a bit of information can go a long way; make an educated decision and purchase. Whether you're buying graphics, business, or word processing software, get plenty of input first. Surf the web, call your friends, call or email those professional contacts. Consult user groups, chat and message boards, and books and magazines to find out what's hot and what's not.

Compare features and prices before you buy, and always test-drive the program first to make sure it does what you want it to do (and is compatible with the software used by your clients and vendors). Fool around with the program on a friend's computer. Take it for a spin at your local dealer. Borrow from a friend or download a trial version from such sites as www.Tucows.com.

One last word about buying from vendors: education and computer consultants may remind you that federal law prohibits any return of opened software or other recorded media to the seller, except for replacement with the same title. "However, this is almost a moot point as practically all software is now purchased as a download," Reed points out.

JUST TELL ME WHAT YOU WANT

Take the time to thoroughly assess your needs before you buy. It will be time well spent. If you can afford the services of one, a consultant is an invaluable ally (see below for more on consultants). Whether consulting the pros or using a DIY method, don't underestimate the time and money involved in keeping your computer system up and running effectively. Here's an inventory of points to consider and questions to ask before you purchase a computer and related peripherals:

- Who will use it? Just you or you and your partner or staff?
- What exactly will you use it for—bookkeeping, typography, creating illustrations, page design and layout, word processing, etc.? What quality of output do you need? High quality—1200 dots per inch (dpi), mid-range—600 dpi, or low quality—300 (or lower) dpi? Do you need to output color? Is your work for the computer screen or for paper?
- When do you want to be partially or fully computerized? How much will it cost? What can you afford? Where will you get the money?

➡ Where will you do input and output? One workstation or multiple? Will you need to deliver material to a service bureau frequently? What kind of scanning will you do (flat art, slides, photographs, transparencies, color, line art) and how much will you be doing? Do you need to network your computer to other machines?

➡ Why are you planning to buy—what specifically do you expect a computer to do for you? If you want to improve productivity or cut costs, how will a computer help you do that?

➡ How will your system be supported: who will train you, help you solve problems (technical support), and fix your equipment when it's not working?

TALK TO ME

Whatever (and wherever) you buy, consider working with a consultant. If you can afford one, it is to your definite advantage to have a consultant on tap. Find a people-oriented expert who knows the hardware and software and who will be there when you need support, training, or advice. To locate a consultant talk to friends, check the phonebook, and then interview. You might also consult vendors or user groups, even though it's a slight conflict of interest. (Vendors will naturally promote use of the hardware and software they sell. User groups—in the effort to promote computer literacy and autonomy—will steer you toward what they know and use.)

You may be able to find a Value-Added Resaler (VAR), a person or dealership authorized to sell some particular equipment, who will act as your consultant. These may be small stores, larger operations, or chains. In either event, look for an operation that emphasizes the relationship they build with the client after the purchase, as part of the purchase. This is the best of all worlds—sales, service, and support all in one—it's worth the search and possibly higher prices to find such a vendor.

Many experts advise you to go local, especially with Macs. While it's not a fact of life, chains or superstores may lack Mac expertise as well as critical in-house support and service.

BUY THE BUY

It's a common complaint that the buyer can't keep up with technology. The lag time in writing this book and when you read it will bear this out nicely. We could wimp out and avoid talking specifics about speed and storage altogether, but let's just fearlessly employ the universal qualifier for all these techy-tacky discussions, shall we? Everything you're about to read is qualified by the statement *at this writing*.

Hardware and software improve so dramatically and so quickly, many users moan that a system becomes obsolete as soon as you crack it out of the box. Because of this situation, any specific information given at this writing may well be ancient history by the time you read it. Therefore we must approach the market in general terms.

Evaluate purpose—what you want to do—and don't overbuy. Consider speed and power. Mix and match speed, power, memory, and storage with some expandability—keep an eye on your future. Get plenty of memory and storage. By the time we go to print, this data will be out of date. But (at this writing) 4 GB (gigabytes. 1 gigabyte is 1 billion bytes) of RAM (Random Access Memory) and a 500 GB HD (hard drive) are now standard; 8GB and 1TB (terabyte = 1 trillion bytes or 1000 gigabytes) is common.

If there's one truism in the world of computer technology it is this: *you can never have too much RAM*. Invest in this absolute essential (and look into third-party RAM—it's usually a much cheaper alternative to factory-installed RAM).

Another rule of thumb here is that you can never have too much storage space. Get the biggest hard drive you can afford!

Trust me on this—make it a priority; get as much RAM and a substantial hard drive. Saying that, external hard drives are a seriously cost-effective means to beef up your storage capacity.

Oh, yes, my mother would also remind me to tell you to backup your data files constantly and consistently. (Please be a good little designer and illustrator and listen to my mother. Please.) "And a word about backups," says Reed. "Consider a cloud-based backup service such as Carbonite or CrashPlan, or establish a *routine* of backing up to a secondary backup and storing it offsite. It's no use having a backup of your files if the backup goes up in flames with the computer."

Purchase a monitor with a screen as large as you need. For graphics, a 17-inch monitor is where you *start* looking, but Vicki Vandeventer says that a 24-inch should be considered the absolute minimum now (there are good buys out there on everything from 19- to 27-inch screens, but they will be more expensive, of course). Most Macs (and PCs) now easily support multiple monitors. How about a two-monitor setup to hot rod your workflow? Or utilize the primary monitor for all things design, with a cheaper secondary for email, web browsing, office apps, and more. Consider a mobile device (like an iPad, iPhone, iPod) to complement your digital arsenal.

APPLES AND ORANGES

A good shopper, of course, can make the actual numbers (and the ROI—the return on investment) vary dramatically. The scenario for either a Mac or PC purchase will play the same—you pay more for extra and better equipment; you do better if you buy smart and shop 'til you drop.

Where to start your shopping? Do your homework and go on a reconnaissance mission: hit the library, browse the web, talk with friends, buy a few periodicals, cruise the stores, and—perhaps most importantly—check with other designers who use computers and software that interest you. Learn what available hardware and software meet your needs and budget.

Then seriously shop around. Many, if not most, vendors offer online shopping. It's easy, fast, informative, and fun. You can buy both software and hardware at that store in the mall, by mail order, or over the phone. You can purchase through a VAR or from a consultant in your local area. Each of these outlets has its fans and critics. Network, comparison shop, research, and read (including the fine print); ask questions. Unless you weigh the pros and cons carefully, and know exactly what you want, you probably won't get a good deal anywhere. But this is true of buying a car, furniture, or stove. The old caveats apply even more to our new high-tech gear: buyer beware, buyer prepare.

While price is important, it's not the only consideration. A great bargain may not be the best computer for you. Inquire about how long the vendor/dealer/VAR/consultant has been in business. How accessible are customer service, repair, and training centers? Can the vendor/dealer/VAR/consultant supply references from previous customers? Check out the kind of training and support available. Do you get any free training? How much? How long does it take most users to learn this system?

What's the cost of the basic system components (versus your budget and in general)? What equipment is really included in that price? What kind and amount of software is available for and compatible with your hardware—at what prices? What add-ons are available? What are the system's requirements in terms of power, space, and ventilation?

What are the policies on returns? What is the system or software's record for reliability? Can it be serviced locally or will it have to go back to the manufacturer? Are service contracts available and how much will they cost?

Get a sense of the top limits on what your hardware and software can handle (number of users, programs, and projects). How are upgrades (customizing to create a bigger, better machine) and trade-ups (swapping to acquire a bigger, better machine) handled? Can you network your system and software easily? Are there compatibility issues with both Macs and PCs on the same network?

To sum up: getting the lowest possible price shouldn't be your sole prerequisite for buying a certain computer at a particular store, and you should definitely shop around. For seriously smart and efficient shopping, organize your information to help you pinpoint the best deal. Info on each component can be gathered over the phone, through the Internet, in person, or from want ads and store advertisements. Remember to research both new and used equipment (if available).

CHOOSE YOUR SUPPLIES AND EQUIPMENT

"Office supplies will often cost more than you think they will," says Kisielewska, "especially once you factor in ongoing disposables (such as toner or ink). Take your time to set up business accounts at places where you get freebies or credits for bulk purchases. Staples, for example, offers free delivery on orders over $45.

"Business accounts for supplies, services—even local eateries—offer discounts, save a lot of time, allow the bill to be paid when it's convenient, and make it less necessary to keep massive amounts of petty cash lying around."

"Like a kid in a candy store" may accurately describe the designer at the art/office supply house, but it's important to realistically assess—and choose—only what you actually need, can afford, and what can fit into your space. Of course, you'll need more furniture, etc., if you're starting up with a partner or associates than you will if you're all by yourself.

A list of supplies and equipment could go on and on. Here are some obvious wants and needs (in no particular hierarchy):

- Storage: shelves, cubbyholes; closet(s) and cabinet(s); file holders and/or filing cabinets, boxes, etc; bulletin board(s)
- Drawing table or worktable (and/or conference table) with chairs; lighting and lamps; waste basket(s)
- Basic cleaning supplies and equipment; first aid kit;
- Analog art/production supplies (includes paper cutter) and office supplies
- Business package (stationery, letterhead, and envelopes) plus business forms; promotional material
- Computer and related hardware, with art, presentation, and business software, plus address filing system (digital, some folks actually still use a Rolodex)
- Phone system
- Handy to have would be a coat rack, hooks, or closet; additional work surfaces and desk(s); a music system; basic kitchen supplies (may include microwave, coffee, and tea maker)
- Decor—plants, framed work, awards help give a sense of permanence and stability.

"GAS" THE WORLD TURNS

In my discussions with the designers and illustrators in this book, we identified a malady common to artists everywhere: GAS, or *gear acquisition syndrome*—the craving to have only the newest and best of everything, from electronics to office supplies and furniture. GAS is a natural "affliction" for many designers. Is this ailment exclusive to the art world? Certainly not, but let the plumbers complain about it in their own book.

If you have the cash available (see chapter 5 on calculating and monitoring your cash flow), an outright purchase is cheaper. You own the stuff (furniture or equipment) without the hassle of ongoing payments, and there are no interest charges. But will you be able to sell an obsolete piece of equipment (if you can't trade or upgrade it) or used furniture to recover part of your investment?

Is used equipment or furniture a good alternative? That's a big maybe. "Buyer beware," says it best. Cheap, previously owned equipment may look like a bargain; but do your homework and shop around before you say yes. Definitely negotiate for a trial period, a repair warranty, and terms for return. It's also wise to, if possible, have the item thoroughly, professionally inspected before you buy.

Before you decide, get your accountant's advice. As we mentioned before, it sometimes makes more financial and tax sense to finance or lease big-ticket items. A leasing company may decline to lease you equipment if you haven't been in business a certain number of years (an indication of stability and ability to pay). They may demand a personal guarantee.

Leasing has tax advantages—you can write off your entire payment—and does allow you to upgrade your equipment with a minimum of fuss. Often you'll have the option to buy at the end of the lease. Investigate interest rates carefully, especially when choosing between leasing and financing a purchase.

PLAY BALL: OPENING DAY

You'll need to gear up for that first day of business. The preconception that a designer just casually strolls into a new workspace and becomes a business is woefully wrong. But any dread of the work required—or planning involved—is also unnecessary.

To get a handle on what to do before your doors open, set up a table that groups items sequentially to help you prepare for your big day. You'll find more information on these aspects of starting your studio in other chapters (and on my website, www. michaelfleishman.com), so I'll only hit the highlights here. For example:

Five weeks to a month prior to opening, you should visit your accountant; work up your first promotion, business forms, cards, and letterheads. If you need permits and licenses, this is a good time to secure all that. Licenses to consider:

- Business License
- Fire Department Permit
- Air and Water Pollution Control Permit
- Sign Permit
- County Permits

➡ State Licenses

➡ Federal Licenses

➡ Sales Tax License

➡ Health Department Permits

Lay down the rent deposit and get the keys. Nail down your web hosting; secure a domain name; create your website; get online. I'd secure any listing in your local phone directory at this time, and list your company in all online directories at this time, too.

One month to three weeks before opening day, see your lawyer; create your business sign or have it made. Print any promo, business forms, and the identity. Business gizmos like refrigerator magnets or stickers should be done now.

Two weeks to opening: mail the promo; place your advertising. Make an announcement via your social media of choice; do an email blast. Dope out your telephony (and buy the stuff) and get hooked up. Hand over your deposits and have utilities turned on; build shelving, etc.

One week to "D Day" finds you picking up your business forms and identity materials; installing the store sign; signing up for cleaning services, etc. Alison Miyauchi says to do another announcement at the one-week mark and the day before opening.

Adapt my form (and timing) to suit your own needs. You will find that following this basic roadmap will get you down the path to opening day easily and efficiently. Of course, you also need to plan expenses carefully so you don't end up over your head in debt before you even open. You don't want your gala opening to be followed immediately by your going out of business party.

➡

RIGHT ON POINT

(PROFESSIONAL VIEWPOINTS IN 50 WORDS OR LESS)

It doesn't matter where I am physically (to do the work), but mentally I need to be in "my space."

—Darren Booth

Always look for time-saving options, even though they might cost a little more. Your hourly rate—even your assistant's hourly rate—[may be] higher than the cost of [automating an] understaffed small office.

—Lara Kisielewska

I had a bedroom large enough to have a distinct sleeping space and a distinct working space, but this actually affected my sleep. I found it hard to "turn off" after a day spent working in the same room I was supposed to be able to relax in.

—Ellie Jabbour

The days of not being considered a true professional (because you work out of your home) are long gone. My clients don't care when and where I work, as long as I keep in touch and hit all my deadlines.

—Vicki Vandeventer

There's a trend toward virtual meetings (for instance, the web service Go-To-Meeting). Video conferencing and web conferencing are other alternatives to face-to-face meetings. But just like during business phone calls, you must eliminate background noise and distractions for a professional presentation.

—Jamie Sharp

MONEY
GAMES

Profiting from the Convergence of Sports and Entertainment

David M. Carter

CHAPTER 7

MANAGING
YOUR BUSINESS

Creating your own design studio is a permanent ongoing project. It could be the best project of your life. The management part can either be learned or solved.

—Ken Bullock

So you think you're organized? Got it together (if you could only remember where all the elements are)? Starting and running your own business is very much like a juggling act. At times you will feel as though you're juggling the task equivalents of a meat cleaver, bowling ball, and cream pie. Just how many minor chores and major responsibilities can you keep in the air all at once? And make no mistake about it, you're going to be so busy you may end up dropping a pin or two.

You know all the clichés. You're only one person. There are just so many hours in a day. You'll be wearing a lot of different hats. These homilies are time-worn, but (to throw in another rickety catch phrase) right as rain.

MANAGING YOUR WORK

Managing your business and the projects you bring in is a matter of zeroing in on priorities. It's also a matter of keeping track of people, services, time, and expenses. To manage effectively, you will need to get organized, set-up systems and procedures and maintain records and files on all aspects of your business.

You must keep tabs on any project to stay on time. Graphic design often involves bringing many pieces together to make a final printed product. Making sure every component of a job is done, and done well, is imperative. As if keeping track of your end of a project isn't enough, you'll also have to watchdog the work being done by your support services.

JACKETS REQUIRED

To keep a deadline and overall turn-around time in mind, break each project down into tasks and mini-tasks. After identifying each task and mini-task, assign an amount of time to each. From there, you should be able to come up with a schedule and a completion date for each task. As each task is completed, record the date so you'll know exactly when it was done.

Create a job jacket for each project. This can be done digitally, of course, on your computer or via mobile device. But if you go old school here—and there's nothing wrong with that—place your schedule into the jacket or tack the schedule (along with the job name) on the outside. This way you will know at a glance what tasks still need to be completed on a given job and whether the job is on schedule. Some folks prefer to use a traditional wall chart, a blackboard, or a bulletin board as a means of tracking the progress of all ongoing projects.

The Numbers Game

Your job jacket will serve as Grand Central Station for all project-related notes and correspondence, as well as scheduling and supplier information. The job jacket can be organized digitally or in a file cabinet; over-sized materials and other project-related art could be stored in flat files.

Categorize projects alphabetically by client. Assign a number for each project. For example, the Caputo Cakes logo might be Caputo #4201, while Caputo's stationery becomes Caputo #4202, and their business cards would be Caputo #4203. By assigning each project an identifying number, you can easily keep track of the chronological order of each project. Use these codes, as well, for identifying charges that are to be billed directly to a project.

Roger Brucker agrees and offers this variation: "Employ a job numbering system using the first two letters of the client's first name and last name (or first four letters of a single name), followed by a serial number that is next available," he says. "For example: ACLE-1432. You could then employ a visual art filing system tied to that job number. All elements—actual physical art to electronic files, etc.—are marked with the job number plus date of entry. Once given a number, that element's number does not change. In this way, all elements can be tracked back to the master job, even when used on subsequent jobs."

GOING THROUGH A PHASE

Regardless of your preferred method or combination of methods, you'll need to keep track of (and come up with completion dates for) the following components or job phases. They are arranged here in approximate chronology of their completion:

Conceptualization and roughs: This is where you do your homework. You'll meet with the client, brainstorm, come up with a concept, and obtain the approval to schedule any other components that go into successfully producing the final job.

Copy, art, and photography; typesetting and layout: Write or commission copy with client availability in mind for consultation, approval, and brainstorming. Whether scheduling setup, location shots, or selecting from client-furnished art and photography, you should factor in time for reviewing imagery (remember to include your client in this selection). Schedule time for image enhancement and manipulation. If you're not the illustrator on this job, provide time for locating suitable talent as well as plenty of time for roughs, revisions, and final renderings. Schedule adequate time for copy fitting, proofreading, and revisions. Be sure to schedule time for client review, approval, and possible revisions as well.

Preflight: Make sure the job—all digital files, color profiles and separations, graphics and fonts, anything essential to the job's successful completion—are the right type for the output device and follow correct specs. Double check that everything is present and accessible. Keep it clean, compatible, appropriately formatted, and ready to rip.

Production: Schedule service bureau time if necessary and factor in hours for getting bids from several service bureaus and/or printers. Factor in production services and time (to collate, trim, fold, stitch, die cut, or other processes involved in completing the job) in addition to the time for the actual print run and shipping/delivery. And if the requirements for the job call for it, don't forget to schedule press checks, possibly including the client in these checks.

MAKIN' A LIST AND CHECKIN' IT TWICE

Getting and staying organized is critical. The ol' grocery list is not just for breakfast anymore. It's important to list—yes, make a list—on a daily basis, of what needs to be done. When that list is written, it is up for argument and grabs . . . at the top of the morning, on the spot, or freeform (how about at the end of the day?). At the end of the shift, you can make a list of tasks for the next day, taking note of priorities and emergencies, tasks that may simmer or stew; stuff that simply needs to be finished now, sooner than later. You could determine priorities by assigning a numerical value to each task (and make sure you tackle the tasks that have the highest priority on a given day).

Keep track of your ideas as well as what needs to be done. You can easily remind yourself about any aspect of a business project or life in general by "recording" it on a central calendar via your computer or a device (cell phone, iPod, iPad, and its ilk). You could even document information in a traditional pocket notebook or on a mini digital recorder. Regardless of when, where, and how you take down your entries, simply sync all information to the master planner.

And whatever it's called—planner, diary, scheduler, log—calendars and to-do lists can help organize your tasks, projects, meetings, and other business-related obligations. You'll find that by maintaining some sort of plan book, you'll be able to follow all aspects of your business on a day-to-day basis so nothing will fall through the cracks.

PEOPLE WHO NEED PEOPLE

Nobody likes surprises. Keep your client posted. No matter how outstanding your design work may be, you will never be able to build a business if you do not have a reputation for a solid (and thorough) work ethic while establishing stellar rapport.

You'll need to communicate frequently and candidly with your clients and develop an understanding up front of what is required of each of you to bring about a positive outcome of any project. With every job, you have an obligation to let your client know what you will produce in the way of roughs, comps, and final, when you will be creating these, and when he or she will be involved in the decision-making process. It is also your responsibility to schedule meetings and opportunities for client approval. It's crucial to establish this with your client at the onset of a project so that you will be able to schedule client approval meetings at different stages of the job.

THE HISTORY CHANNEL

Some creatives feel it is necessary to develop a history on each of their clients. It's not cloak and dagger stuff, Mr. Bond—just facts and figures, background and color: names, address, phone numbers, and contact records; a record of billing procedures, credit, and financial information; any other information you deem pertinent to the business relationship. Any of the client's personal preferences or idiosyncrasies can be kept track of in this file or database, particularly if your past experience with a client's projects has been fraught with a multitude of time-robbing revisions.

It could be argued that the costs of client revisions seem to increase about ten-fold with each stage of production. So if you estimate that it costs $10 to change something on a first rough, ballpark $100 when it is typeset and on your color proof, $1,000 to make the same change even closer to the finish line. It's best to make revisions early on and establish a mutually agreed upon (and documented) protocol at the beginning of a project.

MANAGING YOUR MONEY

Running a tab at your local bistro is one thing. Running a business and not keeping tabs on income and expenses is another. Being a free spirit may definitely be a creative boon, but become a button-down banker with your bucks. It's absolutely crucial to know what money is coming in, how much you have at any time, and where it's going. To do otherwise is simply bad business and financial suicide.

To keep track of business income and expenses, it's essential to set up separate bank accounts for your business. Your numbers will vary, of course, but a practical start-up base might kick off with $2,000 to $3,000 in savings and another $2,000 to $3,000 in a checking account. Online checking is easy, convenient, and efficient, but (at least at this point in time) people are still writing checks traditionally. (So if you are paying bills the old-fashioned way, make sure you have check writing privileges for approximately twenty checks per month.)

Secure a company credit card linked to those accounts. Shop around for the best deal from the banks in your area. Regional banks are usually the best for setting up business accounts as well as applying for loans (see chapter 5). Your hometown banker is more likely to lend money to a neighbor and offer the good service that goes with being a "big fish in a small pond." To compare banks, use account information and total the fees and interest that each bank would charge on the services you need. Break down those fees to determine what your best options will be.

THE ALLEN METHOD

When Brian Allen first ventured into independent business, he knew the shock of an irregular income was just around the corner, so he planned ahead. He calculated what he spent on average each month (bills plus average credit card bill), and says, "That's how much a wife, two kids, and a house costs!"

Next, he created a business checking account and a business savings account. All of his freelance income would go into the business checking account. At the end of each month, he would "pay" himself by first putting 25 percent of his income into the business savings account (for Uncle Sam); the rest he transferred to his personal checking account. "My system," he says, "was to make sure that at the end of every month, after I paid all my bills, that there was still at least $3,000 left in the personal checking account. That way, if the phones stopped ringing for an entire month, we would be able to pay our bills without taking any action. If there was a surplus (over $3,000), we typically put that into our personal savings."

Allen always keeps at least three months of income in the personal savings, just in case a bad month turns into a bad quarter or worse. So far his system has worked exceedingly well. It reduces any panic during a slow month simply because the current month is essentially already paid for. On the other hand, it also helps Allen regulate what should go into savings during the good or great months. "It forces me to put that extra money into savings," he says, "and not into Best Buy."

MONITORING EXPENSES AND INCOME

Income, simply stated, is money coming in. Expenses are obviously monies going out. When you balance your expenses against your income, you end up totaling one column and comparing it to the other. This method is very much like balancing a checkbook and is commonly known as the cash method of accounting.

The accrual method—where expenses are matched to, and directly offset by the income generated by the jobs they are spent on—may be somewhat impractical for a design or illustration studio. Keeping track of watercolor paper or pens used on a per job basis is not practical. For tax purposes, you can choose either the cash or accrual method, but you must stay with that choice for at least six months. Your accountant can help you choose the method best for you.

On the freelance or small business level, bookkeeping (keeping tabs on expenditures and income) may be the only accounting you do, so keep good records. In fact, keeping track of what you're taking in and spending is crucial to supply records to your accountant, bank, and the IRS.

THE GOING RATE

Rates for a particular job depend on several factors. First, off the top: the deadline. A rush deadline always means more money. Second, the clients: are they local, regional, or national? Third, the usage: an all rights or buyout sale should also mean more money. What does the deal involve? One-time usage or multiple usages? Print, TV, Internet . . . what? This small checklist just gets us started; for more on pricing, see chapter 17.

STAYING ON TRACK

Keeping track of your expenses (debits) and income (credits) is easy with a ledger and disbursement journal (also called a payroll journal or cash disbursement journal) that chronologically lists all business exchanges. The ledger categorizes this information according to IRS classifications for tax-deductible business expenses.

In fact, you can order checkbooks that contain their own ledgers or disbursement sheets. And by organizing your expenses into categories that comply with IRS guidelines, you are also complying with the IRS's requirements for a "contemporaneous log of expenses."

Of course, you can go online or digital with a desktop log—computerize your books. There are a wide variety of good, small, inexpensive financial programs to use on a Macintosh or PC (and the gamut of expensive, high-powered packages, as well). Quickbooks or Sage 50 (formerly called Peachtree) come to mind.

You could even fabricate a custom-made ledger, if you're particularly cost-conscious or the digital approach is somehow too high-tech. However, a simple, inexpensive check-writing program (or online service) may be all you need. Old schoolers can use the classic Dome Book (a "general ledger") or another "one-write" traditional system. The good folks at Dome actually advertise with the slogan "No Hard Drive, No Headaches."

But your accountant may advise you that digital technology greatly improves your efficiency and overall bookkeeping by keeping your administrative time to a minimum. These professionals understand from experience that, while it might be hard to break the habit of writing checks by hand, check-writing software or online checking could save you valuable hours in the long run.

I won't strenuously recommend that you toss your checkbook (or get rid of your one-write setup and general ledger pegboard). These venerable systems maintain to this day and only you can determine what's truly "easy and efficient" for your purposes. I can't say that digital bookkeeping is a business must, but that grand ol' (and ever so relevant) saying, "time is money," also carries on. Think it through.

ORGANIZING YOUR FINANCIAL RECORDS

In addition to your ledger and journal, and above and beyond the decision to go digital there, you will also need to maintain files—paper and/or digital—to track client invoices and any other invoices you receive and pay in the course of doing business.

The digital metaphors of files, folders, and a desktop are not accidental. The real world equivalents of such office organization established the template, so my generic wording here should make perfect sense. You can manage client invoices by setting up three folders, one each for paid, unpaid, and partially paid. When you receive full payment, note the date on your invoice and transfer it to the paid file. If you receive partial payment, note the date on your invoice and transfer it to the partially paid folder. When you receive the remaining balance, transfer the invoice to the paid folder.

You will also need to set up an accounts payable file. This would include all project-related invoices you receive as well as your business expenses (phone bills, utilities, rent, etc.). One good method of keeping track is to maintain a file for each day of the month, numbered consecutively. When an invoice comes in on the 20th of a given month, put it in the folder marked "20." On the 20th of the following month, before you insert any new invoices for that day, pull the old invoices that you inserted on the 20th of the last month and pay them that day. This method ensures that you pay all invoices on time, but not until payment is due, which as Lara Kisielewska reminds us, maximizes your cash flow in case of unforeseen emergencies.

It's also a good idea to maintain the following records as a supplement to the accounting systems mentioned above: a cash expense log for meals, travel, and entertainment (if there are no receipts or inadequate receipts); an appointment (and business) event diary as well as a travel log for your car to record business-related mileage and tolls; a method of allocating expenses that are both personal and business (rent or mortgage, utilities, phone and cleaning) if you work at home. Do all of this notation on your smartphone, iPod, or iPad (or similar); on your laptop or desktop computer; or even on paper—but do it.

YOUR IRS OBLIGATIONS

Be sure to put money away periodically to meet your tax obligations. You are required by law to file quarterly returns with the IRS on April 15, June 15, September 15, and then January 15 of the next year. (These dates may vary by a day or two in any given calendar year.) Please note that if you are an incorporated business, you must file an annual tax return.

"Regular corporations can have fiscal year ends," adds accountant Julie Buschur. "The due date of the return is three months after the fiscal year end, so if the corporate year end is 12/31, the return must be filed by 3/15 (you can get a six-month extension)."

By the end of the year, 90 percent of what you owe, or 100 percent of what you paid last year, is due. Be sure that you comply with the IRS on this. You may have to pay penalties and interest if you do not file or estimate your taxes accurately.

Don't forget that you will also need to pay Self-Employment Social Security taxes, based on what you (as your own employer) owe. Your old employer used to make these deductions from your paycheck, but as a self-employed designer or illustrator, you are now obligated to pay this tax yourself. This tax is paid annually and filed with your regular tax return on April fifteenth.

If you are self-employed, anywhere from 25–40 percent of every profit dollar should be set aside for taxes. Self-employment taxes are paid on sole proprietorships and partnerships. At this time, there is no self-employment tax on S Corporation income, but a reasonable salary (payroll) must be taken by the shareholder in an S Corporation. For further information, make an appointment with your accountant to compute your tax liability based on your projected income. Based on this, he or she will be able to prepare your estimated quarterly taxes.

When and if you hire additional designers, understand the ins and outs of payroll taxes for that staff (and know that payroll tax for yourself will also be handled differently). Again, work with your accountant to keep your tax responsibilities on track and in line with all rules and regulations.

WHEN I'M SIXTY-FOUR (OR TWENTY-FIVE)

Plan now for retirement. Deferred savings plans make good sense for your future. But profit sharing is too complicated, and pension plans are right for higher incomes or larger corporations with a great number of employees. But there are alternatives for a small corporation or sole proprietor.

I am not a financial guru (nor do I play one on TV). What follows is merely an introduction to some options, not specific tax advice or financial guidelines. Yes, we live in a great age of information technology. The modern "do-it-yourself, get the job done right" spirit is strong indeed. Maybe you do have the knowledge base and inclination to do your own financial planning. But even the sharpest of my financially savvy compadres seek out a financial professional for current information and counseling.

Needless to say, the economic climate (and forecast) is always subject to change. But the roller coaster ride of our economy can be well managed by those making a living at this sort of thing. And while the best place for your money will vary at any given time (depending on your age and income at that moment), financial professionals know ways to minimize taxes and provide for retirement.

HAVE A PLAN

IRAs (Individual Retirement Accounts) currently allow you to save up to $2,000 of your annual income in tax-deferred savings. SEPs (Simplified Employee Pension) plans allow you to invest more than IRAs permit. These are available to any self-employed individual, and you can contribute up to 13 percent of your net income. There's a minimum of red tape involved—it's not nearly as complex as defined benefit and contribution plans.

IRA contributions must be made by the due date of the return, with extensions. S Corporations are flow-through entities, meaning the entity pays no tax but "flows through" to the shareholder's personal return, therefore due dates are the same as the personal 1040 due dates.

- Roth IRAs permit you to contribute up to $2,000, but it's not deductible on your tax return. The advantage here is that all the interest and capital gains are not taxable, ever. Regular IRAs are deductible on your personal tax return, but all gains are taxed when you receive distributions from the account. With Roth IRAs you can withdraw the principal at any time and not get penalized. Plus, Roth IRAs can be used toward a college education with no penalty for early withdrawal. It is true that you can take your principal out of a Roth IRA at any time without tax, but you must have had the Roth open for five years for the earnings to be tax-free.

- Simple IRAs or Simple 401K plans were created in the mid 1990s to help small businesses provide relatively inexpensive retirement plans for employers. Both are fairly similar. An employee can contribute up to $6,000 per year. The employer has to match only 3 percent of salaries one out of every three years. The other two years, the employer has to match only 1 percent of salaries.

- Keogh, pension, and/or profit sharing plans offer greater tax deductions, but involve more paperwork than the above options. Regardless of whether you are a proprietorship, partnership, or corporation, you can set up a pension plan or Keogh account for your retirement contributions. There are several different types of plans available exclusively to the self-employed:

  - Money Purchase Pension Plans (MPPPs) allow you to contribute 20 percent or up to $30,000 a year. When you set up an MPPP, you designate the percentage of your income you'll be putting in each year and stick to that percentage.

➡ Profit sharing plans are similar to MPPPs, letting you save up to 13.04 percent or $30,000 annually. The amount you contribute to this plan can vary from year to year and might make more sense if your income is inconsistent.

➡ Defined benefit plans are based on calculating how much you need to contribute annually to receive a specified amount once you retire. With a plan like this, you can contribute any amount of your income, even 100 percent, but because they are costly to set up (an actuary needs to make the calculations), these plans are recommended only for those who have high incomes and are close to retirement.

TWISTER

Health insurance and life insurance and disability insurance. Oh my. Health insurance and life insurance and disability insurance. Oh my. Health insurance and life insurance and disability insurance . . . wait.

Perhaps, when contemplating insurance, you feel like you've entered the Enchanted Forest, completely ignoring that blatantly ominous sign warning you to KEEP OUT. ADULTS ONLY! Gee, Toto—you certainly won't get much of an argument from a rational individual that the American health-care system is indeed a scary Wicked Witch of The West.

But, insurance is, shall we say, a necessary evil. And that same reasonable soul should carry insurance. Should you use different insurance carriers to meet specific needs? This works for many, but if you bundle plans (life insurance, disability, and health care) together with one carrier, you'll usually get better rates overall. Shop around for the right agent by checking out recommendations and referrals.

Let's skip down the Yellow Brick Road and do a light physical of some basic insurance coverage. And not to worry, you're still in Kansas.

AN APPLE A DAY

Skimp elsewhere if you must, but get the best health plan you can afford. Don't make the mistake of thinking you can go even a day without medical coverage. You never know when lightning may strike and, with the exorbitant cost of hospitalization and health care in general, you don't want to have to pay for medical expenses from your personal funds.

Group insurance rates are frequently lower than those you can obtain as an independent. Many group health care opportunities are available through professional organizations. Perhaps your local Chamber of Commerce can offer better rates than the group insurance available through design-affiliated professional organizations.

Some have speculated that this situation exists because insurance companies view those involved in artistic professions as a high-risk group. Like it or not, professionals in the creative arts (including the visual arts) have been excluded in years past from the kinds of preferential rates available to other professional groups.

Investigate alternative sources (like locally based, self-insured funds for printers and those affiliated with the pre-press end of the graphic arts industry). An independent insurance agent in your area can usually give you the needed information on such group opportunities.

FOR THE LIFE OF ME

Do you really need life insurance? That's a complicated question that demands critical research and solid financial counsel. Life insurance is an investment. As such, life insurance may offer various investment options (even cash accumulations or payments). It can be the financial safety net for your dependents in the event of your death—protecting or paying off a mortgage; replacing your now "lost" income; covering the benignly labeled "final" expenses (funeral, burial, medical costs); paying off debt or real estate taxes, buying a partner's business shares; maybe providing funding for your kid's college bills.

Term life insurance covers you for a specific range of years (typically ten to thirty) and pays out only during that term. Whole life (also known as permanent life) pays off when you die. Premiums depend, of course, on the type of policy you elect.

As with anything, how much you need varies by individual: how much you earn and how much you've saved; how much—and what—your family will need and for how long.

TEMPORARILY ABLED, PERHAPS?

It's also crucial to evaluate disability income insurance. If you are laid up, you not only lose your salary, but risk losing your business as well. When determining what kind of coverage you should look into, take into consideration all of your personal obligations, such as mortgages and dependents. Shop for the best coverage rather than the lowest premium.

Consider a non-cancellable policy with guaranteed renewal. This will forbid the insurer from terminating your policy or increasing your premium after an initial two-year contestability period has passed. Also, check out policies with a cost of living adjustment that will help you keep pace with inflation.

The Best Policy

Finally, if you are in good health, you might even find out from your agent that an independent policy is an attractive option. A better deal than group benefits? No promises here, but a new business staffed by a young designer should be able to buy life and disability insurance at reasonable rates. Ensure you will obtain the best rates by bypassing obvious risk factors (don't smoke) and preventing peril (install safety equipment).

Consider a number of alternatives when shopping for the best deal. For instance, if you feel your only need is to cover yourself in an emergency, you may want to opt for low premium payments on a health policy with a big deductible. On the other hand, if you have a family to take care of, a Health Maintenance Organization (HMO) can provide for emergencies as well as offer reduced rates for check-ups and other medical needs.

And once you've found an insurance carrier, diffuse hassles and make sure you are adequately compensated for claims by making personal copies of all claim records.

COVER ME

When considering the overall picture of insurance for your business, investigate these standard areas of coverage when you're starting up:

➡ **Valuable papers:** Compensates for loss of stolen or damaged artwork and files by covering research time, labor, and materials involved. This type of insurance is extremely important when you consider the replacement value of original artwork (digital or otherwise), transparencies, films, and general files.

➡ **Property and liability:** Covers damage to your studio's contents in the event of burglary, robbery, vandalism, or fire and water damage.

➡ **Liability:** Covers injury to any non-employee on your premises.

➡ **Business interruption:** Replaces lost profits if your business is temporarily shut down because of damages to the premises

➡ **Auto insurance:** If you're using your car for business and let others on your staff drive it, you'll need to add them to your policy.

➡ **Disability and/or workman's compensation:** Covers injuries incurred on the job by anyone employed by you (required in most states).

➡ **Computer equipment:** Additional coverage beyond general contents in the event of damage by such things as fire or vandalism. This might also cover the cost of renting replacement equipment while your equipment is being repaired.

➡ **Finally,** if you're working out of your home, you'll want to add a rider on your current homeowner's or renter's insurance to cover damage and theft of your studio property.

PUTTING MONEY BACK INTO YOUR STUDIO

Unless you've hit a windfall of profits after operating for a very short period of time, and feel the additional business justifies a loan, you'll need to plan for future growth by regularly investing some of the profits of your business into various accounts.

You'll want to invest a portion in a liquid account (a passbook savings or money market, for instance). Although this type of account won't yield a high interest rate, you'll still be getting some return on monies that are just as accessible to you as the cash in your checking account.

From there, check with your financial advisor, but consider divvying up the remainder of your savings into a variety of CD options, stocks, money market accounts, and mutual funds. The best return on any of these investments will vary at any given time, depending on the current economic situation, so shop around and look for the best alternatives to satisfy your short- and long-range goals. Lock in on the best interest rates available for the savings options that fit your unique needs.

HELP . . . I NEED SOMEBODY!

At start-up, odds are you'll be doing it all. Salaries can take a big bite out of your budget, but at some point you just may need to hire a staff.

No doubt, when the time comes, you'll know what kind of help you most need. However, consider the following: as studio principal, you might bill out your time at $100 per hour, but you find yourself spending much of this time answering the phone, studio organization, and doing clerical tasks. You'd want to free yourself to do the work that generates the most income, so generally it makes good economic sense to fill an entry- or intermediate-level job rather than a more qualified position.

Don't hire another full-time designer unless you are sure you can keep that person busy. It's better to cover a temporary crunch by farming some work out to a freelancer than to hire an employee. You'll not only save the costs of the salary but also the benefits, heavy tax payments, and the furniture and equipment for that person to use.

IS BIG BETTER?

No matter how grandiose your vision or how diminutive your scale, you must maintain a high quality in your work—sound advice when you consider that keeping the dollar value of your work up there is the fastest way to get to fat city. High-quality work is best achieved through carefully managing the growth of your business. Businesses that make it past the initial hurdles often come to failure because no provisions were made for growth. Grow too slowly and you may find yourself in debt and scrambling for work. Fail to anticipate the workload and you might be unable to meet client demands.

There's an old axiom that says, "Be careful what you wish for—you just might get it." Many of the founders of "big" studios I interviewed waxed romantically about the "good old days" when the company was "small": a less hectic calendar; a daily schedule with more breathing room; nominal travel; simpler management styles and procedures; moderate overhead; intimate assignments . . . the list goes on and on. More than a few yearned to downsize (or had done so already). Our economy taught life lessons to some who were financially forced to retrench or cut back. Several cautioned that a loss of quality often accompanies rapid or great growth.

Everybody started on a modest (or more modest) scale, many working out of home. A number of designers remain situated there, in front of the fireplace, because they prefer a more personal business habitat. Others have endeavored to preserve a warmer, more congenial atmosphere in offices outside the home with loosely constructed, friendly environments designed to foster an open exchange of ideas as well as hard work. Small potatoes or big cheese, the creatives interviewed for this book are highly regarded for producing superior work and providing superlative service. The size of the operation has little to do with success—it's an individual thing.

LOANS: MAYBE NOW, MAYBE LATER

See chapter 5 for our initial discussion on loans. But to recap, if you have a good credit history and are of sound character, you may have a good chance of getting a loan after having established yourself in business for two to three years. You might be able to finance a small loan for a piece of equipment after one to two years in business.

Start your studio with a solid plan for money management and then consistently follow through to improve your chances of getting that loan. Keep good financial records from the beginning so you can easily demonstrate to a skeptical banker why you deserve a loan.

Here are eleven steps you can take to become an educated loan applicant when you need additional funds:

1. Be realistic. Sorry, but for a freelancer or small businessperson, the odds of getting a bank loan are just not good. Should you be looking elsewhere for that start-up money?

2. Go to your accountant for referrals. He knows you; he knows your business; he knows the banks. Get some advice. Even ask him to make introductions and open doors for you.

3. Shop around. Visit three separate banks (or more). Evaluate and go with your best deal. A small bank may be the best bet and your local bank is probably your first stop. Lay the groundwork. Build and maintain a loyal relationship (savings and checking accounts) with your bank of choice.

4. Make friends. Build a professional and personal relationship with your banker long before you need a loan.

5. Clean up your house. Reduce your overall debt before you apply for a loan. Establish a solid credit history—repay other loans and pay them on time.

6. Do your homework. Write a complete business plan. Or, at least, prepare a loan package (see below). Have current fiscal statements (plus past financial summaries) ready for inspection. You'll also need to explain why you need the loan. How much do you need?

7. Demonstrate exactly how the money will be used. What kind of loan do you want? Be specific and put it on paper as a proposal. If you need to make a bona fide presentation with your facts, figures, and visuals, do so.

8. Know how and when the debt will be repaid, plus conditions of payment. Be comfortable with the structure of the deal. What about the term (the duration) of the loan? To the best of your ability, make it as easy as you can.

    Depending on your cash flow, you could elect to repay this loan as a single payment. Or pay off the loan in chunks or monthly payments that decrease the principal with remaining interest computed on the unpaid balance.

    What you pay on a monthly basis must fit in with your cash flow. A four-year loan lowers your monthly payments, but will ultimately cost you more in interest. Can you pay off the loan early or will you be hit with prepayment penalties?

9. Understand your total loan agreement completely. Don't just look at the dollar cost of the loan—it really comes down to getting the best rate and terms you can get (and live with). Turn down the extras.

    For instance, you don't need the bank's credit, life, or disability insurance. These options—they're not mandatory—only jack up the end costs of the loan. And decline a loan calculated under the so-called "Rule of 78s." Avoid this strategy, as it's decidedly unfavorable to the borrower. Stated simply, under the "Rule of 78s," if you pay your loan off early, you'll be hit with a prepayment penalty. It's legal, but a bit underhanded, and most folks don't check their paperwork or fully understand their contract.

10. Evaluate the rates, study the terms, and assess your options. Most loans these days are simple interest loans. Should you go with a variable rate, fixed rate, or semi-fixed rate loan? If you go with a variable rate, is there a ceiling on how high that rate can go (and a floor to which it can fall)? If you get a fixed rate, will there be an annual adjustment? Does your

lender say, "Well, Mr. Simon, I'll give you a fixed rate, but I'm going to fix it annually at 5 percent over prime"?

Uh . . . and what the heck does that mean? The "prime rate" is the consistent rate of interest—the oft-called reference or base rate— at which banks will lend to credit-worthy borrowers (customers with good credit). Some variable interest rates may be expressed as a percentage above or below prime rate. Make sure that the "prime rate" you are quoted has been established by the Treasury Index.

11. Go for it. Yes, it is true that little percentage points add up to big bucks, but you can't predict if (or when) interest rates will go up or down. You could lose your best opportunity by waiting until rates are at their lowest point.

PACKAGE GOODS

You'll need to prepare a loan package before making your presentation to the bank. Refer to chapter 5 for more on all this, but here's a checklist to prime that pump. The formal document should cover the last three years (remember the current quarter, too) and include:

- Company history (keep it to just one page)
- Principals' résumés (again one page per individual)
- Statement about use of loan process (a simple but specific list of categories and amounts is fine). However, when applying for that loan, a comprehensive business plan would be a big plus. (See chapters 2, 3, and 6 for related information, and chapter 5 for a more specific discussion on business plans.)
- Profit and loss statement, including balance sheets and a record of current accounts receivable and payable
- Cash flow statement
- Three-year cash flow projection
- Statement of your terms, pricing, and company policies
- Personal and business tax returns (ask how many years)
- Equipment index
- Customer and supplier references (three to five for each)
- Personal guaranty. A word here: unfortunately, most lenders will insist you personally guarantee a loan. Neither the tight relationship you've established with your banker nor the heavyweight business you've set up will spare you this considerable risk. If you need the money, you'll just have to bite the bullet. However, you might just look at a personal guaranty as yet another means of showing the bank that you are a good risk.

DEVIL'S ADVOCATE

You're no doubt aware that, when starting out, you need to get familiar with laws protecting your copyrights and gain understanding of intellectual property, fair use, and work for hire, etc. It's only smart, and professional designer organizations like AIGA push this all the time.

And Kristine Putt agrees completely. But she's also not afraid to walk a bit on the wild side and says, "However, you should also know when to break the rules." It's a topic Putt says she's well aware of, but something most designers won't even discuss (and based on her experience, it's even somewhat taboo). Here's Putt's story:

"When I first started out," she says, "I was a stickler to 'policy' and actually wound up losing clients. Ouch! I thought that maintaining a strict code of ethics was doing the right thing; the only thing. But I eventually developed a rep for being a 'difficult designer.'

"You have to know when to lay down the law, but also realize when to trust your instinct and walk away. Understand when—and where—you'd be willing to bend in good conscience before your professional reputation takes the hit."

Putt admits it's a tricky conundrum, boiling down to knowing yourself, understanding your customer base (and what kind of customer you are committed to serve) plus, as she puts it, "how personally you take what some may deem as—rightly or wrongly—abuse. It may come down to a question of balance—the balance between what you know is right, and what you feel is best."

"We're creatives," Putt says, smiling. "We are emotional. We take things personally . . . and then pretend that we don't. You have to let stuff go sometimes or it will eat your soul. Be flexible. I know it's hard. It can make us feel we've been taken advantage of.

"But you must realistically step away from those feelings and separate fact from fiction and a binding 'emotional ownership' of your design. If you can't, you'll only wind up upsetting yourself (and everyone involved) and possibly tarnishing your good name in the process."

Putt proposes that, when you make a mistake, just own up when it's your error. Let it go when that's prudent. Learn from either scenario, and then don't allow it to happen again. Go to the mat with a customer when necessary, obviously, but make sure client squabbles are completely and realistically grounded in professional ethics and practice.

And she adamantly advises you to pick your battles carefully. For instance, usage rights must be scrupulously negotiated—and agreed to—before the agreement is signed and work commences. You live in the present, but think "big picture," and plan for the "long run."

Now, when it boils down to payment? Putt steadfastly says to make no exceptions. "Be absolutely ruthless about collections," she says. "I once made a surprise, unexpected visit to a client's office and sat in his lobby for three hours while I waited for him to come out of a meeting, just so I could get my check."

THE SHAPIRO REPORT

Are you putting in too many hours, not making enough money, and overwhelmed with paperwork? That's a problem for many designers just starting their own businesses. I queried Ellen Shapiro, a longtime design firm principal (and the author of many magazine articles on the design business, plus two books on working productively with clients), who filled me in me on how she would counsel a fellow designer who found him or herself in that situation. The following is what she told me:

TIME MANAGEMENT

You should be able to devote at least half your time to actually doing the creative work that you went into business to produce. Of course, some of your time will need to be spent finding and grooming new clients, generating proposals, and doing some office administration.

However, if you're like many of us, you may find your days filled with small tasks that eat up too many hours (like answering every email that comes your way). Here's one suggestion: triage your email and phone calls. During business hours, answer only those emails and take those calls that are essential to (a) getting new business (b) doing a better job on the business you already have.

Sound simple? Try it. And no looking at Facebook more than three times a day.

BY DEFINITION

You might need to sit back and try to define—or redefine—your role. Write a job description for yourself. What are your strengths? How will you best utilize your time?

As the firm principal—the person whose name is on the door—spending face time with clients is essential. Never give up that role, but Shapiro suggests you might not be able to do everything else by yourself.

Many illustrators are successful as solo operations, but graphic designers who are responsible for larger, complex projects need to build a team and effectively manage, lead, delegate, and nurture the people on the team.

"Very few of the great creative directors and designers (whose work you see in annuals and probably admire) can and want to do it all themselves," Shapiro says. Most likely, at some point, you will need to tap into a pool of freelancers for adding new creative solutions to the mix or completing jobs when the workload is high. Eventually you may need to hire one or more part-time or full-time designers.

PROJECT YOUR FUTURE SUCCESS

"Although it seems that every year the competition gets tougher, prices get lower, and clients demand more in less time, it's still possible to make this your best and lucky year," Shapiro says with a smile.

How? First, know what kind of work you have now and what kind of work you want to have in the future—a question only you can answer. For example, if your clients now are small retailers, restaurants, and individual service providers, there may be bigger fish in the waters of opportunity: health-care and educational institutions, high-tech businesses, manufacturing companies, and more. Bigger projects with larger budgets, stuff you can really sink your design teeth into. What's preventing you from going after them?

Oh, your portfolio doesn't include work that those clients could relate to? Take that as a challenge and proactively show what you would do if you had the chance.

"No, not work on spec!" Shapiro says emphatically. "Just take the time to create some outstanding portfolio pieces that showcase your thinking and talent. Many successful designers and advertising art directors have done just that to attract exactly the kind of clientele they wanted."

Yes, it will take time, but consider the potential rewards. Not only bigger budgets and higher visibility, but less paperwork too. "What if you sent out six invoices for $10,000 each instead of sixty invoices for $1,000 each?" Shapiro asks. "Would your life be easier? Would your business be more profitable?" Something to think about.

EVERYTHING HAS ITS PRICE

Pricing is a challenge for all design firms. An hourly rate—say, $100, as an example—is fine. But most design jobs are not estimated on hourly rates alone.

The fee is based on a combination of factors—including the worth of your perceived value. You can research formulas and suggestions; the *Graphic Artists Guild Handbook: Pricing & Ethical Guidelines* is a good start; and you can network and attend seminars and conferences.

One rule of thumb: The larger the client, the exposure, the audience, the higher the fee. Set your fee considering those factors, plus the time you will really need to put into completing the job beautifully and correctly.

"The best pricing strategy is a mixture of common sense and getting a straight answer from the client," Shapiro says. "Be direct. Ask: 'What is your budget?' If they say they don't know, then say, '$10,000.' All of a sudden, they do know that it isn't $10,000." So what will it be?

To set fees accurately, know how many hours you spend on similar projects. Stay on top of your timesheets. Take the few minutes every day to fill in your hours. Insist any employees (and freelancers) do the same.

"There is no magic formula," says Shapiro. "Every successful creative business estimates how many hours they will need to spend on project D by knowing how much time it took to complete similar projects A, B, and C."

I BID YOU A DUE DATE

Talent alone is no guarantee of success. Rather, the key is your ability plus lots of elbow grease, coupled with intensive customer service, energetic marketing/self-promotion, and a sharp business strategy.

And a keen-edged business acumen embraces the chops to smartly discuss bids and estimates (whether you are working with new or established businesses).

Don't be pressured into talking money or cutting a deal on the spot; when you need the time, take it. Don't be afraid to ask for what you really need to do the assignment; be prepared to say no and maybe lose the job. Approach all negotiations with open eyes and mind. Remember that negotiation is a bit of a game and it's all a learning process. Nobody's shooting at you. Actually, life is one long negotiation, so you're fairly seasoned already.

Always get a contract on the outset of an assignment and do it from your end. A letter of confirmation may be wise, and it could even be a short thank-you note outlining the terms of the agreement and job specifications. Simply describe what you expect to furnish, how much you expect to be paid, and when—no legalese needed, just plain, polite talk spelling out the agreed arrangement.

If the client looks shaky for some reason and you still take the job (brave soul), you can minimize your risk by asking for payments at various key points along the road to completion.

SIGNED, SEALED . . .

It's true, you can always build a "pain-in-the-butt" factor into your bid, raising your prices accordingly to compensate for the inevitable conflict you're about to endure. But why bother?

If your experience, radar, or research tells you that a buyer is dubious, you don't really need the aggravation or the bucks. There is no adequate compensation for time spent in hell, despite the invaluable lesson learned. Better to politely decline and move on. If the potential pay-off proves too alluring, know what you're getting into and strap on your seatbelt—it's going to be a long, interesting ride before you see any money. And then get it down in writing and signed by the client. Make sure your proposals and estimates state specifically what is included in the fee, including the number of meetings and presentations as well as the number of revisions the client can request.

And make sure the client understands that additional work, presentations, revisions, etc. will be billed as additional and that out-of-pocket expenses are not included in the fee. It's standard practice to add 15 to 20 percent to the price you pay for everything purchased on the client's behalf—printing, photography, illustration that you negotiate rates for, hire, and supervise—even stock photos and messengers.

... AND DELIVERED

Then you have to deliver the goods—and provide clients with the high level of service that should come with a relationship with a real, live designer and not just an online, anonymous crowd-sourced "vendor."

And, of course, make sure you get paid for everything you've done and get paid on time. Late fees are not uncommon and I've heard designers who give their clients a discount of 1 percent for paying early. Plan and bill your work in phases. At the completion of each phase, send an itemized invoice with clearly described line items—the quoted fee; billable client-requested additions and changes; itemized expenses (marked up); and sales tax, if applicable.

How about uncollected or late funds? If anything goes over thirty days, send the client a friendly email reminder (or pick up the phone).

BY THE NUMBERS

Finally, if you protest that all this sounds like it's going to take the fun out of being a freelance designer, that you are not a "numbers kinda gal," you may need to find someone who is (to work with you).

For many small businesses, a part-time bookkeeper or accountant may be able to handle your numbers-oriented tasks for a year or two. And if all goes well, you'll grow into needing to hire an administrative assistant—an honest, trustworthy, numbers-oriented person who can let you get back to doing what you do best—designing.

Don't despair, getting to that point is a mark of success!

SUPPOSE I PROPOSE

First, let me recommend a wonderful resource for you: Ilise Benun's Marketing Mentor site (www.marketing-mentor.com). My thanks to Benun for allowing us access to the superb content found within and for her accompanying expert advice. Consider this side-bar your 8 a.m. Monday class: Proposals 101. The vital "text" for the course is *Benun's*

Designer's Proposal Bundle (purchased and downloaded at Marketing Mentor site). Don't leave the art building without it

But an interesting note here is the caveat Benun will start you off with. As she says: "Don't put too much weight on [a] proposal itself because there is more to the process than what's on paper. What matters more is how well you communicate and follow through, how reliable you are, how you speak to [your clients], and how well taken care of they feel."

So, people, here's Benun's checklist of what should be in your proposal:

THE CORE

All proposals, no matter the type, no matter the size of the project or length of the proposal, should have these five key elements.

1. Description—what the client needs and what you are proposing to do
2. Deliverables—what they get, when, how many, etc.
3. Costs—creative fees plus expenses, expressed as ranges rather than fixed prices to provide a cushion in case things change (as they often do)
4. Timeline—realistic production schedule
5. Sign-off—the client's approval of agreement

LONG FORM

In proposals of more than three pages, consider including any or all of these elements, depending on how well your prospects already know you and/or your firm and who will be reviewing the proposal.

- Information about you and/or your firm. This includes your biography and those of any other relevant contributors and freelancers on the project.
- Samples. Include the most relevant ones here, even if your prospect has already visited your website or seen samples of your work. By the time your proposal arrives (along with a few others), it will help your prospects to see relevant samples again, while they're deciding. Also, the proposal may be reviewed by others involved in the decision-making process who are not familiar with your work.
- Client References. To enhance your credibility, strategically choose as references one or two clients whose projects have something in common with the one in question. Then, let your references know that you're passing along their names. (It's a great excuse to make contact and see if they need anything from you, too.) Tell them a bit about the prospective project, and give them some details about what your prospect may be most interested in hearing about.
- Usage rights. Briefly clarify how and where the work will be used, per your discussions so far. You will go into more detail about this in the contract.

➡ Client responsibility. This is a list of what the clients are responsible for, which also makes it easy for them to see the level of their involvement. Some proposals double as contracts by adding terms and conditions. But unless you're certain to get the project, your proposal should not include any legal language. Simply include a phrase at the end such as, "Upon approval of this proposal, we will send a contract."

➡

RIGHT ON POINT

(PROFESSIONAL VIEWPOINTS IN 50 WORDS OR LESS)

Selling is not bullshit, it's problem solving.

—Paul Melia

The bad news may be that we're never sure how the bills get paid, but the good news is that life is an adventure.

—Jennifer Berman

I am a solo agent at heart—I enjoy the freedoms. It's risky going out on one's own, but the rewards are all yours.

—Peg Esposito

Don't overspend. Don't overbuild. Be cautious as you expand—take small steps. Avoid runaway growth. Keep your overhead low. Think flexibility—plan ahead for expansion.

—Mike Quon

Serving your clients is the best way to build a solid business. And even though you have to jump off a few bridges to make that happen, you try to make it look very easy.

—Dan Johnson (deceased)

I prefer to pick and choose my clients, and I've determined that there are types of clients I don't want to work for. I've learned that I can say no to a job—even if it's the only offer I've had for a week. Some people are hard to work with.

—Adela Grace Jackson

"Selling it" is less about being a used car salesman; more about meeting people. Be creative about where and how you network. You can't hide in a dark corner, you must engage. Be fluid. Adapt. Respond.

—Allan Wood

SECTION II
TO MARKET

CHAPTER 8

FINDING CLIENTS

There are multiple ways to find clients, you just have to offer something they're looking for—and do it better than the guy standing next to you [who's] trying to get their business, too!

—Kelly White

MATCH GAME

Finding clients who need your services is a bit like working with a dating service. You're matchmaking, pairing your special abilities with the folks who have the greatest need for them. This sounds simple, but figuring out where to focus your energies involves some thought and planning. It might be best to first break your possibilities down into several business groups to isolate where potential business may be. Certain enterprises—and the assignments they offer—may be more applicable to designers than to illustrators (comic book publishers, for example), but if the shoe fits, that's a good problem to dope out.

In addition to thinking about where you can market your work, also reflect on your level of proficiency and match your skills accordingly with prospective clients. Consider your design style and how it matches up with those potential customers. Does the work in your portfolio display trendy design that could direct you to the national (or global) stage? Could your stuff interest the owner of that new boutique in SoBo (go ahead, Google it)? Is it lean, traditional, and conservative? Or more appropriate for a law firm or doctor's office?

If you're just starting out in your career, it may be prudent to sound out smaller, local clientele before you approach national concerns (or even larger vendors in your city). Baby steps are quite okay—and nothing to be ashamed of—but if you tack towards "no guts, no glory," I still say go for it.

I'm rather the gut-level, free-range kind of marketer. While you don't need my blessing, it's just wise to realize that until you've gained some experience and credibility, your design skills may be better suited to smaller locals than to those multimillion-dollar corporate yokels (found downtown anywhere).

BUSINESS IN MIND

We've talked in earlier chapters about why designers may not be as business-minded as they should be. Likewise, many might not be exceedingly functional salespeople either. Perhaps the problem is really one of attitude rather than a lack of ability. Maybe designers fear the image of some high-pressure huckster peddling sub-standard, unwanted goods. Perhaps they hold the mistaken notion that any sales activity is below their creative station.

Total bull. In truth, sales are the lifeblood of our business; so how do we get past these counter-productive notions? It might help to develop this mindset: You are calling on clients *to see if you can help.* So think, "How can I help you?" instead of "Do you want to buy?" As Ellen Shapiro points out, "As soon as I can, I change the meeting from me selling work to me helping them with their communication problem."

You need to sell. If you're convinced that by doing so you're reduced to pushing snake oil, your business will go nowhere. It's crucial that you believe in what you are doing, and what you are doing is solving problems—a most valuable service and worthwhile endeavor. If you must sell something to make a living, creative solutions make for a wonderful product. Don't you agree?

In this chapter, you'll learn more about how to sell this potent elixir, where to find clients, and how to make effective—no, truly dynamic—presentations. You'll find out how to keep clients hungry for more so you won't have to go out on a sales hunt with every new job. Let's get busy!

GET A JOB

"I wish I could say that 100 percent of my clients have been great," says Pittsburgh designer Rick Antolic, "but that's not the case." For the most part, Antolic's customer relationships have been super, an experience with clients he summed up as open-minded, flexible, very supportive, quite helpful, and certainly task-driven. "It's been clear that my clients expect me to accomplish a job in a professional manner and operate from this strong suit themselves," he says with a smile. "It seems to me I've enjoyed some near-perfect working relationships." Working from that vantage point, any gigs that fall short of this high benchmark just may stay with the Pittsburgh native. "I still think about certain projects from time to time," Antolic says.

Yes, obviously, the client matters, and the assignment does count. Good work is always important, and the finished product is perhaps the actual main event. "But," says Antolic, "what the client does with the art—within the bounds of ethics and legalities, of course, and once it's out of my hands, doesn't have to be the heart of the job."

BALANCING ACT

There is no such thing as "job security," whether you're on staff or on call. "The value in having a talent or skill is that you can always freelance at your will if you must keep a day job," counters Antolic. "All artists I know who work a day job also freelance on the side. There's a positive upside, obviously . . . the extra income, choosing what kind of assignments you take, avoiding jobs that don't advance your career direction (focusing on gigs that build the portfolio that *you* want). And a day job is not for everyone," he continues. "If you do have a day job, don't walk away from freelancing." I like that Antolic steered away from the usual advice here: don't quit your day job.

But either way you put it, and especially as a freelance designer, you'll have to accept that freedom to do "exactly what you want" isn't necessarily a constant or given. But there is *always* a choice to do exactly what you want—*no* is an easy word to say and spell. And what results after you say that simple no (or yes, for that matter) out loud is, well, what we call life.

You can always just play nice or be difficult; you can follow or ignore instructions; you can decline a job itself. The trick is to thrive in all these situations in any direction. As Antolic puts it, this is not a boring job and never has been.

MEET THE PUBLIC

An offshoot of this that can seriously test your power of yes and no is collaboration. Okay, you've already agreed to the gig. Now, can you work together as a team? More over—and, dare we say it—who's in charge? "Many professionals," says Antolic, "including myself, can work effectively in both situations. Sure, you'll obviously prefer one over the other, and personally, I like depicting someone else's idea more than I like coming up with my own from scratch. I enjoy the opportunity to take the client's design and improve upon it—add, subtract, enhance, or even understate . . . change a little here, a little there to maximize its effectiveness."

Antolic recommends you definitely seek out clients open to collaboration, but at the same time work on your comfort level to handle restrictive work climates—you'll definitely run into these situations. However comfortable you are working with either scenario, court both types of clients and build your career around them all. "Be prepared to work for all kinds of folks—Joe and Jane Public," Antolic sums up, but then adds: "I know this sounds cliché, but the greatest plus in doing all this is being in the public arena."

Now, let's clarify in this instance: here, the clients are not Jane and Joe, the *audience* is Jane and Joe. "But sometimes, somehow," Antolic says, "Joe and Jane hire you, and they need the greatest amount of education about how we work (and they generally are the clients who pay the least). I tend to avoid those clients whenever possible."

Antolic will also tell you that no matter how professional the client, the target audience is almost always Jane & Joe Public. Who knows better how to communicate to them? Here, Antolic almost always defers to the client. "Unless or until they show me that they don't really understand what the public responds to," he says, "which doesn't happen often when working with true professionals."

A TO-DO LIST FOR CLIENTS

- ▶ Do a job well. Do it right; do a good job for them—whenever they need you; whatever they need you to do (within reason, honestly and ethically).
- ▶ Set limits. Ellie Jabbour has some specific instructions here: "Designers just starting out should establish boundaries," Jabbour states from experience. "If you answer

your phone every time it rings on one weekend, you have may have set the expectation that you can be reached any weekend. Ultimately, you will do better work,
and the client will respect you for setting boundaries that allow you to do your
best work."

- ➡ Become known for presenting accurate and thorough cost estimates (clients love this).
- ➡ Deliver on time (or early).
- ➡ Check in; check back (even after the job is done). Maria Piscopo recommends you
check in again *after the job is in place* and find out how useful your work has been
for the client. It's one thing to like your design and another to benefit from it!
- ➡ Show you care—demonstrate that their best interest is your first priority; listen.
- ➡ Reinforce your work through actions, not words. Show that you want the job to succeed. Better yet, demonstrate that you want the client to succeed—show interest in
their business. You're a team; you're in this *together*.
- ➡ Keep your name fresh in the client's mind. Remind them you're there if they need
you; ask how things are going. Wish them a Happy (whatever holiday, or otherwise).

BUSINESS CHOPS

We examined how to manage your business in chapters 5–7, of course, but
in in light of this discussion about clients and the client relationship, Kelly
White chuckles a bit here. "Business skills are extremely important, after all it
is a business—*your* business," she emphasizes. So, how important are business
skills? And what business skills do you need?

It bears repeating that the label *business person* may simply speak to your
basic management skills (or maybe lack of): Are you forever late? Do you constantly change appointment times? Forgetful? Disorganized? Do you have a bit
of a problem responding (to emails or phone calls) promptly?

"No client wants to do business with people who come across like they don't
care," says White. "The sense of any project kicks off right here. Gain their business by demonstrating your interest and desire to help. *Show* you care about what
clients have to say, how they think. *Treat your clients like you were the one calling
for advice or help.* Be responsive and respond quickly.

"Work hard to understand your clients' needs," she says, "what they are trying to accomplish—and stress how you can help. Listen attentively and intently.
Be open to discussion."

A client's learning curve—and thus, a job's positive progress and successful
conclusion—may well be expressly based on what he knows (or doesn't know)
about design and the design process. So patience is the proverbial virtue.

Along those lines, keep your problem solving chops honed to a fine point as you'll need to explain the options clearly and completely. If you can't, don't, or won't, how can you possibly expect to really help your customer? "You must know how to achieve the results that lead to the solution," White concludes.

ALL ATWITTER ABOUT SOCIAL MEDIA

Using social media is one of the favored methods to find work now. But we don't even need 140 characters to qualify that understatement.

"I think everyone has their own method of finding clients," Kelly White says. "Social media is absolutely a huge resource these days." She mentions that Facebook, Google+, Twitter, and now Pinterest and Instagram, are all used by designers to find clients. Another resource for finding work would be a local BNI (Business Network International) chapter. People swear by this group, as well as business-oriented social networking sites, like LinkedIn (especially LinkedIn groups). You build a community around your practice and get people engaged in what your business is about and what's going on.

"Craigslist might come to mind immediately, and most art blogs and design websites have job boards," White reminds you. "I have also heard of people doing searches for freelance jobs while using Tweetdeck (a social media dashboard application for managing your Twitter and Facebook accounts) or using Google Alerts to find the newest postings of jobs for freelancers."

"I do most of my work remotely," Nadine Gilden says, picking up the thread. "I don't meet with clients much anymore, and I use online tools infinitely more than traditional methods for making contacts." As Gilden will also tell you, this takes some righteous time; you'll need to be "on"—actively engaged and dedicated to—social media, seriously getting to know people. But such concerted networking pays off by keeping you squarely on a client's radar.

"And for me," says Gilden, triangulating off the basic discussion, "when I do need to bring in outside resources on a project, I would sooner hire someone I know through Twitter. That is indeed how I usually find them." Gilden also qualifies that she doesn't do much print work, which she thinks requires more of an in-person relationship than online work.

Ellie Jabbour suggests you consider creating an online portfolio at sites like Behance (www.behance.net). In a later chapter, we discuss such sites as a way to directly present your work to prospective clients, but Behance and its sister sites are also utilized by clients searching for designers.

Finally, Kristine Putt joins the conversation here. Putt makes the point that, suffice it to say, most designers could accurately be labeled tech-savvy. So it may be easy to forget that not everyone is comfortable with digital communications, and not everybody will be tech-comfy because that's how *you* operate. "People may hire you for your design ability," Putt says, "but they will only be loyal to you for the manner in which you treat them. Make it easy for them to connect with you and they'll be your biggest fan for life."

NATURE OR NURTURE?

"Some designers use outsourcing sites to bid on projects and build a portfolio that will attract new business," says White. "Other designers actually find clients through family and friends."

Beyond looking for business potential within your immediate sphere of influence, you should seek specific opportunities for networking that will yield referrals and leads. In addition to providing a good support system, professional groups, locally, nationally, and globally, provide splendid opportunities to find potential markets in your area (or the world).

Of course, don't pass up the rich benefits of simply "joining the club": for example, the AIGA and/or your local Art Directors Club. When you attend meetings or events, especially local get-togethers, schmooze. Find out who's working for whom. Get some insider's information. Are the clients busy? *Are the designers busy?* Let your mates know you're ready to help them out and/or the customer—you'd appreciate their consideration as well as any referrals. You're not scrambling for scraps or sifting through the dregs, but wrangling overflow is another story.

Contact professional groups affiliated with the communications field or other executive organizations. Local groups for editors, writers, public relations specialists, and ad clubs are often looking for support services and members (or the organizations themselves) may need your good design skills. The aforementioned collectives frequently publish and distribute directories for members and other business professionals as a source of services in the community.

LEADS

Look for potential business wherever you go. Remember that, while you are certainly offering service, you're not selling that service so much as you're solving communications problems. All professionals you know or could do business with want to improve their visibility and profitability. In fact, you may already have the inside line on business possibilities through a former employer. (Any situation where you once worked is bound to hold potential business opportunities on a number of levels. Contacts, sure. Advice . . . I would think so. Overflow . . . why not?) Don't forget, you're already familiar with the folks, the work, and the work habits of these people, and—if you left amicably—they should see this familiarity as a plus. Let's discuss some other "leading" suggestions.

PUBLISHING

Print is still viable, despite the reports of its imminent demise, so let's lead off here. Age before beauty, maybe? Every town has a newspaper and most cities have at least one publisher of books and magazines. If you're not on staff, you're in a great position to handle any overflow, special needs, or crunch time crisis requiring more from the in-house art staff (for short or long duration). A little targeted research will reveal the demanding occasions for those publications in your area (for instance, a special holiday issue or charity event; an election special insert; a magazine commemorating a bicentennial event; the promotion of a revered local charity; pitching for a good cause or noble charity). Contact publishers when you think the production for such peaking periods is in the planning stages; be on tap (and on top of your reminders).

PARTNERING WITH SUPPLIERS OF GRAPHICS AND PRODUCTION

Yep, such places can still be found and can still get busy, and these days they have diversified to embrace all aspects of commercial and private ministrations. There will be an emphasis on author assistance—paper and digital—including self-publishing, ebooks, and apps; printing and binding, production and technical services. Oh, just a note: please don't confuse these vendors with places that offer framing, printing, and/or art materials.

Starting close to home, local printers may find themselves in need of production skills when a client "dumps" a job on them that was supposedly ready to rock 'n' roll. Even if a printer has typesetting and production facilities (plus service providers), they will frequently need to provide more design work than their suppliers or staff can handle.

AD AGENCIES; OTHER DESIGN STUDIOS

When you're on your own you're in a good position to handle the overflow coming from any and all aspects of an ad agency's business. Possibilities include: design and illustration, of course; art directing or production assistance; calligraphy or typographic design; visualization and storyboarding; photography or photographic enhancement and manipulation; and more.

BUSINESS AND PRIVATE ENTERPRISE

Here you will find interesting possibilities. Is the real estate market booming in your area? Think of ways your skills could be used in creating promotions for realtors trying to sell property. Do you have a flair for restaurant identities and menu design? Does your oral surgeon have a hard time explaining surgical procedures to you? Could he use a brochure or handout that explains these procedures? It's getting close to tax time and your accountant jots her number down on scrap paper because she ran out of business cards. If she's too busy to take care of getting them printed, could you do it for her? Could she increase her business if you cleaned up her image by designing a new card? You get the picture—think about where your skills can best be applied.

PROMOTE YOURSELF

Self-promotion can take many forms. Of course, a web presence is mandatory. You can still consider advertising your services in creative directories (print and/ or online); local phone and business directories; via snail mail and email; even contacting prospects by phone. But these days a designer will most likely promote via the ubiquitous web outlets, networking in its diverse incarnations, and, yes, word of mouth.

A designer can do *so* much—wildly disparate dispatches for paper and electronic communications; graphic digital presentations and vivid physical displays that entertain or sell or inform or promote. Perhaps your first order of business is to look at your marketing and self-promotion as the savvy method to better advertise your unique customer service. You should promote by posing—then answering—the question, "How can I help you?" and not by shouting "Hey— look at me!" Think substance, not flash.

I've always firmly believed that you must show *what you love to do* as the hallmark of the work you are soliciting. This, as Piscopo says, will also bring you clients that love your work. Choose samples wisely, of course; target your approach and select work of yours that is only of the highest quality and marketable value (obviously). Push a consistent presentation across your advertising ventures. Emphasize straightforward substance and solid content. If you're not sure what customers are buying these days, do your homework. Look at potential client websites and check out the portfolio pages of your competition. As Picasso might have quipped: "Good artists steal, but great artistes *research*."

Promoting on the Internet is different in many respects (as in, theoretically more cost-effective and time-efficient) from how it was back in the day of good ol' printed mailings. Of course, there are still folks who tap into the combination of tried-and-true networking, modern cyber-marketing, and even classical direct mail.

You could go the one-stop shop route. Agency Access (www.adbase.com) offers FoundFolios and Emailer. Workbook (www.workbook.com) offers lists, sourcebooks, a blog, as well as a website with "comprehensive features and resources for ... designers ... serious about reaching the most active and important art buyers in their fields."

As just an example, Workbook features *Workbook Print* (a creative directory also available online), *Workbook Portfolio* (a fully searchable collection of designers), and *Workbook Directory* (an online resource of creative industry contacts and targeted mailing lists). So, for instance, your options could mix and match the premium

Workbook services and self-designed email newsletters as generated through plat-forms like Constant Contact (www.constantcontact.com).

THE SELF-PROMOTION PIECE

Back in the (good ol' and legendary) day, we'd be talking about a self-promotional *mailer*. Literally mailed. You may be of an age when—gasp—there was no omni-present Internet. Working the mails was the only real game in town. Today, when done with style, wit, and smarts, actual *physical stuff*—a brilliant mailer (or drop-off) can still capture the complete attention of a busy art director inundated by a sea of mundane emails. So regardless of how you promote, and as a nod to a great tradition, let's just utilize that handy term "mailer" as a generic tag for a conveyance of business communication.

The primary purpose of self-promotion is to dazzle and entice its recipients and to have them keep your promotion piece around—the fabled and hallowed "keeper." As such, creative license should know no boundaries. This showcase of boundless artistry can exhibit as unique forms of wine and beer bottles with custom labels, fortune cookies with clever messages (or delightful surprises) enclosed, even hula-hoops have been utilized to spin a campaign. And this is just some of the mild stuff that comes to mind. The play is to keep the format handy and accessible to improve chances that your promo will be on tap rather than tossed.

The point is that even in this jaded, digital age you can take a basic concept and morph the idea into something more, something different.

So-called conventional notions—creating a show reel (also called a demo reel), posters, and calendars—should not be casually written off as old hat.

If your video portfolio is, well, *moving,* or the calendar concept is eye-catching—as in smart *and* useful—you just could get it front and center on a client's wall or desktop, doubling your promo's visibility (as both a physical reminder and design showcase).

Really clever mailers are frequently passed along. ("Look what I got today, I know you'll appreciate this.") This takes on new meaning in the age of email, links, Pinterest, YouTube, Twitter, social networks, and Facebook. A seriously great piece almost invariably will expand its impact beyond the initial recipient.

If you're looking for inspiration, just fire up your computer and check out your email. I'll bet you have more than one email veritably shouting at you to "Check it out . . . you'll love what I just got!"

I would still scope out both digital and print monthlies, annuals, and crea-tive directories, as well. Within these pages you'll view today's most creative and beautifully designed self-promo pieces. Magazines like *CA, Print,* and *How* (as well as most local competitions) include a category for self-promotion. *HOW* magazine has devoted an entire competition to self-promotion, featuring the winners in an annual special issue.

There are almost as many reasons and occasions—or excuses, even—for mailing out self-promotion pieces as there are types of self-promotion. Seasonal (not necessarily just holiday) greetings, a change of address, acquiring a partner; industry conferences and trade shows you know clients attend . . . all these tip the iceberg of opportunities for you to showcase your best work in a self-promotion piece.

Self-promotion functions as either a rather blatant or oh-so subtle means of letting people know you're in business and that you're looking for clients. Either way, you want to intrigue a prospective client with a promo that demonstrates the exquisite caliber of your work, and regardless of how you package and present it, you obviously want it to be beautifully designed and exceedingly well crafted.

THE CAPABILITIES PRESENTATION

Yes, the advent of the website plus the show and tell of online portfolio sites—like Behance, Dribble, and Carbonmade, to name only a few—has revolutionized designers' marketing and promoting. But even in today's digital, high decibel design, I'm going to make the pitch that you feature some old school as part of your repertoire.

Back before the Internet (and yes, there was such a time), a generic self-promotional vehicle was often presented in a brochure configuration and frequently used by artists for its versatility. A capabilities brochure was designed to provide a tantalizing glimpse of your portfolio by offering a representation of some of your best work.

Sounds exactly like what you want an online portfolio or website to do, eh? And you'd be exactly correct here. But don't be limited by the concept of a defacto online presentation. Nor should you be rooted in the traditional tri-fold, bi-fold, or bound-with-a-cover brochure, if you go that route.

So it could be a compelling online solution, a single, folded 11"x 17" sheet, or some rock 'em, sock 'em custom size, shape, or structure. Balancing creative expression with the information prospective clients need is where experience (or the lack of it) comes into play. If you have worked with many high-profile clients, you'll want to play up *credibility*. But, if you're just starting out, you'll want to demonstrate *potential*.

Your self-promotion capabilities presentation is an ideal solution to show what you can do or have done. In essence it says, "I got you to notice this marketing piece and consider hiring me. I could help you be noticed by your prospective clients." Trust your gut on juggling the desire to demonstrate your creativity with the need to communicate that aforementioned credibility. And do keep your marketing piece clear and concise. "This credibility," says Roger Brucker, "is established by several vehicles; for instance, examples of what you've done, a description of how you do it, or the testimonies of satisfied or delighted clients."

Perfectly Capable

A capabilities presentation will offer some standard information:

1. Client information: You'll want to provide a list of the firms you've worked with, making sure to lead with (or at least include) the ones that have the most prestige and recognition. If you are just starting out, generating a client list may be difficult to do, but if you were a staff designer before going out on your own, you have a right to claim the design and production work for which you were responsible. Check with your former employer to find out if he or she would be opposed to your listing a few of the clients with whom you have worked. Make sure you add a few client testimonials, too!

2. Background: Think of this as your résumé. You'll want to include information about your education and your awards. Include any experience or achievements that will enhance your credibility as a creative professional.

3. Capabilities: You want to spell out everything you can do and leave no stone unturned. Whether it be handling a major identity program, outdoor advertising, magazine illustration—if ya got it, flaunt it. If you enjoy doing calligraphy by hand or love to create custom typography, if you can provide top-notch copywriting, or shoot your own photography, mention it.

4. Your artistic philosophy: Now do your best to convince prospective clients that your work can be more beneficial to them than any other designer's or illustrator's work.

5. Contact information: Don't forget your address, phone number, website, and email addresses. This sounds silly, but it happens. Without this most basic info, your promo is essentially useless. Hey, and don't forget your Twitter feed, Facebook page, and any other social media you want your client to follow.

6. Lead-in: This introduces your studio to the world at large, and sets the stage for your presentation to tell anyone and everyone what you can do and what general benefits you offer to prospective clients. You go generic out of necessity, but to multiply the effectiveness of any pitch, cover letter, or intro, do your homework—know the market segment that you want to canvass.

If you're mailing the package, here's where a *cover letter*, tailored to a company and an actual name, personalizes that mailing and lets you spell out the benefits that are specific to the prospect's needs.

Online, an intro or intro page does much the same thing, but, of course, it cannot be client-specific (you could target a specific niche with common bullet points to address that market, however).

A video could address specific viewers (theoretically the party responsible for making the buying decision) *personally*. Here, you *directly tell* your prospect why you're most qualified to do this work.

OLD SCHOOL

I am reticent to dismiss any marketing strategies offhand—some practice that seems archaic to me or inefficient to you invariably appeals to somebody else. Cold calls, for instance. Every time I hear from a source that loathes this practice, I simultaneously come across another smart guy who advises you to hit that up.

The Internet, of course, has spun marketing on its very axis, but to give you a well-rounded picture, we're going to look at a number of options.

COLD CUTS

Let's talk about cold calls right upfront. A cold call—person-to-person, by email, letter, or phone—is a contact without request and often without referral. It's essentially selling door-to-door, and as such can be pure frustration. Cold calls are a stellar way to test your tolerance for rejection, and for many art directors, these calls are a certified nuisance. Persuasive (not obnoxious) salespeople may get decent returns for their troubles, but you may equate cold calls with the flood of those "courtesy calls" you receive just about dinnertime every day—sound like a familiar scenario?

If you're intent on this sales tactic, you need to build a list of contacts. Use resources like Yahoo, Bing, Ask, Google, and LinkedIn like mad. Consult the yellow pages. Go to the library and bookstore to research annuals, directories, and publications and scan client names. Attend trade shows (and read trade publications). Send for annual reports. Join your local ad club. Join a local service club like the Lions or Rotary. Visit the Better Business Bureau and the Chamber of Commerce. Take a stroll through the business district. Talk to your friends and colleagues.

Cold calls are indeed another avenue for pursuing more business. Getting in the door to see your prospect is the initial hurdle, so getting on the horn is not an illogical first step. However, if nothing else (and even if you never do the deed), the cold call is a great metaphor for solid, general contact communication. Thus, I thought back to (and adapted) my cold call criteria to come up with an appropriate to-do list.

1. Do your research.
2. Be completely prepared. Right off the top, are you contacting the right person? *Your* contact information (name and spelling of that name,

gender, job title, address, phone number) must be current and correct and readily available. Have all your information and recordkeeping in front of you. Be flexible enough to rearrange your schedule, if necessary.

3. If you land a meeting or score a next step, get the details right—an exact address, good directions, and contact name (and how to say and spell that name).

4. You are never selling anything with a first contact. No pressure now, so relax. Don't get easily discouraged. Learn from your rejections.

5. In closing, says marketing guru Maria Piscopo, "Plan and prepare your conversations and questions to the extent that you avoid *closed* questions such as 'Can I call you?' and use *open* questions, such as, 'When is the best time to call you?'"

MAIL LISTS

Utilizing a "store bought" mail list is a marketing strategy that the Internet has virtually killed (head over to Agency Access, BikiniLists, and Mailchimp, for instance). But if you somehow have the time, energy, and inclination, you could still pursue it to various degrees.

For instance, just by heading over to your local Chamber of Commerce, you can obtain a list of new businesses and compile an inventory of prospective clients. That's a mailing list. Your mailing list needs will depend on the nature of your skills and on who you think will buy your services. "Depending on your area," says Maria Piscopo, "you may find bigger and better clients in your county Chamber of Commerce if you feel the city chamber provides too small a 'client pool.'"

Check out the *Artist's & Graphic Designer's Market* from the local library (or just buy it at the bookstore). But, says Piscopo, "The unique aspect of this directory is that it only lists clients actively seeking artists and designers (so it's not a list of everyone)."

You could also consult the various phone directories for possible leads. Head to the library or the bookstore and browse any creative annuals and talent directories and review client names. Special interests and their specific publications may have mail lists for your review (and perhaps for sale). Lists may be available through a list broker.

Purchasable CD databases are long gone. Oh, you might still be able to find a purchasable CD database *somewhere*, but why bother? These search tools have certainly been replaced by online and email subscription services doing the same thing—providing phone numbers and addresses of all the restaurants, dentists, or ice cream parlors, within twenty miles of your front door, for example.

Note: If you create a list of potential clients, database software (like Excel or Bento) is very useful for maintaining, organizing, and evaluating results, as well as for preparing you for sales and follow-up calls.

TALENT DIRECTORIES

Talent directories may also be called creative directories. These resources—with a national scope, as well as in major metropolitan regions—offer contact info for designers, illustrators, and photographers by service and geography. Art buyers of all stripes can browse through the catalogue as an easy way to spot a look, then order the stylist of choice.

As I mentioned previously in this chapter, resources like Behance, Carbonmade, Dribble, and Workbook (www.workbook.com) represent an online approach to this marketing option. When considering these directories, you would want to consider the advantages of such an avenue for start-ups. Do you have a particularly unique look or a specialty that someone is likely to buy—either as the main event or as a support service (like typographic, calligraphic design, or calligraphy)? Can you push that vantage at this point in your career?

And when you network with other professionals on your home turf, become aware of whether a local directory is available in your region. If so, determine how useful it is to you in your community. Again, the insights of other designers or illustrators are your inside line to the best opportunities in your area.

THE PHONE BOOK

I previously mentioned what just might be the most overlooked opportunity for taking names and representing close to home: the phone directory. And don't pass up the business-to-business phone directory as a ready source of categorized business listings. In terms of regional visibility, local accessibility, and plain fact finding, I wouldn't take this route for granted.

TRADITIONAL ADVERTISING

You may want to consider local media advertising as another marketing and promotional tool. Radio to sell graphic design? Sure! A sharp, creative radio spot fuels the visuals of the imagination. If done well, your message will definitely get across. Television time will be pricey, but a good fifteen- or thirty-second spot may be money extremely well spent. You might even consider an announcement on your cable channel's community calendar or a late, late night television spot (when ad rates are dirt cheap). How about a punchy press release?

COMPETITIONS

We looked at design competitions and crowdsourcing contests—with all the associated ups and downs—back in chapter 3. We won't repeat this discussion or debate—I simply bring it up here as a possible part of a general, potential marketing game plan.

If you enter a competition and come out with a winner, get some mileage out of this happy event. You could enter your crowd pleaser in other competitions (if you're still buying into the very concept) or push the tangential promotional opportunities (including a press release). I am not advocating for these competitions, only suggesting that you ride the wave of any accolades and recognition.

PRO BONO WORK

Lightly repeating what we examined in chapter 3, *pro bono*—volunteering or donating your time and services—can be an effective means of generating publicity (or simply doing a good turn). While we said that the concept of pro bono work is not universally loved, you shouldn't necessarily dismiss pro bono as a simple giveaway or write it off as merely paying your dues. Establish ground rules, define limits and clarify expectations, and pro bono could be a healthy investment of your available time, energy, and spirit. "Don't forget," adds Piscopo, "pro bono gives you real-client experience, samples, referrals, and testimonials."

SPEC WORK

Last, and certainly least, spec work. Avoid this. This may be easier said than done, especially if you're just starting out. Mock-ups, design contests, and crowdsourcing further muddy the already murky waters. In a word: No. Work. For. Free. No. Spec. And No. Work. For. Hire. Don't. Period.

Professionally, "spec work" rhymes with "risky business." There is a vocal constituency who would use the term *unethical* (or put it even more colorfully) to describe the practice: "Rip off?" You'll hear that one, for sure. A kindred soul may simply label it as a "mistake." As with everything, there are always different takes on the subject, many sides to the issue. But think about it for a second: Rick Antolic asks in an earlier chapter (about competitions) if your plumber would enter a competition to install the pipes in your new home? I ask: will the doctor who performs your colonoscopy work on spec? How ludicrous!

But I am also not afraid to present another realistic take on all this. Ellie Jabbour's design career is off to a rousing start, which puts her plum in a middle-front row seat for the whole pricing pageant. "Spec work is common in New York. I think it's because there is so much competition and intense demand for jobs. You sometimes need to do it. Of course, I see the negative side, but I have always learned from the experience and stretched my abilities."

We're all professional adults. No one should suppose they fully understand what *you* truly need professionally, personally, and financially. You gotta make the call; so no judgments here.

KEEP THE CLIENTS YOU GET

The silver bullet here would be inscribed with all of one word in it: Service. Serve your clients well. It's all about reliability, returning phone calls promptly, following up personably, effectively, and efficiently, personally ramrodding the job. Call it every cliché in the book: going the extra mile, handholding, TLC, bending over backwards, doing whatever it takes. Cozy, and oft used, these homilies, nevertheless (if I dare use one more cliché), hit the mark. Some other things you probably know or suspect about dealing with clients include:

1. A prima donna with an I-don't-care-about-you attitude, no matter how good he or she may be, will only generate and keep business for so long. Given a choice, a client will prefer the designer known for good work and personal service.

2. Unless they're masochists, people don't honestly want to work with someone who doesn't care about or won't take care of them. Would you?

3. Consider the amount of time you spend in acquiring business, how promoting yourself and cultivating new accounts eats into your billable time. Getting and keeping clients who keep coming back will free you up to bill out more of your time. Clients who keep coming back because you reliably take good care of them are also more likely to do everyone a good turn by passing your name on to those with whom they do business.

It is entirely possible to keep your studio going with small- to medium-sized accounts. Obviously, your volume of business will have to rise accordingly. However, "big" is relative. Your bread-and-butter account may conceivably be another designer's bargain basement. All things being equal, how many "big" clients should you get? As many as you can handle of course, but be careful not to put all your eggs in one basket.

You should set a limit on the percentage of income derived from any one client. If your firm is predicated on the business of one or a few major accounts, it will mean disaster if those accounts pull out for any reason.

Maintain a broad client base for that same reason. If the print publishing industry is taking a hit (as we know it is), you know may be in trouble if all of your business is in this troubled sector. In the event of problems within a particular industry, a troubled economy, or the pullout of a big client, you need to be flexible enough to regroup and work in another arena with a minimum of damage.

THE MESSAGE

Allow me to caution you on using proper etiquette when contacting art directors (or potential clients). I trust that you know this instinctively, but I'm going to err on the side of prudent business savvy and play this out with you here.

First, always identify yourself to whomever takes your call or receives your letter, email, phone, or text message. Especially if you can't get through, leave a detailed, but concise, message stating who you are, what you do, and how you think you can help this individual. If you have made contact, go through the same identifying process, then clear this person's time by asking, "Do you have a moment to talk?" or "When do you have the time to chat?" If the contact is unavailable, ask for a specific time when you can contact her again, and follow up promptly at that time. By doing this, you'll be demonstrating courteous and timely communication skills.

So you landed an actual meeting? Great! You've done your research, right? You have found out all you can about this prospect before the scheduled appointment. You're completely prepared. Face to face, blend a straight-laced business discussion into a friendly, informational conversation. No hard sell—try a softer approach, avoid the sales pitch. Simply chat to learn more about the prospect and the project. You're just seeking an exchange at that point.

Obviously, show your portfolio. Use an initial get-together to present design solutions that suggest how you can solve the client's communication problems. Observe closely and keep your ears open. And here's the critical key to the kingdom: *talk less, listen more.* At this point, you're just trying to determine if the potential for doing business exists. So genially probe for information with phrases such as, "I'm curious about . . . I'd like to know . . . Please elaborate on this . . ." Lightly schmooze a bit with just a touch of flattery: "Tell me more about your good work at Amalgamated Anagrams. What's it like to be employed with such a dynamic company? What are some of the thorniest communications problems you've encountered?"

If there is a definite assignment up for grabs, you could say: "I'd like to hear more about your great product and what the firm has done in the past. Can you tell me about this exciting project? Why are you taking this new direction? What'll be tough to explain? What are your goals?"

Once fact finding about the project is over, then talk money. You will eventually have to inquire about fees. Simple, direct inquiries work well: "What's your budget on something like this?" or "How much do you want to spend here?" The client may volley the ball back to your court and inquire what you would charge for such an assignment. Your reply might be: "All clients are not the same. Every job is different. For projects similar to this I've charged $XXX; this is based on . . ." Then detail your pricing structure and related particulars. By the way, certain advisors tell you to give a range between X and Z, while others warn you to never ballpark—always state a firm figure. You'll have to decide what feels and works best for you.

Of course, you will ultimately ask for the prospect's future business at some point. Make it easy for both parties with phrases such as, "Great, what if we . . . ? So where do we go from here? Does this sound doable? Let me run this by you . . . Shall we . . . ?"

RIGHT ON POINT

(PROFESSIONAL VIEWPOINTS IN 50 WORDS OR LESS)

Great work to a client is generally more about marketing. How pretty the art is and how it won a design award is less important in the client's mind. Does it say what we want it to say? Does it accurately reflect what we do and who we do it for-profit?

—Ken Bullock

You're going to deal with the whims of all sorts of clients. My "best" design work was actually done for my absolute worst client ever.

—Jason Petefish

In regards to keeping clients happy, one of the most important things to do is simply to check in. Keep customers informed. Communicate. Respond.

—Nadine Gilden

Satisfied customers are not loyal; delighted customers are loyal. You wow customers by exceeding their expectations. When they perceive that they have received sacrificial service from you, they are delighted.

—Roger Brucker

Seek clients who are serious. You are being hired to emphasize the brand's best attributes, but be willing to walk away from clients you don't believe in or if you can't do your best for them.

—Kristine Putt

CURATTI ▼

The best way to handle a deadbeat or difficult client is to never acquire one. Easier said than done? Establish a screening process. Figure out your client base. Qualify your leads.

—Gerald D.Vinci

Word of mouth has played a large part in helping me to create and sustain my practice as a designer. Referred clients have been some of my best customers. They know what I do and want to work with me.

—Allan Wood

The privilege of serving great clients is a given. When our creative work is appreciated, it's like I'm a little kid again and my mom sticks one of my pictures on the refrigerator.

—Nick Gaskins

CHAPTER 9

THE PORTFOLIO

The war is over, digital media has won.

—C. J. Yeh

ABOUT THE PORTFOLIO

We make a point back in chapter 2 that your design education—learning the basics, picking up the right tools (creative, critical, and technical)—provides the foundation of your practice. A stellar résumé is all well and good, but you should consider your vitae the documentation supporting an absolutely competitive portfolio. Some designers will tell you *fuhgeddaboutit*—sending a résumé is actually a waste of time, but all designers will tell you your portfolio will speak sheer volumes for your abilities as a graphic designer, regardless of where you are perched on the career ladder. It helps gauge how a client (or employer) can benefit from your abilities.

In person or online, a portfolio is a collected display of samples, a planned presentation of your work, used to communicate your abilities—call it your gift—to that potential client. It cannot be said too frequently—it is the portfolio that counts—whether it's digital or physical, you just want someone to look at your work.

When you graduate from design school, your portfolio will be awash with fitting student samples and you'll be faced with a real conundrum: have you done any real work, out in the trenches, under actual field conditions of seriously demanding deadlines and consequences?

And whether online, left with an assistant, or opened across the table from you at an actual interview, your portfolio must offer as descriptive and effective a presentation as possible. The playbook will vary with your method of presentation, so let's open up the book on portfolios, shall we?

THE REAL DEAL

No matter how it's seen, be selective about what you include in your portfolio. Young designers tend to show their best work, but dilute it with anything they have that's been "printed" (and here, I'm using the term loosely).

Maria Piscopo asks you to remember that you will not show "everything ya got" unless you are meeting with a rep. "Keep in mind," she says, "that clients only care about what they need from you, so find out what slice of your portfolio pie that is and just show that work."

The number varies slightly from expert to expert, but a dozen of your most representative pieces should be sufficient. An exact setup also fluctuates from source to source, but generally you would organize the presentation so that your best and most eye-catching pieces are the first and last shots viewed.

One train of thought says a portfolio—or portfolio presentation—should be viewed as a design project in itself. We'll play with this in a moment. Your portfolio presentation can demonstrate display and packaging opportunities as well showcase your capabilities in this department. Thus, you obviously want to imply an intelligent strategy to market a most important concept—you, the *designer.*

Your portfolio or online presentation should be neat and well crafted, too. You don't actually need more bells and whistles; you want less flash and glitz . . . far more substance. This means ease of maintenance for you, ease of use for the viewer.

Al Wasco re-emphasizes that some employers still want to see a physical portfolio (even interactive designers), "because it gives them a sense of their craft and attention to detail. It may be debatable, but as mentioned previously, a back-up physical portfolio never hurts."

Hey, you want be a contender. A sloppy book, or one that is not unified or organized—in execution as well as navigation, and whether that be digital or analog—will get you a one-way ticket to Palookaville. Did you want to suggest that you care little about craftsmanship? Do you intend to convey the impression of a designer who doesn't think logically? Will you seriously want the client to say, "You don't value your own work, how are you going to value the work you might do for me?"

ASSEMBLING THE PORTFOLIO

Let's begin by saying that it's best to present a solid, consistent style (particularly at the beginning of your career), especially when selling in the national marketplace. Now, repeat these three words while putting that oh-so-consistently-relevant portfolio together: "only my best." Generally, small is better and less is more. Think in the neighborhood of ten to twenty pieces. Focus. Be highly selective. If in doubt about a particular piece, don't use it.

Nothing less than your best work should be in your portfolio; you're only as strong as your weakest sample. Think pacing. Think flow. That one inferior piece sandwiched somewhere in the middle of your book will be remembered first—it will detract from the "good stuff" and diminish the impact of the entire portfolio. Don't include anything of which you're not proud. Don't include any style or technique you don't really want to do. Don't include work just because someone paid you.

"Never ever put in a sample just to show you can do (whatever) unless it's *great* work," says Wasco. "Don't try to simply show how well-rounded you are unless every piece is absolutely top-notch. It will only call your judgment into question. As in 'Why the hell is *that* in there?'

"This applies to logos, book covers, package design . . . anything and *everything*," he says. "Never try to show that you can do it all. It will backfire on you unless you're one of the rare people who *can* do it all. Even then, if you don't love the thing, why show it?"

As you develop, so grows your portfolio (we're still talking quality, not quantity). A portfolio should never be stagnant—update it regularly. Samples must be well-protected but portable, and easy to change and examine. Make it

THE ONLINE PORTFOLIO

Wasco and I would say that *all* designers will emphatically tell you an online portfolio is *the* critical element of your whole program. It's simple: a web presence is mandatory. The online portfolio helps you promote and market. An efficient, good-looking, easy-to-find website keeps you ahead of your competition and helps you to stand apart from the crowd.

You may want to consider a blog instead of a traditional portfolio. There will be a host of decisions to make (and jobs to do): doping out smart keywords; using the right domain extension; coming up with a good name; going with the right publishing platform, choosing a killer theme; downloading and installing that theme correctly; selecting plug-ins; organizing structure, navigation, and content; optimizing your imagery; and savvy promoting.

The topic of the online portfolio is introduced here, but I expand on it in the next chapter, "On The Web." So, for a far more detailed discussion of the online portfolio, head to chapter 10.

CD OR NOT CD, THAT IS THE QUESTION

C. J. Yeh points out, "CD was once 'cool'—remember those uniquely shaped CDs?—but it's now a dated concept." Yeh stopped asking students to prepare digitized portfolios on a CD about five years ago, and, as you know, most new Mac laptops don't even come with a CD or DVD player anymore.

"The way to go is to a PDF file," Yeh says. "Send it through email. As long as you know how to prepare it properly (which is a required skill for graphic designers), the file weight will, or should, be manageable.

"If your work is on a website, email the URL. I've been working with recruiters, creative directors, and art directors over the years, and email is their preferred method of communication."

simple to carry (with or without handles), of uniform page-size, and lightweight. A leather or leather-like ring binder (open or zippered) enclosing the transparent sleeves offers the simplest answer here.

There is no distinct advantage to either a vertical or horizontal layout, and it's not written in stone that you must go with a traditional, conservative portfolio format. But your portfolio should not be a lazy Susan or circus ride. By this, I mean that the portfolio review should *not* be a physical workout (a compelling, visceral experience is another thing entirely). So, you want to make sure the art director isn't swiveling your book—or his head around—from page to page; have one consistent page orientation throughout. (If this proves impossible, group all horizontal pieces into one section and vertical samples into another. This way the art director cranes his neck only once.) While such good organization is a must, I don't necessarily subscribe to the notion that says one must lump all color pieces together (and the same with black-and-white pieces).

It's a given that solid craftsmanship is crucial. "Neatness," as applied to structure, is not arguably relative, but crisp, clean samples wrapped in a professional package, all presented with style and taste, are the orders of the day—a portfolio cannot be a haphazard affair. There should be a planned arrangement and logical progression to the sequence of samples. Your credentials will be highly suspect if the presentation shines brighter than your samples.

For identification purposes, the portfolio should be clearly—but tastefully—labeled. No neon lights, just complete identification inside and out. As for the order of individual pieces, you can approach the pace and flow of the portfolio in a variety of ways. Chronological (or reverse chronological) organization shows progression and development. Organization by subject matter works for many designers. You could take a graphic approach and group by technique. You might want to organize thematically and demonstrate problem solving within a specific body of assignments.

Always start big and end strong. After a trenchant beginning, some portfolios will build to an exciting finish. Wasco says that one rule of thumb is to start with your strongest piece and end with your second strongest (or vice versa). Many books rise to the middle and slope to a big bang. Others are like a roller coaster ride—with many visual peaks and rests culminating in a stunning climax.

A UNIFIED FRONT—AND BACK

The best way I know to unify a presentation is to make all the elements consistent. When the portfolio is presented in an actual binder (box, bag, or whatever), you must unify sizing via consistent presentation (mounting and matting), keeping appearance, plus exterior and interior dimensions the same. Subtle touches and elegant materials, if you can afford them, add a touch of quality and could convey the image of a successful designer who can afford the best. It might be wise to make such an investment if you're trying to impress high-profile clients. However, the container cannot outshine the contents. "I've seen too many students spend *big* bucks on a portfolio case that looks cool," Wasco comments, "but not be willing to invest the time and money for flawless printing and mounting of samples."

While designing your portfolio, you might want to consider putting together interchangeable components so your portfolio can be tailored to a variety of situations. For example, if you were trying to sell your services as a book jacket designer, you would want to include more samples of the work you've done in this area than samples of brochures and annual reports.

While not all employers want to see sketches and "process" work to gauge how you think, you may want to demonstrate your sketching ability, rendering talent as well as design capabilities. Show sketch layouts for proposals, maybe a comprehensive layout with the finished printed piece. This way a client can see how capably a designer can present concepts before they are committed to print.

But Wasco suggests you fully think this through. "If I only see a half dozen sketches for a logo design, I know this student doesn't really explore an idea widely," he says. "I've also seen preliminary sketches that were stronger than the final piece—at which I'm invariably told, 'Well, my teacher didn't like that one.' This leads to a discussion about trusting your instincts or the glories of presenting multiple ideas."

Which gets us to this: when given the opportunity to discuss your portfolio, we can make a case for you to explain how you solved the problem at hand for every project you present. Be clear about what your responsibilities were—if you handled the overall organization, say so. A lot of customers will not be familiar with the design process at all; they'll want to know the specifics. "Here's a rough layout of what we did on the XYZ project. Here's the comp, and here's the finished piece." The client will thus get the impression that you know what you're doing every step of the way.

TARGETING A PORTFOLIO

Should you change your portfolio for each type of market you show it to? A "market" can be many things: the type of industry; a type of client; the style of work; a medium or technique; or the geographic market. Many designers work in concentrated markets. Some cannot relate to changing their portfolio à la carte. That is not the same as updating, of course.

If you have many pieces from which to pick and choose, you may want to orient your portfolio to particular markets. There are many ways to approach this. A binder with simple, interchangeable sleeves can easily facilitate this process. At the beginning, you may not have many pieces targeting your various market options. This means a somewhat generic portfolio that addresses a wider base—not a sampling of divergent directions, but an overview—a portfolio that meets a variety of needs.

Let's use greeting cards just as an example. Your quirky, hard edge, line-oriented design work reproduces great and complements tough, driving news stories. It's strong and compelling. However, the art director at Ballpark Greetings may not relate to your portfolio of black-and-white editorial samples.

If you add color and humor (and present card mock-ups to further sell your case), that Ballpark hotdog could visualize how that type of design could work for him. By the same token, your cute greeting card designs for Ballpark may not pass the mustard at *Rolling Pin*, a magazine about marriage counseling. The imagery you show for this must be in context with the content.

Yes, sometimes different markets overlap, but people will tend to classify your work. It's a little tough to break barriers and preconceived ideas. The rule of thumb is to always show what's relevant—to the client and for its market.

LABELING PORTFOLIO PIECES

Let your work sell itself. Saying that, labels *could* be used as efficient identifiers or as elements of page design. Such compositional devices can be effective if used with purpose; a brief description noting the title, client, and project can be entirely appropriate.

But, think smart about this. As Yeh reminds you, "Designers today should be problem solvers, not just visual artists. Reviewers always like to see short, concise descriptions for each project. With two or three sentences, you should explain what the problem was, and how your design concept solved it."

In other words, your note should enhance the visual wallop that carries your portfolio. "I think that the label should state the design challenge and goals to give the reviewer a way to evaluate its success," says Wasco. "An ad aimed at existing customers, for example, might use an approach that would be a disaster for attracting new customers. Also, the role the designer played is useful information: did they do just the visual design or design plus copywriting? For websites, it's also helpful to some employers to know if the designer did the coding as well."

CREATING OPPORTUNITIES

Next, we'll chat about presenting a portfolio, which may very well be in person—or not. Chances are good your work will have to speak for itself. So, make sure that it does. And that's as it should be. Requesting and scheduling a portfolio review may ultimately, of course, be two different things. Scheduling—for a review of your book or for an actual meeting—hinges on an affirmative answer to that request and either can be done by letter or telephone.

A phone request is informal (even intimate), quick, and—regardless of the response—right to the point. A written or emailed request can be backed by visuals—after all, you're selling product not patter. Both methods have their edge, so take some thought to determine how you want to communicate with the art director. Texting feels a bit too casual, but any time you say, "oh, definitely not" (to whatever), you'll hear of somebody somewhere making that happen. Wow, there are always surprises, but I wouldn't advise texting to set up portfolio reviews.

Some folks are natural writers; their polished words are powerful and persuasive and not to be ignored. Others prefer the immediate and individual interaction only the telephone provides. As you'll be spending lots of time on the phone and at the keyboard (business generates correspondence and vice versa), you'll have plenty of opportunities to develop the many facets of your communication skills.

PRESENTING YOURSELF

What happens during a portfolio review . . . it's just like a job interview, right? There are all kinds of "portfolio reviews." The accessibility of your work on your website or blog—think Tumblr, Weebly, WordPress—constitutes an obvious "review" situation. There are dedicated portfolio sites (for instance, Behance, Cargo Collective, Carbonmade, Dribble, Indexhibit) and national, regional, and local portfolio events (as sponsored by the AIGA or Behance, for example). And, of course, there's still the classic one-on-one meeting—a real person looking at real stuff (with or without a real you present).

Generally, when and if you can get a face-to-face portfolio review, it's less formal than a job interview. Alison Miyauchi, chair of Communication Design at Alberta College of Art and Design (Calgary, Alberta, Canada), tells her graduates to try and get as many of these "full contact" reviews as they can. "It helps them refine their books," she says.

The game rules don't vary much. Common sense tells us that what counts first and foremost is *great work*—backed by self-confidence, a positive attitude, and good personal appearance.

But folks have disputed even this. Yep, many art geeks dress rather (expletive deleted) *casually*. However, it would be irresponsible to insist that an iconoclast dress code will work in *your* situation where *you* live. Sure, your mom's not dressing you now, but the bigger picture still says to dress appropriately, fashionably, and neatly.

But these days, can you actually get such personal face time? Getting in to see art directors has always been a tough gig; that is, after all, why the demigods of design created drop-offs for busy, busy mortal art buyers. But regardless of the odds, don't write off the prospects, opportunity, or rewards.

And, just a note . . . personal contact is not old school, it's really more old *cool*. When you get right down to it, to quote the late, absolutely great

Simms Taback, "This is still a business of people." I say good people skills will go out of style only when people disappear. So . . . whether a lefty or a righty, carry your portfolio in your left hand; be ready to shake hands with the art director without fumbling or shifting your binder. Eye contact is a sign of confidence—look your client square in the face, open your book, and knock some socks off.

TAKE A MEETING

Ken Bullock suggests you consider hardware for client meetings (especially meeting on-site in a client's office). It can basically be boiled down to two options:

A. Go with a traditional laptop computer (Mac or PC—your preference). "Bear in mind," Bullock says, "that most of your creative team will be on a Mac, but most clients will be PC, so there may be some compatibility issues if you do not plan ahead."

B. Tablet computers. This could be an iPad, Android device, or similar. Yes, there's a "coolness" factor to consider here. Like it or not, it can also speak to your level of sophistication with technology.

In either case, it would be a good idea to have your own projector if you can budget that in. "You would want this in case you end up with a client that doesn't have a projector or at a client's office in a conference room that doesn't have one," Bullock points out.

Trust Bullock's seasoned experience, if not Murphy's Law; both the afore-mentioned situations are very possible. Please note: work out ahead of time how your tablet or computer links to the projector before the meeting. "Oth-erwise," Bullock states wisely, "that coolness factor goes right out the window." It should be said that having your technology fail during a client presentation isn't the end of the world, but certainly doesn't help build a client's confidence in your abilities.

Wasco echoes this. "If at all possible," he says, "be entirely self-contained, i.e., bring whatever technology you need. The iPad is becoming more common, but bring the correct video adapter to plug in to a projector or monitor . . . don't expect the client to have the proper cables/adapters."

Wasco also cautions you to be careful with an online portfolio in a meeting: what if the Internet/wireless isn't working where you have your meeting? Be sure to have an up-to-date *local* (offline) copy of your presentation on your laptop/tablet, just in case. Better safe than sorry: have a print version on board if all tech fails. "I'd rather show color prints of websites I've designed," Wasco points out, "than to sit there with a dead laptop, trying desperately to explain how cool my work is."

WE'LL MEET AGAIN

MaryAnn Nichols, Yeh, and Wasco offer these pointers to make a client meeting more productive (and profitable):

1. *Do some research.* Who are you seeing? What do they do? Who are their clients? What do they need? Can you provide a service they need? If so, then tell them how you can benefit them.

2. *Look presentable and be courteous.* You have only one chance to make a good first impression—use it. Always shake hands, make eye contact, introduce yourself, and be polite.

3. *Be confident and listen carefully.* Point out your strengths, have a positive attitude, and suggest how your skills can benefit that person. Listen attentively for advice and suggestions.

4. *Organize.* There is the concept that you should keep like assignments together—logos with logos, posters with posters, and packaging with packaging. So, if you have designed a logo and are showing applications of it, keep it together. Don't be redundant—it's not necessary to show the same design in twenty different color combinations.

   But many industry professionals prefer to see a portfolio or portfolio website that's not compartmentalized into categories. Instead, they *much* prefer to see design concepts that are executed across multiple formats and media channels. For example, a branding system of logo and packaging; a website, accompanying signage and advertising—a "360" advertising campaign offering print, video, direct mail, social media, and viral video (and more).

   Designers today are taking on the role of the strategist—a steady navigator who can steer clients in what is essentially a vast sea of choices. Note here that your mastery of conceptual thinking beyond one given task is essential.

5. *Never apologize for your work.* If you are dissatisfied with a piece in your book, take it out or redo it. Never show anything that is not your best. A few excellent pieces are far better to show than many mediocre ones. After all, your goal is to leave a good impression.

6. *Thank the interviewer and leave your calling card.* Always thank the people you have seen for their time and help. Remember to leave behind a copy of your capabilities brochure and a business card or your résumé and a printed sample of your work. This helps the interviewer to remember you and associate you with your work.

7. *Always follow up.* Piscopo recommends *you* ask for a follow-up (don't count on the client doing it for you) with an open question such as "How would you like to keep in touch?"

Then you do just that. This capsulizes the follow-up you both agreed to at the end of your meeting. Follow up with a thank-you email the next day, and after that, consider a hand-written note on a card of your own design. Not only will the person be amazed to receive an actual letter in the mail, the card will be yet another sample of your design skills (so it needs to be your best work).

DROP-OFF POLICY

Wasco doubts that this happens very much, mainly because it is the age of the Internet and art directors are busy (and you respect that, of course). Back in the day, you might have viewed a drop-off as simply saving everybody's time and eliminating uninteresting prospects (from the art director's point of view) and uninterested vendors (from yours).

But it *is* the Internet age, and online is all about efficiency, time- and energy-saving, and ease, is it not? But I never say never, and there *may* be those art directors—if they are looking at physical portfolios at all—who want to look at your physical portfolio right off the bat (and may look at portfolios only at specific hours on certain days).

If you are, by chance, instructed to leave ("drop off") your book, you will, well, drop it off—then have to pick it up later, again at a scheduled date or time. Yes, you read right; you won't be there. This caveat still applies everywhere: if you feel your portfolio is not ready for prime time, strong enough to "speak" for you in your absence, don't show it yet; get that book in shape.

As for any results, if you are requested to drop off your portfolio, there *may* be a written reaction—which just might be impersonal, generic, a photocopied form, or handwritten on post-it notes—or possibly a critique or suggestions. If the art director is interested, an assignment might at some point come your way—bravo—or maybe an appointment will be arranged to get together to chat about a job—great!

Or you might receive nary a word . . . no clue about any reaction, and you may have to politely follow up for a response. And even then, you may still get no response. Here, Piscopo smiles a bit ruefully. "And do *not* include the leave behind," she tells you. "It is too depressing when it comes back with the portfolio because they 'forgot' to pull it out and keep it. Mail it later with your follow-up."

As far as portfolio reviews are concerned—no matter how you slice 'em—there are no guarantees and no obligations. Considering the ROI—your return on investment—what's the smartest way for you to peddle your wares?

IT'S IN THE MAIL?

Your online portfolio is vastly preferred. And for many designers, sending a portfolio through the post harks back to the age of the dinosaurs. Snail mail? Your ol' pal, Fred Ex? Actually doing the rounds? Some harried art director mauling real pages of an actual portfolio? Ha—straight out of Drawassic Park!

Indeed, Mark Monlux says, "I haven't done it in years. However, I field continual requests for my website, and I point people constantly toward my blog. My online layout and presentation is equally as important as a physical portfolio and is seen by far, far more people."

Wasco states he'd be surprised if one in a hundred clients or employers ask for a physical portfolio. The online portfolio, in his experience, is virtually *always* the first level of screening. "If your online portfolio isn't good, there's no way you'll get an interview," he says unequivocally. "Like it or not, and for all types of designers, a strong online presence is the ballgame."

TAKE ME OUT TO THE BALLGAME

But not so fast. I coached Little League, and I'm one of those folks who understand the practicality of hitting all the bases, so I'm going to make sure you are covered either way. Now, after concurring about the importance of your fastball (aka your web presence), go back and touch third base. If you *must* mail portfolio materials to a prospective client, here are some guidelines:

1. Obviously pack it up right and tight.
2. Organize for a neat, clean, focused, clearly labeled logical presentation when opened.
3. Send an expendable binder and samples; nothing irreplaceable.
4. Submit work to the appropriate person, when promised. "Find out *now*," says Piscopo, "how long they expect to keep the portfolio."
5. Include a personal cover letter; keep it professional, brief, and friendly.
6. Include an SASE (or a prepaid Fed Ex shipping label) for its return.
7. Be patient; you won't get your work back immediately. Follow up with a card, email, or phone call. Do not give up, but don't be pushy.

BABY, IT'S COLD OUTSIDE

A cold call, as you'll remember from chapter 8, is a contact without request or referral. It could get you a portfolio review without the preliminary wait involved with written correspondence, but cold calls require time and energy you may not want—or have—to expend. Factor in that busy art directors will consider cold calls a distinct bother, and what do you have?

What you have is essentially door-to-door sales and perhaps pure frustration. For some designers, the very idea of the cold call is unthinkable. Others hate them, but still accept making them as a necessary part of business; they view cold calls as just another avenue for pursuing yet more work. It's a sure way to test your tolerance for rejection, but a super salesperson may get a decent return for the trouble.

RIGHT ON POINT

(PROFESSIONAL VIEWPOINTS IN 50 WORDS OR LESS)

Make sure every piece in your portfolio is as good as it can be: no halfway accomplished tasks. Offer samples that solve a wide range of problems with stylistic consistency as well as mental latitude. Avoid the mediocre. Be very critical. Stay detached.

—Fred Carlson

Art directors are looking for good thinkers when they review a portfolio.

—Kathie Abrams

If I had listened to everyone when I was first looking for a job, I would have taken every piece out—so I decided to go by my own instincts. It's a hard balancing act. Be willing to listen, but [present] your best work and stand by it.

—Elwood Smith

Self-editing is very difficult and very important. Focus on your strengths and what you do best…what you love the most. Resist the urge to include a sampling of everything—as in, "I can do it all!" It comes down to quality over quantity anytime.

—Al Wasco

Having a website is very direct—a portfolio review that is instantaneous and international. Of course, you must continually update and pay attention to all the details, be very sales-oriented, and stay on top of everything.

—Isabelle Dervaux

Your portfolio is a bit like a profile on a dating site; you want to put your best foot forward and you want to generate interest. Never place weak work in your book—it only brings down the overall quality. Fewer pieces: all jewels.

—Alison Miyauchi

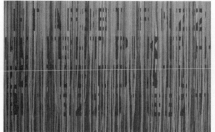

CHAPTER 10

ON THE WEB

My website is the best self-promotion I've ever done.

—Randy Glasbergen

DEAL DIRECT

"What we are beginning to see," says Rebecca Hemstad, "is the realization by many companies that websites must work on *all* devices; it's increasingly becoming a necessity." Hemstad (originally an aspiring historian), switched career paths into design when, as she tells us, "Computers emerged on the scene."

Her foundation is in print design, but she embraced multimedia/web from the beginning—working on desktop software design, digital publications, web application design (and most recently mobile application design).

The shift Hemstad refers to is indicative of an overall cultural move to mobile computing with the general presumption that the desktops are dying. "It's indicative of us moving into design for *systems* (not pages)," she says. "It's the notion of digital ecosystems."

Equally critical in a global perspective is the recognition that many third-world countries are now embracing mobile technology and will never experience the desktop phenomenon.

From her wide perspective, the design field is, putting it mildly, in flux, due to significant technological changes and, more importantly, to cultural changes in response to that technology. Hemstad—who would *not* advise students to think about a design career exclusively in print collateral—says, "There is no long-term future (in print collateral).

"What will our world be like in twenty years? Can you imagine?" she asks and poses the relevant question: "Will you still be reading printed newspapers, brochures, magazines, or books?" That, indeed, is the *Final Jeopardy* question. You supply the incredibly relevant answer (but bet wisely).

CALL AND RESPONSE

Hemstad says that with this cultural sea change—and this is important for designers to know—comes a shift away from *graphical* user interfaces (GUI) into a *natural* user interface (NUI) that pushes ease of use and a straightforward learning curve. "Web designers are not only producing websites for desktops, but also on mobile, tablets, and different gadgets," says Rigie Fernandez. "And with the growth of outsourcing and crowdsourcing," he comments, "marketers are seeking the help of freelance web designers to produce their web marketing collaterals."

Responsive web design (RWD), as Hemstad points out, has, at this writing, been around for three years now. There is also a rising need for social media design and applications, e-commerce, and ebooks. Marketing on the web nowadays no longer relies solely on traditional email marketing and web ads. According to Fernandez, social media—Facebook, Twitter, Google+, LinkedIn, Pinterest, Tumblr, etc.—now dominate the marketing industry, and marketers are tapping into the millions of customers out there.

"But," as Hemstad qualifies, "this is all associated with Web 2.0. Web 3.0 is an entirely different beast and quickly becoming a reality." To understand a little of Web 3.0, think along the lines of Apple's Siri. Siri is software that, as the company promo touts, "lets you use your voice to send messages, schedule meetings, place phone calls, and more. Ask Siri to do things just by talking the way you talk. In other words, we want our devices—our tools—to be an extension of us."

Hemstad also points out that one of the biggest debates on the web has been whether Google and Facebook will actually be dead in five years. Along with the rise of the aforementioned social media platforms, applications like HootSuite (which Fernandez personally uses), Crowdbooster, Buffer, SocialOomph, and others help marketers create, plan, and monitor (as well as simplify) their social media strategies.

But perhaps we should qualify this statement, particularly when one considers web design from the all-important perspective of user experience. Paraphrasing Vincent Flanders (author of *Web Pages That Suck: Learn Good Design by Looking at Bad Design*), Hemstad says that, "Nobody cares about you or your site. Really. What visitors care about is solving their problems. Now."

"CODE" IT BE MAGIC?

Now let's make this discussion even more interesting. As C. J. Yeh says, one of the biggest arguments in recent years has been whether web designers need to know how to code. Yeh tries to make it simple for his students. "If you are an industrial designer who designs cars," he points out, "you are not going to be the person putting the nuts and bolts together, but you do have an advanced understanding of how car mechanics work under the hood. Otherwise, you are just drawing pictures of a fantasy. Same thing with web design, if you do not have an advance understanding of the technology, you are just drawing pictures."

Yeh also points out that Adobe has been pushing WYSIWYG (what you see is what you get) web page construction tools for ages. Indeed, Adobe Muse and Edge—of which, Hemstad and Yeh are not big fans—both generate HTML, CSS, and JavaScript codes automatically.

But, according to Yeh, the biggest problem with computer-generated codes is that these codes are never *DRY*, which stands for "Don't Repeat Yourself." The concept of "dry code"—and the most fundamental tenet in programming— pushes for the elimination of duplications wherever possible: cleaner and more efficient code.

"This requires human intellect," Yeh explains, "and computers just cannot do it—at least not yet." Yeh goes even further by posing this interesting thesis: "To be blunt, I think Adobe tries to keep designers away from codes so the designers have to rely on Adobe products to survive in the industry.

"Most successful web designers I know eventually move away from Adobe products because all these WYSIWYG functions just clog up the interface and get in the way of it all. If you know how to hand-code, you can use just about anything to program (and you don't have to pay Adobe every year)."

Hemstad will tell you that in an era where "design thinking" is widely (and wildly) bandied about, we ignore the fact that design is an *act*. "The inevitable predicament is not about how much code you should know," she says, "but literacy itself."

HEAD CODE

Yeh states emphatically that every designer today should learn HTML, CSS, and JavaScript. He speculates that people often regard HTML, CSS, and JavaScript as mere production tools. However, Yeh would have you reconsider that mindset. "Learn programming," he says, "and you learn a new way to think. As designers, we must allow ourselves to be inspired by the media that we use as well as our craftsmanship."

Yeh points out that a return to craft was one of the most important concepts driving the Bauhaus movement, that in the *Bauhaus Manifesto*, there was no essential difference between the artist and the craftsman. The artist is an exalted craftsman, and proficiency in a craft is essential to every artist. "Therein," Yeh says, "lies the prime source of creative imagination."

However, Brad Reed fundamentally disagrees with Yeh about designers learning "to code"—that they absolutely need to know it's there, have a general idea of how it works, and, most importantly, understand how code-based platforms (whether desktop or mobile) limit design options. "If you apply the same logic to coders," he says, "that they should all learn 'to design'—then where does that leave you, the designer?" And the Bauhaus movement? "Legendary, and much revered, yes," Reed comments, "but it resulted in drafty, unlivable houses filled with furniture no one would sit in."

So perhaps we are simply arguing about *literacy* again. As Hemstad tells me, maybe the new literacy *is* code.

CODE READ

There are great resources online, and, certainly, many people learn to code just by researching online. Books can also give people a structured course of study. Yeh recommends the following books for learning how to code:

➡ *CSS3: Visual QuickStart Guide* (6th Edition) by Jason Cranford Teague; Peachpit Press

- ▣ *Introducing HTML5* (2nd Edition) by Bruce Lawson and Remy Sharp; New Riders
- ▣ *jQuery in Action* (2nd Edition) by Bear Bibeault and Yehuda Katz; Manning Publications

Here, Hemstad feels that you can read all you want, but you need to be engaged in the act itself. "This is why software like Rosetta Stone is much more effective at teaching languages. I personally advocate online, gamified environments that teach you, such as:

- ▣ TeamTreeHouse
- ▣ Code Academy (www.codecademy.com)
- ▣ Code Racer (coderace.me/#)
- ▣ Code school (www.codeschool.com/courses/journey-into-mobile)
- ▣ W3C schools (www.w3schools.com)."

DIGITAL HOME SCHOOL

Fernandez is a self-taught web designer. He says that most of what he knows now was learned from tutorials on the Internet. Indeed, there are MOOCs—massive open online courses—offering free online college-level classes open to all with the available time, energy, and inclination. Udemy (www.udemy.com) and Code Academy (www.codecademy.com) come to mind.

"Personally and professionally, you have to be committed to learn," Fernandez says. "Technically, it takes a lot of research, reading, study, and hands-on practice." Fernandez says he easily gets bored reading long text, so he investigated and found video tutorials (Adobe TV, Lynda.com, and Wordpress TV were his resources here). "If you are dedicated to learn, you can make it happen."

Fernandez, like Hemstad and Yeh, suggests learning basic HTML, CSS, and diving into Adobe Dreamweaver to get the hang of how to design for the web. Places like W3Schools and A List Apart are not without critics, but Fernandez has found such sites to be a good resource for beginners. "But eventually," Fernandez points out, "if you really want to pursue the web, learning how to code is imperative."

Hemstad emphatically agrees. "Actually, this is becoming more and more important," she states. "In order to design websites you absolutely must understand the medium you are designing for. The days of a designer just making a Photoshop comp and thinking they can hand it off to some developer to create are gone, especially with our shift to mobile."

BACK IN THE DAY

"A lot has changed in how I market myself and promote my work since my school days," Fernandez says. "Before, all you needed was a good portfolio and the necessary contacts to promote your work (and get clients).

"Now, aside from a solid web portfolio or a website, one should have a strong web and social media presence and personal branding," he follows up. "It's not enough that you're a designer with a solid portfolio—that's simply a given—you must be very visible on the web. You should have a blog. You need to establish an account/page on Facebook, Twitter, Google+, LinkedIn, Pinterest, Tumblr, etc. . . . . You should be networking with a lot of people to gain visibility and snag clients."

VISIBILITY

As Fernandez mentions above, visibility on the web is crucial in getting clients, and social media is extremely important when promoting yourself as a contemporary designer selling modern services. "If you want to go viral," Fernandez says, "get into social media."

Fernandez isn't talking about simply signing up for an account. You should set up a page dedicated to your brand (and that's *you*). Sure, create a page in the major social media websites. That's great. But creating a page is not enough. You must gain followers. How? "Post consistent and timely content that will interest your followers," Fernandez advises. "Interact with your followers. Your page going viral depends on those followers. The more you interact with them, the more visible your page will be. You should have a carefully planned social marketing strategy."

Fernandez personally used (the now defunct) Google Reader and other sites to find content, which he then reposted. And consider that video content may attract even more attention than still images. If you're a writer, a blog is probably your best bet to create relevant content. "Don't forget to integrate that on your social media account," Fernandez points out, "and link it to your website."

WEB PRESENCE: THE GOOD, THE BAD, THE UGLY

A big thank-you to two of our chapter gurus, Rigie Fernandez and Rebecca Hemstad, for brainstorming the following pointers for this sidebar:

THE GOOD

1. Having a web presence means you can promote yourself without maintaining a physical presence. Your website, blog, Facebook page, Twitter, and LinkedIn accounts work together to present a marketing tool promoting your brand and services 24/7.
2. A web portfolio can be a moving experience—literally. You can show motion graphics that a traditional portfolio cannot.

3. Create a responsive website portfolio. Make sure this site can be easily viewed on all devices (desktop, tablet, and mobile). Hemstad tells me she's even heard the argument for a responsive résumé.

4. Maintaining a blog promotes your work; it adds traffic to your website and it's a good outlet for practicing your writing skills.

5. Be a social butterfly. Establish your own social media page and post useful, consistent, and fresh content. This material—and how you interact with your followers—can build your personal brand.

6. Network. Connect with designers, developers, marketers, and clients. Whether in social media or face-to-face interaction, network contacts can help you navigate the course of a tricky project, offer you a much-needed job, or refer you to someone who may need your services.

7. This is a real moment for the web. Rising statistics of Internet users have prompted companies to channel efforts and resources to promote their brand for web users. This means more opportunities (and work) for web designers. Of course, a lot will depend on your expertise and what you want to pursue. Remember Hemstad's earlier advice: start thinking in terms of "systems" and not "sites."

THE BAD

1. The web moves on a fast-paced track. If you can't keep up, you'll be left behind.

2. You have to be up to date and updating in an instant. Timely, yes, but also expedient. Think fast, faster, fastest—like it or not.

3. Cross-browser incompatibility and a failure to thoroughly test your website on all browsers (and on different platforms—PC, Mac, tablet, mobile, etc.) before submitting to the client may very well lead to an unsatisfied client.

4. Keeping your eye on project timelines and the budget will be critical. Don't blow a deadline—or go over budget—because your information architecture is faulty or because you didn't allot enough time to fix bugs or other technical issues through adequate testing.

THE UGLY (but in reality, not *so* ugly in the cosmic scheme of things)

1. It is critical to design across platforms/media/channels.

2. Gaining web presence is all about *content*—what you post and the personal branding you want to promote. Savvy web designers know that the user experience is key, for as Hemstad wisely cautions, "It's about solving your user problems. Remember—it's not about 'you.' Along those lines, professional etiquette is required. Keep in mind what is appropriate to post and share (and what is not)."

3. Designers need to focus on both design and functionality. It's too easy to fall into the trap of producing a visually engaging website that reeks of poor web structure. An engrossing site needs to serve that content. As says Hemstad, "It cannot scream 'look at me, look at me—am I not cool? Am I not a cool designer? Don't you want to know how I did that?' Great web design is invisible."

4. It's a non-stop learning process. You not only need to learn how to create a website, but can you say (and spell and fully understand) the terms SEO (for web, mobile, and social media); HTML5; SMA (social media application); CMS (Content Management System); Video; 3D, etc.

5. Don't forget that a website is not only about visuals, but also about the user experience. Any website that is not driven by User Experience Design principles is poorly designed.

6. Good web design means a solid (and planned) information architecture, a user-friendly interface, and straightforward navigation. Brand and service must meet user experience head-on for serious communication.

7. Accessibility compliance is becoming vital—backed by legal requirements in many countries and for certain industries in the United States. Websites that fail to meet accessibility requirements are coming under more scrutiny and litigation.

BACK TO THE FUTURE

Let's consider a few pressing concerns:

1. "The notion that a wannabe web designer can do it all alone is gone," Hemstad remarks, "especially for any data-driven site requirements. It is easy to give voice to the idea of e-commerce, but there are backend requirements (such as security) that must come into play." Hemstad goes on to say that a web designer today will likely be working in a team context and that being able to communicate effectively with other members of the team is vital for ongoing respect (especially for web developers)."

2. "We are also in the very early stages of the movement toward 'big data'—particularly data visualization skills," Hemstad notes. "It's another huge jump, and in my opinion, quickly becoming a hot area of specialization—mainly because good UX/design of data is a necessity for the positive user experience. Content is increasingly dynamic and fluid and web design should be as well."

3. Hemstad also makes the point that today the terms *websites* and *webpages* are fast becoming obsolete—what we are beginning to see increasingly is the design of *web systems*.

4. Traditionally bound applications—once only tendered as standalone desktop software—are now being delivered (with HTML5/CSS3) via the cloud. "This means we are going to increasingly see more and more sophisticated web applications," Hemstad says. "This is the *future of software.*"

5. Native IOS applications have a corner on this market but as more and more browsers become compliant with HTML5/CSS3, the opportunity to "write once/run everyone" is becoming critical. "The problem with native apps is you need to create a 'unique' app written in a proprietary context for each device," Hemstad explains. "RWD (responsive web design) means create just one and it should work on anything."

THE ONLINE PORTFOLIO

Just a preface: I introduced this topic in our previous chapter, "The Portfolio," and expanded on it for this chapter. So, here's the detailed discussion promised in chapter 9.

Ken Bullock feels that a great portfolio is right up there with a good work ethic, talent, and a love of design. For this designer and art director, the word *portfolio* means so much more these days than it did when he was coming up. As Bullock ponders, "When I graduated, a portfolio was a bound (usually leather) book or case with a bunch of blackboard mounted pieces. These days when I am looking at a designer to hire, I still want the book when they come to interview, but I want a web portfolio even more."

Bullock looks for a URL on a candidate's résumé so he can instantly check out what the designer has to offer, get a preview of their capabilities, and catch a sense of style and presentation skills. "I'm actually a little worried about a candidate who doesn't have a web presence of some sort," he says. "I think to myself, 'Really? In this day and age . . . you don't promote yourself or showcase your portfolio online?'"

Consider this for a moment. As a professional designer, *you* are all about image and promotion. Your charge is to make the client—the people, the company—look good. "To attract attention to the customer or the customer's product," Bullock continues the thread, "make the concept legitimate and professional. If you can't promote yourself, how can you help me do the same for my clients or their product or service?

"It isn't like it was years ago when you had to code, or slice and dice imagery," Bullock states. "You don't even have to have web hosting; not with services like Behance or WordPress (or even something as simple as SnapFish or Flickr). A customized, personal URL is a nice thing—but even some of the previously mentioned services allow you to do that for free. Having a web presence isn't asking too much from a would-be designer."

And these days it's so easy (and essential) to have an online presence; "important" may be too tame a qualification. "Having a web presence is basically a *requirement today,*" Yeh sums up.

Many designers highly recommend WordPress. "WordPress is awesome," says Yeh. "Especially, if you know HTML and CSS well enough and can customize your template." Note: "customizing" is the keyword. Yeh points out that WordPress websites can look too generic if you don't know how to customize your template. Here, Al Wasco says that having your own URL speaks volumes. "It may cost extra, but definitely pay to use your own, rather than 'something. wordpress.com.'"

THE CRITICAL LIST

Designers (and illustrators) Mega and Al Wasco tell us that launching an online portfolio is a pivotal component to both your creative and marketing programs. These days, a web presence is a simple, mandatory artyfact (sic, huh?) of modern design life, but let's not assume the obvious too quickly, okay?

"Many designers don't really pay attention to their website," Mega fills in here. "Some don't even have one! Bad move. An online portfolio helps you promote your art and brings in potential customers—often the first thing a future customer sees from you. Put up a slow, ugly, and messy website, and viewers may assume you're simply not very serious, maybe even unprofessional."

Yes, you could use a simple image service (like Flickr or Pinterest), but to stand apart from the crowd of artists in the marketplace, here's some solid advice on creating an efficient, good-looking—and best yet, easy to find—website that will distinguish you from your competition.

LIKE ROLLING OFF A BLOG

Actually, Mega recommends that you create a blog instead of a traditional portfolio. Why? Two words: fresh content. Let's say you have an online portfolio somewhere, and perhaps this is complemented by a social network where you interact with colleagues, friends and family, and hopefully clients, too. This interface is a good thing, but not enough.

"How often do you update it?" Mega asks. "Be honest and critical. Ask yourself, if I saw your portfolio once last year, why should I return? Why do I want to come back? And if I don't come back, why would search engines (like Google) do that?"

The problem is that if normal (but obviously critical) viewers don't— or these all-important search engines can't—visit your portfolio regularly, you'll quickly be missing in action. And you do not want to become impossible to find.

FULLY CONTENTED

As Wasco will warn you, be careful about the content you post. Alison Miyauchi agrees and says, "It never ceases to amaze me what people will post, thinking that it is okay."

Wasco cautions that talking about your work is a relatively safe bet, but that the very nature of a blog implies a certain amount of personal opinion. It is one thing to discuss a famous designer who's been a major influence on your work, but yet another matter to wax on about that rowdy St. Patrick's Day bash with your designer buddies. "Let your personality show," Wasco advises, "but be discreet."

"Facebook and LinkedIn are now filling the role of what used to be relegated to blogs and websites," says Roger Starnes. "It might be worthwhile to note that both these social media sites could be utilized for the purpose of sharing info and skills."

Starnes considers the casual nature of a Facebook post to be less effective in managing what he calls your professional "portrait." And if that is the case, a combination of your blog (with posts) added to Facebook is a way to cover both bases.

"Potential employers today will be curious about your history on both LinkedIn and Facebook to see who you 'really are,' not just who you say you are," he adds.

BE THE CEO OF YOUR SEO

The letters SEO stand for Search Engines Optimization, and we're talking about the science of jockeying for the best spot (aka ranking) with search engines such as Google. And that's actually a really good thing.

Of course, offering a premier showcase of work that viewers will positively buzz about is the main key to success. "It should be obvious," says Mega, "that beyond the SEO, what your viewers want (and what your search engine must reveal) is great content—creating amazing art is your job; *that's* what people will talk about."

You want to give your beautiful work the best possible exposure you can. Thus, it's wise to learn a few basic tricks of optimization. Both you and your users will benefit.

Establish the proper environment to efficiently show off your material by learning good production habits from the onset. If your imagery loads fast and your site design boasts effective navigation, you control how your work is seen. You'll be in the ideal position (literally and virtually) to shoot for a big, bigger— the biggest—audience. Read that: maximum exposure and repeat customers. Let's see how we can do that.

GOOD SAVE

Roger Starnes has a good tip for you.

"If designers are using Photoshop, it is best practice to save the images at the size they will be viewed on the page featuring them," Starnes advises. "When possible, I recommend using images saved as JPGs exported via 'Save for Web & Devices' from Photoshop at '60' [image] quality. If images need to be small, it might be good to link them to larger images."

As noted earlier in this chapter, using WordPress for your site will cover this to some extent, but overly large images still may slow a page down. "WordPress allows larger images to have smaller 100-percent thumbs or down-sized images to help with this," says Starnes. "A one-to-one image will always be the crispest for the viewer."

A HOST OF DECISIONS

Start off by choosing the right web host (the place where you will store your website, sort of like the house where you blog lives). "When I started my own art blog," Mega remembers, "I didn't know about hosting and chose a local provider. This eventually proved to be a bad move—ultimately too expensive and decidedly unprofessional."

Ah, ha! Cheaper does not always translate to mean a bargain. Just as expensive isn't always better. But no matter the costs, nobody wants to live in a dilapidated structure. So how do you find the best host for you? Here are a few items to consider when choosing the right match:

1. It's not a bad idea to go with a big, trusted name. "Look for the heavyweights," Mega confers. "Mr. 'Big and Famous' didn't become respected and well known through sheer luck. Great customer service is vitally important and can't be underestimated. You want (and need) fast and efficient solutions—a host who will reliably help you solve the inevitable problems."

   Here, Wasco advises you to pay more, if necessary, for 24/7 live phone support, especially if you're new to web design or hosting. You probably don't need to be reminded that tech support can be agonizingly slow and frustrating, especially if your problem isn't fixed on the first go-round. "There's no substitute for talking to a real person," Wasco says, "when it's 4:00 a.m. and your website is down for no apparent reason."

   Wasco also imparts a good test to try before you sign on the dotted line with a hosting service; try to find the tech support phone number.

"If it's hidden away somewhere," he says, "that's an indication they don't really want you to call. Now when you've found it, call and see how long it takes to reach a human being. Ask some beginner question to see whether they're willing to help you or only offering gobbledegook. If it takes too long to reach a person, or you can't understand what they're saying for any reason, keep looking."

The more established hosts have built solid reputations over the years only through superior customer service. This reliability translates to user satisfaction. Everything is hyper accelerated in our Internet era; if a provider's products or service is bad news, there *will* be talk—fast, deadly, ubiquitous—and it will catch up with potential buyers. It's pretty simple math, so keep the above equation in mind: do your homework to narrow your field of choices.

Look for chat support, too, and do the same experiment there—try to see if you can get answers quickly. "A good host will have a great chat support," Starnes says. "It may be difficult, but see if they can speak and understand English efficiently, too!"

2. The aforementioned "house" you're building needs a substantial foundation (a good server), solid doors (security), and a waterproof roof (as in, spam-free). "And you want to be able to repair your plumbing (infrastructure, general settings of the website like redirecting a page) if needed," says Mega.

And let's mention that you need those pipes (and any ductwork) to work smoothly and productively. In other words, your site should run fast. Downtime or slow run times most likely point to server (mis)management. There's not much you can do about that, but the unfortunate outcome will be disgruntled, impatient viewers who may never come back. A way to prevent this is to hitch up with a trusted and reputable host with a proven track record.

It's also to your advantage to see how much you can add on to the site if you need it. Some questions to consider . . . Does the host offer SSL (secure hosting)? Do they offer e-commerce solutions that you can add later? Do they offer email; and, if so, how easy is that to add on?

3. Be a savvy shopper. Reliability, tech support, and cost are the most critical issues. Don't worry about how many email addresses you'll get. "A handful is seriously all you'll ever need," says Wasco. Don't covet oodles of disk space. "Unless you plan on uploading hundreds of large images, zillions of gigs are really unnecessary," he adds.

Good hosting need not be expensive. It bears repeating that expensive doesn't necessarily mean better, and cheaper may be too costly in the long run. What you'll find is that reasonable, quality service can certainly be found (and the research here is worth all the necessary time and effort).

At this exact writing, I have been able to find great price breaks for excellent hosting packages. This money spent should get you up and running quickly and efficiently. The companies I researched—and there were many—reviewed well and boasted strong reputations. They offered valuable services, good customer support, and the abilities to grow with you.

BUILDING YOUR BLOG: THE RIGHT STUFF

You found the perfect host. Time to create your blog and upload killer content. Keep these tips in mind:

1. Smarts

Starnes leads off with this simple, but absolutely critical piece of advice: "Keep your hosting info in a safe place, and be aware of updates and renewal times."

2. Keywords

When choosing a URL, create a catchy, short, and indelible URL by using memorable keywords that best describe your activity, in the right position. "Put the most important term first," Mega advises. "Then the second, etc."

Wasco tells you to try for something that's easy to spell—a seemingly simplistic but intrinsically smart thought. "Imagine telling someone your URL over the phone," he elaborates. "You want it to be absolutely straightforward—easy to spell; and remember.

"For example, CuyahogaValleyNationalRecreationArea.org is a tricky mouthful, and CVNRA.org is eminently forgettable," Wasco rightly states. "They use 'dayinthevalley.org': easy to remember, easy to spell." By the way, Cuyahoga's URL redirects to http://www.nps.gov/cuva/planyourvisit/events.htm—which, of course, no one would ever remember handily.

3. Domains

The preferred domain here is obviously .com. If you can afford it, Starnes suggests that it's wise to spend the extra bucks to get other "default" domains. Consider a .org site, as well as .com, and .net domains, too. "They can point to the 'real' site," he says. "This protects you from others buying these domains later and sending your users to bad or competitors' sites."

But Mega cautions against .net and .org if you want to target a global audience. "Most people assume that .com is the place to go," he points out. "Don't lose them. To achieve a good position with your country name, buy both (i.e., .uk and .com)."

Sifting through the points and counterpoints, both Mega and Starnes are really saying to use the appropriate domain extension. A regional domain suffix address (one that ends with .fr, for instance) according to where your activity is located is okay and will make your blog easier to find in your own country.

4. Naming

Be distinctive, but it's still best to choose a simple name. "Set yourself apart," says Mega. But keep in mind that hyphens and numbers may be hard to spell (or keep track of and remember), and terms like *top or best* are too generic. There's no real advantage here.

Check to see who is using very similar domains already. Why? If a user mistypes your URL, what will they see? "You don't want to choose 'cmm.com' as users may go to 'cnn.com'; it's simply too hard to hear the difference if spoken out loud."

5. Platform

Now choose the right publishing platform. There are lots of fine choices (Tumblr and Weebly come to mind), but like many in the know, Mega prefers WordPress, and I can see why. Everybody—as in, most web designers—uses it, but you don't have to be a web designer to create solid content.

A note here: Starnes suggests you consider the differences between labels. The tags in question are "platform," "solution," or "service." "One may see 'platform' as the server," Starnes says, "LINUX or APACHE or the software it runs on—such as PHP, ASP, dotNET, etc. Others see 'solution' more as WordPress, Joomla, etc."

And about WordPress . . . WordPress, like anything, is not unequivocally, universally loved, but generally, there's a lot to admire. After all, search engines like Google adore it because Wordpress code is clean and easily understandable. It is flexible, good looking, and feature-rich.

And while some WordPress themes are responsive (and some are not) WordPress is updated and maintained regularly, and it is simple and user-friendly. It looks beautiful on desktops, laptops, iPads, and iPhones (or other smartphones), and even on your TV.

6. Download and Install

Download and install your chosen platform on your server. It will probably take only a few minutes and you won't need to be a technical genius. At this point, we should make a strong case to learn and fully understand your chosen platform.

For instance, if you go with WordPress for your CMS (Content Management System), when you log in for the first time, you'll encounter the Dashboard, which is the place where you track your recent activity, manage your visitors comments, and create content. You will see sections called "Posts" and "Pages." What's the difference between these? "A Post is an entry on your blog," Mega instructs, "where you talk about new artwork, a new exhibition, or other daily news. A Page is something static like the 'About me' section."

It's also wise to note that good hosts should offer a Quick-Install function for adding WordPress (or Joomla, etc). Don't forget that these programs will require the host to support that solution, and perhaps require a content database with username and password. But, as Starnes cautions: *always* keep that login information handy.

7. Choose a Theme.

A "Theme" is the basic look of your blog. WordPress offers seemingly millions of themes created by users. You can fashion your blog exactly the way you want to, but Mega wisely cautions you here.

"Hold on, don't go crazy," he says with a smile. "While there are a lot of themes available, stick to the basic, default option. You don't want to put a Ferrari in your garage when you don't know how to drive it. It might sound cool to have a fancy car, but what about in the future— when you have to replace a wheel nobody sells?"

Mega also strongly advises you to choose the Twenty Eleven default theme. It's created by WordPress (WP), which means they'll fix any potential bug, update it frequently, and that's it is secure and built on solid code.

"A WP theme is a good way to start," Starnes chimes in, "so long as users know that customizing any of the code or pages without changing the theme or theme directory could be overwritten by future updates."

8. Select Your Plugins

A "Plugin" is a tool created by a user that offers something extra for your blog (like a badge or action). Locate the Plugin section of your Dashboard, and the click the "add new" button; it's pretty simple.

Putting it mildly, a wealth of plugins are available, but once again, stick to the basics. Plugins present a ton of potential features, but you won't need most of them. "Plugins will make your website slow and messy," Mega says. To name only a few, he recommends, "*WP Google Fonts* (an easy, simple, and efficient way to choose a great font for your blog. Your blog can look pro without complicated coding); *Digg Digg* (so visitors can share your content on their social network); *FeedBurner* or *FeedSmith* (which create an RSS for your blog); *Google Analytics for WordPress* (which allows you to see how many people visit your blog everyday); and *the* best plugin on WP: *WordPress SEO*—the perfect SEO solution to help you check your content and much more. A must-have."

"Akismet and *Captcha* are good plugins as well," Starnes adds. "Both help users reduce spam that will come with any measure of user attention."

9. Get Organized

Your blog should now be ready to rock and roll. Here's a good thought about structure and navigation: choose your WordPress categories and tags properly. Consider the following suggestions for choosing your categories and tags.

A. Define your categories. Categories mark the sections of your blog (e.g., a "Logo" category, a "Poster" category, etc.). "Choose wisely," Mega continues, "Stick to four or five categories. Don't create a new category every week because it will confuse visitors. Future content should be relevant for each one of those categories." A little tip: Add a keyword in the name. Use labels like "Fleish Business Cards" instead of simply "Business Cards."

"This will add a tighter focus," says Mega.

B. Tags are complementary information. Search engines rely on your categories and tags to define your page content. For a "Poster" category, a tag could be a sub-category like "Music."

"After publishing posts, you'll have a selection of tags listed in the 'Choose from the most used tags' somewhere," says Mega. Mega says to stay with this automatically generated selection instead of creating new tags. Having a "Logo" tag and a "Logos" tag creates two lists of posts for the same topic. "Be specific: choose 'Logo with paintbrush' instead of just 'paintbrush.' Go to the 'Tag' and 'Category' sections in the Dashboard and add relevant and precise descriptions for each element."

10. Organize Your Content

You obviously want to create successful and interesting content. On a blog, new content is called a "Post." The common mistake many designers make is to upload a lot of unrelated content at one time. The result is a messy portfolio that visitors have a tough time figuring out, which is also indecipherable for the search engines. It will sound like a lot of work—and to be honest, it is—but follow these recommended practices to ensure optimum results. Every time you upload new stuff, you should do the following:

A. Come up with a descriptive title. Instead of "Cool New Designs," go with "New promo for the TV show *Ancient Ohio Cook Pot Roadshow*." Viewers and search engines should easily understand what you are talking about.

B. Tell what the post is about. Begin with "I designed this promo for a PBS Television special that examines long-buried cooking utensils accidentally discovered on farms near Cincinnati."

C. Do the same for the "ALT TEXT" associated with each image. "ALT TEXT" describes the image for visitors to your site who can't see. Your alt text will be read to visually impaired people and, of equally importance, it will be utilized by Google and other search engines for image searches. "Most of my Google-based traffic on my own website (www.theviewfrom32.com) comes through image search," Wasco says. "Good, descriptive alt text is critical."

D. Make it enticing so that I really want to read your post. Highlight important information and organize style and content with bold and italic emphasis.

E. Don't be too brief. Explain why I should care—who, what, when, where, why. Mega will tell you to write at least three hundred words of relevant information in every post.

F. Use relevant words or phrases people would search for in Google (but keep a natural tone). Use proper grammar and spelling, not slang.

G. Be polite. Be unique. (Credit images you borrow. Never copy and paste content from other blogs, but if you do, cite your sources and always credit images and photos. Stealing is a no-no.)

11. Quality Control

"Quality content is everything," Mega tells us. "Create at least two new posts per week. There are no secret strategies to attract visitors and rank well in Google. . . . Interesting content is the most important aspect of your online success."

To which Wasco adds, "Don't try to make it 'cool' or 'high-tech' unless that's your area of expertise." To which *I* would throw in, think *substance* before *flash*. Relevant content trumps pure razzle-dazzle every time.

12. Optimize Your Imagery

"Not too large, not too many. Not too heavy, a proper title, captions, and tags," says Mega. But how large is too large? "That's tough to say," Wasco joins in. "In most cases an image roughly 600 x 800 pixels should be fine." In terms of file size ("weight"), Wasco tries to keep imagery from 100–500 kilobytes. He cautions that folks must pay attention to optimizing their images, and choosing between the JPG or GIF formats can make a huge difference in both image quality and file size.

"Remember that even though we assume fast Internet access [is ubiquitous]," Wasco says, "work to keep file sizes as low as possible, in order to keep your site fast. Sites that are slow to load will annoy the hell out of visitors, and if you have a lot of images on a page, this can be a real problem.

"Some people go all GIF or all JPG," Wasco says. "Big mistake!" Why so? The play is to experiment and evaluate which file format works best for each individual image, as there can be dramatic differences between the JPG and GIF (and PNG) formats. (Hint: Photoshop makes it simple; you can fool with the "Save For Web & Devices" command and explore multiple formats and sizing easily.)

Starnes has a problem with a "use all" method for imagery. He recommends users to go with the most appropriate image format and stick with what works the best on all devices and browsers. "There are places where a 24-bit transparent PNG is ideal," he points out, "but it results in a larger image size and older browsers [or] users may not be able to see it."

Along those lines, when using the JPG format, the quality ranges from "0–100" (sometimes shown as "0–12"). Wasco tells us that he has optimized thousands of images and has found that for most images a setting of 50–60 (6–7) is more than adequate. "Using a higher setting yields larger file sizes with little or no visible difference," he states. "Multiply this unnecessary increase in file size by dozens of images, and your site can really slow down."

"When using Photoshop," Starnes instructs, "users can see the preview of what the image will look like for each image setting. If the image is starting to blur or distort, consider using a higher setting."

"Many hosting platforms will automatically optimize your images as you upload them," says Brad Reed, "creating large, medium, and small versions to be used as appropriate, based on your audience's browser and bandwidth. Yeah, *they can tell.*"

"Viewers don't want to wait around for your huge website to load on an iPad with their data plan expense," Rebecca Hemstad adds, candidly bringing to your attention that "you will not be that important to them."

SELL IT, BABY!

So it's time to tell the world about your portfolio. Here, Mega and Wasco weigh in on promoting your blog. While the two designers are not in complete accord, they still offer a pertinent overview and solid, valuable advice. Let's hear them out.

1. Mega says that, whatever "SEO experts" tell you, links don't matter (much). If you create quality content, you will get a good ranking.

He cautions you not to obsess over links. By that same token, don't exchange or buy links. "If people enjoy your blog, they will link to it; it's that simple," he states.

But Wasco disagrees. "You have to work to be found among the millions and millions of sites out there," he says. "My website typically gets sixty to ninety visitors per day, and a link from a hot site like www. DesignObserver.com will instantly ratchet it up to 800 visitors (or more)."

Wasco does tell you to be *selective* about asking people to link to your blog. "Find the best design sites and contact them with a brief, personal email asking them to look at your work and link to it if they think its valuable."

2. According to both designers, it is smart to get natural inbound links (links pointing to your blog); to find applicable outbound links (links to pertinent external sites); to cite appropriate reciprocal links; and to create internal links to your relevant previous posts.

3. Both Mega and Wasco will tell you to share and promote. Use social networks, related forums, and websites, and share every post you create on your social networks. Create a newsletter (for instance, on www. MailChimp.com). Don't put your link on unrelated websites. Spamming is bad!

4. Both designers think it's a good idea to add your website URL to your email signatures.

POINT/COUNTERPOINT

Wasco tells you knuckle down. "Work at it! Find the sites you like and contact them. With a little luck they'll link to your site. Write articles about design on your site; then send links to those other great design sites. There are so many designer sites out there you *must* actively let people know about yours. In the real world, networking is critical. This is simply online networking."

But Mega says to sit back and relax. "If you create good content, they will come. Don't give up. Your blog will not gain a good rep in one week. You gain trust once it has been around for a while. Hang in there. . . . Popularity and authority loom large at your doorstep."

THE NOW

As Yeh will tell you, digital is no longer the future. It is how *everything* is done now. He points to the *Occupational Outlook Handbook*, where you learn that computer system design and related services (web design, app design, etc.) is expected to grow 61 percent while print publishing is expect to shrink another 4 percent.

"In the job prospects session," Yeh points out, "the *Handbook* states: 'Graphic designers are expected to face competition for available positions. . . . Prospects will be best for job applicants with website design and other interactive media experience.'"

It's probably a no-brainer that the market is saturated with designers who know how to do print. So it makes strong sense that young designers looking to break into the industry would be wise to show what they can do with digital media. Websites, motion graphics, social media marketing campaigns—these should be the meat of a chunky, tasty portfolio.

SURVEY SAYS

From a 2012 survey, after a senior portfolio review at New York's FIT (Fashion Institute of Technology), Yeh reports that comments overwhelmingly indicated respondents wanted to see more examples of web and interactive design.

What Yeh and his colleagues heard was that, based on portfolios reviewed, too many focused on struggling platforms (such as posters and publication) and not enough on new media. They were told that digital work and a corresponding practical education for the digital world was deemed crucial; that designing for the web is seriously important; and that the lack of user-experience design (UX) and overall web design in a portfolio gives the distinct impression of an incomplete submission.

"Young designers who can design beautiful pages and write clean code will have the best chance [in the job market]," Yeh says. "Companies and design studios looking to hire designers who design for web will look at the source code of portfolio web pages."

"Already," adds Starnes, "some employers or managers that I know like to see a physical sample from web or digital designers. Digital is easy to copy or even steal, so a personal letter/note/sample can do well to validate and/or point to online samples (just in case)."

FOR WEB DESIGNERS

Right off the bat, if you are primarily a web designer, be sure you are using current industry best practices in design and coding. As of this writing (2014) the hot buzzword is "responsive," meaning that the best websites automatically adapt to different devices: desktop, laptop, phone, or tablet.

"Simply being able to discuss this will help," Wasco tells you, "even if you can't totally implement it." Wasco suspects that in a couple of years we'll need to design every site for *touch* since more and more people are accessing the web with phones and tablets. Designers don't—or won't—*need* to code, but it stands to reason that if you have a solid understanding of HTML and CSS, you'll be decidedly more employable.

Dreamweaver would be the current software of choice for web development and should be considered as an essential tool to master. However, if you can create a website *only* with Dreamweaver, you are less valuable to most employers. "And, not to mention," Wasco says, "you're shooting yourself in the foot if you can't troubleshoot the code behind any software."

Use web fonts to create beautiful typography. Check out font services, such as Typekit, www.Fonts.com, Font Squirrel, and Google Web Fonts. A *somewhat* recent technique (it's actually been around since the 1990s) that you should be aware of, called a "rule," is @font-face. Look into it, as @font-face may be particularly helpful to tap into "web-safe" fonts.

But the whole shebang comes with controversy and politics. Type foundries (font creators) have an issue with @font-face: the basic conceit—the logic that governs the concept—is that font data would be free to download. No DRM (digital rights management)! Ahoy, matey—can you spell the word *piracy?* Web designers want easily accessible fonts that legally and—shall we say—economically, don't bust EULAS (End User License Agreements). *Yo, bud*—can you spell the term *trust?*

THE D. VINCI CODE: THE TEN COMMANDMENTS OF DIGITAL DESIGN

There's much involved in art and design outside the digital medium, and Gerald D. Vinci is very much the creative pragmatist. He sees digital design as just one extension, one arm with which to communicate an idea. He will tell you that an effective digital designer needs to be well versed in *all* areas of digital design, and that you cannot—or certainly should not—function *only* as a digital designer.

So it's from this vantage point that D. Vinci shares his guidelines for establishing yourself as a digital designer in the following list.

1. Play with your toys. Understand and become familiar with all types of display devices that could potentially display your project. Designers often spend too much time focused on creation and do not play around with the end product as much as they should.
2. Offer full service when possible. Develop a diverse skill set and try to supply the majority of your customers needs in-house.
3. Get help. When learning or adopting additional skills is not possible, partner up with a reputable colleague who can help offer this skill set.
4. Research. Spend at least an hour a day educating yourself on the latest technology, products, software, tools, and techniques. This will lead you to more services or features to add to your bag of tricks. (A note: Hemstad advises you to continue this

important practice even after you are employed, even if it means nights and week-ends. She does her research on her lunch hour.)

5. Design responsibly. Keep the project focused on the customers' needs and the end user's expectations.

6. Always think about UI/UX (user interface/user experience). Digital design is more about form *following* function than form *over* function. A design must serve a purpose; otherwise the end user will be disappointed.

7. Network and contribute. Establish a strong network of peers you can bounce ideas and projects off of. Having an unbiased group of professionals who can help you weed out good ideas from bad ideas can be a life-saver when you are stuck on something. Don't forget to contribute to this group so they won't think twice about helping you when the time comes.

8. Adopt forward thinking. Plan your project specs according to the device or devices that will be displaying it, and think ahead, as certain devices that are not displaying it now, might be very soon.

9. Pay attention to what others are doing in your continuing iniative to educate yourself and stay current.

10. Educate your customers. Show them all available options and state your case, with their best interests in mind, according to which ones make the most sense for their project.

FLATLINE

Finally, it should be said that the whole UI/UX thing is a very hot corner of the playing field. And take note of a rather hot spot of that warmy, warmy corner, which is trending as of this writing: the prolific rise of *flat design* to enhance the user interface.

The move towards flat design is the direct counterpoint to *skeuomorphism* design. Skeuomorphism designs assimilate the textures and evoke the look and feel of the object rendered. You know these: digitized versions of stitched, Moroccan, leather-bound books on an oak bookshelf and calculators with rounded buttons that appear to depress are just two of the usual suspects.

The movement toward stripped-down flat design focuses on the clean and smooth—pure color; simple icons, lines, and shapes; basic type—and on a straightforward, minimalist utilization of UI elements. We're back to essentials with the accent on functionality: no embellishment, no conflated 3-D.

Flat design goes hand-in-hand with responsive design. Easy reading and navigation are the buzzwords. But, as Starnes points out to us, responsive designs are less about the designs of the sites and more about how they appear on each device. "So a site can still be very well designed," he says, "but it must be simplified, as each device shows less."

FLAT OUT

And like the new car that depreciates drastically as soon as you drive it off the lot, some wonks say that flat design is now passé.

"What it really comes down to is designing for user needs," Hemstad says. "Designing a site on the premise that it is the hottest and latest in thing won't work. Whatever style you choose needs to serve the content, and the content is all about solving those user problems."

RIGHT ON POINT
(PROFESSIONAL VIEWPOINTS IN 50 WORDS OR LESS)

Technology has been a boon to the freelancer. But don't let yourself be trained by the computer; be aware that solving compelling graphic problems requires artistic lateral thinking. Educational and life experiences must lead you forward. You have to have "been there" to know your subject.

—Fred Carlson

When the web was in its infancy, I perceived a niche and tried to fill it. Sounds intuitively obvious, but it's not as easy to do. I became Peter Zale Paradezign. Like a paralegal, I stepped in and assisted designers in finishing projects, whether it required design, illustration, or production.

—Peter Zale

Your site should appeal to the most design-conscience viewers: designers. And if your site does not function properly, has missing links, is hard to navigate, or looks like an amateur created it, someone is just a click away from a jump to a competitor.

—Jay Montgomery

In my experience, striking a good balance is the goal, but it's very hard to do. In my view, a student should learn software skills first, along with some design, then move to a school where the emphasis is on design. This, to me, is the best of both worlds.

—Al Wasco

We as designers (or developers or as both) need to wake up and realize it's no longer about my code being better than yours, or your design being better than mine. It's about information and accessibility, simplicity and minimization. It's about affordability. And it's always about the end-user experience.

—Gerald D. Vinci

Artists tend to think that websites are a "business card" for the showcase of their art (either through exhibitions or via commission). I would say, in reality, it's the other way around.

—Mega

When creating your online portfolio site, don't include "everything and anything." Your website needs to express the essence of your personality but remain professional. Design is about solving problems. Focus on showcasing your capabilities in this capacity. Don't overwhelm. Provide enough to get invited to an interview.

—Rebecca Hemstad

NATIONAL
BRONZE
SCULPTURE
SYMPOSIUM
YELLOW SPRINGS
OHIO

© Maxwell Fleishman 2014

© Rebecca Hemstad 2014

CHAPTER 11

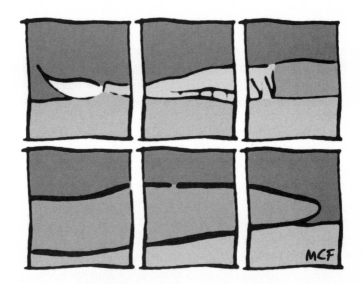

DESIGN IN
SEQUENCE

In the end, it may simply come down to that most generic and correct answer for how to break into comics: hard work and commitment—par for the course with all and any sort of comic work.

—Mike Maihack

ART IN SEQUENCE

As you've been reading throughout this book, you have heard numerous professional testimonials about how the general field of design has been changing. Comic books (as well as cartoons and comic strips) are certainly a specific venue witnessing a remarkable metamorphosis—a clear demonstration of evolution in the industry. They just don't make 'em like they used to? Indeed.

In some circles, the terms *comic book, cartoon,* and *comics* may still be considered lowbrow. The term *sequential art* was coined by the legendary Will Eisner in 1985. (By the way, please find a copy of Eisner's *Comics and Sequential Art,* published in that year; it's essential reading.) Eisner is the veritable father of the *graphic novel* (another tag elevating the cachet of the ostensibly humble *comics* or *comic book*).

You might say that comics, cartoons, and comic books—sequential art—is an angle tacking more toward illustrators. On the surface of it, I tend to agree. But actually there's a @&#% load of design involved: cover, page, and typographic design; characterization (character design) and color styling; illustration style and technique; and visual treatment. And while not under the design umbrella per se, writing and editing—integral and inextricably linked to the comics design process—must be mentioned here, too. *Shazam,* y'all.

So in this book, and particularly in this chapter, we'll conduct a general conversation of sequential design, but won't be doing an in-depth analysis of, graphic novels, comic books, and comics. Please, hang in there though. We'll dive deeper into that pool with our sister title, *Starting Your Career as an Illustrator.*

FUNNY BUSINESS

There was a time when cartoonists and comic book artists had a rather specific venue—print. You had what were tagged "the funny pages"—newspaper syndication; comic books (obviously); magazines and zines; self-publication. You were faced with intense competition and limited (though I wouldn't say limiting) options.

But the rise of webcomics with the Internet as a medium changed all that. At this writing, print is not yet dead. In fact, as was recently reported (at this writing) in newspapers like *USA Today,* print comics are actually *thriving. Boom! Pow!* Faster than a speeding iPad; more powerful than the locomotive of digital media. Able to leap tall measures of quality and quantity. Print sales keep going up, up, and away.

While we certainly want to point you down the right digital path, we also want you to practice some positive, big-picture, splash panel-style thinking. Can you say *crossover,* kids? Let's predict the success of your webcomic and visualize the great demand for all those eagerly anticipated print spin-offs of your wildly popular work (books, calendars, posters, greeting cards, etc.).

At least for now, it will be prudent to design simultaneously—and establish a workflow—for print *and* digital (and in that order, print *to* digital). As you produce your hard copy image, routinely convert the design to digital. No extensive redraws; no bulk scanning saved for a rainy day or slow week. Safely store and organize hard copy and electronic files for easy access when you become the Queen (or King) of all media.

THE BIZ

How and where to break in? True, at this writing, the newspaper industry appears to be in dire straits and newspaper syndicates are faring no better. Again, we can blame or applaud the Internet for this game-changing business model.

But currently, *there are still newspapers*—traditional and alternative—as we know them. So yes, stay the course, one can still submit a cartoon feature to the syndicates (or self-syndicate) the "old fashioned way."

Traditional print comic books are still exceptionally viable, and the path to publication remains equally established. Here, the same o', same o' is still operative: submit to publishers. (A note: small presses here may be the way to go.) You schlep your stuff to comics conventions and book shows. You network with pros. You promote.

Web comics have busted out. Digital publishing is booming. Self-publishing is enjoying a true renaissance. Why not create and post your own comic? Do some research. On great sites like CBR (Comic Book Resources; www.comicbookresources.com) and Comics Alliance (www.comicsalliance.com), you'll find both comics creators and hopefuls discussing the current, hot topics like the importance of building a fan base and a reputation online or cultivating the interesting European markets—comics have always been big the world over.

All across the web, the debate over competitions remains in full swing. Approach the online syndicates—digital sisters to traditional newspaper syndicates—like GoComics (www.gocomics.com/explore/sherpa). There are webcomics blogs *about* webcomics (Fleen is one; www.fleen.com) and organizations dedicated to the webcomics venue (like Vancouver's Cloudscape; www.cloudscapecomics.com). Comics history, news and opinion, networking, and just pure gossip forums are mere clicks away. (The gossip sites are not so "pure," by the way. However, I'll let you dig up and dish the dirt your bad self.)

As with traditional print comics publication, basic legwork mentioned previously remains the same. Do consider advertising. Think about possible merchandising. Don't forget copyrights, which means officially registering your work, not just posting a © notification. You get good; you get known; perhaps you'll get a distribution deal.

You could enter contests, if you're of this mind (please read chapter 3 and chapter 8 in this book.) And, of course, while it's never been easier to promote and market, getting noticed and making a living at all this—via any route—may still be a job for Superman.

ONE'S SIGHS DO NOT FIT ALL

Discussing how to break into comics is an interesting proposition for Mike Maihack because he doesn't feel there is one standard, defining experience to point to.

"The last thing I want to do is misinform someone," he states. "There is no 'this is how you do it' pep talk. But regardless, I can say that my big break came from self-publishing." When he says "self-publishing," Maihack means having actual, physical, printed books available along with a simultaneously available webcomic.

"I wasn't drawing the webcomic out of a desire to do 'bigger' things," Maihack comments, "but I did consider that if any work came my way, it would be because of the webcomic."

After all, as Maihack estimates, thousands of people around the world were reading his webcomic while his printed books just sold here and there at various conventions. But it was one of these conventions (the San Diego Comic-Con, in fact) where one important publisher did pick up the print version of that webcomic, saw something he liked, and precipitated Maihack's blossoming comics career.

ALTERNATIVE THINKING

I highly recommend two great books, both written by Jessica Abel and Matt Madden: *Drawing Words and Writing Pictures* and its follow-up *Mastering Comics* (both from First Second Books). Beyond standard, old school submissions, if your traditional marketing comes up short, Abel and Madden suggest some alternative means to get your work out there. Let me paraphrase some of their best advice:

- Consider trading with your colleagues and donating to schools and libraries.
- Send your stuff to established comics artists for possible feedback and inspiration. I'd inquire first before any blind or cold networking, however. (Always err on the side of personal and professional courtesy.)
- Dream global; go local. Sell to your hometown bookstores.
- Attend and/or exhibit at comics conventions. Speak on a panel or offer a workshop at a comics convention. For that matter, organize your own convention.
- Launch your website. Join an online portfolio gallery. Kick off a blog. Tweet. Do a podcast. Obviously, create your webcomic; sell and distribute it ASAP online.

"Hey, I'm drawing comics for a living," he smiles. "You could say, 'right place, right time'—which would be true—but had I not put the product out there to begin with, no specific time or place would have mattered."

GRAPHIC NOVELS

As I say previously, a graphic novel tops out with a rich mix of design-related projects. It's a gig that tips all your hats: Writer. Penciller (illustrator). Colorist. Inker. Letterer. Layout artist. Designer. Editor. Publisher. Promoter. You certainly don't have to do it all, but mix or match, the job *will* keep you busy.

You can always approach publishers (both mainstream and indies) and create under their brand. You can sell to comic book shops. This is what's called the *direct market*, and it's the dominant distribution and retail network for North American comic books. You could aim high and try to snag a grant or snare an agent.

You can do it yourself: perhaps create a feature for an online magazine or serialize on your blog or website. Maybe you are compelled to produce your own e-magazine. However, do you *want* to run the whole show? Producing an entire magazine is a massive undertaking—not highly recommended for the faint of art. However, modern self-publishing *is* convenient and affordable. But that's

SIDELINES

Currently, animation as a genre of sequence design is flourishing—a real *reel* renaissance. The old school of stop-motion, claymation, and traditional cel animation has never gone away. Of course, computer animation and general CGI (computer generated imagery) is smack in the middle of the sprocket.

There are opportunities in game design, hardware and software, plus films and television (special effects, commercials, programming). Sequence designers are also finding work in print and in the fine arts.

Publishers are enthusiastically tapping into the burgeoning world of apps, digital books, and cards (as ebooks and ecards, obviously), as well as online magazines and news reporting.

Designers considering alternate jobs in this field might explore careers as editors, web software and app designers, typographers, distributors, or even publishers (but do see my previously mentioned comments). Last, but definitely not least, think about teaching (read chapter 18). Designers who can teach graphic storytelling or animation, game and character design, or special effects are hot commodities.

still not saying that it's *easy*. Of course, tap into social media (essentially word of mouth on steroids and another revolution in marketing and promotion) to get the words out.

If "just" getting your opus to print is your goal, twenty-first-century technology is certainly on your side. Modern photocopiers and general *print on demand* (POD) capabilities make self-publishing a viable vision.

RIGHT ON POINT

(PROFESSIONAL VIEWPOINTS IN 50 WORDS OR LESS)

I think about it; maybe sleep on it and wait for something to inspire me. Sometimes it comes together in the first twenty minutes; sometimes it takes a day or so. One idea evolves into another; you might stumble upon it in the middle of the process.

—Chris Haughton

If you are going to be an image-maker, you need to make images for people to interact with—on paper, the web, Facebook, tablets, Tumbler, Instagram, etc., not to mention upcoming technology (like the new wave of web comics coming soon).

—Brian Fencl

I think it's the duty of the artist to be more than a creator of images. It helps to be conscious of what the client is thinking about, the image she wants to convey, and the limits of the chosen style within what the client wants to accomplish.

—Mike Quon

You need to keep your mind open just wide enough to let the interesting stuff in. Don't worry about what is trendy or hot. Follow your intuition for the solution of each project.

—Ilene Winn-Lederer

CHAPTER 12

MAGAZINES, NEWSPAPERS, BOOKS

Remember that magazine, newspaper, and book publishers don't ask much—only that it's absolutely clear you know how to design for their product. No sweat, right?

—Melvin Potts

IS PRINT DEAD?

Well, if you're reading these words by turning a page, obviously it ain't dead yet. That's not to ignore the obvious—nor the handwriting on the south wall of the *New York Times* Building—but let's uh, turn the page and look at the following markets with an open mind and cautiously optimistic outlook.

MAGS

How many different types of magazines are there?

We can approach this from an historic angle and accurately state that the golden era of the magazine is, after all, *ancient* history. You could cite the numbers and point to the hard reality that (at least, as I write this) magazine newsstand sales have been crashing while digital circulation is, to put it mildly, soaring.

Plummet. Drop. Fall. Crash. *Wipe Out*? You're hearing all these words (and more) connected to another word: sales. Make that two words, actually: newsstand sales. I am not a scaremonger; I'm only doing some research and reporting facts. By the way, single copy sales indicate a magazine's popularity. They are a traditional benchmark in this industry and are the key factor magazine publishers consider when establishing ad rates. At the same time, I am reading that *current* overall circulation has balanced out, due to subscriptions and strong online sales.

Rather than being an alarmist, one could quit sucking on the lemons and offer the lemonade of heroic optimism. New magazines are still starting up and taking off. It looks like magazines are, *at least*, doing better than newspapers, and fresh form factors—the iPad, for instance—offer interesting opportunities and revitalized hope. Along those lines, modern technology is prompting publishers to push the envelope of subscriptions, explore branding and licensing, tinker with design formats both online and in print, examine diversification, and explore innovative business models.

Maybe the better answer to my original question is that there are only two types of magazines in any platform: those that take your designs and those that don't.

TYPECAST

Yes, magazine circulation looks to be on life support, or even flatlining, as readers migrate online and advertising bucks are thrown at the Internet. But the pool of the magazine market is still wide and deep, and the depth of basic categories remains constant no matter how you swim to the content.

The following venues are real; the titles are all fictional. You'll find local and regional publications: *Ohio Every Second, Yellow Springs Today*; trade journals: *Velcro World, Industrial Strength*; general audience or consumer periodicals: *American Laughstyles*; special interest magazines: *Spelunking Gerbil*,

Contemporary Antiques, *Starting to Stop*; and in-house or company organs: *Inside This Company*.

ZINES OF THE TIMES

Online, oft called digital, magazines are, obviously, produced on the web. These serials may be called *webzines* ("web magazine") and I have seen the tags *cyberzine* and *e-magazine* also in use, as well as various alternative spellings in play. There are *e-zines*—smaller forums or newsletters that could also go out via email—and blogs, as well as online newspapers that plainly tap into the magazine format.

As mentioned previously, the big fish are diving into the waters online and offering digital variants of their print titles in both HTML—which mirrors conventional web pages—and Flash versions, which boast fancier graphics, navigation, and interactivity.

As with print publications, online magazines are directed to a particular reader. And like their print counterparts, these Sisters of the Immaculate Pixel are bellwethers of society and culture; academia, science, and politics; as well as first alerts for trade or industry.

THE LOOK . . .

Different magazines require different kinds of design. For example, even though the *Saturday Evening Post* has been currently reconfigured for today's demographics, you won't find the unorthodox aesthetic of *Juxtapoz* within the pages of the *Post*; it simply wouldn't mesh with a more conservative audience.

Every magazine—digital or analog—has its own editorial tone and visual tenor. There will be magazines (consumer, special, and general interest publications) that lean toward a conceptual approach. Some periodicals, such as regional and trade magazines, will be journalistic in nature.

Some publications ostensibly focus on a particular genre, but really offer a much wider palette; *Rolling Stone* comes to mind here. Safer to say that design, art, and text must zestfully blend together to consistently enhance the flavor of the magazine and appeal to the general, but particular, tastes of the readers.

. . . AND FEEL

A magazine must establish a consistent, distinctive look. Its style—the "tone"—should be evident at first glance. When you go to the library, look at all the recent issues available. At the bookstore explore every magazine displayed within a particular category. Consider editorial content; think about the subject matter. Is the magazine conservative or progressive? Hip or traditional? Is it politically left or right? Does it specialize in hard-hitting exposés or typically feature lighter stories on food, travel, or fashion?

At the same time, study both illustrations and photography. Are the visuals appropriate? Are the art and photography conceptual or realistic?

Compare any two magazines. Take *Automobile* and *Sports Illustrated*, for example. You should instantly get a sharp impression of what these periodicals are all about—and how they utilize design to directly address a target audience. If you don't (and it doesn't), the magazine is in trouble (or will be).

WHAT MAGAZINES NEED

Design, copy, art (illustration and photography), and ads share the pages of any magazine. To varying degrees, a magazine may employ designers, photographers, and illustrators; stylists (hair, food, and fashion); prop builders, prop masters, and model makers; production artists; typographers and calligraphers; editors and copyeditors, as well as copywriters; and cartoonists.

The Internet has certainly morphed or bumped off the above job descriptions; but as a designer for magazines, you just may be hands-on for any or all job-related tasks. Back in the day, a tight schedule was simply business as usual. In our Internet era, this frame of reference is hyper-accelerated, and you still must deliver at the highest quality, in whatever time given.

Freelancers are usually called in when the workload is heavy: versatility, speed, and accuracy are critical. If you can create strong informational graphics and lay out an elegant page with lots of text and other components, you could be in high demand. You should have a thorough knowledge of page-layout software and should use keyboard commands automatically. "Your initial job with a company will let them know how efficiently you work," June Edwards says. "Dependable and talented freelancers will receive many repeat calls, and eventually can be selective and only take the most rewarding jobs."

RESEARCHING THE MARKET

How to find out if a magazine accepts freelance design? Looking to work on the design staff? This homework has never been easier. First, simply open your eyes: surf the Internet and browse the library and bookstore.

Check the masthead. Read credits and bios; explore what kind of work is done by staffers or contributors. Make contact. Email, call, or, yes, even write a note to the folks at the creative helm—editors, art or design directors, the art staff—and simply ask.

Consult references like the annual *Artist's & Graphic Designer's Market*. Scour creative annuals and trade magazines. Pore over content, interviews, promotions, and advertising. Look for any client contact info to cull an informal catalog of potential business this way. Another plus—looking at all this design and studying all these designers will be very inspirational.

RECON

Remember that you're not at the public library, but you shouldn't have any trouble doing some research in any bookstore (or newsstand) where browsing is welcome and accepted.

The goal is to discreetly jot down information about a new publication. Take a moment to clear this with the clerk or owner beforehand. Introduce yourself, state your purpose, and express your thanks.

And speaking of which, listings of magazines can be found at most libraries. Consult the following: *Artist's & Graphic Designer's Market, Writer's Market, The Standard Periodical Directory, Gebbie Press-All-In-One-Directory, Gale Directory of Publications and Broadcast Media, Ulrich's Periodicals Directory*, and the Standard Rate & Data Service (SRDS).

Here are some publications that cover the magazine industry: *HOW, FOLIO, Print,* and *Graphis; Advertising Age, Adweek,* and *Communication Arts.* It would also be worth your while to research the classic but, alas, defunct *U&lc* (Upper and Lower Case) and *STEP Inside Design.*

Research contacts and addresses for potential customers from these listings.

THE APPROACH

Most magazines will have an art director or creative director (perhaps this person is called the design director). Depending on the size of the publication, there may be someone with the title of *associate* art director or *assistant* creative director. They'll obviously have an editor or publisher, often one and the same person. Dope out who reviews art submissions and send to the big Lebowski.

If you're sending some kind of hard copy (or a physical portfolio) and you want it back, include an SASE (or a prepaid Fed Ex shipping label) for its return. If not, leave it (and trust the disposition of your submission to your contact). It will get filed, tossed, or tacked.

Don't send an unsolicited portfolio (returnable or otherwise). It bears repeating: Do your homework and establish the appropriate contact, with a specific name plus the correct department. Some active research—a phone call or email—should do the trick.

If you cannot come up with a name (perhaps the position or its occupant is in transition), you could label your stuff ATTENTION: DESIGN DIRECTOR (or DESIGN DEPARTMENT) or DESIGN BUYER (or ART BUYER). At the outset, if you have no recourse, this is okay, but it is not highly recommended. When you want to establish a personal connection and maintain communications, make it a priority to get the name of the art buyer as soon as possible.

STARTING BLOCK

Where to begin? Which type of magazine would be good to start with? Think about the publications you enjoy most. Browse around, look all over, then dream a little—visualize where you'd like to work with whom you'd love to work.

It can be argued that there is no "best" place for the beginner to start, that all the markets are good. Hey, if you're good, why not start right at the top? But trying to start your freelance career at *Time* will probably be like kissing the business end of a shark—best of luck to you, mate.

We could recommend a conservative gambit. Start with local periodicals; work your way up to lesser-known mags, and eventually to larger or more prestigious publications. Begin with small staffs, operations where you won't get lost or mired in the red tape of the big companies. Work at the modest end of the scale. Initially accept low fees to get published credits and gradually breaststroke up to the churning frenzy of Shark Week.

VARIETY

Don't limit your submissions to one type of magazine, or worse yet, one magazine only. Approach as many magazines as you have a mind to, as many as you can.

Freelancing is a numbers game. Your livelihood depends on the bigger picture of how much you sell. In all likelihood, one client (or one type of client) won't support or sustain your business. The term "exclusivity" is pretty much inoperative in this market. Your style must meet the needs of a variety of magazines if you're to succeed here.

GOING POSTAL

Art directors are incredibly busy people, so receiving samples through the mail will probably *not* be a rather efficient use of their time. I say *probably*, because there may be those art directors who prefer to initially review your actual work in their hands. *Maybe*. But I will bet that most art directors are inundated with submissions from all angles and aren't plowing through piles of actual portfolios stacking up on their desks.

Safer to say, the initial review of your work will be via your website, blog, or portfolio gallery. This has everything to do with time, energy, and finances. It's much cheaper and easier and far more time-efficient.

If something clicks, you might be asked to send a follow-up whatever. If you're local, you may be requested to come in, bring your book; perhaps discuss a bona fide assignment. Of course, there are no guarantees you're going to get a job out of this communication, but that's called doing business.

ORGANIZATIONS

Professional organizations you might join are Graphic Artists Guild, Society of Publication Designers, or American Institute of Graphic Arts (AIGA). You could consult the City and Regional Magazine Association (CRMA), the Society of Photographers and Artists Representatives Inc. (SPAR), the Society of Typographic Arts (STA), and your local art directors club.

THE NEWS

Many cities are losing the daily newspaper, as we once knew it. As newspaper operations close, scale back, or change business and presentation models, it's evident that this market is changing and business is down. These comments are understatements to some analysts and complex exaggerations to others.

Blame it on the economy and/or digital media, but don't sound the death knoll or break out your black duds quite yet. Are you a veritable news junky who feeds a daily fix at the local library? Or maybe you're just someone who enjoys perusing the *Sunday Times* over a lazy brunch. Whatever your habit (and there are far worse addictions), folks want—still need—to get the news, and journalists still get out—want to report—the stories. But how those bulletins break and get delivered is at the root of the real conundrum.

SAVING TREES

On the web, news sites and news apps for mobile devices are revolutionizing news delivery and consumption. Ad revenues are migrating to the web. But you hardly need me to tell you all that, or how. I made the statement previously that newspapers are faring worse than magazines and the hard reality of the eight-hundred-pound digital gorilla in the newsroom is as clear as black and white.

Technology will ultimately write the headline with a happy ending dependent on what side of the story you're on. I myself optimistically adhere to an earlier sentiment that embracing new-generation opportunities may actually offer revitalized hope for a challenged market. I don't think it matters much if management failed to see (or ignored) the writing on the screen. Will the evolution of technology give literal meaning to the old ink-stained declaration of "Stop the Presses"? Perhaps. But I'm betting that the news simply survives through innovation and a different business protocol.

INSIDE STORY

Once again, I'm back to this basic train of thought: there will only be two types of newspapers: those that embrace your design aesthetic and those that don't. Makes it easy, doesn't it?

But of course, you might just engineer a modest career track: begin with a community newsletter, then work your way up to the local level and beyond. Start with small-staff operations working at the modest publications. You may have to accept low fees for published credits. Rack up experience and gradually climb the ladder. Consider pro bono; think about doing a few "freebies," as long as these loss leaders are not conducted with highly capitalized, major-market players. Understand the arrangement and make sure there is a measurable benefit from giving away your work (and refer to the index for more information on pro bono throughout this book).

I can't say that *all* roads lead to the Internet, but it looks like we're getting there, and when in Rome . . . With print formats currently offering a bumpy career ride, it may be easier to market your design services—full-time or freelance—to web newspapers (and magazines). But don't write off the print market quite yet.

Regardless of format, content will be the wild card, Ace. You're going to find neighborhood newsletters, local and regional news (*Dayton Daily News*), big-city newspapers with national circulation (like the *Times*), newspapers with a national scope (*USA Today*), tabloids (the *Enquirer*), plus general or special interest newspapers (*Funny Times*.) Of note: online news services, like The *Daily Dot*, which, by the way, bills itself as the paper of record for the web, the Internet's community newspaper.

Wrangling the pages of any news site or newspaper you will find, as Robert Zimmerman tells us, "extremely busy people working on very tight deadlines. They do not want to be guessing as to style. They'll hand pick the person who best suits the assignment. Whatever it is you do best, that is what you should offer."

NAME THAT TONE

The basic structure of a newspaper—digital or traditional—doesn't really vary much from one to another. Because the primary function of a newspaper is to report some kind of news, even the *New York Times* and the *National Enquirer* are still editorial sisters under the skin. Okay, I'm snickering, too, but without comparing apples and oranges, do their websites honestly look all that terribly different?

Compare two newspapers (coming down to earth somewhat, the *Washington Post* and the New York *Daily News*, for instance) to contrast those qualities that make each publication unique and individual. Determine a newspaper's philosophical content and political position. Analyze subject matter while examining writing style. Do you agree with the editorial stance?

Evaluate all the visual aspects—design, illustration and photography, info graphics . . . is the art conceptual or straightforward? Do design, graphics, and copy elegantly harmonize to better convey content? In your evaluation, does the design succeed here?

Tom Graham says, "I think it is important to objectively analyze the look a newspaper is currently printing. Chances are, they will not stray far afield from that look. If what you see really turns you on, and you feel you would fit right in—maybe even do it better—then proceed."

SKILLS FOR NEWSPAPERS

Copy, photography, and art share the pages of the newspaper or news site. You'll be working as a page designer and production artist (if the position is not filled by staff). Depending on the size of the operation, you may be doing graphics as necessary. This could include illustration and photography; typography and calligraphy; informational graphics (maps, charts, and diagrams); maybe some project research and development; perhaps a bit of writing even. Online, these job descriptions may morph or blend out of necessity and economics.

Way back in the day, black-and-white was the bread-and-butter of newspaper illustration, but you can thank the influence of *USA Today* (and the computer) for the explosion of color as we know it in the newspaper industry. However, "retro" (the large dot, halftone look, including that intentionally off register thing) is popular. Black-and-white imagery abides.

Staff designers will handle the daily grind—probably the fast-breaking stuff and extremely tight deadlines, of course. But another side of that coin is that late-breaking jobs *are* often assigned to those freelancers with a reputation for dispatching short turnarounds under high pressure, especially in an overload situation. When there's way too much on the drafting table, reliable freelance designers will be brought in to relieve the stress and strain. Features or magazine sections that are planned well in advance of publication (and most likely dealing with upcoming events, ongoing trends, or timely ideas) also are freelance possibilities.

SEND IT TO ME

Do you send samples to the editor or the art director? As a general rule of thumb, you may want to send samples to the art director or design director, unless instructed otherwise. The "unless instructed otherwise" is the key, that it's quite okay to submit samples to the editor, publisher, or a designated staff contact.

CHECKING IT OUT

To find out if a newspaper accepts freelance work? Call, email, or simply ask the art or design director (or staff). Consult *Editor & Publisher* (www.editorandpublisher.com). *E & P* is "the authoritative journal covering all aspects of the newspaper industry, including business, newsroom, advertising, circulation, marketing, technology, online and syndicates."

You could contact The Society for News Design. The SND (www.snd.org) is an "international organization for news media professionals and visual communicators [whose mission is to] enhance communication around the world through excellence in visual journalism."

Also consult *Artist's & Graphic Designer's Market*, *Writer's Market*, *Gale Directory of Publications*, and *Columbia Journalism Review*.

The editor and publisher are one and the same person at some newspapers and news sites, especially at the smaller ones. Likewise, small operations may not have an art director. Maybe job titles and administrative responsibilities are coordinated, shared, or rotated amongst staff members. A chief designer acts as art director. The assigning editor also designs. Establish the appropriate contact at the newspaper by doing your homework. As said before, don't forward a portfolio unless you have a specific name or know the correct department accepting submissions.

BY THE BOOK

Forgive the clichéd heading. It was so obviously *obvious*, I fearlessly gave into the inevitable. The book market offers a rich and rewarding arena to practice your craft. To begin, let's discuss conventional differences between traditional trade books, textbooks, and mass-market books. According to scholarly glossaries, trade books are "books intended for the general public, and marketed through bookstores and to libraries, as distinct from textbooks, subscription books, etc." A textbook is "a book used for the study of a particular subject; a manual of instruction."

Textbooks are educational materials sold directly to educational institutions. Trade books are sold at retail and appeal to a select audience. They can be scholarly works or professional titles, special interest books, instructional manuals, biographies, serious fiction, larger format books, cookbooks, or juveniles (often, but not necessarily with a teaching motive).

Mass-market books are sold at newsstands or bookstores and other retail outlets and are produced in high volumes at lower costs (to hopefully generate big sales). These books are more commercial looking and created to appeal to a large audience. Mysteries, spy novels, gothics, fantasy and science fiction, and historical and modern romance novels all fall into the mass-market category.

EEEEEE, BOOKS!

An electronic book is a book in digital format. Well, that was plain enough. What makes for a good ebook? The same stuff that makes for a compelling read in hard copy applies to ebooks—distinctive, interesting content.

Mobility, availability, shelf-life, ease of use—ebooks create a delightful reading experience for couch potatoes and hot trottin' taters on the go. Devices like Amazon's Kindle, Barnes & Noble's Nook, Canada's Kobo, and of course, the Mac Daddy of them all—the iPad—are driving booming ebook sales off the charts.

The obligatory turf wars (embodied by proprietary hardware and software like Apple's exclusive app for ebooks called iBooks and its sister sales service, the iBookstore) led to new models of production, cost, sales, and distribution; not to mention the art of navigating the business deal for a new sales direction. Throw in the hot button issue of Digital Rights Management, and all this builds a platform that becomes all the more interesting for consumers and creators alike.

IN THE HOUSE

A publishing organization, with its various subsidiaries and divisions, is called a "house." Publishing houses can publish several genres. Many have various specialized imprints. Imprints can range from, let's say, cookbooks to spiritual non-fiction, from sports books to children's and cartoon books.

PLEASE ALLOW ME TO INTRODUCE MYSELF

What is the best way to break into this market? Let's assume you've looked at books. You've done your research by patronizing the library and the bookstores, browsing the newsstand, visiting schools, and attending trade exhibits. You've studied covers, interior layouts, internal illustrations, and technical drawings. You've analyzed book design—compared trade books and textbooks, children's books and adult titles, and examined the mass-market paperbacks. You've located addresses, names, and phone numbers and are ready to mail your promotional pieces.

What—and how—to send? "I would definitely advise you not use snail mail to send samples of your work for the publisher to keep on file," says Vicki Vandeventer, "unless of course it's a promotional piece designed to get some extra attention. I absolutely think that the best contact method is email. I would include a brief introduction in your message with a link to your website, which should contain a résumé or bio. You can also attach a PDF file of a few appropriate work samples to your email," she says, "but as an art director myself, I really want to study a designer's website."

What you show or send obviously must address your strengths—art directors generally want to work with specialists. Publishing credits can add credibility and parallel experience is a plus; actually, any work that even remotely resembles publishing responsibilities can only help. Follow up with a phone call or email at some point shortly thereafter. Ask if they'd like to see more or talk further. Perhaps they'd like to meet in person and see more of your work in hand?

It breaks down to this: determine where you fit in; then get your marketing and self-promotion in gear. And while it never hurts for you to have a spiffy interview outfit hanging at the ready (and to polish your in-person routine), Vandeventer confesses that (at her staff gig) she actually never uses the phone on her desk. She'll speak with a freelance designer occasionally on her cell, but all communication with outside vendors, including printers, is accomplished through email. "It works great, and I really think it's the most efficient way to communicate. You automatically have a record of everything that's discussed, which often comes in handy down the road."

COUNTERPOINT

But here we should also listen to Kristine Putt, who says, "Many freelance designers operate under the notion that they can communicate with clients *strictly* via email or social media. A friend of mine, another designer, tells me, 'If I need to talk to a client on the phone, I don't want their business.' I don't believe this attitude is smart freelance–business management.

Putt feels that you can't force clients into communicating with you solely on your terms and still expect to be appreciated. "You need to be flexible and meet customers on their terms. Some people simply prefer to discuss projects with their designer via phone. If you want their business, you need to make it easy for people to connect with you, and they will love you for it and refer you to their colleagues."

The outcome? Telephone and in-person meetings may create a solid, more intimate relationship between the designer and client, establishing a personal connection that reduces the chances of conflict and chaos.

WHOM TO CONTACT

Hmm . . . editor or art director? Research, research, research (see our sidebar later in this chapter titled "House Hunting"). If you can't initially find the person's name, dig deeper: send emails, make calls—ask questions. Find out who accepts submissions and ask specifically for that person's name, title (editor, submissions editor, art director, etc.) and department. Get the correct spelling of anything and everything.

The editor probably has more control than the art or design director. But the art mafia may be more supportive of your cause, and dealing with them (if they like your work) may be easier. In general, send an art submission to the art director.

LOCAL FIRST?

Although unlikely, there may not be a publisher in your area and you'll need to cast your net out wide. But homegrown is neither completely necessary nor mandatory, and working with "out-of-towners" is common practice, certainly these days. But I always feel it is best to start locally—simply because, hey, you live here, right?

If nothing else, your shot at person-to-person, live contact and interaction is more feasible. And there is the thinking that publishers may try new or inexperienced people exactly *because* of their accessibility. But regardless, as a stranger, newcomer, or unknown quantity, if soliciting publishers with your work anywhere and everywhere, make sure you offer experience and chops that the publisher needs.

BOOKED SOLID

Other than books, what do publishers produce that might need freelance help? Publishers use freelancers for illustration (on jackets and covers, as well as text), design, in production and technical areas (such as interior layouts for book dummies), as photographers, stylists, and model makers.

Publishers need freelancers to create ads, direct mail, and promotional pieces. Freelancers will also work on newsletters, brochures and catalogs, and point-of-purchase displays. Many book publishers also produce activities (coloring books, for instance), educational aids (flash cards), and games and posters that provide educational opportunities.

You will find that most publishers use freelance help, especially the larger houses. The easiest way to verify this is to contact an art director and ask. "I'd recommend sending an email instead of calling," Vandeventer tells you. "The in-house design staff at a publishing company is much smaller today than it used to be. The good news is that freelancers are used extensively, both for

HOUSE HUNTING (DIRECTORIES, ORGANIZATIONS, TRADE MAGAZINES)

How do you locate those publishers that best suit your talents? You can always approach a publisher directly and request a catalog. Look for work that resonates with you—chances are, if you like their work, they'll like yours.

"But," as Vandeventer tells us, "the best way to do research on publishers is to look online. All publishers have a company website these days."

You can always haunt the library and the bookstore. But Vandeventer points out that it may not be so easy to find a big bookstore and wander around anymore. "However," she says, "you can basically do that online via Amazon; it's a great resource."

There are various directories and publications you can scour for possible contacts and contact information. Explore the *Literary Market Place (LMP)*. Research *Writer's Market; Novel & Short Story Writer's Market; Poet's Market*; and *Artist's & Graphic Designer's Market*. Examine *Publishers Weekly; Writer's Digest; Print; Communication Arts; HOW*; and *Graphis*. Write to the Children's Book Council.

Here are some good links to publishing organizations:

▶ Book Industry Guild of New York (formerly Book Binders Guild of New York), www.bookindustryguildofny.org

▶ Bookbuilders of Boston, www.bbboston.org

▶ Midwest Publishing Association (formerly Chicago Book Clinic), www.chicagobookclinic.org

▶ Publishing Professionals Network, www.pubpronetwork.org

▶ Association of American University Presses (AAUP), www.aaupnet.org

▶ Publishers Marketplace, www.publishersmarketplace.com

▶ Society for Scholarly Publishing, www.sspnet.org

Check out your local Art Directors Club. Other organizations you may want to join, network with, or simply be aware of might be the Graphic Artists Guild, and/or the American Institute of Graphic Arts (GAG and AIGA boast local chapters and a national membership); the Society of Children's Book Writers and Illustrators; Guild of Book Workers; Boston Book Festival group.

By the way, the Publishing Professionals Network mentioned above is a non-profit organization founded as Bookbuilders West, and rechartered as PPN in 2012 to "reflect the changing nature of long-form content publishing and embrace all the partnerships that exist within our industry [and to provide] educational resources and opportunities for all individuals involved in book and book-related publishing." Talking point: is this change in monicker a handwriting-on-the-wall scenario, anyone?

design (and illustration). The bad news, possibly, is that no one has time to talk on the phone with prospective freelancers. But if you email something to an art director, it will definitely get looked at."

Digital submissions are the way to go. And this definitely makes it easy to work long distance with a publisher. Usually, deadlines are reasonable to generous in book publishing, and book projects are typically extended affairs—rarely rushed into, seldom rushed through.

The house publishes many books, and evaluates far more than ever see print. A manuscript may be tied up for two months or more while it is reviewed and evaluated by any number of people before a decision to publish is made. Matching the appropriate designer with the right project is done thoughtfully and over time. Electronic and online submissions dovetail right into the work schedule of an extremely careful, but exceedingly busy, art director.

JOBS FOR DESIGNERS

There is not a large market in *all* cities for book designers, but it does exist. However, it's a toss up whether publishers prefer their designers to be local, if not in-house. And when they do look out of town, they may prefer to hire freelancers from big publishing centers (New York, Boston, and Chicago).

INSIDE JOB

Any designer can design covers, but the interior is a specialized area and requires specific training (often on-the-job). A design studio may create a cover, but it will usually be the specialist—the book designer—who designs the interior.

Does a house find it preferable to hire one book designer to do both cover and interior? Vandeventer weighs in here: "I've never found that a publisher actually *prefers* to hire one designer for both the cover and interior," she says. "I've always thought that was unfortunate, but maybe that's specific to the education market, where function can dominate form and budgets are minimal.

"These days, simple book interiors are often template-based; the typesetter just follows the template. This is obviously not ideal and is not the case for books that contain a lot of art, but it's the norm in scholarly publishing at the university level. Elementary, high school, and college textbooks are more complex and are more likely to be individually designed.

"In my experience, selecting a cover designer will often involve the marketing department, and someone who specializes in covers is often chosen."

Yes, the big publishing centers employ a lot of book designers who work with all the major publishers. "But I don't think you need to live in a big publishing center or even a major city to make it as a freelance book designer," Vandeventer says. "I do think you need to have experience working at a publishing company or two to be taken seriously. That should prove that you know what you're doing, and it will also give you a lot of good contacts in the publishing business."

INTRODUCTION

For your introduction, focus on examples of page design where typography is a crucial design element, and present this body of work to the appropriate art directors or editors. Actual, produced work will be best or better, but bright ideas and enthusiasm may be appreciated. However, keep in mind that smarts coupled with knowledge and experience is what the publisher needs and demands.

A designer—one with a good education (let's say a BFA with graphic design concentration)—qualifies to be a book designer at an entry level. Publishers will only use freelancers in book design if they have a lot of experience. You may only be able to learn book design by working on staff at a publishing house; otherwise your design work could possibly be limited to covers.

RIGHT ON POINT

(PROFESSIONAL VIEWPOINTS IN 50 WORDS OR LESS)

Address the needs of your marketplace. Accept the fact that you won't get the big money or high-profile work (*Time, Esquire,* etc.) right away. Get exposure, but more importantly, explore your media and the way you see the world.

—Sam Viviano

Concentrate on a standard of excellence and keep it up. It doesn't matter which media you work in.

—Bill Mayer

Curiosity—I think it is the most important quality you need to succeed in this marketplace. If you aren't endlessly curious, wanting to know how to do things and how things work, you might get frustrated by how quickly this industry can change.

—Nadine Gilden

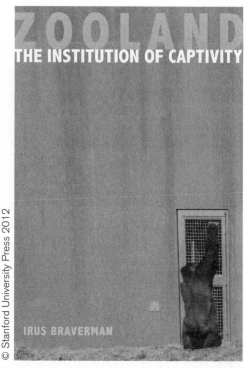

© Stanford University Press 2012

CHAPTER 13

WORKING WITH
AD AGENCIES

After twenty-five years of working for a large advertising art studio and preparing myself for a year or so, I announced that I was freelancing. The transition was fairly easy since my employer had encouraged me to meet and deal with clients.

–Paul Melia

IS AD ALL THERE IS?

What does an advertising agency do? That depends upon the agency, of course, because no two agencies are alike. In general, advertising agencies solve marketing problems by communicating what the client wants (and needs) his market to know.

To do this, ad agencies develop copy and appropriate graphics for web-based, multimedia, and interactive resources; marketing *collateral* (the collection of media propping up product sales or client service); newspaper ads, radio, and TV campaigns. They create: lettering, logos, and branding; signage and billboards; packaging and product development; film and audiovisuals; sales catalogs, brochures, literature, and direct mail; book and magazine design; public relations to market research; internal corporate communications; sales and channel marketing; and social media marketing and promotion.

A full-service agency is a multi-media agency that, as the term implies, does it all—broadcast, print, and online. A majority of agencies make this claim, but few perform equally well in all areas.

APPLY WITHIN

Small ad agencies sometimes require a great deal of freelance help. Big agencies may use freelancers only when staff is on leave or when they have an overflow of work. Good freelancers often fulfill design and production needs, but you may find that the "fun stuff" stays in-house while the tedious "grunt work" goes to the independent contractors.

In a large city, many agencies rely on good freelance help. In smaller towns, not only are independent contractors called when a "special look" is needed, but when the regular staff is on vacation, sick leave, maternity leave, or if the agency gets a temporary overflow of work. For instance, around the Christmas holidays, an agency with many retail clients may be inundated with work—freelancers may be called in to help through this busy season (obviously, when the holidays pass, work levels revert to normal and extra assistance may no longer be needed).

I am told that there is also a trend in smaller agencies to become "virtual"—i.e., they maintain a small core staff, and use contractors or independents to provide nearly all creative and production work. "This shift," says Deborah Budd, "has been enabled by wireless technology and 'the cloud,' so agency staff may work seamlessly with remote employees and clients over the Internet."

FINDING SUITABLE AGENCIES

In the age of the Internet, knowing what a particular agency does (and who its clients are) won't take much digging. First, you network. Check out the Internet—this is an enormous resource for finding suitable agencies. Be sure to explore agency websites, including their Facebook, Google+, LinkedIn, Twitter, Pinterest, and other social media pages. Furthermore, you could phone (or visit) the chamber of commerce and Better Business Bureau for information about local agencies. Talk to your colleagues, check with printers; touch base with businesses that advertise (and isn't that everybody?). Ask around; get as much background information about the local advertising scene as you can.

The next step is to contact the agencies. Again, begin online. If you can't find what you need on an agency's website, you could call them. You don't even have to ask for the art director initially; talk to the receptionist. If he or she doesn't have the answers you need, you'll be directed to someone who does. Simply ask, "What are your specialties? Can or do you use freelancers? In what capacity?"

Remember the three distinct virtues when selling yourself: be persistent, be polite, be positive. If your communication skills are professional, you shouldn't have any problems. You'll find most people are friendly and helpful. Robert Zimmerman agrees and says, "I would suggest a fourth virtue (even though this truism doesn't contain the letter P): do consistent, excellent work." He's right. Without good stuff, persistence may be deemed annoying, politeness only gets you in and out the door, and being positive won't compensate for quality.

On the website, you'll be able to see the agency's book—and all the work that snagged all those awards last year. See what the different agencies are doing, then make up your own mind. Once you evaluate the nature (and caliber) of their product, plus the measure of their clients, some decisions will be made for you. But remember, ultimately, someone at the agency—usually the creative director or art director—will determine whether *your* talents suit *their* needs. However it works out, make sure you're aware of the players first so that you can get into the game.

ADVERTISING AGENCIES VERSUS PUBLIC RELATIONS FIRMS

What's the difference between an ad agency and a public relations firm? Public relations firms assist clients by increasing public awareness of their clients' existence, presenting a new image, or even polishing a tarnished reputation.

PR firms attempt to keep clients in the limelight with reportage (reporting news online, for the press and broadcast media) and interviews, lectures, events, book signings, and autograph sessions. They'll even *create* media events and publicity stunts. They may also handle social media marketing, which could be an opportunity for a young designer. The hopefully high profile created by a PR firm helps position a client favorably in his or her particular market, works to counteract negative publicity, or establishes a new career direction for that client.

Often, assignments from PR firms parallel those of ad agencies. For example, public relations firms produce "indirect advertising." Since the full-time staff usually concentrates on marketing research and consulting with clients (and generally don't have art departments), PR firms may be good places to get work and would be more likely to use freelance designers. And Deborah Budd points out that since many agencies partner with PR firms, rather than offer PR services themselves, PR firms can also be a direct network to ad agencies or design studios.

DO TELL

How to tell if an ad agency works with freelancers? How do you know when they *need* one? It might depend on the size of the agency (a large agency doesn't use—or need—as many freelancers as a small one). The answer to both questions is simple: ask them—make inquiries.

It's yin and yang, really. You won't know when they need a freelancer until *they* do. You do the requisite homework; you gather the necessary background info. Your work is out there online. Maybe you've had a shot at showing your book in person. They may share your interest in producing work for the agency. After interacting with them, they certainly have a good idea of your capabilities.

Theo Stephan says you can drop the art director a short note of thanks after a meeting, but a common rule of thumb is, "Don't call them, they'll call you. You don't grovel; no starving artist's war stories. Act successful! Everybody likes working with a winner."

PLAYING THE FIELD

There's at least one art director at every agency, and big agencies often have a number of art directors. The art director may answer to the creative director. Whom do you talk to?

Again: ask. One email or phone call, and you'll know for sure. Don't hesitate to ask the receptionist who the art buyer may be. The more people who know you—or know about your abilities—the better. "The first person to try is the creative director," Michael Wooley, president of Weber Geiger & Kalat Inc, recommends, "but also contact art directors, production artists, copy chiefs, and copywriters." You might also ask about the production manager, who may be responsible for calling in extra freelancers.

Obviously, you should work for as many agencies as reasonably, humanly possible. Get as much work as you can, when you can, where you can, depending on the size of your town and the temperament of the advertising community.

One caveat: it would not be wise to do an assignment for one agency, then go directly to the competition and create work of the exact same creative or

THEY'RE SPECIAL. YOU'RE SPECIAL.

When considering ad agencies, something to think about is whether you should specialize in a certain product area. Use common sense. You know best where your strengths lie. Stay busy, but enjoy what you're doing.

Some agencies find a comfortable niche and stay there, believing that specialized experience allows them to create better work. This can be true, but there is a danger of falling into a rut. This also holds true for the freelancer. Don't limit yourself. More flexibility means a wide variety of assignments; greater assignments mean better money. Keep all available doors open; only specialize if you freelance in a big city that has more than enough work to support your specialty. Flexibility and variety will allow you to gather pollen from a wider range of flowers.

What does an advertising agency mean when it says, for instance, "We specialize in food marketing and pharmaceuticals"? What this says is that the agency's accounts bracket the food industry—from fast food restaurants, food manufacturers, grocery, and wholesalers/retailers—to pharmaceutically oriented clients. You'll need to be familiar with related terminology and visuals, as well as the particular marketing needs and tactics of these clients. Studying several websites can quickly educate you.

Do you enjoy designing whatever is needed to sell chuck roast and carrots? Can you supply five visual metaphors for the effects of stress on decision-making ASAP? Food and pharmaceuticals are lucrative facets of the advertising game. If this is your forté, you'll do well.

conceptual stripe. Don't expect either agency to welcome you back with open arms afterwards. "Agencies typically address confidentiality and restrictions in contracts," Budd says. "If they don't cover restrictions when they hire you, it's a good idea to ask so you are both clear about policies and preferences up front."

And consider that agencies may view each other with some paranoia. Agency "A" might wonder if you share marketing strategies with Agency "B." Ask yourself if there is any conflict of interest—creative or otherwise—between two rival accounts. You may never have to deal with this situation, but be aware that it does exist.

BREAK IN

Agencies use a lot of layout comps (comprehensive sketches of an ad or concept) during client presentations or when pitching an idea to prospective buyers. If you can create a good comp (or thumbnail concepts), including examples of each in your book would be an effective way to break into the market. Use your layout skills to pave the way for bigger, better, and more diverse assignments.

Networking is always smart. Cultivate referrals; drop names. Join the ad club and any organization frequented by local art directors and creative individuals. (Consult the chamber of commerce regarding the names of such associations, meeting places, and times.)

"Consider blogging as a good way to build your online reputation," Budd recommends. "Write about work you do (respecting client confidentiality, of course); ads and design work you like; your influences and design heroes; and industry issues. Promote your blog on LinkedIn, Facebook, and Twitter. Try emailing agencies you want to work for and share your latest blog posts or new work."

CLEVER, CLEVER

Put your self-promotion and marketing plan into action. Establish contacts and then don't let them forget you—follow up; stay in touch! Budd reminds you that if you have the budget, clever direct-mail promotions can also open doors. "Try creating an intriguing mail piece (possibly with a 3D element)," she suggests. "Selectively mail one or two agencies you want to work with each week, and follow up with emails or phone calls asking to meet face to face."

APPROPRIATE SAMPLES

If you want to do advertising work, I wouldn't necessarily mix apples and oranges. The operative word there is "necessarily."

Ad agency art directors won't *necessarily* be interested in your card samples *as* greeting cards, per se. Warm and fuzzy bunnies don't usually sell sports cars. Hmmm . . . are your clever-but-risqué cartoons appropriate for young buyers of refrigerators? Are you seeking a writing gig, too? If so, are those marvelously smart puns good for a hearty snicker about candy bars?

The play is to show how your greeting card material can be developed as a full-blown, marketable ad concept (in context with type) and demonstrate that your work meets the real needs of an agency's clients.

LOCAL TALENT

In advertising, time is essential. How true. It makes sense that local talent may be sought out (perhaps even preferred), especially if you're needed on a regular basis or to meet tight deadlines. But, as Zimmerman points out, "Today, agencies are looking for an exact visual fit for their client. They don't give a hoot where you live."

As an agency's freelance assignments develop very quickly, art directors soon get to know who's good, who's dedicated, who's reliable, and who's available. Location will be a definite non-issue if you offer and routinely demonstrate those skills. Conversely, if you live next door, but can't deliver, you won't rise above the friendly neighbor status.

Be prepared to work remotely through project-management sites or using online file-transfer services. "You may also need to know how to use online conferencing and virtual meeting services," Budd says. "Having current technological skills can only enhance your design skills."

BUYOUTS AND WORK-FOR-HIRE

Buyouts are frequently requested in advertising. In writing your contracts, decline to use this term. State the sale as a package or bundle of specific usage rights that are carefully defined. There is no true industry consensus about the definition of the word, only confusion. The term needs to be defined specifically, and you should include the precise usage rights the client wants to buy.

In a "buyout," the client controls and determines how, when, where, and how often your design can be used. You're invariably forfeiting all rights of ownership and subsequent compensation for continued use, plus you'll have no say in the fate of the work (remember, the buyer owns all reproduction rights).

If you can't negotiate your way out of a buyout, and the client insists on owning all rights despite your best efforts to sell only the rights that are needed, you can:

1. Say no thank you and be prepared to walk away from a bad deal.
2. Accept a trade-off, if you can live with it and if it's to your advantage for the future: is it a good credit to have or a great vehicle for your work? Will it be a dynamite portfolio piece? Is it an entry into a new market? Is the art so specific that you are unlikely to be able to sell it elsewhere after the terms of use expire?
3. Make it worth your while. Remember, the more you sell, the higher the sale should be. Don't be shy or afraid to price accordingly.

The artist should also be aware of the circumstance known as work made for hire. In a nutshell—*and in the eyes of the copyright law*—a work-for-hire contractor effectively becomes an employee without any employee benefits. As the creative's "employer," the client owns the hire and controls the copyright. This is unfair at best, but perfectly legal; the work-for-hire provision robs you of your just due. It is definitely a worst-case scenario and is to be avoided.

Budd weighs in here: "Please note: Work for hire should only apply if a freelancer is hired as a *temporary* employee—e.g., to fill-in for someone on a leave-of-absence, to work regular hours on multiple projects just like a full-time employee.

"Contract language should explain when work for hire applies," she states. "If the freelancer is hired via purchase order for a specific assignment, the freelancer remains a contractor and should be able to dictate terms on copyright."

And do remember: *Full copyright is never transferred except in writing by the designer or artist*—and the designer or artist sets the price as well as the terms of use. You probably don't need us to remind you that, should a PO ask for full buyout, you should negotiate the price accordingly. "Most agencies know about work-for-hire at this point," says Budd. "Any agency that attempts to circumvent copyright law should probably be avoided in future."

But, sigh, this is still the real world, and if your baby is down to her last diaper just when you're offered a work-for-hire contract, you may understandably be tempted to take it. I would never condemn those artists who accept these deals. Don't rally behind any cause if you can't reasonably justify the principle. Just know what you're getting into, and accept the consequences of your decision in the light of your situation.

ORGANIZATIONS AND READING

There is a wealth of material and discussion on the Internet about pricing, ethics, standards, and practices. At the library or bookstore, look for *The Graphic Artists Guild Handbook of Pricing and Ethical Guidelines* (a book that should be on every designer's bookshelf, actually).

Also consult Tad Crawford's *Legal Guide for the Visual Artist* and *Business and Legal Forms for Graphic Designers*. A very old reference book, but still worthy of examination, is the out of print *The Artist's Friendly Legal Guide* (North Light Books).

On a national level, the Graphic Artists Guild has chapters across the country. Many large cities and colleges have local chapters of The American Advertising Federation, The American Marketing Association, or American Institute of Graphic Arts (AIGA). Most cities of modest size have an advertising club, art center, or art forum. Explore memberships in your region or city, and select a few that seem valuable as networking or information resources.

➡

RIGHT ON POINT

(PROFESSIONAL VIEWPOINTS IN 50 WORDS OR LESS)

Agency art directors—they'll say, "Beautiful work, but how can we use it?" So you think, "What's wrong here? It's the art director's job to visualize how a particular style would fit into their work." But it's one of the best pieces of free advice I ever got.

—Mary Thelen

Your ego is on the line. Always. It's part of you; something you created. When it's rejected, it's difficult to keep in mind that it's not you, it's the work that's being rejected. You develop confidence, but in the beginning I had a hard time with that.

—Mary Grace Eubank

You have to convince an art director that she needs you, so demonstrate your creative process to advertising agencies. Convey to the art director an equilibrium of ideas and techniques—your style. The art director wants to pigeonhole you; make it easy for her—emphasize consistency.

—Chris Spollen

© Mega 2014

CHAPTER 14

THE GREETING CARD MARKET

I got an office job—and I hated it. I don't know what possessed me, but I printed up sixteen postcards. And I did it all the wrong way—I had no idea what I was doing. But I knew that anything would be better than working in an office.

—Jennifer Berman

GREETINGS

A point of clarification, folks: in the greeting card industry, a "design" is essentially the same as an "illustration." A finished card design is not *always* about the illustration, of course. Splitting one wild hair, the finished product represents the concept as expressed through the visual.

Let's elaborate a bit here: the term *design* refers to the visual element that accompanies the editorial (the copy) on a card. This artwork may be used for a single purpose—a select card, one page or individual spread in a booklet or calendar. The design may be a basic character study, a particular scene or still life. It could be an abstract composition, a simple pattern or border; perhaps a concept composed entirely of calligraphy or type.

Any medium can be used for a card design. You'll find designs done digitally, of course; prepared in pen or pencil, water-media (including acrylics and gouache), cut paper/fabric collage, and embroidery. A design could also be paper or clay construction or hand tinted photography. It could even be executed entirely in what is termed "finishes"—gold leaf, die cuts, embossing, etc.

THE COMPANY YOU KEEP

Bill Abbott has licensed stateside to greeting card companies like Renaissance, Marian Heath, Pictura USA, and internationally to Hallmark UK and For Art's Sake (Australia). I consulted with this pro on a market segment he says is still financially rewarding, but nonetheless in a period of slow change.

The first item of business we discussed was how a greeting card company chooses the cards it will publish. From my experience, a card company targets production to selected markets, such as the young and trendy in specialty shops or the generally middle-class shoppers at the drugstore. Keeping a deliberate finger on the pulse of current popular culture, card and paper product companies do extensive market research to determine what categories of cards the public wants to send. Pre-market testing determines which visual styles and messages the buying public prefers.

Abbott cautions here that it's critically important to remember one simple fact of life: a greeting card isn't being produced to highlight your art; your art is being used to sell the card. If your art doesn't work within their framework or context, you're barking at the wrong moon.

"Provide card companies with artwork tailor-made to their needs," Abbott says, "and they'll come back to you over and over as a reliable source of good, functional material well-suited to their buying public." Typically, a submission of six to twelve samples is ideal. Too few and the creative decision-makers can't develop a feel for your work; too many becomes unwieldy (considering they've likely received hundreds or even thousands of other submissions that month or even that week).

HOW MANY TYPES OF CARDS ARE THERE?

Basically, card companies produce two types of products: occasion cards for standard holidays and established events (birthdays, graduation, anniversaries, friendship, sympathy) and non-occasion or everyday cards.

Within these two primary lines, look for these general categories: traditional (an established and long-accepted and rather realistic approach); studio (contemporary and sophisticated with biting wit); humorous (also funny, but usually simpler and not as caustic, leaning toward the cartoon); romantic (hearts and flowers, decidedly sentimental); juvenile (appealing to children); cute (adorable characters in charming situations); stylish (a modern and chic look); and alternative (often labeled as edgy, risqué, or provocative).

I've seen statistics that say 80 percent of the card buyers are women, and Abbott points out that the most abundant card-buying demographic reflects women over the age of fifty. "The younger generation tends to be less interested in cards as a form of expression," he says. "Many billions of dollars are still spent on greeting cards each year (over $4 billion sold by Hallmark alone)." For the big picture and some relevant facts and figures, go to the individual websites of the GCA (the Greeting Card Association, as located in the United States, United Kingdom, and Australia).

Abbott will tell you that publishers like Hallmark and American Greetings aren't sitting still, waiting to see what happens with the changing face of their market either—these industry leviathans (as well as their competition) are aggressively seeking new opportunities to bring social expression into the new millennium.

DIGITAL

Often free or provided for a nominal fee, eCards are hardly worth the paper they are printed on (that's a joke, kids). Being serious for just a moment, eCards (electronic greeting cards) are a booming product line for card companies.

This is smart marketing. ECards paint a positive picture of an environmentally conscious greeting card company—and you, by (or buy) association. ECards are also a savvy loss leader attracting viewers to the company's website. The need for artists and animators to create them grows exponentially.

CARD ALTERNATIVES

A note here: the term *alternative* actually has a, well, alternative definition in our present era of environmental awareness. "Alternative"—as in "durable" (as in recycled or recyclable) and "functional"—products (and production processes) are high on the agenda for eco-sensitive companies seeking to utilize resources responsibly. At this writing, as print is not yet dead, this is a good thing.

Let's backtrack, shall we? For a company to sell more *durable* (as in shelf life) and *functional* (as in user friendly, commercially viable) product, their cards must reflect contemporary subject matter and topics of special interest to the card buyer. Current trends and the changing lifestyles of American consumers dictated the development of a genre that stretched the parameters and attacked old taboos: the alternative card.

The alternative market is not so new, now. Almost every company markets so-called alternative cards, so it's safe to say that the label is somewhat out-dated. The alternative card phenomenon gave us cards dealing with left (and right) wing politics; women's rights; gay and lesbian lifestyle; gay marriage; the dysfunctional and/or extended family; the singles' scene, as well as divorce and remarriage (for all orientations).

There are cards helping you cope with everything from receiving poor ser-vice to retiring; celebrating (or commiserating about) your diet; congratulating you on that promotion. You'll find discourses on technophobia, rants on high (or low) finance, and soft testaments mourning the death of a beloved pet. If the subject is somehow relevant and current, chances are you'll now find a card addressing the situation.

Yes, you'll still find the "warm and fuzzy" cards carrying cuddly or bubbly copy, and heartfelt messages of hope. But today's product lines also approach subject matter with new, deeper sensitivities and frank, honest sensibilities. Modern cards also act as small doses of psychotherapy, delivering concerned counseling or gentle expressions of advice, support, and compassion.

Of course, and I say this with a smile, "naughty" sentiments have been a sly staple of our culture and society, as well as the publishing industry (under or over the table), since the birth of publishing. There are practically no limits here; today you'll see cards catering to all manner (and levels) of erotic tastes and practices. I phrased that delicately, didn't I?

TAKE MY CARD, PLEASE

Cards these days are rife with sly wit, biting sarcasm, and decidedly offbeat (even downright strange) humor. They may make you blush, and you'll read language previously found only in graffiti.

Humor sells in this market. Seriously. Do an online search; you'll find busy and talented creators whose quirky (and exceptionally funny) portfolios generate big laughs and bucks in the greeting card market.

"If you can't find your funny bone with a GPS, but can create aesthetically pleasing images, all is not lost," Abbott says. "Work with a gag writer and either pay them a flat fee for gags sold or arrange a royalty. Do an Internet search for 'gag writers' or contact groups like the National Cartoonists Society for mem-bers who offer this service."

AT VERSE YOU DON'T SUCCEED

Here's a logical question: generally, should you write copy or verse to accompany your samples as a way to demonstrate how your designs can work in a greeting card format? Humorous copy ideas can be submitted in the form of a card dummy with rough art (especially if the visual sets up the joke, when said words and visuals cannot be conceptually separated).

Mediocre verse or bland copy as placeholders won't sell the design—you're not promoting yourself as a wordsmith, correct? Thus, if you are talented with text and wish to be considered as a writer, make this perfectly clear in a cover letter (sent to the right person at the appropriate department, of course). Create a separate package of sentiment or verse suggestions, and make sure your lines are strong enough to stand on their own two syllables. Supporting visuals here may be an added-value option, but generally, serious copy is submitted on its own merits. And in this instance, you're not selling art, right?

SUITABLE ART

The greeting (often called the sentiment) in a card defines the art and of course, vice versa. Different art styles are preferred for different types of cards. Think *South Park* as done by Norman Rockwell and you'll easily get the point.

A card company must consider its entire card line when choosing what to publish. The aim is to achieve an overall stylistic balance, visually and editorially, throughout the product line. Visually, you will find a range of the highly traditional to the very hip, and a great variety of art styles and media in between.

The trendiest, most avant-garde or ultra sophisticated modes may not necessarily be incorporated into a product line, however. Subject matter (for example, unicorns or teddy bears), a particular style (a minimal drawing approach) or technique (digital caricature) must prove to be more than a fad to be considered for the line. Greeting card art directors and designers have often looked to the fashion and interior design markets to gauge the success of an available look or theme or even of a color palette.

Small card companies are often on the cutting edge of new trends. A smaller card line means shorter lead time in preparing product. This translates to a much slighter financial risk should a fad prove short lived. Because of this advantage, these small mavericks may set the pace for the industry at large.

MANY HAPPY RETURNS—RESEARCHING CARDS

How can you research what type of cards a company produces? Abbott responds: "You can't go to your local chain grocery store, major national retail store, or mom-and-pop gift shop without encountering racks of everyday and seasonal greeting cards!"

Abbot's reminder points us to this obvious first wave of research that, arguably, may be the best method to check out greeting card wares and markets. I can't say "hands down" here—initially, an online exploration will be more immediate—but logically, a *hands-on* experience with this type of product is still smart (and a good thing).

Go to every outlet you can find (some shops may carry one company exclusively, but most stores carry lines from many different companies). Spend lots of time at the card racks investigating the type of cards each company offers. "See any cards that present a style similar to yours?" Abbott continues. "The names of the manufacturer are printed on the backs of the cards. Is there more than one card company where your artistic style might be suitable?"

Buy the cards you like best and that seem closely related to your own style. Check logos and get a feel for which companies put out the kind of cards that most appeal to you. If you're not purchasing today (or didn't record pertinent info from an earlier visit to a company's accompanying website), jot down the corporate data while browsing.

"It's worthwhile to have a pen and paper handy to gather information," says Abbott, "or use a device such as a smart phone with a notepad function to record your observations. When you get home, visit—or revisit—the websites of those card manufacturers and seek out their submission guidelines, usually provided somewhere on their home page."

A few notes here: your fact finding shouldn't be a problem at the store, but always clear your intentions and actions with a clerk or the owner at some point. You won't have any trouble if you just introduce yourself, state your purpose, and express your thanks. Oh, yes—come prepared—don't borrow envelopes for notepaper.

PAPER CUTS

A first visit to the company's website or the card shop will give you an initial overview of their product. If for some reason you can't find a particular company's wares online or at the stores, call or email them and ask where to find their cards in your area.

You could also write to the company's creative department. Blasphemy! A real letter? Sure—send them a custom greeting card; utilize the opportunity to market a mini-portfolio, as well. When writing an actual, more traditional type of note, use your letterhead, enclose a business card, and toss in an appropriate promo piece—this will provide the reasonable evidence that you're not a spy for the competition.

To research virtually all the greeting card companies at once, attend the National Stationery Show, held in May at the Jacob K. Javits Convention Center in New York City, NY. Here you can interview and show your portfolio, market and promote your work, network, and examine every aspect of every company—all at one time, under one roof.

PAY ME NOW OR PAY ME LATER

Let's discuss royalties versus flat rates. Typically, greeting card companies pay creative providers via one of two forms: flat fee or a royalty percentage (and often with an advance).

"Flat fees will vary and could be negotiable, depending on the company," Abbott says. The benefit of a flat fee is knowing precisely what you'll receive for your work, and that you'll receive it (usually) upon delivery of the completed art. The downside, when compared to royalty-based arrangements, is that there's no follow-up income from that sale.

With a royalty arrangement, you earn a percentage of net sales. This, in Abbott's experience, has been anywhere from 4–10 percent and usually is paid quarterly. Additionally, you may receive a modest advance on royalties (for Abbott, this has ranged from $150 to $300 per design sold). "This is sort of a guarantee for your efforts," says Abbott. "Once sales surpass the amount of the advance paid, you will receive the quarterly royalties for as long as the card remains in the marketplace. If the card sells well, you may continue to receive payments for many years after the initial sale. Should you have the good fortune to have multiple cards under license, the quarterly income could be substantial."

RIGHTS (AND WRONGS)

"Among the more critical elements to the business end of your art are the rights associated with its use," states Abbott. Should you sell all rights to your design or negotiate for royalties?

It's hardly uncommon for card companies to purchase all rights to designs. Let's examine the company's rationale behind this. Let's imagine the negotiator—for, let's say, the fictitious Has Bean Greetings—handling such a sale: "Card designs are invariably done quickly and in volume," she might say. "We don't see your design(s) offering much marketability in other areas, and we don't usually sell an old design to another company. You're not offering us a unique character or fresh concept, a hot look, or a more recognizable style . . . but we like your stuff, and we want to buy your card designs outright." Do you buy into this buyout?

What about royalties? Keep in mind that royalties on a single design could add up to less than an outright sale. Now, a *line* of cards (or products utilizing your imagery) is another story. If the control of your artistic vision in either scenario is justifiably a hot button for you (and it should be), selling all rights is certainly not *your* best deal.

Ilene Winn-Lederer tells us this: "In the greeting card industry, where so many images are continually produced, it is very difficult to consistently follow up on what royalties are due . . . especially if you are working with a small company that may or may not maintain diligent records. Large companies often have formal accounting procedures, and they will send regular statements. Nevertheless, I prefer to get paid a fair use price upfront whenever possible."

"The early stages of courtship," as Marti McGinnis labels beginning negotiations, "is a good place to determine just what kind of rights the greeting card company expects.

"In gentler times, it was no problem to retain the copyrights to their work," she says. "But with the explosion of corporate giants and global marketing on the Internet, it's getting increasingly common for large and small companies alike to demand 'All rights throughout the universe.'"

No, she's not making this up. Don't be a space cadet, however; fully understand this little licensing moonwalk. "If you're willing to grant a package of (literally universal) rights," says McGinnis, "Make 'em pay up!"

What's that you say? You don't mind seeing your creation become the next hot fashion trend? Okay . . . sign off on all rights for whatever it is they're paying you per t-shirt design and watch them—not you—rake in any licensing royalties.

McGinnis isn't telling you to be contrary or forfeit the deal if you can help it. If there's no extra money to make it worth your while, then make other reasonable demands: perhaps it's your signature as part of the design (at least your name gets out there every time they use your creation).

McGinnis also has this wise advice: no matter how wonderful the art director may be (and you will work with plenty of absolutely great people), the paperwork will be issued by company lawyers protecting corporate interests. These people generate a distinctly anti-artist document; they often have no idea (or plead innocent or play dumb) as to what it is they're asking you to agree to. "They may not—or will not—be ready to comprehend your concerns for your rights as a freelance artist," McGinnis says.

A good contract is an artist-friendly contract. Educate yourself as to what this means (and means to your career). Refer to previous chapters in this book to begin your contracts homework (listen up; there is reading and writing involved, and there *will* be a test when you negotiate your next contract).

Read up on licensing online, at the library or bookstore. Consult the *Graphic Artists Guild Handbook: Pricing and Ethical Guidelines* and look for Caryn Leland's *Licensing Art & Design* for great, practical information and an extended

SWING!

The majority of US greeting card markets, in Abbott's experience, are royalty-based. Here, possibilities across the spectrum of card companies (and their outlets for distribution) are remarkable. Do the math: a greeting card that nets you, let's say, royalties of $300 per quarter means $1,200 per year. Let's go big or go home: if you sell fifty designs—each earning $300 per quarter—you'll earn $60,000 a year in royalties.

This simplified scenario would be a real home run, but it just establishes our field position. Your batting average will vary wildly depending on a score of factors, but Abbott reasonably argues that it's a fair scorecard. "If greeting cards represent only one facet of a well-rounded business," he says, "a comfortable living is certainly within the ballpark."

discussion on this subject. It's slightly dated at this writing, but nevertheless still comes up as your first choice on an Amazon query and is a good place to start. Another positive thing you can do for your business education is to become a member of The AIGA (www.aiga.org) or the Graphic Artists Guild (www.gag. org).

EASY AS PIE

"When you think of rights," Abbott advises, "imagine them as slices of a pie. You've created a design that might be viable in a number of markets, one of which is greeting cards—one slice of a much larger pie. If you license your work to a card company, and they don't already specify it in their agreement, seek to offer *greeting card rights only*."

This is wise counsel. Abbott is suggesting you get the most financial mileage out of your work—you may also be able to license your art in other categories, exponentially expanding your sources of revenue streams. "If you don't," he continues, "and the agreement offered by a greeting card company states *all rights,* that work has run out of gas as a vehicle for income, and it didn't travel very far."

Another stratagem is to negotiate a time limit on rights offered. After a mutually agreed, contractual period, the rights revert back to you. "Remember," says Abbott, "you own the art—you don't have to agree to *anything* you're not comfortable with. But of course, once you sign on the dotted line, it's too late to rethink how you really wanted the rights used and for how much."

UK MARKETS

Abbott says that the larger, more established greeting card companies in the UK tend to offer a flat fee rather than royalties. This may initially seem a disadvantage (when compared to US markets), but it's not uncommon for rights to revert back to creators after a relatively short, contractually designated period of time. So, the deal for a popular design will be renegotiated and the company will offer further compensation, or you are free to shop the design around elsewhere.

SUBMIT

Regardless of how you submit, your samples must demonstrate your excellent color and design sense plus the superior technical chops you've honed to perfection. Showing off good drawing skills wouldn't hurt either.

Compile imagery pertinent to cards and to the particular recipient (determined by your exhaustive research). If your art style, personality and creative wits are suited to greeting card work, it shouldn't be a big chore to determine which of your samples are appropriate to send.

If this chemistry is right, the only inappropriate samples are those irrelevant to this field. Let's say you do meticulously detailed line work. If all your samples are cross-sections of airplane engines, don't expect many assignments from a typical greeting card company.

You don't necessarily need a track record of sales or clients, and if you have the chops, you can score a deal. At the card shop, you'll see some cards done in black and white, so black-and-white samples are okay for showing line work, but by and large, you really need to present color. Samples of layouts are not really helpful, unless you're applying for a position as a staff designer (or in the production art department, a crucial part of any card company, by the way).

You know the drill. Busy art directors need to get a sense of your style and skill. A first contact should be prefaced with a query letter. And while it's up to you to follow through with periodic updates, don't pester. They don't have a lot of time to view portfolios, read your chatty emails, or gab on the phone at your convenience.

About hard copy submissions . . . yes—there are card companies that still request physical samples: brochures, tear sheets, postcards, even photocopies and photographs. Often, copies are made for the files, but if you're sending hard copy, it's best to send samples that the art director can keep. If you want something back, say so, and include an SASE. They won't have any time or inclination to return samples sent without sufficient return postage (and don't make the unreasonable request that the card company insure the return package).

If you're worried about the security of your submission, copyright your stuff and submit a non-disclosure agreement (however, there's no guarantee that they'll sign it).

COMMISSIONED DESIGNS

Card companies are open to submissions, but marketing single concepts can be a tough sell. You may have a bright idea for a single card (or theme), but that doesn't mean it will fit the company requirements of the product lines currently being assigned.

Card companies, as opposed to buying over the transom, usually *commission* designs. Company policies may vary, of course, so check with each. Each company has an individual philosophy and program, every studio has their own way of doing things, so it's not so prudent to create finished art and to try to sell it for publication.

A series of cards within a consistent theme is called a *card promotion*. A company must devote a larger share of its new designs to a single, specific look. Marketing a series is risky to the greeting card company putting many of its eggs in your one basket, so it's not always desirable. If your card promotion is your initial approach to a company, you may not get very far.

A company's entire product line—for instance, counter cards, promotions, designs by caption category (birthday, anniversary, and so forth)—is all determined by management and marketing and based on myriad decisions. Except in small operations where two or three people run the whole show, the creative staff is never totally in control.

Staff art directors and line planners give out the assignments and are, presumably, paid well to develop ideas for promotions and other products. It may be difficult for you, a raw unknown, to usurp their function.

THE BACK DOOR

It might be more efficient (and smarter) to actively pursue assignment work first and parlay that into commission work with Has Bean Greetings. Become an indispensable freelance hire while developing lines and themes on the side.

A fruitful (and hopefully, long) business relationship with any company can begin when you receive and complete your first assignments. Show that you're competent, dependable, and a pleasure to work with and I bet they will be open to your bright ideas. If you're reliable and your work is good; if you can follow instructions without being heavily directed; and if you can still add your own special touch to your assignments, they may look to you for new product concepts.

When you've established a track record with this studio, present your designs with your foot firmly in the art department door. This could be a more fruitful path to success without undue heartache.

Now after having said that, if you're convinced you've developed an absolutely killer idea for a promotion, if you have absolute faith in this concept, don't sit on it. Keep in mind that you buck the odds, but full speed ahead—submit your brainstorm or mention it in a submission for future consideration.

USING FREELANCE HELP

Generally, small companies use freelancers because their output can't support an ample or full-time art staff. But many small companies are literally small operations, and maybe one-person operations, at that. There are also complaints that small companies don't pay as well and may not pay promptly.

Large companies may use fewer freelancers because they have extensive in-house art staffs. If you're right for Has Bean Greetings, you may get the nod for a particular job, but you could indeed be viewed as the proverbial "little fish in the big pond." When you walk with the giants, size does not always equate with monster job opportunities (or harmonious relationships), and the red tape can be particularly colossal and frustrating.

The medium-sized competitor is probably your most dependable and reliable source. Since they're slugging it out with the big kids in certain product areas, these mid-range companies have busy staffs; they may actively welcome and court outside help—card designs are always changing and the demand for new art, plus the desire for a variety of looks, is often more than the in-house staff can handle.

The greeting card industry has a voracious appetite for bright ideas and innovative stylings. According to the Greeting Card Association in Washington DC, greeting card publishing is the largest user of creative talent next to advertising; and freelancers may very well be considered the fresh air that keeps the card industry breathing.

JUST ASK

The easiest way to find out if a company uses freelance design is to simply contact the company. Check out the website (it's quite common to list job opportunities and guidelines online). Send an email (or call the personnel office or creative department) and ask directly: "Do you use freelancers? To whom do I send my samples? Would you please send artist's guidelines for submission?"

Another avenue by which to gauge the size and dependability of a company may be through researching blogs that cover the field and industry organs like *Party & Paper* (www.partypaper.com) or *Greetings, etc* (www.greetingsmagazine.com). You can find listings in the annual publication, *Artist's & Graphic Designer's Market* (North Light Books). Card companies that don't have a listing here are not likely to need much free-lance help.

CARD FORMATS

Abbott says that card companies need new and engaging art throughout the year to keep their various lines fresh in this highly competitive arena. Submission guidelines are typically very specific and should be used as a template for presenting your art to their creative teams. "An important element to consider is the layout of your art," Abbott states, "the needs of which are entirely unique to this industry."

I'll go out on a not too dangerous limb and say that while most designs are vertical, you will see some horizontals. But when you look at a card rack, which portion of the card is visible to you? Answer: generally, it's that third to upper half. So when creating for greeting cards, this consideration should immediately top your list of design concerns.

Card sizes vary; there is no true standard for the industry. Submission guidelines will instruct you as to that company's size specifications and requirements. In general, it will be in proportions similar to a 5"x 7" format.

Create with the caption in mind. No matter what the format, build your design around that part of the card that will show in the display. This top third to half is important and must look particularly attractive.

"And if the upper half is devoid of interesting elements or color," says Abbott, "what compels consumers to pick the card up and look closer? While you may be exceedingly proud of your portfolio showcasing card designs in a modernistic, square format, if your slick creations can't be reduced to the typical greeting card dimensions—you're wasting your time, as well as the time of an extremely harried creative staff (which won't help endear you to the review team receiving future submissions with your name on them)."

The vertical card has more "rack appeal" because the vertical format best displays captions clearly. Not to fudge the point, but with that (and modern display cases) in mind, layout may simply be a matter of company preference. However, certainly consult individual artist's guidelines for this pertinent information. Of course, if you've got the right look for the line, an art director will direct you on these specifics when you get an assignment.

OTHER PAPER PRODUCTS

Many greeting card companies also produce other paper products (such as note cards, stationery, party goods, and giftwrapping) and even collectibles. For example, our Has Bean Greetings offers their card vendors a complete line of paper products and certainly wants to fill all the product space in their shops (remember, such vendors may be called *card* shops but they invariably carry a wide range of eclectic items).

But if Has Bean only makes cards, the stores they service will buy other merchandise from the competition, who we'll call Maxxed Out Designs (MOD). If MOD produces cards and more (including collectibles), they will likely snatch a larger share of the card shop trade.

Depending on the specific company, freelancers may or may not be utilized as frequently on these other paper product lines. But just as you may find a company that produces only greeting cards, there are folks who specialize in stationery and note cards, giftwrapping materials, or party goods. These may be better outlets for your art.

TRENDS

To research greeting card trends, look at fashion, home decoration and furnishings, and advertising in general. When the research gets tough, the researchers go shopping. Get out and have some fun: to truly study current design, graphics, color, and pattern, you must visit the penultimate consumer-testing laboratory, otherwise known as the shopping mall.

Of course, you can obviously go online! But wherever, whenever . . . the play is to keep your eyes on popular culture and your mind open. The keys to the kingdom are available merely by being alert to what's happening all around you—in your neighborhood and across the globe.

So, here's more entertaining homework: watch television; read for both news and entertainment, business and pleasure. Especially look at women's magazines, since the target market for cards is female, eighteen to forty years old. Play at the toy store. Listen to the radio and go to the movies; observe popular local, national, and international celebrities. Talk to friends and family about feelings and values important to them. As mentioned before, for an overview of what's new and hot in the industry, go to the National Stationery Show in New York City. Other gift shows are held in other cities around the country, too.

THE WORLD FROM YOUR OWN BACK YARD

I'll close this chapter with this: we work in a truly global marketplace. As I've said previously, in our digital age, technology has spun creative process, product, and delivery completely around on the very axis of opportunity.

As Abbott reminds us, wireless connectivity from virtually anywhere and instant communication means that there are no cost-prohibitive geographic limitations on where you could be submitting your design. The United States has a massive greeting card market, but we're not the only game in town. English-speaking greeting card markets—the United Kingdom, Australia, New Zealand, and Canada—have voracious appetites for quality art. "Add to that," Abbott says, "European creative directors you can connect with online via a medium like LinkedIn.

The Greeting Card Association, a tremendous resource in the United States, also has equally helpful chapters in the United Kingdom and Australia. On their respective home pages, you'll find links to their members and to those that are actively seeking submissions. All this could yield excellent results."

INDEPENDENCE DAY

Finally, truth be told, do you even need to deal with the middleman of the greeting card company? How about going the independent route? Could your interactive web storefront, combined with solid content, good search engine optimization, and diligent social media marketing, map your progress of world dominance in the greeting card market? Think about it.

"More so than ever before," Allan Wood tells us, "being an independent card designer–producer presents a very viable prospect. The advent and accessibility of high-quality digital printing presses that can produce on a variety of paper–card stock makes generating small runs of cards a reality, both practically and financially."

Wood also points out that there are also many quality offset printers who can produce runs of as little as 250 at very cost effective prices; do your research and shop around. With small print runs, it's also a very practical option to incorporate mixed media (paper cuts, glues, stitching, foiling etc.) along with unique cutting and folding techniques. "Finish your card off yourself—by hand; this could be just the thing to differentiate yourself," Wood advises. "Marketing your work may be all about fulfilling a local niche market—talk to your local florist, national park, or tourist center—as the place to begin your card business."

RIGHT ON POINT

(PROFESSIONAL VIEWPOINTS IN 50 WORDS OR LESS)

I've been a freelancer doing greeting cards for years and lately have been exploring ways to both reinvent myself and venture down other creative avenues. I strongly suggest you investigate possibilities and opportunities you have not yet explored—for instance, I am trying my hand at writing cards as well.

—Tim Haggerty

Certain events you cannot miss; one of them is the New York Stationery Show. There you can meet reps who sell to specific geographic areas. They sell the cards for you. A rep gets you the orders, and you fill the orders. My reps are my national sales fleet.

—Jennifer Berman

"Shall I paint you less old and wrinkly?"

"I'd have gotten you a nicer card if you'd had more money in your wallet."

"I figured you should have breakfast in bed on your birthday. Can you reach the stove okay?"

You may be really good at greeting cards, but don't limit yourself to just that. Take advantage of every opportunity.

—Randy Glasbergen

It's important to research what greeting card art directors want to see. It saves you work and lets you know where you should put the extra effort.

—Mary Thelen

Be sure to include in your written contract that your signature be integral to the overall design, so at least you get free advertising. Now's the good time to develop a signature that's legible!

—Marti McGinnis

"I'm going to close my eyes and count to three. When I open them, ten of those candles better be gone."

"I hope you came with a receipt."

"When I grow up, I'm going to have a mustache just like you, Grandma."

"Bring me more 'Death Gray'!"

CHAPTER 15

SELLING TO SMALL BUSINESSES

Many people don't realize that a good designer can, with the right information, design just about anything. It's your skill at defining a problem—and your ability to creatively solve it—that you're really selling, not just your ability to put together a book, brochure, or whatever.

—Vicki Vandeventer

RIGHT AT HOME

Illustrators or designers just starting out may find the old axiom "less is more" an appropriate business metaphor. One might think established businesses would be the best bet, but that keyword *established* does not necessarily translate into more opportunities for creative freedom. Indeed, your fresh, bold ideas may find a very happy home with small businesses.

"Right from the start," says Allan Wood, "I knew I wanted to run my own design business. The main question was 'where was I going to get the most comprehensive experience to develop the skill set necessary to do that?'"

For Wood, the answer was working within a small print design business for a few years. As opposed to working within an agency—where you are usually a link in the chain and gain very little exposure throughout the entire process—Wood found that working within a small business, by necessity, gave him first-hand experience in every aspect of design.

"My responsibilities ranged from dealing with clients, developing briefs, and running quotes; creating designs and press-ready artwork; I benefited immensely from the whole pre-press experience and gained invaluable knowledge of print, binding, and finishing techniques. I did everything from digital and web design to sourcing and negotiating with production–supply specialists (and trouble shooting the myriad issues that naturally arise). For me, this formed a rock-solid foundation that still serves me well today."

WHAT TYPES OF FREELANCE HELP DO SMALL BUSINESSES NEED?

More than a few folks consider working with small businesses to be bargain basement, low-budget, "clip art"-type grunt work. We can be more creative and industrious than that, can't we?

"When I started out," says Wood, "I decided I wanted to specialize and provide my services to small businesses. For me, small business clients play a large part in our local communities. They often provide niche or unique resources; they help create diversity, both in choices and culture, and are usually members of the local community itself. For me, it was a proactive and subversive move against big business, but maybe I'm just an activist at heart. All those small businesses along the street are just blank canvases waiting for you to draw on; you can transform the world one shop at a time."

Your job could be creating a logo for the comic book store in town. That logo is incorporated in a new business card and on the website you're building for them. They also need an upcoming newspaper ad. You may design and paint bold interior graphics or use that new logo for the shop's exterior sign. Perhaps, while adapting both logo and ad for a direct mailer, you'll be working up a poster at the same time.

How about interior signage? Pricing and sales change regularly and the store owner's hand lettering just won't cut it. Besides, he loves the character style he's seen in your book (you're an illustrator, too) and wants you to incorporate that look into the store displays. This might also lead to tags, bags, or other in-store "signage."

UP THE BLOCK

But you get where I'm going with this. Small businesses are not only the little hardware stores down the block. There are a lot of independent companies out there performing all sorts of business functions that are quite small.

All small businesses have some sort of visual needs, from simple stationery and business forms to advertising and marketing, display and signage. Perhaps you've noticed a business that doesn't have a graphic profile—that might be a good place to start. Maybe it never crossed their mind to use certain promotional vehicles to get their message across.

The wise small businessperson knows that good graphics sell products. A store owner may carefully watch the advertising budget, but is conscious of the fact that successful businesses probably got that way through advertising. If the business is on a limited budget, the owner isn't working with an agency. He or she probably has no art background and will certainly not have your design sense or technical expertise. Smart enough to know *something* is needed, but with no idea exactly what (or how to get it together), the small businessperson turns to you for quality, affordable graphics.

IN DEMAND

A small shop owner's graphics may not justify employing an agency, but it's these advertising agencies in town that just may want you. As local talent, you're able to meet tight deadlines and will understand the needs of your buying community. Your hometown sensibilities are a big plus on regional accounts.

The same thing applies for neighborhood newsletters, town newspapers, and city or regional magazines. Often these publications will only work with regional talent because these artists are neighbors who understand the issues and the current events that affect the local population.

A shoe store employs you to devise caricature-based buyer's incentives. One happy customer, a restaurant manager, loves the gimmick and asks you to design something similar for his bistro. A vendor for the eatery enjoys the concept so much she hires you to do the same for her business (and even commissions a personalized version for a family event).

Think of it as your big graphic design block party. Your whole town is fair game—the public television station, the local community college, your favorite deli, or even your dentist. Any small or local business with communication, marketing, and promotional demands—and that's every business that advertises, generates correspondence, and interacts with customers—can use your help.

These initial prospects are no small potatoes in the bigger stew of your business. Good assignments are where you find them, and some tasty ingredients for success are rooted right in your own backyard.

INTRODUCTIONS

How do you find out if a local business needs freelance artwork? The best way is to simply introduce yourself by publicizing your services. Yes, marketing and self-promotion again. Your local program is important. You have the decided advantage and incentive of knowing the home turf, so take a direct and aggressive approach.

"Aggressive" does not mean obnoxious or overbearing; it means a keen and concerted effort. Establish and maintain a web presence. Advertise in city (or regional) newspapers and magazines, plus neighborhood weeklies or monthlies. Mount mini-posters on bulletin boards; mail your brochure. Follow up with postcards and phone calls. You're figuratively, if not *literally*, in the neighborhood, so don't let a contact go cold.

Chatting up the main avenue of the business district will probably take no more time than your usual stroll when shopping; it could be the most lucrative window shopping you ever do. If you're out and about, ask for a storeowner or manager. Introduce yourself. Make sure a brochure arrived (if you've done some preflight strategy) or trot one out at a first introduction. Tell this person you've been making the rounds and took the opportunity to say hello. If the timing is not good, indicate you'll be back in the neighborhood on a certain day, at a certain time. Ask if it would be okay to return and schmooze, perhaps show some samples too.

You're obviously after an affirmative response. But even if there's no job—when you get some sort of a positive reaction, simply gather information. Deborah Budd suggests those of you with a blog (ideally, one that has resources and suggestions for local business marketing), share the URL on your business card or brochure. And when you do get a shot, bring your portfolio but forgo a big sales pitch (for now). Lay the groundwork for a *continued* promotion. Chances are, when there is a need, they'll remember that person with the pleasant smile and beautiful art.

Of course, if they ask not to be bothered, believe them. These are busy people, so don't pester. Say, "Perhaps another time, if this is inconvenient?" or "May I keep you on my mailing list and call again for a future appointment?" Obviously, if they instruct you to *never* bother them again, take that to heart. Here's where you decide to be patient, persistent, or practical.

FINDING NEW BUSINESSES

How do you find out when a new business is about to open? New construction or reconstruction is an obvious tip off. Keep your eyes open, wade through the dust, and make inquiries.

Check the Yellow Pages for names of local businesses. The Chamber of Commerce and the Better Business Bureau should be able to supply you with a list of new businesses in your area. Business trade publications in most markets publish corporate announcements; business magazines on a local level like to welcome new businesses to that market. New businesses about to open often issue press releases to the local media; watch for that. Check the newspaper for grand opening announcements or lists of incorporations. Join your local art directors club.

Whom do you contact at a new, small business? The store owner or manager is your best bet. A sales clerk, while receptive, won't have the authority to commission your work. However, as the sales staff have the ear of the storeowner, they could be allies to your cause. If the boss is presently unavailable, begin with the clerk and make a date to return when the boss is likely to be on site.

SAMPLES

The small businessperson is interested in how you can help their business—the store, their revenue, the bottom line—so your samples will have to generally relate to the business environment. Fred Carlson says, "I've found that, while some clients buy style and some markets buy subject matter, they're probably more subject matter-oriented. Small businesses buy subject matter that relates to what they're doing.

"The visual should be easy and economical to make—online or on paper. You can't present an extremely complicated, tricky to reproduce image to a small business owner; they're not going to spend the money on those kinds of things.

"Small businesses have fairly simple needs and relatively small budgets," Carlson sums up, "so show design that fits in with lower budgets."

AWWW, GO DIRECT YOURSELF

Small businesses generally don't have an art director. This means that you may have to not only create the design, but also get it published (print or digital). Don't pass up an opportunity to work with a printer because it just means more work (grumble, grumble).

If you're worried about the finished product or merely want to further your graphics education, it's to your advantage to see the job through to the end. Why not factor added responsibilities into your bid and have a fun learning experience at the same time?

As Carlson says, "You may very well be asked, 'You can design the thing, but can you do the production. Can you get it printed?' This falls in your lap sometimes because the buyer isn't that sophisticated about the division of labor in the graphic arts. They might just assume that you would—or should—know all these other things. What you should say is: "Sure, I can do all those extra things—how about if I estimate production management separately so you can see the cost? And I'm happy to recommend a few good local print vendors."

"If you maintain this relationship with certain local clients, it keeps the checks coming," Carlson says. "The more you specialize, the less chance of a relationship with a small business. They're going to have the most basic needs, and if you can service those basic needs, you're going to do all right."

And let's not give the wrong impression. Understanding how to get a piece effectively published online is one thing. Knowing how to prepare print files or work with a print vendor is not merely a matter of putting in a little extra quality time at the printer's. As Matt McElligott says, "In terms of print, a knowledge of inks, separations, dot gain, line screens, film, paper, etc. all contribute to getting a piece done right. A good graphic designer understands this and should have put in time learning the ropes."

LOCALS PREFERRED

Are small businesses open to freelancers who *don't* live nearby? Realistically, you don't have to live down the block to service a small business account. However, if your distance from any theater of operation complicates the job or delays completion of an assignment, location can be a liability.

And maybe you know several local businesses that assign their work to design studios. Does this mean they wouldn't need any freelance help? Not necessarily. This shouldn't discourage you from showing your work to a small business owner (the owner may even encourage the studio to use you for some aspect of a job). Find out about the design studio and show your work; it will certainly help the cause. If the studio doesn't have an exclusive arrangement with the business, you may want to approach the owner regarding other graphic needs around the establishment.

PRINTERS? YES, PRINTERS.

As I write this chapter, print is still not dead. And at this writing, the print *business* is also not terminal. So let's ask this question: do printers need freelance help? Not really. By and large, if a small business goes to a printer to get the complete job done, the outcome is probably going to be very simple. Printers are not going to want to spend a lot of money on a creative solution, so they tend to price out low and zoom through the aesthetics. Chances are, they'll probably use somebody on staff.

Wood says he has found a variety of opportunities in networking with local printers. They sometimes get inquiries about work they don't do (ie. branding, logo design, illustrations, diagrams, etc.) and may refer the client to you (if they know you'll steer the print work back to them). Or they might get busy and need some projects accomplished. I've done many freelance jobs and obtained quite a few new clients this way. This has really helped maintain cash flow."

Printers can also be clients. Even struggling printers must practice marketing and self-promotion and may barter services with designers. You may be asked to design a catchy promotion piece, trading your fee for free tearsheets and valuable publicity. Perhaps it's an even exchange for their producing your promotional brochure. Getting your work printed on a slick promo is good advertising for both you and the printer.

"Use signed agreements," Budd says, "just as you would with any client. Don't work with printers who drag out payment for your services or renege on barter arrangements. The exchange should benefit both parties, not just the printer."

FOLKS JUST LIKE YOU (LIFE IN THE TRENCHES)

START HERE . . .

Judith Lauso believes that it is best to work for a small studio-type business in need of your talent from the beginning. Lauso herself feels that, based on her exceedingly positive experience in such a situation, you can completely express your artistic side to communicate important messages and ideas on the ground level, through project completion.

In the early part of her career, Lauso worked with a local community newspaper, where she was lucky enough to be exposed to industry-grade layout processes and organization. Working for a professional publication helped her interest in design blossom. The creative elements of designing (and illustrating), the feedback from peers as well as the readership, the satisfaction of knowing that her work was being distributed to a wide audience—all of these things provided an environment where collaboration, common goals, and the inevitable education that results, prepared her to enter the freelance market.

"I enjoy working professionally at something that I truly love to do," she says. "Each job allows me to grow and learn about whatever subject matter is currently in front. Working independently and choosing my own hours are features of freelance that I like."

. . . AND END UP HERE

At the beginning, your first position could be as an intern or even a consultant. "You will learn to be honest and sincere rather than saying what you think the client or boss wants to hear," says Lauso. "A stalemate about a design issue or content gives you the opportunity to be honest with your thoughts on technique and honest with yourself about dealing with the client's wishes. You try to compromise and remain within the clients overall plan, all the while tactfully explaining the ifs, ands, and buts of why the project should be done differently."

This is all part of developing a process that helps you maintain a productive work-flow. It also allows you to maintain positive relationships with clients and your collaborators. Without such organization—encompassed by the organization of time, materials, and costs—frustration (for any and all parties involved) can set in.

In other words, educate and share. Lauso's point here is that, when working in a creative field, it is absolutely essential to share your talents with others. With clients and employers, obviously, but this includes taking the time to advise, mentor, and assist colleagues and those new to the field. Such good work can effectively be done through local professional affiliations (for instance, AIGA, the Graphic Artists Guild, and Lauso's own affiliation, the Pittsburgh Society of Illustrators).

And with this education—in such a profession of people, process, and product—will come the inevitable opportunity to learn and grow through failure and rejection. "There will be moments where you will not, let's say, achieve the outcome you desired," she says smiling. "But this is not a time to quit or become discouraged. Rather, it is a chance to improve your craft and benefit from the experience. Decide what didn't work. Always make it a point of learning."

BUT IT'S A SMALL WORLD AFTER ALL

"Most of my clients are smaller businesses," says Nadine Gilden, "and I think many of these people want a flat rate. Because they have a budget, they want to know how much it's going to cost them before they get involved—it's very important to them. I screen clients and try to work with only those who share my aesthetics (and are comfortable paying my rates)—I've learned to walk away from those clients who don't meet these critical criteria.

"Yes, in the beginning," Gilden states, "sometimes you do have to work for free. You haven't proven yourself yet, so people don't really have a reason (yet) to pay you an industry wage. Until that happens, you come up with ways to give yourself more work—find sites that you don't think are well done and do a redesign; offer your services to a non-profit (if you're going to work for free, at least it's for a worthy cause)."

Budd advises you to always draw up a "scope of work" document (that applies to *all* clients, not just small local businesses, and yes, even non-profits.) Scope of work details what the client will get in return for that flat rate, including a set number of hours and a limited number of revisions.

"If the client exceeds the scope," she says, "you can insist, 'We need to discuss increasing the budget if you want more changes.' Scope of work sets some boundaries and helps clients new to working with designers understand the design process and related costs. That puts the relationship on a professional footing from day one."

Gilden also makes the astute observation that, with seasoning, you will come to realize that it isn't actually about you and your fabulous talent. It's not even really about the client . . . it's about how best to serve their audience, their readers, and their customers—all the while representing the client's brand in the best way possible.

CAREFUL DOES IT

It behooves us—I do love saying that—to close with a bit of brass tacks. We must soberly evaluate the previous commentary (on working for free) along with other professional opinions. While she does not disagree with Gilden outright, Jamie Sharp says, "Be careful about underselling. It can do a disservice by devaluing your work and the industry as a whole."

When Sharp offers a price break, she indicates what the full price would have been and shows the discounts right on the quote (and invoice). This helps teach her clients about the value of good design (more on this coming up).

"For any potential customer," Sharp continues, "it is important to do your homework and familiarize yourself with the lingo and buzzwords of their industry. Set yourself up as an expert—someone who can speak to their audience and portray them correctly."

This gives the client confidence in you and is especially true for small businesses that, in all likelihood, have never dealt with professional designers. "Your interactions with your customer offer opportunities to educate them about the true worth of quality design," Sharp is more than happy to repeat. "You don't have to beat them over the head. Spelling out the time requirements, hourly fees and any extras (like editing and changes) in your quote helps the client see your value, which only supports the long-term viability of visual communication as a career."

RIGHT ON POINT
(PROFESSIONAL VIEWPOINTS IN 50 WORDS OR LESS)

Be prepared to do a lot of educating when dealing with small business owners.

—Marti McGinnis

Style has everything to do with vision, and this is never "small." What you see—the way you put that down on paper . . . every single job should be an enormous learning experience. Make this personal growth a career-long goal.

—Sam Viviano

When working with small businesses, one challenge is convincing them that your rates are fair and reasonable. How you convince them is an individual matter, depending on your style of work, the temperament of the client, and other pricing examples you can point to.

—Randy Glasbergen

Working with small local businesses can be a real education, providing opportunities to sharpen both creative and business skills.

—Ilene Winn-Lederer

Whatever you can do to get your foot in the door is a step in the right direction. I think it's best to build up experience at a local level. Work with people who are right near you. You can go back and forth; there's a give and take there.

—Roger DeMuth

I work with mostly small to mid-size businesses. And for these clients, a modern designer can only be described as a jack-of-all-trades. Gone are the days of the specialist.

—Gerald D. Vinci

Everyone's Favorite Place!

Take a stroll through Yellow Springs, Ohio

YS OPOLY

YellowSpringsOpoly.com

© Bing Design 2014

CHAPTER 16

WORKING WITH DESIGN STUDIOS

How do you break into this market? This isn't the right question, because there is no easy way. What is the best way? A lot of hard work. Fill a need. Factor in talent, speed, and competitive pricing. Be there when the work is there—you cannot create the work.

–Dan Johnson (deceased)

YOU ARE WHO YOU ARE

The days of the dedicated illustration shops, generating just that—art, usually in the form of illustration—are behind us. Design studios still flourish, however.

A design studio concentrates on visual communications that utilize copy, illustration, and photography. The design studio conceptualizes a piece, designs it, commissions the copy, and farms out the art and photography, as necessary.

Chances are that you are (or you're part of) a design studio—an entity with a definite name and identity (Sue Jones, Freelancer; Chicken Soup Graphics). You work primarily out of your place of business (at home or away) or you may work in someone else's studio, agency, or "graphic design department." As such, your primary business is design, from concept to completion. You might focus on the production of design.

But let's say, you don't consider yourself engaged in running (nor even remotely connected with a "real") *design studio*. You still want to know how to work with these folks. Read on . . .

WHAT A CONCEPT!

Many design studios like to see the way you "conceptualize." Conceptualizing is the vision to see—and show—a sparkling diamond in chunks of raw coal. Most likely, you'll be showing thumbnails or roughs. Maybe it will be the complete transition of a particular assignment, from the germ of an idea through the initial thumbnails, rough sketches, comprehensive layouts, and final piece.

In general, the skills needed for a successful tenure at a design studio are speed, intelligence, technical skill, and a unique point of view combined with a fresh approach. Design studios—and, sure, any art studios still out there—will demand solid layout capabilities, exceptional computer savvy, and sharp rendering skills (to execute thumbnails and roughs).

And what's your specialty? What's the hook and bait that reels 'em in? Is it a pervasive visual elegance? Does your design aesthetic blatantly challenge the viewer smack in the (type)face? Or is it more steady, reassuring, even practical? Maybe your taste is positively snuggly and cozy, down-home and even folksy? Loose? Casual? Whacky or whimsical? Bold, flat color or nuanced and textural? Busy, busy, busier or stark and minimal? Do you love collage? Are you crazy about hand lettering (or letterpress) and old school retro?

Whatever your bent, in your portfolio, the ample evidence of excellent design and production skills should be a given. Drawing and painting prowess, a fine color sense, plus an advanced technical repertoire are all excellent calling cards.

Your portfolio must boast finished, polished skills. You could offer a range of looks or a focused approach. It's whatever gets the job done, as long as it's obvious your individual touch is stamped on every piece.

DESIGNER LABELS

How do you present yourself as a designer in person? One solid piece of advice I've been told is to first *sell yourself*. This begins with making the other person comfortable. Project a feeling of well-being and the prospect will feel good about you. Next, observe closely and listen carefully. Talk less, listen more. When asked, "What do you do?" answer with a layered response: "I'm a graphic designer. I design (such and such) for companies like (so and so)." The key is to make meaningful contact. Remember, you are not selling anything at a first meeting; rather you are attempting to make a good impression and generate interest.

At this point, Tom Graham says, "A good question to ask of an art director is 'What are you working on?' or 'Working on anything interesting?' Chances are they'll love to talk about their latest project, maybe ask what you think. This takes the focus off you for a bit. My experience early on was: I was nervous and talked too much."

Now, according to consultant David Goodman, comes the moment of truth: the exchange of business cards (the design of which, Goodman maintains, says more about you than the words printed on it).

To sum up: it's not so much where you are on the ladder, but how you communicate where you want to be. As Goodman says, "Selling design actually has little to do with design. It has to do with people. Selling is a person-to-person activity."

LOCAL TALENT

Are local design studios dedicated to working with local talent? This, to me, is a toss up these days. I think there may be advantages for local talent if face time is important to a client, but if you live on the corner of Reliability and Efficiency, modern communications and delivery systems make location virtually a non-issue.

I wouldn't pigeonhole my business locally and I wouldn't limit myself to only regional design studios. If you're just starting out, perhaps your track record, confidence level, or comfort zone indicates where you'll be working; in these instances, one-on-one with local studios is certainly reasonable (and makes sense). But certainly keep your eyes peeled for opportunities beyond your city limits. Once you've established yourself (emotionally, mentally, physically, professionally), it will be easier to expand your horizons.

BEST INTRODUCTION

Your website sets all this up—the proverbial one-two punch. First, grab their attention with your eye-catching, captivating online portfolio and get your foot in the virtual door. Then, the quality of the work within shows off your effective communication skills.

Clients aren't too concerned about how a freelancer might interact in a group; nor do they care what you might bring to the organization (or where you see yourself in their organization over the next five years). Likewise, the information on your résumé is not key—credits and work experience can be hyped—it's the portfolio that counts.

"There are always several people who can do the job," said Dan Johnson. "So you have to be in front of the contact's mind, or you have to be there at the right time. Now, factor in talent, speed, and competitive pricing—these are some of the best ways to [break into] this market."

If you are new in town or just starting out, establish a web presence—that's just de rigueur, a given. Crispin Prebys advises you to ask for a simple portfolio review with a mailed query letter—you're not asking for a job at this juncture, just a look-see and advice—and then follow up with an email or phone call.

There's also the practical aspect of simply walking through the front door of this gig—work on staff for a few years. Get some actual experience at a studio before attempting to go out on your own. Learn the way a studio operates; get an idea of the type of projects design studios handle. Establish a network of contacts and a body of skills. Join organizations pertaining to the field, *then* freelance.

YOUR BOOK IS *YOUR* BOOK

Deborah Budd was very adamant that we make a strong case here for an absolutely critical bit of business: be extremely careful about including work in your portfolio that is not entirely "yours," but the product of a team effort. Art directors, and especially small studio owners, are sensitive to plagiarism, which clashes with the unfortunate tendency among younger designers to be less respectful of intellectual property.

"We owe this to the 'free' and 'open' Internet, and the sense that 'copying' and 'referencing' are the same thing," she says. "When we share ideas online, they become temptations for non-professionals to 'borrow.' For a professional designer to do this is career suicide.

"If the idea was not yours, don't include it," Budd continues. "If you are very proud about your role in a team project, explain clearly what that role was, so studio owners know you are not claiming others' work as your own. And if you're unclear what constitutes plagiarism, do some reading and educate yourself. This is the design industry's cardinal sin."

'ROUND AND 'ROUND

Should you send a disc or other medium? There are a couple of trains of thought here: forwarding media that is packaged attractively and prepared correctly may get your great work the stand-out attention it deserves and needs. Or it could turn out to be a clunky and terribly time- and cost-inefficient exercise for both parties.

Often, with all the ugly, rampant computer viruses out there, strange (as in foreign, not weird) media may represent a real danger for the recipient. Swish—nothing but net: your disc (or flash drive) goes right into the circular file. "Bulletproof" Macs notwithstanding, how many gigs (job bites, not bytes) will you get from the client whose computer crashed when they inserted your funky disc in their precious laptop?

Of course, if the prospect *asks* for a portfolio—or requests a follow-up—on disc, go for it; but take pains to create a dynamic and expertly produced digital portfolio a client will ultimately swear by, not swear at.

If you are mailing your work, make it easy—and safe—for your prospect. You could mail (or email) a sample and tag it with a link to your online portfolio, or send the sample and follow up with an email that offers the link. Or, as Budd suggests, try an email with a really clever headline and a great image, plus a link to a customized slide show of some work that "fits" what you've learned about the studio's work or client base. Better yet, make the link a video of you talking directly to the studio owner and sharing images of projects you feel are relevant to the studio, with an invitation to follow up. Whoa . . . a pitch disguised as a portfolio—hey, bacon wrapped up in bacon.

DIRECTORIES, ORGANIZATIONS, AND MAGAZINES

Looking for design studios? I suggest you ask the Chamber of Commerce or call the local Better Business Bureau. Try your regional Business to Business Yellow Pages. Check the members' directory of your town's ad club. Consult the membership directory of the American Institute of Graphic Arts (AIGA). There are various design firm directories online.

Organizations you can join to get to know more designers? How about the Graphic Artists Guild, the Society of Publication Designers, and the American Institute of Graphic Arts (AIGA)? Tangentially, look into the City and Regional Magazine Association (CRMA), Society of Typographic Arts (STA), and your local art directors club. You might also want to contact local universities.

Magazines focused on design? Read *Print, HOW, Communication Arts, Graphis, Advertising Age, Adweek,* and *Graphic Design: USA.*

RIGHT ON POINT
(PROFESSIONAL VIEWPOINTS IN 50 WORDS OR LESS)

First realize that [art directors at design studios] are going to say things that you don't like. You just have to put yourself into your work and make it your own thing. If you enjoy what you're doing and you create for yourself, then it really doesn't matter what other people think.

—David Catrow

Whatever you can do to get your foot in the door [of a design studio] is a step in the right direction. I think it's best to build up experience at a local level. Work with people who are right near you. You can go back and forth; there's a give and take there.

—Roger DeMuth

Put yourself in your clients' shoes; (try to) see from their standpoint what they are looking for. A designer must set up the situation that says, "I'm the expert—let me do my job." However, it's crucial to get the client involved, to establish their ownership.

—Bennett Peji

Special Relations

The Americanization of Britain?

Howard L. Malchow

SECTION III
ACHIEVING SUCCESS

CHAPTER 17

PRICING

It's easier to lower your prices than it is to raise them, but if you must—you must.

—Norman Fleishman

(My Pop. He also advised us to always rotate the stock.)

Pricing—there's no ancient incantation, secret formula to discover, or tried and true family recipe to fall back on. Many designers will tell you that cut-rate pricing ("working for chickenfeed") devalues the industry. In the bigger picture, this view is absolutely correct. Just as true is that lofty principles can't purchase diapers or formula today and don't make the mortgage next week. It's a tricky conundrum and I can't—and won't—presume to preach. (But please keep reading to the end of this chapter.)

Freelance rates for graphic designers will vary depending on the designer, of course—availability and schedule; timeframe, deadline, and budget; many things—but when it comes to pricing your work, is there really a "right" or "wrong" way to go about it?

PRICING FACTORS

In my conversation with Kelly White, we identified all the above and several other factors. Here's our pricing laundry list—in no prescribed order at any given time; my priorities are not yours. You must set your own agenda.

1. *Docket*. How many assignments are you working on simultaneously? Multiple projects in progress at the same time might mean someone approaching you with a rush job may get charged more.

   And work, in my experience, has a fine propensity to spawn more work. Stay busy, even if you have to generate your own assignments.

2. *Time*. How much time do you estimate you'll invest in a project? How long did you really work on a particular job?

   "If it only took you three or four hours to work on the assignment," says White, "don't be a jerk, charge only for actual time spent on that assignment. It's not fair to overcharge; especially when the other person is trusting you to honestly estimate the amount of time it took to complete their request."

3. *Deadline*. The trifecta of due dates, time, and docket! The sweet harmony of this trio makes every job sing a distinctively different tune. Reasonably, a screaming drop-dead date *should* secure a much higher fee than a deadline with a ton of breathing room, right?

4. *Revisions*. How many revisions will you do? This component may involve a somewhat retroactive exercise. Historically, how many revisions have you typically done (for this client; in general)? The more revisions you do—will or might do—the higher the cost.

   But White cautions that there's a bit of a catch here. Some designers throw in a certain amount of revisions *gratis* (for instance, three free changes built into the contract, and, say, $50 an hour for revisions after that). Additional charges kick in only if the client asks for more than a stipulated quota . . . not unusual (and your mileage may vary).

Revisions can definitely eat up a job and spit out the fee in fugly widdle bits. To address such a dreaded scenario, you could charge by the hour. This can readily rein in a waffling, revision-happy client.

When you charge by the hour, set a comfortable, fair, hourly rate that is utterly accurate and based on *your* situation and needs. Work with the client and negotiate a livable contract (for both parties). Establish deadlines under the umbrella of a reasonable estimated range. Build in a bit of wiggle room (quote a twelve-hour job at twelve-to-fifteen hours, for instance. This actually can pad everybody's comfort zone). And play nice. To the best of your ability, when and if you can, work with your client's budget restrictions.

5. *Challenge.* We're talking about examining the project itself: what *kind* of assignment are you dealing with? Is it a flyer, poster, logo, website, or . . . ? "Different projects obviously should be billed out at different amounts," White emphasizes.

And be sensitive to the *nature* of the assignment. How's it all *feel* to you? Heed your gut. What's your client radar telling you about the customer and the job? Any red flags being thrown? Anything warning you away from the gig or this guy? It may be something you can't quite put your finger on, but it behooves you to pay attention and ask questions.

Know that your "Spidey sense" will not be infallible. Here, experience really helps; life is a great teacher. You learn—or you'll quickly learn—that a fee by itself is frequently not worth your time, energy, and, yes, sanity. Having said that that, if you feel it's okay to throw caution to the winds, charge accordingly; draft a bullet-proof contract, and then it's "brace yourself, my dear; I'm going in."

And along those lines, do you see this job offering any fun at all? I'm not saying the *fun factor* should be the only reason to take a job, although it certainly can be. I'm not suggesting it should be *the* reason to refuse a job (although it should be duly considered; joy is underrated). What I know is that if the project makes me miserable (to any degree, in any way), and the fee is my sole reason to fire up my hard drive in the morning, that particular paycheck always lands in my bank account with a distinctly hollow *thunk*.

6. *Stature.* An "if-the-shoe-fits" rate structure based on a client's size and position in their market.

7. *Audience.* Pricing based on the intended audience: local, regional, national, or international?

8. *Value.* "When I first started," recalls White, "I remember freaking out and thinking, 'Okay . . . I don't want to charge too *much*, they won't work with me.' But then at the same time this other thought pops up: 'But

I don't want to charge too *little*. They'll think the work is going to be cheap looking.'

"*Sheesh* . . . it was a constant back and forth. I finally decided, although I was a little uncomfortable doing so, to ask my instructor at school what I should charge." And while her former mentor didn't quote an exact price, White never forgets what her mentor told her. He said, "Just remember, this is your art. This is something you worked very hard on. If you took your car to the shop because it wasn't working properly, it would cost $75–100 just for them to look around and check everything out—and that's *before* they fix any potential problems.

"Think about your design kind of in the same way," White's advisor continued. "Don't shortchange yourself. You're offering a service; doing something for people that they can't do for themselves—just as a doctor does, or like a car repair man, or furnace service person."

Certainly, it wasn't the answer White expected, but this gentleman's response made her realize that no one can actually give you an accurate "one-size-fits-all" hourly quote or tell you what to generically charge. White's instructor slyly opened up another learning opportunity for her. She subsequently found that weighing all the factors above made a difference in her pricing structure and procedure.

9. *Money*. Last here and patently not least. So, love, what do you think you're worth? What do you *need* to be making? Trick questions, I know. Charging too little? Perhaps. You'll know soon enough when there's more month than money staring you right in the calendar. Charging too much? Maybe—until your networking reveals you could be charging twice or three times as much.

10. *You. If you believe you are worth it*, name your price. Bargain basement fees ultimately only low-ball your self-esteem. Establish minimums, based on your bona fide facts of life, if you need to. If you have to fudge from your baseline, do it by choice, not under pressure or from fear. As Paul Melia says with a laugh, "Hey, maybe you're having a sale this weekend."

THE PRICE IS RIGHT?

In researching pricing, I found designers who priced by rounding figures to whole numbers. I've done that—it certainly makes it easier to split payments (halves or thirds would be typical).

But it never fails, other designers dispute this practice, countering that round numbers (oh, say, $600) may be seen as an easy fabrication to quickly make a generic bid. Those designers maintained that a more complex number—something like $527, for example—is a better response; such figures appear to be exactly determined—an ostensibly "bona fide" price.

Regardless, you should strive to be as accurate as possible. Any number that, on paper, *looks* pulled out of your, uh, hat—$666, for instance—may give the distinct impression that lazy you actually pulled it out of your, uh, hat. Best to slow down and seriously think through your quote; actually do solid arithmetic that reflects honest labor.

That's only common sense. But there's no guarantee, mind you, that such due diligence will dissuade your client from dickering. You have absolutely no control over how a client perceives *any* quote, regardless of how scrupulously you sweat your math. So, be completely prepared to justify your bid; your client may very well ask, "Hey—why does *that* cost *this?*" This is not an unreasonable request; they have every right to do so—and to which you offer a meticulous, rational response.

Many designers suggest you try out different pricing tactics for size. Excellent advice, prudent you—test various strategies and evaluate what works best for your business. Nothing wrong with that, rather astute you. Good business thinking, too.

But even your best professional intentions may come to naught. Those rather reasonable rationales. The careful homework. All that transparency. The upfront, straightforward negotiations. *Fahgettaboudit.* The client won't budge from her low-ball offer and your negotiations sputter and fizzle out to an impasse.

When that happens, David James says to walk away with dignity. "After explaining that your price is as low as you can go without compromising the project," James advises, "and if it's still too high, maybe this customer is not ready to hire a professional designer.

"Whatever you do, don't buckle to their demands to go lower, you'll only regret it. With any client, especially a new prospect, you have to be prepared to walk away if the relationship isn't working—which doesn't bode well from the outset."

RATE HIKES

When you're charging project to project, you are no doubt keeping close tabs on your bottom line. So it should be said that, eventually, you may be in a position where your rates must change to make ends meet.

Designers bat around what comes next, but I err on the side of forthright communication. I think it's good business to let existing clients know that (a) as the song goes, a change is gonna come and (b) when that change is going down. Current jobs under preexisting contracts are obviously exempted from any rate massage, of course.

Is an apology needed? How about regrets? No and no—this is not an expression of your failure or you admitting some kind of offense. Is an *explanation* necessary? Now here's another point up for debate. Like many designers, my thinking is that you're under no obligation to do so, and my feeling is that it's not an absolute necessity. But you may want to extend the professional courtesy *when asked*.

Don't attempt to rationalize a frivolous, for-the-hell-of-it fee bump. But there are valid scenarios for fee increases: steady inflation running roughshod on the cost of living; a change of business direction facilitating a fresh opportunity that requires more expertise—the real world, in other words.

You may just want to give a simple heads up (as in "on September 23, 2014 . . ." or "come April 29, 2015 . . ."). Optionally, you could establish a time-frame and extend a traditional thirty-, forty-five-, or sixty-day notice.

You should utilize a system of multiple, timely notifications: that initial emailed or mailed note with follow-up reminders (email or snail mail); a disclaimer on promos, invoices, and estimates can be efficient; an actual phone call to special clients, if feasible, could be in order.

And as your clients are real folks first and, one hopes, hopefully cognizant businesspeople, as reasonable individuals they should at least understand, if not empathize. These guys are also adults. If a client has a problem with your new rates, he or she can move on (as can you). That word *no* is a beautiful and powerful little thing.

PRICING . . . BASED ON WHAT?

Varying schools of thought address the complex machinations of pricing. If we are first, and rightly, assuming that pricing is the foundation of running any business, Gerald D. Vinci says that it's important initially to define the difference between running a creative business and being a creative freelancer—also known as the proverbial hired gun.

STANDARDS AND . . .

Solid companies uphold and adhere to relative standards across the board. You determine and set costs and provide the same exact level of service across the board. Yes, each job will be different and the scope and scale of services may vary, but your quality of service remains a constant. "Your pricing should not vary greatly for the same end product," says D. Vinci. While comparison shopping can sometimes be in the eye of the beholder, doing the apples-to-apples thing reveals the differences and explains variations in costs. *Transparency* is key in pricing. Do not make the customer wonder or give him the chance to make assumptions.

"By that same token," D. Vinci continues, "if a client tells you their budget is $5,000 (but what you build will cost only $2,500), do you increase the cost to align with their budget? Some creatives will admit to pricing according to your client's budget, but this is not a fair method to establish pricing either. This is more of an ethics question than a pricing question. The obvious answer should be *no*, but many people price according to what their clients can afford. I believe we should charge for the work and time spent and not pad expenses to reflect a customer's budget."

... PRACTICES

When working with new clients, D. Vinci always asks what their budget range might be—not to determine what to charge, but to come up with a reasonable group of options for the customer within their price range. Asking clients for their budget also determines if they are realistic about the costs associated with developing their project.

"Just a heads up," says Roger Starnes, "clients tend to think that you are trying to figure out what to charge when asking this. I suggest that freelancers explain the question."

CREATIVE FREELANCING/CONTRACTING

Freelancers, of course, can go from assignment to assignment, merely develop one segment of a project, or work for numerous customers, outsourcing their needs. Freelancers may not be tethered to any one company. They might be working at one or several companies simultaneously, free to work with whomever they choose.

"I don't really subscribe to this method of getting work," D. Vinci states. "I'm an entrepreneur at heart and don't think this generates the same level of satisfaction, business opportunities, or residual income that you can acquire running a business.

"While you are free to work with whomever you choose and charge whatever you want (per project, per client), freelancers tend to charge what they think customers will pay versus a design firm, which will have fairly set pricing for a similar project. Freelancers typically have much less overhead than a creative business would. Unlike business owners, they may not advertise as much (if at all) and do not typically offer as many services as a creative firm."

Thus, the cost of working with a freelancer looks on paper to be lower than that of a design firm on average. The majority of freelancers may get their work through networking, creative job boards, previous employers and coworkers, and various forms of self-promotion.

Because of the flexibility freelancers offer in pricing, completion times, working one-on-one, and many more advantages, a customer might find working with them much more desirable.

A BONNY RATE

According to D. Vinci, putting a price on creativity is easy, and it will probably come down to two methods: pricing based on an hourly rate (prices based on your time) and project pricing (still based on the value of your time, however).

You avoid talking about the hours it takes only because clients may not value an hour of your time as much as you do. But basically: you provide a service, and there's accountability for what that service costs. You establish that your work has value and you ascertain the basic cost—whether it's hourly or per project—on a particular type of valuable service.

You identify your target market. You know what it costs to be in business, to stay in business. You get a handle on your workload; evaluate when you're busy, when you are not. Ruling out the simplicity of choosing an annual salary as a basis for your rate per project, you will continually be adjusting and readjusting for ebb and flow, thus putting too much pressure on you and your business. D. Vinci tells us that the easiest way to establish pricing is to figure out an hourly rate on which to base all your work.

"Pricing must be based on time in any creative field," D. Vinci says with conviction, "since only you know how long it takes you to create—and how much that time is worth."

D. Vinci advises us that even if you establish a base cost for a particular product, that cost should still be built on your time. So how do you get to this figure? Now comes the homework: research other competitor websites, online forums, professional groups; consult friends, colleagues, and peers who work in a similar field; approach design companies directly and ask how much they charge. "This might seem a bit devious," says D. Vinci, "but there is no ill-will meant when finding out pricing. Any reputable business should be willing to give you a ballpark cost."

Confer with your local Chamber of Commerce. Look outside of your own profession for inspiration. Consider your competition; compare, contrast, and compete.

Now find your sweet spot; set your sale price, but be flexible. Budge when and if you must. Call it a starting price and go from there. "Come up with a base cost that works for you and doesn't scare away customers," says D Vinci. "Doping out a fair price can take time and you may have to test it out on several clients to see what seems reasonable across the board."

RIGHT ON POINT

(PROFESSIONAL VIEWPOINTS IN 50 WORDS OR LESS)

Price too low and they'll question the quality or service. People equate quality to price even though that's not necessarily the case. Understand the difference between offering a fair price and pricing to sell. Never price to sell unless your product is in such high demand it generates pure profit.

—Gerald D.Vinci

© 221 by Viv 2014

Practice "value exchange" when negotiating. A client may want you to reduce your cost. Don't merely agree to a price cut and be done with it. Instead, "exchange" the value in some other way. If the client still says no—walk away. At least you gave it one more shot.

—Kristine Putt

A note to potential freelancers: think about taxes before you spend all their customer checks. A good rule of thumb is to save 30 percent of all payments for Uncle Sam.

—Roger Starnes

Interior designer

© Optimum Design & Consulting 2014

CHAPTER 18

TEACHING

If you maintain a creative and flexible approach to the communication of ideas; if you love what you teach and enjoy working with people, your enthusiasm will be communicated to your students. They will respond in kind and will be engaged in your class.

—June Edwards

ADORABLE

Perhaps, like Ken Bullock, you simply adore *learning*. The expression "be a student of life" really fits the guy. That's very cool. Could be, you too have always been hungry for knowledge. And maybe you simply love sharing what you know and helping to enlighten, educate, inform—even in some cases *to lift up*—the people in your life. If so, teaching, formally or informally, will be not only incredibly gratifying, but also the ideal way to pay it forward.

JOY AND EFFECT

Bullock enjoys teaching and has done a lot of it. Maybe not in a traditional academic role, but in the corporate setting, as an internal trainer, within professional development programs, and just casually hovered over a colleague's desk and around conference rooms. Anywhere and everywhere colleagues wanted to know what he knows.

If you know something, and know it well, you just may be an effective teacher. "Teaching brings a different level to your knowledge," Bullock considers. "In your design practice, you've figured out what works best for you. But when you teach, you must be able to come at a problem from multiple angles, not just the way *you* solve a problem or learn. If you don't, there will be a student out there that challenges you on it. There's always more than one way to get a thing done. As a teacher, your job is to enable your students to ascertain what works out best for *them*."

BE PREPARED

Bullock has approached this long enough that he understands teaching is also about preparation—something folks who don't teach rarely see nor fully appreciate.

He's been there. He knows that most great educators spend numerous hours preparing to teach. Outlines and lesson plans; working up handouts and developing demonstrations; devising curriculum and generating assignments; strategies for questions and answers; contingencies . . . all create a road map for the teacher to better lead students in the best direction.

And of course, the longer you're at the front of a class, the more preparation. A two-and-a-half-hour studio twice a week over the course of a sixteen-week semester takes a lot of prep.

SPECIAL

"It takes a special person to be a teacher," Bullock states. He doesn't say this to snag a pat on the back. He considers himself only a part-time academic. You'll need extended or specialized training and designated certifications.

A CONSULT

Informally teaching or tutoring students, colleagues, friends, or family is one thing. On the job (or freelancing from home) you must, of course, be graced with the time, energy, and inclination to act as the de facto "help desk." You obviously don't want to be taken advantage of. Nor should your status as go-to guy interfere with your job or home priorities and responsibilities.

But if you are poised to establish your credentials as the team trainer, resident expert, or just an invaluable problem solver, it could definitely be parlayed to your advantage. Knowing your way around tools and toys can create a new job title for you: consultant. This is something to consider, as these professional advisors command good coin.

We should point out that the money is generally, uh, not so great. But Bullock embraces teaching because he loves it. And, if you're of a like mind, so should you.

MARKS, BROTHER

As a teacher and designer, as well as a writer, I am rather a full-time evangelist for visual thinking and translation. At the base of that lofty perch is the *mark*. That mark is the very core fire of what I would call *designed communication*.

Your marks should unmistakably reveal your thinking and your world. I believe you must love the life of the "mark" and the creative passion it ignites. One might say that the mark sparks—the rhyme is unabashedly intentional— the flame of creativity. To fan that flame, you should tell a visual story that invests the viewer in your narrative process. Empowering the audience in this manner gets you one step closer to making the art you are meant to do (more on that later). You strive for meaning and relevance by getting to the marks directly, through open reflection and hard work.

So, as an academic and a designer and writer too, it is important for me to teach—and for students to reconcile—the mechanical with the intellectual process. Why we design (or draw) is often what and how we design or draw and vice versa. I am frequently asked the million-dollar question: "Can you teach me how to design (or draw)?" The answer: a teacher's real charge is to show students how to make their own marks from personal observation, particularly not to mimic the instructor and certainly not to ape the currently popular design trend or hot designer or illustrator. Becoming a real artist is an exploration that's not taught, but rather developed, encouraged, and coached.

STAY THE COURSE

So, if becoming a true artiste is an exploration that's not taught but rather developed, encouraged, and coached, then it's reasonable to assert that teaching is a collaborative affair, and this approach must then take into serious account the big responsibility falling on an educator who is asked to create a class of lasting value.

I think a teacher's job is to empower students and get them one step closer to making the art they are meant to do.

Thus, "teaching," to me, must be a true two-way street between student and instructor. I believe a strong art course is structured to teach fundamental principles through an empirical series and wide range of building experiences. A "good" teacher exuberantly relays information, sure, but he or she also mentors knowledge, craft, and technique through solid example and deep demonstration.

It's not just preaching from the pulpit, either; you reflect on what you know as the grist of what students are learning. You inspire, engage, and encourage with wit, a thorough command of your materials and a keen grasp of the challenges of *communicating* to students. In other words, you understand the market; you know your audience.

WAX ON

From the other side of the teacher's desk, I believe that design students are obviously burgeoning professionals, and they have to reach high. They must, or we are not tracking a basic definition of the word *professional* itself.

I also believe that making art means you must exercise all your strengths—the physical, mental, and emotional muscles that will power up your career, as well as enable you to stretch (as in head and heart).

Old elitist paradigms don't work; selling is not selling out by simple definition. If you embrace design as a calling, if you make art because you have a primal need to do it, then you will create regardless of compensation. Being paid for your passion is honest motivation.

When students question why we create, I put it this way: as a kid, a box of crayons and a blank sheet of paper were probably all you needed. A new box of crayons was downright thrilling.

Current art technology is our veritable big box of sixty-four crayons—and just as exciting, no matter what your chronological age. Add in any classical training and the study and exploration of modern visual communication is like discovering that crayon sharpener built right into the back of the box. How cool is that?

It's about seriously listening to your inner voice and determining what drives your process of self-realization, knowing and reaching for what you want. But you have to be committed to continued learning through a lot of investigation and hands-on practice.

I equate both life and art as true user experiences. Metaphor alert: today, professionally, you must be a social butterfly and a creative bee. It's a non-stop learning process with—to paraphrase Rigie Fernandez—the personal and professional focus on both design and functionality.

You design your world, personal as well as professional, built on solid and planned information architecture, a user-friendly interface, and straightforward navigation. In art, as in life, your brand (you) and service (your work) must meet user experience head-on for serious communication.

WHERE TO START

To kick-start any creative journey, I always advise all within earshot to employ an elegantly simple (and simply elegant) mantra I learned from my colleague, Jenny Kostecki-Shaw. It's just two wonderful words: Begin Anywhere. But on the practical note, to obtain a teaching position at the schools Fred Carlson lists in chapter 2, we need to filter Kostecki-Shaw's elegant mantra a bit. June Edwards helps us here.

"In general, search committees look for candidates who demonstrate experience and skill in the discipline," she tells you. "Résumés and portfolios are examined first, and applications that do not meet the minimal qualifications will be set aside. The quality of work in the portfolio, and the extent of the work, publication, and exhibition experiences will be considered for each candidate. A teaching philosophy, artist's statement, and references are usually required. Teaching experience is a plus, and if you taught courses similar to the ones listed for the position, you will have an advantage. The strongest candidates will be contacted for an interview and often a teaching demonstration."

Please note that at four-year, state-affiliated colleges and universities, and at most private four-year institutions, a terminal degree is required. An MFA is the terminal degree for the arts: most schools do not accept an MA. If you are hired with an MEd, MS, or a similar degree, you will need to obtain a PhD or an MFA to gain tenure. Tenure and promotions are based on three components in state-affiliated schools: excellence in teaching, scholarly growth, and service (committee work, etc.). Private institutions usually require less service or committee work.

"At community colleges, two-year degree institutions, and on-line institutions, either a master's degree or PhD is required," Edwards says. "A stronger degree might be the deciding factor if there are a lot of applicants for a position. There are usually fewer full-time positions available at these schools."

LIFE IN THE CLASS LANE

William Jaynes cautions that, from the outside, teaching looks easy. His initial thought was, "Hey, I know this art stuff—I've been to *art school*." That's when he found out just how *much* work goes into creating and instructing a class.

"You learn that your meticulously prepared lesson plan covers only about half an hour of a three-hour studio," he says. "Eight hours looking for the right sample may translate to a mere fifteen minutes of class time. And this doesn't include grading and critiquing or working with students *outside* of class."

And then there is the problem of actually finding a way to enable student learning. After years as a practicing professional, Jaynes states that "seeing as a beginner," is not an easy task. The focus must be on the students' work, not your own. "You're not the star," he points out, "you become the humble facilitator."

Jaynes wisely (and honestly) points out that balancing the professional gig with an academic career is problematic. Perhaps, it's because the same type of creative energy fuels both endeavors. "There is a fight for attention much like romancing two lovers at the same time," he muses. "You can end up just tired and heart broken.

"But I've found that art-making makes me an authentic teacher in the classroom. During periods when I'm not pursuing my craft, the teaching becomes hollow."

WHAT ARE YOU TEACHING?

So why attempt this tough juggling act? Why teach? Well, it could be said that all great treasures are guarded by dragons. Many consider teaching the ideal way of giving back; certainly, the rewards from this gig are, in fact, tremendous.

For some of us, it is all about carrying it forward. "Certainly, I recognize the need to be a role model and a facilitator for my students," says Lampo Leong, "demonstrating my passion and devotion to my art, while at the same time communicating as clearly as I can in order to challenge and inspire. My ultimate wish is to open a path for students that will lead them to discover and actualize their own values."

It's much like solving a puzzle; a commissioned design is always about communication. Fundamentals, style, and technique are only the underpinnings to the creative event. Brainstorming is the place where the vision comes to life, the first step—where the artist revs up his thinking and gets his creative juices flowing. Roughs, thumbnails, and comprehensives could be tagged as the place "where the ideas live." These preliminaries kick off the life cycle of most designs. A design begins, takes shape, and gets refined here on the way to complete the journey: the final.

I mention all this because, in my teaching philosophy, what we are designing, the subject matter, may well be the major focus of the whole exercise. Whether your art hawks bottled water, whips up emotion, or pushes opinion—even if the design is simply a mechanical workout or an exercise in pure concept—"What's this picture all about?" should indeed be a core issue of your education.

But just talking "subject matter" means we are only examining a big picture in a wide frame. Subject-making presents the opportunity to address that million-dollar question mentioned previously. It's the chance to grab the viewer's or reader's attention, to be a strong *communicator*. Visual translation should work to amplify or clarify concepts. Concept spins both composition and mechanics and confronts process and product. Conceptual skills are all about communication and problem solving. Creative expressionism, both intellectual and technical, is a visually active idea. This art tests interpretation, often offering unexpected insight and meaning.

For me, at the heart of the exercise is a welcome test intrinsic in every assignment: a learning opportunity for *both* designer and audience. Making art is a euphoric exploration to push forward. Teaching art extends that ambition. The teacher teaches the teacher and the student simultaneously.

A teacher's technique and imagination are charged to find the best way to help students make their statements, even if it means simply getting the hell out of the way and enabling the students to do what they do best. Making that point effectively can be the real fun. There is the real excitement of problem solving.

My language here is purposely ambiguous; those last two sentences work from both sides of the teacher's desk. Student and teacher work together to articulate what the design is all about—what's really said—and to enable the student to distill ideas and get these concepts across with minimal, effective language: to entice an audience and maintain viewer interest, not say too much while saying just enough. The teacher facilitates the hand-off of inspiration to concept, the segue of composition into technique, the juggle of representation with interpretation.

Even the most straightforward answers can involve exhaustive process (and perception)! There must be a pure dedication and a consistent commitment to successfully catalyze these tasks. It's easy for some students to misinterpret the intentions of a so-called "tough teacher" and view a rigorous classroom regimen as restrictive. But the challenge of creative restrictions and intense process produces interesting results and expands your boundaries. A demanding instructor should always take students in a different direction if the goal is to push them toward the possibilities and open doors as a result.

Perhaps you're just enabling students to explore the stuff of it: the toys, tools, and materials. That's okay. Go right ahead and have them fool with concepts and play with rules, but the work ultimately begs some relevant questions: "What did you teach here? What did they learn here? What did I learn as a result?"

Remember also that, on his way to turning on the lightbulb, Thomas Edison regarded each failed experiment as simply what not to do again. A brilliant mantra that brightens up the classroom, say watt?

THE TEST LAB

Art teaching offers a nice little perk: a wonderful give-and-take that sweetly enhances your professional practice, if you're doing it "right." As Alex Bostic tells us, "Art is one of those things where you have to *do it* to *really* teach it well. You have to be 'in the trade' to know what you are talking about. You have to be in the game.

"Teaching (and working with students) brings a distinct vitality to my life," Bostic says. "The isolated artist who stays in his shell, enjoying little or no personal contact, often struggles with the outside world.

"I understand my business as well as academia. I have my routine," Bostic continues. "It's *the students* who bring fresh challenges into that mix. Problem solving for the classroom can cast a new light in the studio. Helping students solve problems helps me solve my problems as well. I see teaching as a constant learning process.

"Students are looking at everything in a new way. To keep up, *you* must also look with that fresh perspective. This forces you to evaluate the state of the art, to appreciate change, *and* the here and now.

"Students want to know what's going on, so *I* have to know what's happening to report back. Without a doubt, students are *my* best learning tools."

WHOSE LEARN IS IT ANYWAY?

Matt McElligott agrees. He thinks that working with students has opened him up to new ideas, new approaches, and more. He's discovered that teaching, not surprisingly, has been an excellent education in itself. "As anyone who's ever tried it can tell you," he comments, "there's no better way to really learn something than to try to show someone else how to do it."

Let's flesh this out a bit. When students focus on something they haven't seen before—the new or unexpected—great change can occur on both sides of the teacher's desk. A truly savvy educator should be open to learning from students and should recognize that teaching is a great counterbalance and outlet. In fact, at the end of an earnest day in the classroom, it could be difficult to say who benefits more—the pupil or the professor.

I've always felt, wholeheartedly, that one learns so much from whomever *you think you are teaching*, whether that be a parent with his child or some seasoned career pro working with a newbie. I can't imagine a smart teacher refuting that; few folks are so pompous that they think they teach and don't learn at the same time.

WORKS FOR ME

For some, teaching simply rings just right. As Stan Shaw says, "Teaching allows me to indulge my love of history. The research and reference combined with my personal, creative experimentation gives me some insight into how I work.

"I also get to see through the eyes of the students—who may or may not be familiar with what makes a 'good' or 'successful' piece. The constant job of breaking down what I know, taking a good look at it while quantifying for those students, provides a fresh take on this process."

Greg Nemec tells us, "I used to tutor inner-city kids in reading and writing. I was always attracted to igniting that spark of learning. There's a quote that resonates with me here. It goes something like, 'Figure out what you're passionate about: do it, and the money will follow.' However, it took me a long time to figure out that I should be teaching these same age kids to make *art*. So I then started art classes for local grade-school kids.

"I tend to dive into preparation, research and learn as much as I can before I switch over to the intuitive side and start being creative. I need that foundation to begin. With teaching, I am less structured.

"I always draw from my experience, knowledge, and prep," Nemec states, "but I like to see what organically unfolds in the classroom—let that influence what we do next. One thing just leads to another. Teaching kids has helped me be more open to change and unpredictability in my own work."

COME ON IN. THE WATER'S FINE

Isabelle Dervaux was new to teaching when we first chatted about the subject. "I was a bit afraid," she candidly admitted. "You jump through all these hoops: maybe I'll have the wrong mix of students; I won't handle it well . . . I'm out of my league—I'm not cut out for it."

But friends convinced Dervaux otherwise. "It's fine; just go ahead," she was told. And Dervaux was glad she listened to them. "I got a lot out of it," she says, "how to articulate or think; how to say something, in plain words, logically, *out loud*. You see that what you learned along the way is tremendously valid, that what you're doing is honestly good, and you feel more confident. You notice that you know *much more* than you think. You gain new perspectives . . . a fresh look.

"I didn't expect to really enjoy teaching," she says, "but I actually loved the connection."

THE FRONT LINES

Developing content for your class can absorb a great deal of time. Within the parameters of any subject exist a wide range of possibilities to be explored. Edwards says to compose a course description and draft an outline that initially gives *you* an idea of what should be covered in the class and summarizes, of course, the critical information ultimately offered to your students.

"A big part of your job is to make that content relevant and interesting," says Edwards. "The more you explore and plan, the better your class will be. If you are excited about what you present in class, your students will likely be excited as well and will produce better work." Real world alert! Make sure you include information learned from working with clients and art directors: your students will gain a deeper understanding by hearing about your practical experiences. Flexibility is also important. As the semester progresses, you might decide to scrap some of your original plans to incorporate an idea better suited to your students' needs and interests.

If you are teaching a class for the first time, Edwards reminds newbies that it is always best to take a few months to prepare *before* classes begin. In addition to determining what should be covered, creating a logical sequence for that content is key. Synch with the school calendar to decide how to fit the various units into the semester.

Is it a no-brainer to remind you that your approach to the content of your class should reflect the needs of your students first and foremost? "Find out as much as you can about them," Edwards says. "Do they all have the same technical skills? Are they all at the same level and in the same program? If your assignments require specific technical skills, you might develop a short questionnaire for the first day of class to determine if you need to include additional technical content."

Next, decide how many projects you'll assign and what the grading rubric will be for each: students should have a clear understanding of your evaluation system. If you will include only a few major assignments during the semester, consider breaking projects up into two or more grade modules while providing early assessment and progress checks for each student. "It is best if grading occurs early and often during the semester so students have a clear understanding of how they are doing in your class," Edwards advises. "You could also give grades for the various components of a finished project. Your final grades will be that much fairer if students are given a variety of opportunities to succeed."

Critiques, obviously, are an important part of the evaluation process. Students need to have the experience of presenting their work, absorbing and processing feedback, and assessing the work of others. The tone of a class critique should be nonthreatening and positive; however, students must be led to recognize the successful components of a project, identify areas that fall short, and how to improve those areas. Creativity and effort should be acknowledged and encouraged. "Discussion and analysis leads to a deeper understanding of the design process," Edwards states. "This helps your students develop the skills they need to succeed in a competitive field."

Most colleges and universities have a system for students to evaluate the effectiveness of each class at the end of the semester. Which projects and presentations were most effective? What information was vital; what not? Any problems? Students should be asked to evaluate their own performance in your class. How well did they fulfill their responsibilities: attendance, preparedness, effort, etc.?

Just as students must find their own voices, teachers must also find their own creative ways to communicate ideas and information. "The best classes are the ones taught by artists who recognize the craft of teaching," Edwards sums up. "These teachers are always learning—seeking new and better ways to engage both clients and students in the process of design."

RIGHT ON POINT

(PROFESSIONAL VIEWPOINTS IN 50 WORDS OR LESS)

Yes. Maybe at times, the saying, "Those who can't do, teach," is true. However, in my experience, I've also seen that "Those who can do, can't teach." Professionally, how do you transfer your skill and knowledge from one to the other?

—Bill Jaynes

When I first started teaching, it was a way of giving back. You have to have something to teach and it's not so theoretical. You have to be "in the trade" to know what you are talking about. You have to be in the game.

—Alex Bostic

Fine teachers push other avenues of thought—you learn from each other. Training and learning never stop; art education is a two-way street. I learn more from my students than they learn from me.

—Paul Melia

A good teacher pushes you forward, providing critical feedback you cannot get while working on your own. School provides a sense of community and networking—eyes, ears, and minds that can help students set their work free.

—Ulana Zahajkewycz

Talking to students revived my passion for the career. I heard myself talking and realized how much I had invested in that career and how much I knew. It was a pivotal experience.

—Lizzy Rockwell

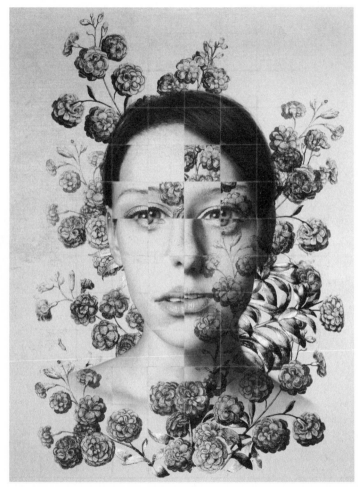

311

CHAPTER 19

IT HAPPENS

You are invariably off balance, but you have the aim.

—Paul Melia

COPING

I want to tell you something. While I haven't taken a poll, I believe most creatives I know will say the same: friend, this is a tough business. That begs a fair question: if it's such a hard slog, what are the reasons I'm doing this, then?

I do what I do because I *adore* making art and always have. And if I can make some money following my dream and passion, that would be the icing on the cake. I saw that if I wanted to stay in there for the long haul, which eventually became the realistic desire to support a family, I needed to diversify, stay flexible and wide open to inevitable change (aka growth). And I soon realized that I need to be an entrepreneur—even if I couldn't spell or pronounce it correctly—now, more than ever.

Coming up as a kid, art was "my thing." In school, I wasn't a scholar and not much of an athlete. But I could draw with the big dogs. It made me feel better than anything. If you think and feel the same, then no matter how difficult it is to "break in" and stay put, you *must* go for it. Repeat that please: "go for it."

Notes to myself and you: have a plan; be determined, stay focused, learn to bounce softly—be kind to yourself. I don't mind spewing the traditional clichés here to make the point: you're the best you there ever was. Love that guy (or gal). Make him *work*; but keep reminding him that if it's not fun, if it doesn't make him happy, there are always options and choices; you *can* move on. After all, life is the big box of crayons, isn't it?

IT'S PERSONAL

It's hard not to take the ups and downs of this profession personally. But maybe "taking it personally" just means personally taking it in a positive direction. You can succumb to the hard knocks or look at a downturn as the trumpet to charge. Either way, you'll have to approach your challenges from left or right of that center.

"It makes sense to explore. . . . Change is refreshing," Mike Quon says. "My career dream was to be a designer and an illustrator. I realized that dream by working almost continuously, juggling the creative side with a heavy dose of promotion and marketing.

"But when my design and illustration business grew to where I was spending more time selling and managing than I was creating or working on other parts of my life, I realized it was time to downsize."

Whether it was having a smaller shop or the perceived "downturn" in the industry, a less consuming work life made it possible for Quon to start a family and do all the things that go along with having kids and a home life. "A new approach to work can help you answer some tough questions about what you really want your life to be about," Quon advises. "What is success?

What do you really want? For me, it was realizing that raising children was my biggest design project—too big to miss."

Quon certainly advocates you going for the proverbial brass ring. He's telling you to take the chances. But have the nerve to move on to something else (big or small). Keep moving, learning, and making adjustments; keep fine-tuning it. Remember, it's all an experiment anyway. And it is about the journey as much as it is about the destination.

We know life's not fair. There are a lot of talented folks not making it. Quon knows a designer who works at Home Depot in the evenings to make ends meet and says so be it. "This is only a discouraging story to me if he stops making art due to this outside employment." says Quon. "Honest work, if done because it's part of your action plan, is just part of keeping the machine moving forward." I agree with Quon wholeheartedly. Keeping diapers on the baby, putting food on the table—making all the ends meet honestly—only makes you a big mensch in my book.

FOLKS JUST LIKE YOU (LIFE IN THE TRENCHES)

ORGAN RECITAL

Around Thanksgiving 2010, life got seriously in the way of everything else . . . big time. I had a chunky ol' heart attack and angioplasty procedure (two stents). This event was more than a profound shock as I was (and am) in good shape with a decent lifestyle. But it runs in my family, so that's the wild card. My angels were watching out for me—the coronary actually happened *at the hospital while waiting for a stress test*. It all went well, which is a glorious understatement, as I am, at this writing, still here to tell you that news. My care was incredible; my lovely wife, Joanne, was—and is—the head stateside guardian angel.

At this writing, I'm well into the big bounce back. You take it low and slow at first; then keep it steady as you go. You build shelf life and oomph, with everything humming around what I call the flab four: diet, meds, exercise, and stress relief. Reasonably, you understand it's always "so far so good," but you *must* make the commitment to firmly go the greater distance. Yes, there have been a few more quirky rides on the cardio roller coaster, and I work daily with natural wear and tear—we are amazing, albeit imperfect, machines—but my heart is fixed. And I can honestly say my recovery has been an unequivocally life-affirming, game-changing journey of positive outcomes.

"Remember it is about creativity," Quon says, "and creating keeps you evolving in so many different ways. It *might* mean doing something new, instead of the same thing you have been doing for all those many years . . . what a concept! Just make sure you are doing enough of what you want."

"And," as Quon sums up wisely, "do be careful what you wish for (you just might get it)."

WEAR AND TEAR

Beyond the daily stresses of being that "best you there ever was" and the logistical challenges of putting bread on the table, there are the physical manifestations of a potentially long tenure at life's drawing board. It's inescapable—we all rust or flame out. And then stop.

In discussions of this sort, the sports metaphors don't just border on cliché; they literally annex the conversation. With luck and maintenance, you'll run comfortably in what is indeed a marathon and not a sprint. But physically, mentally, and emotionally, how *are* you running your race?

Over the years, on the road to knocking out a career, you will no doubt swerve on a slippery patch of health, professional, and personal challenges. It will seem like the events hit like buckshot, but one hopes you will gracefully dodge the truly big bullets.

So what's my point here? Besides fully acknowledging life's little blessings, if nothing else, you will be reminded that control is ephemeral, fleeting; that it takes only one moment for "all that" to change to "all this," and then you have to just deal.

If you have to, please accept help with gratitude. As you must, try to be more aware of what you can do and *not* do and work to keep each action in its own state of grace. Acknowledge frustrations and own your fears and attitudes. And in the middle of that little run of bad luck, remember that maybe it seriously could be really, truly, absolutely, much worse.

BETHANY

For some people, the comparative "worse" is sincerely relative. Bethany Broadwell said that she was one of a fortunate few who could honestly say it was a practical decision for her to go freelance.

Broadwell, who died in 2009, two years after I interviewed her for an earlier book, was in her thirties at the time of our chat, weighed a mere forty pounds, and battled a neuromuscular condition called spinal muscular atrophy. The disease progressively weakened Broadwell's physical strength and caused her to rely on a wheelchair for mobility. Simple tasks like speaking on a telephone or arriving at an appointment on time involved massive organization and planning. Completing every aspect of even the simplest effort usually meant she was forced to depend on someone for help.

"I need enough flexibility in my work routine to maintain my stamina," she said. "It made sense for me to seek out home-based employment that can largely be accomplished in front of a computer."

As her arm and hand movement was extremely limited, technology made it feasible for Broadwell to circumvent her challenges. Her fingers never passed over a keyboard. "I strictly use the mouse and click key-by-key on a virtual, on-screen keyboard," she told me.

"Once I am positioned in front of my system, I can work independently for the most part," Broadwell continued. Her favorite communication methods were email or instant messages, both of which would offset her slightly unclear speech and allowed Broadwell to interact with clients.

Working on a project basis gave Broadwell the leeway to attend to any personal care needs she may have had. "As long as I keep careful watch on my deadlines," she stated, "I can complete assignments at my own pace. Providing I meet or exceed my clients' expectations, the matter of how or when I accomplish their project is immaterial."

Pushing practicality aside, however, Broadwell felt it was more interesting to reflect on why artistic freelance projects can be a good match for people with disabilities. "In my case, the main philosophical reasons have to do with the three C's of control, connectivity, and continuance," she said.

But no, she wasn't a control freak. As she told me: "The reality is I can get a little down if I dwell on my physical condition being out of my control. When I am disheartened by my limitations, my art can help me cope with these helpless feelings. It gives me the power to shape images into the creative arrangement of my design. I have an outlet I can mastermind."

Broadwell professed that her work also pushed her to be more outgoing. "A disability can contribute to a sense of separateness and inadequacy," she said. "In order to keep my flow of projects steady, I am constantly networking, brainstorming, and asking questions to stockpile creative leads for future endeavors.

"I am put into a position of needing to take initiative, exude confidence, and demonstrate my capabilities. The repetition of these tasks helps me become a more vibrant, positive contributor."

Did she feel she had a calling; was she "making a difference"? "This is the mission of all kinds of people," she pondered. "As someone deemed 'frail,' the idea of impacting others is a factor I contemplate. How can my small self influence others in a positive way, when my existence itself is so precarious? Through art, I am comforted to think I am creating a means of continuance. Whether I am here or not, my perspective is established."

Although gone, Broadwell's poignant and inspiring message still resonates and lives on, as does her powerful and determined spirit. Thank you for your not-so-small self, Bethany, we miss you.

ERIN

If you want to talk about coping skills and bouncing back, we should chat about Erin Brady Worsham, who points out that disability is a possibility for all of us. "If nothing else," she says, "it brings about the profound realization that art was never really about the pencil and paper or the paintbrush and canvas. Whatever the challenges, artists will find a way to express themselves."

It's not just happy talk and another smiley face moment, folks. Worsham knows. "I was an artist before I got sick, but my work lacked focus," she will tell you. "When I was diagnosed with ALS in 1994, I knew it was only a matter of time before I would no longer be able to use my hands, and I lost the need to create."

Only after Worsham found out she was pregnant did she recognize her desire to live and make her mark on the world for her child. "Thinking that visual expressions were beyond me," she says, "I began to paint images with words on my communication device in a journal for my son. I think this was an important period for me, because it forced me to fine-tune my descriptive skills.

"In 1999, when we discovered how I could work on the computer, my mind went wild with the possibilities," Worsham remembers. "I had taken the simple

FOLKS JUST LIKE YOU (LIFE IN THE TRENCHES)

REST, REFRESH, RELAX

Ali Douglass's creative vision is 100 percent, but she was having some physical issues with her eyes. Her condition affects her work, but while obviously connected, is not directly *because* of the work.

In her care and treatment, Douglass discovered that her optical problem was a learned behavior caused by staring at the computer too long or focusing at her drawing board so intensely. She ultimately learned to take a break every twenty minutes and focus farther out, thus protecting her precious eyesight. That was something she had to practice, she says; reminding herself to take five; stretch her body out, concentrate somewhere else beyond that visual hot zone.

"I was twenty-nine years old at that time," she remembers. "And I felt like I should be invincible. But of course, I'm not." And to the reader of these words, a friendly caution—make this perfectly clear (apologies to Douglass, and pun intended), you are not, either.

act of putting pencil to paper for granted. Now I have to use a painstaking process with a sensor taped between my eyebrows, but it seems a small price to pay to draw again.

"I am confused when people ask how I cope, because I don't see the alternative. I am as I am, and I am who I am—and that is an artist," Worsham flatly states. "My art has given me an identity outside of the ALS. It lifts me above the physical limitations in my life to a place where I can work—just like any other artist."

SISTER ACT

Without minimizing the very real impact of these conditions, let's talk about some lesser demons (and only on the cosmic scale of things). You know 'em, you love 'em, you deal with 'em everyday—the sister-act of mistakes and failure, often in cahoots with their little brothers: panic, anxiety, and insecurity.

"Usually the first thing I do after reassuring the art director that I can handle this job—*hey, no problem*—is panic," says Tom Graham. A seasoned professional, Graham is reticent to admit it, but doesn't deny this fact—the anxiety of "being in deep water, up to my eyeballs" is *very* real.

After about an hour, Graham says he settles down. "I read the text, and start thinking—rationally and objectively. I again realize solving an illustration problem is an *intellectual* as well as an *artistic* job (maybe more so)." And then the fun kicks in and his confidence returns.

Scott Jarrard also owns up: "I totally fear failure," he says. "I want to succeed. I want to be the best I can be. Failure is not an option. I keep on moving. I deal with failure by working harder. By taking a deep breath. By taking a break, pondering, doing the dishes, going for a walk. I'll do something else—and then go back and rework whatever my problem is."

Ken Meyer, Jr. says that if you always succeed, you are not really learning. And Lizzy Rockwell has learned to walk away from a problem when the answer is not revealed after an honest effort. "It is impossible to be creative and frustrated at the same time," she says. "Frustration can be agonizing, but I trust the solution will ultimately come to me."

DAMAGE CONTROL

When you *really* blow it, how do you face that fact? How do you deal with it; what is your recovery process? Dan Yaccarino notes he becomes very conscious of what just happened; he examines his motivation, looking hard at both failures and successes. "I sit down and take a good, long look," he says.

"When mistakes happen, my first reaction is flat-out anger," admits Jarrard. "I'm a perfectionist, but once I settle down a bit, I can honestly analyze the situation. I'll ask myself a lot of questions: 'Exactly what was my glitch? *How* did I blow it—where did I go wrong? What was really expected of me? You come to a happy middle ground when you share expectations."

This means that Jarrard talks over concerns before any drawing begins. He works to avoid conflicts on the job by working everything out in clear, comprehensive, written agreement. He believes that good communication skills—especially right from the very start of the job—are vital. "If it is truly my fault, or I was completely off track," he states, "I'll start over and suck up the time. If we're in a gray area, I will listen first, *then* share my point of view. I will talk through my process and concept to explain why I did certain things."

AN ORGANIZED SELF

Such positive, preventative practice (and creative chicken soup) entails some serious organization. Part of that discipline, and a big block of bouncing back peacefully, involves, as PJ Loughran points out, "Learning when to go forward and knowing when to pull back or in another direction." And a sizeable chunk of this self-knowledge is a sense of humility.

Be aware of your strengths and your shortcomings, for as Loughran says, "This is the opposite of entitlement; no matter how talented you are, regardless of how easy it all came to you. And while you may be good (or *great*) at something, arrogance is a dangerous thing.

"We all make mistakes," Loughran says, "especially in a creative discipline. You're never going to knock it out of the park every time. Everybody does both good and bad work, but the way to bounce back is to be consistent *over the long haul.*"

Your mom was pitch perfect: even though you crave a challenge, you must live in the present. And your dad was exactly right: failure or disappointment is a learning experience. So when you make a mistake, you pick yourself back up. As long as the quality of your work is consistently good, one healthy mistake shouldn't be the end of your career.

EMBRACE FAILURE. LEARN FROM IT

Could've, should've, didn't, wouldn't. Can't, and *don't,* and *maybe not.* Are these big buzzwords in your daily vocabulary? "There are too many whiners out there," Loughran says with a laugh. "Get motivated! Look for opportunities; pursue them; *make* something happen. Create opportunities for yourself or seek them out. There's no lack of talent in the world. If anything, there's a lack of discipline and ambition."

Branch out and go out on that limb, too. The old cliché may be shopworn, but is still a truism. Mistakes are always an occupational reality, but so are lofty goals and great success. If things go well or head south, you're responsible. Such empowerment can provide a huge sense of your daily worth. This is not an Olympian trait; it's within all of us. It's that balance and control that makes the difference.

Some folks do feel there is a certain safety in failure. There's no pressure if you're convinced that you'll just boot the game, regardless. Hey, why take the risk, you *know* the outcome. So you don't take the shot or you dog it, certain of the results. And sure enough, the self-fulfilling prophecy comes true.

Jarrard tells you to wholeheartedly learn from your mistakes. "Hopefully by accepting a mistake, I can avoid making the same mistake again," he points out. "If I can now avoid that same mistake, I have progressed. If I have progressed, it means *I am learning*. And if I am learning then I am enjoying life.

"If my life was 'easy,' or if I didn't struggle professionally, I am shortchanging the future. By heeding my faults *and* recognizing my progress, I have something to look forward to—I look forward to being a better person and a better artist."

To which Ulana Zahajkewycz adds, "The long, hard road of making your own mistakes to get to your true, final destination is always open to everyone at all times." Julia Minamata chimes in that we get far more information out of mistakes than successes anyway, and what you learn from failure is completely dependent on what you're willing to take from the experience. "The most important thing we learn from our successes is that success is possible," she says.

FAIL TO FAIL

Once, in an interview, I was asked to cite my biggest professional failure (and how I overcame it). But for me, this wasn't a specific event. From my point of view, it was the challenge to resist the tricks ego can play with your self-perception.

For better or worse, the quest for recognition, approval, and rewards (not to mention big bucks) are a part of a designer's—actually, any artist's—reality. The competition is fierce in most creative fields. The level of ability out there is simultaneously intimidating and inspiring.

Accolades and achievements are certainly desirable, undeniably cool, insanely great, and guaranteed to clear your complexion while improving your SAT scores at the same time (maybe just *half* a joke). But that's not what being an artist is *really* about, right? Surely that's not really why we scribble about all day, is it?

Well to me, at least, it *shouldn't* be—you do design because you love it. You create because of the little rush and big tickle you get when you realize, "Hey, I made this. *Me*. No one else can do it quite this way."

There will inevitably be moments when you need to remind yourself of that. And getting to that actual heart of the matter is what's *really* desirable, cool, and insanely great. However I'm still working on my complexion and improving my SAT scores.

FLIGHT OR FIGHT

Life, professionally and personally, can get more than a bit daunting. Call it a dry spell, but you may hit stretches where not much is happening . . . business spirals down; work drops off or simply evaporates. Been there; done that, thank you.

You could sit around to piss and moan, or you could do something about this mess. Granted, it may be hard to keep the faith, but that is why it's called *faith*. If you actively believe in your personal power to make the changes and upgrades on all fronts, personal and professional, you have a clear shot at turning it around.

How? I can sum it up in three words: *resolve, diversification,* and *action.* If you haven't diversified early, it's really never too late. Really? Really. I doubt seriously that you're a hopeless, one-trick pony. Hell, even I can walk and chew gum at the same time.

Diversification is simply figuring out what else you're good at. And what else ya got means basically looking at, well, what else you like to do. We bandy about that term *creative* so . . . well . . . creatively. Here's your chance to dip into that creative *well*; what Vivienne Flesher labels as that whole spirit of being an entrepreneur—and come up with other job descriptions for your multi-tasking self.

I am also a firm believer that work begets work; that it is easier to find work when you have work. For me, I can pull my thumbs out of a number of pies: design, illustration, and fine arts; teaching (public and private; full or part time); writing assignments; speaking gigs and lectures (large and small . . . including school and library visits); consulting.

I'll risk sounding like a late night TV infomercial to say that a good attitude and positive mindset, strong work ethic, plus active marketing and promotion make the difference. It has for me. And I'm not going to say "at least," as it was, and is, hardly a minimal effort. I believe it can make a difference for you, too.

So when the creative well dried up for me, could I have worked the midnight shift at the local mattress warehouse? Sure. And while that is honorable work, I had different ambitions. And so did Ray-Mel Cornelius, who will tell you the story of his former student bemoaning a hard time deciding whether to enter the communication arts or go into business with his uncle, who had an air-conditioning/heating repair business.

"I told him that there was nothing wrong with air conditioning and heating repair," remembers Cornelius, "and that if he felt he could make that choice, then AC/heating may well be for him.

"I would have made an awful heating and air conditioning tech, and probably a terrible *just about everything else*," Cornelius states unequivocally. "There's nothing else I could or would want to do with my time than make images."

DISTRACTIONS

What? Hey, I'm sorry—I got pulled away for a second. Now *where* were we . . . ahh, yes—how do you deal with distraction? Kelly White tells us that distractions are bound to happen, stealing your attention away from vital tasks. It's everything from the phone ringing at inopportune hours (or non-stop) to your children playing around the house while your dog barks incessantly. The weather, too—the thunderstorm and lightning strike that took your computer out; a dreary day's irresistible nap seductively beckoning you away from your desk. "There are many things that can happen," says White, smiling, "and they will. The best thing to do is to plan ahead a bit.

"For instance: you know you have a deadline coming up in two days, but you rationalize, 'Hey, I only have thirty minutes of work left to do. No sweat . . . I can run through it quickly the day before I send it off.' You are making a *big* mistake and will learn that the real world will quickly get in your way— anything can happen 'the next day': a loved one in the hospital, unexpected revisions on another project. Even if you only have 'a little to do,' don't procrastinate; *just do it.*"

As White points out, nothing is worse than missing a deadline due to poor planning, especially if it's due to the proverbial thirty minutes of work. She recommends a three-pronged attack. Plan A: think ahead. To the best of your ability, recognize potential distractions and be ready . . . take care of the situation; sit back down and try again. If that doesn't work, there's Plan B: take a second to opportunistically step away and deal with those distractions; put out the fire (figuratively), regroup, and hit it hard again.

This, however, as White points out, will never be a foolproof operation. There will always be days that no matter what you do, your strategies just won't work. So here is White's Plan C: it is extremely important that if this is the case—after you've gotten to the place where you've sent that nagging email, made the long-overdue phone call, or skinned the lunkhead cat (just a joke, no animals were harmed during the making of this chapter), and you're still distracted—just roll with it. A note here: emergencies are just that. If you were pulled away in the middle of a conversation, make sure you take time to follow up in timely fashion; explain what just happened. "You'll find that people will not only understand and be appreciative that you were honest," says White, "but will also sympathize."

"I deal with distractions by hiding in my office," Jarrard adds, with a laugh. "I have a home office and I absolutely *love* being able to spend time with my wife and kids. But if I need to get a project done, I will turn on some tunes and shut my office door. If the door is closed, my family knows not to bother me.

"But if my wife wants the family to go camping and a client calls with a rush job that can't wait, she knows that the clients are paying the bills, and we'll go camping tomorrow night. So I try to deal with my distractions by prioritizing my clients' needs with my family needs."

DESIGNER UP!

I say this earlier in the book—it's always easier to say it out loud then to put it into actual practice—but it bears repeating: *try* not to get easily discouraged. Learn from your rejections. Every rejection will be a distinct challenge. You will have plenty of opportunities to develop some bark, also known as a thick skin.

As Shaun Tan says back in chapter 4, most problems and rejections result from creative cross-purposes rather than actual disagreements. He advises you to stay open to discussion, revision, and compromise while still maintaining your own artistic integrity.

Tan comments that staying true to your school while playing nicely with others are not mutually exclusive actions, as many people often believe. He also asserts that clients may be right about things as often as artists are and that it's important to appreciate outside viewpoints, beliefs, and standards.

At the risk of sounding like your Psych 101 textbook, dealing with rejection filters down to the solid advice your mom and dad laid out for you back in grade school. You know this sandbox game plan from your years on the playground. I can hear your mom's voice right now: "Stay objective." Actually, your mother probably simply said, "Try not to take it personally. Don't be so hard on yourself. Don't let 'em get to you. Everybody gets rejected. Shake it off, pick yourself up; try again. Rethink it. Be patient. Let's not be hasty. Be flexible. Roll with it or do something else."

And, oh yes, didn't your mother begin or end with "Think positive"? It *can* work. At these trying times, honesty and self-respect are lovely, productive sisters you should get to know. Try to acknowledge your strengths. Pay heed to your victories and understand your goals. Refrain from playing the blame game as your emotional escape route.

Take care of yourself and your relationships. Tend diligently to life goals, both personal and professional. And finally, consider this: is it really all about you? Truth be told, you're neither the center of the known universe, nor the mega-misery magnet you may imagine. Really. Self-importance is not character-building. Wallowing does not become you.

A GOOD FIT

How's your health—your overall mental, physical, and emotional well-being? For me, it comes down to the three stooges, uh, *stages*: relaxation, exercise plus diet, and play. All three, often combined, are crucial—especially for board jockeys. You're only a stooge if you don't promote your general fitness.

The following is all old news, but absolutely true. Your program of diet, exercise, and relaxation may be far different from mine. But what I know is that the balance of work and play rounds off the edges of stress and hyperactivity and supplies me the nutrients and endurance—mental, physical, emotional—to sustain my juggling act.

I'd bet you know all this and probably admit it when your other half's not around.

- ▣ Fact 1: You *must* exercise—you have to fit it in. We all need to embrace some sort of physical activity. So, butt off the chair, get away from that desk and *move*—move more than just your wrists. You are more than just a wrist, right?

- ▣ Fact 2: Man does not live by board alone. You are obliged to pursue outside interests; we should actively seek diversion. In reality, you are not actually indentured to InDesign. You can take a break.

- ▣ Fact 3: Likewise, you must figure out how to chill (down *or* out). It's not the stress that rocks and rolls our lives, it's how we deal with that tension.

- ▣ Fact 4: Sleep and food are vastly underrated. Your mother knew what she was talking about. It goes without saying that adequate rest and good eating (both of which are choices and habits) are paramount to your personal and creative health. This *should* be a no-brainer, but many young guns *and* old hands still try to defy time, nature, and gravity.

- ▣ Fact 5: For some, the work itself is ideal therapy. Creatively, there is nothing more satisfying then getting into the "zone." The "zone" is quite addicting. Your mind focuses intensely and on only what you are doing for that very moment. Such pharmaceutical-grade concentration means that everything else—including time itself—just falls away, often for hours on end. Incredibly, it's simultaneously pure stimulation and complete relaxation.

- ▣ Fact 6: Now, don't forget to brush. And hey—flush next time, will ya?

STAY WITH THE PROGRAM

I am far, far from perfect in the life maintenance department. Don't get me wrong, the agenda makes good sense, and I strive to practice what I preach. Generally, the machine hums pretty smoothly. But I blow it. Frequently. And so will you. However, I *have* doped out the secret to keeping the program going for the *long haul*: forgiveness.

I'm not talking about rationalization. I try hard not to beat myself up when I fail, at least, not *too* much; brute force guilt in small doses is sometimes an effective motivator. When I stumble or hit a pothole, I strive to acknowledge and own my mistakes. I give myself the leeway to wallow in the muck for a brief spell. I then remind myself to be kind to the most important cog in the wheel: me. Then I work to clean up and *move on*.

Moving on also means thinking ahead and envisioning the fabled bigger, better, brighter tomorrow. But I also believe that to manifest this future, you should take action *today*; you must live in the here and now.

RIGHT ON POINT

(PROFESSIONAL VIEWPOINTS IN 50 WORDS OR LESS)

Learning from mistakes . . . Can I ever relate! "A lesson is repeated until it is learned." If I don't find anything to take away from an experience, then clearly I haven't evolved. I can expect to continue facing the same problem again down the road. Keeps me on my toes.

—Kristine Putt

I relish testing my limits to see how far I can take things (personally, artistically). I enjoy the challenge; I never want to say, "I could've or should've." I want to be able to say, "I did or I didn't."

—PJ Loughran

© Dermacyte 2014

We artistic types can be a sensitive lot, and we can take it personally when someone doesn't like our work. You will have to get over that or you are done.

—Nadine Gilden

I found the more I push through it and work with it—excitement mixed with pressure and challenge are what I consider "good" stress. I can comfortably go into almost any situation and feel relaxed (I did say almost).

—Allan Wood

Business entrepreneur consults

What's truly important in my life is not my career—but hanging out with friends or hanging out with the dog. My priorities have always been my dog, my husband, and then my work.

—Vivienne Flesher

You have to figure out what's important in life. Is art important, or is it something else? If you are like a lot of people, you'll fight about it in your head. Not worrying about such things will allow you to go a lot farther.

—Ward Schumaker

I don't believe there are any "mistakes"; mistakes are labels of personal judgement. If you're fearful of making mistakes, this gets in the way of learning through problem solving, which gets in the way of the pure joy of creativity. There's no single way to view (or do) things.

—David Julian

Phone calls interrupt; car pools and meetings need to be arranged; shopping and household tasks demand attention; children have their own set of needs—all of which no one can afford to ignore. I used to think, "I don't even have time to die, too many people depend on me."

—Ilene Winn-Lederer

CHAPTER 20

ON YOUR WAY

The second best friend you can have (the first being someone who can give you a good job) is another designer.

—Ward Schumaker

COMPLAINT DEPARTMENT

I observed earlier that the design field has changed dramatically in the past thirty years with the advent of desktop computers. And while it's a challenging slog for most everybody, I can speak from experience. Backed up by my correspondents in this book, and exploring this hot topic on online forums, the fact is it's no easy trick getting work if you're older.

Sorry, somebody's got to talk about it. As an older designer, if you are not on top of all the latest technology (as younger designers certainly are), your prospects of gainful, fruitful employment will be dismal. We can fret about the poor economy, and burnout but, *boo hoo*, let me direct you to Isabelle Dervaux who asks a simple question: "What would I do if I didn't do this job?" she ponders. "Frankly, I don't know what else."

KNOW YOURSELF

My point here is that we can weigh in on, and weigh ourselves down with, life's challenges. But I'd rather make all this *tsuris* an opportunity for self-examination. I will take the hits for coming off as *Little Miss Sunshine*, but, hey, somebody has to do that dirty little job.

The small print first: it starts with *you*. Recognizing what you do, can or can't do doesn't always mean that you *can*—or will—do it. It may not be economically viable or you may not have the time (nor the energy) to go in a particular direction. You may not be cut out to be a *full-time* anything from the get-go. Better to ease into your path, wherever you're going, slowly and deliberately.

Or you can think of yourself as a brand. Advertise yourself that way. Redesign your website to tout this. Get clients to write testimonials. Create a portfolio that reflects just that. Name your company to appropriately indicate your identity and position your aspirations. In essence, you become the brand.

Gung ho or go know—neither scenario plays out as a general rule of thumb for those starting out in business. Rather, both are just out there to demonstrate that thought and preparation can take you down or up any number of streams.

ALTERNATIVE REALITIES

When one is described as "alternative," what does that mean? Alternative to what? Aren't artists in general an alternative to "regular" folks? Is there a perception or reality conundrum involved with this label?

The next question I would ask is, when you're part of the "establishment," what exactly are you establishing? Is it actually a roots kind of thing? You know, it seems as if the most alternative lifestyles and practices have magazines (or websites, these days) dedicated to that culture. These devotees sum up a certain "establishment," as I see it.

FOR THE TEAM

Kristine Putt has a designer friend whose work recently got ripped off. Putt encouraged him to pursue it, but ultimately her friend chose to do nothing and simply let it go. He didn't think it was worth the hassle (lawyer fees, the fuss, etc).

"I get that," Putt laments. "Truly. It's a pain in the . . . neck to pursue legal action for copyright infringement." But, then she pauses, collects her thoughts, and carefully speaks her mind: "There's this precedence thing that weighs in so very heavily at this point," she says. "Every time a designer chooses to 'let it go,' they are making it that much harder for the next victim of copyright infringement to win a case.

"We owe to our industry," she continues, "and especially to our own ilk, to do what is right, just, and moral. If not for ourselves, for all the other designers out there that are struggling with this issue. Only by following through on the principles of an ethical code can we expect to change the mind frame of society that stealing from talented graphic designers is not only unethical, but downright illegal."

Putt next makes a clear, sharp point: "I hate seeing anyone's work, especially young designers, getting hijacked. And, okay, maybe sometimes experience is a good teacher. But if you don't care enough to do something about it for yourself, then at least do something for the hundreds of thousands of other designers that have been taken advantage this way.

"It's in your power to make an example from your case and deliver a strong message that stealing is wrong and there will be consequences," she concludes emphatically. "My hope is to prevent, or at least reduce, digital thievery in this way."

More questions: Does "establishment" really translate to a "pecking order"? Or does it equate to the status quo? Perhaps, a simple frame of mind? Aren't artists in general a common fraternity or sorority and wouldn't this be the establishment? And how sharp is the "cutting edge"? Well, how'd it get so sharp? And while we're at it, who's this "avant-garde" we're always hearing about? Hey, is the avant-garde keen on this cutting edge? Even with all the alternatives within the avant garde, isn't there an establishment here as well?

"No matter what anybody says about my work, I can only be what I am," Paul Melia wisely says. "I can't force it. Oh I'd love to think of myself as avant-garde, but I'm not—I just do what I love to do. I'm *progressive*. I am with the times or ahead. But I wouldn't consider myself cutting edge, that's not me. And those are *just words*, they don't bother me. I do what's inside *of me*. If someone accepts it or pays me for it, or has a positive reaction, I'm lucky."

Thus, a last question: are there any alternatives to all these labels?

SQUARE PEG/ROUND HOLE

Is it important to fit in? By classical definition or perception, aren't artists *expected* to be "different"? But, as PJ Loughran says, "Titles are just so silly. It's a way for people to categorize, to simplify, to make sense of somebody (or their work). I try to avoid that stuff as much as I can."

And, Rick Sealock says, "It used to be the standard to be *different*. Now it's called 'quirky' because it may not be as commercially viable and tolerated as before."

Such folks were always the most interesting creatives to Sealock. Never boring, always original thinkers; these creatives challenged and pushed cultural boundaries, and thus, educated the public. Maybe political correctness and corporate philosophies of our society, in our culture, created and imposed adverse labels in an attempt to curb originality.

On the flip side of this is that school of thought that rails against any or all conformity: the idea that, if you "fit in," you'll actually lose the (creative) edge. Personal or professional compromise may be real or imagined, but according to Sealock, artistic *integrity* must be maintained.

As Sealock cautions, if integrity is not maintained, and thanks to an ever-increasingly educated populace, we steadily run the risk of dumbing down the industry.

KEEP YOUR AVANT-GARDE UP

Reiterating what I express a bit earlier in this chapter: within the avant-garde lies the dreaded "establishment." After all, the most alternative lifestyles and practices have magazines (or blogs and websites, these days) dedicated to that culture.

"You can go wild and crazy on the page because it is the acceptable thing at the moment," Greg Nemec points out, "but [that avant-garde hook is only] whatever's hip *at the moment*: 'Hey, look at me, I'm edgy.' That seems pretty establishment to me."

"You might have to deal with this, play the game, certainly pay attention to it," says Paul Melia. But, he offers a counter as he reaffirms his previous sentiments: "I do what *I* do as honestly as *I* can do it. I don't let the tags influence me too terribly; I just don't think about it that much. You can't worry about the labels; you simply must do what you do. You let the chips fall where they may."

WHERE IS THE MIDDLE OF THE ROAD?

When one is described as being "in the mainstream" or "middle of the road," what do we mean? Are these two different things? What *is* the mainstream, and is this positive or negative? Is the "middle of the road" actually a perceived ditch off the "cutting edge"? Can you get anywhere in the middle of the road?

Sure, you can. I'll play devil's advocate for the AAA (Artmobile Association of America) and ask, isn't the middle of the road the straight road to somewhere? It is the safer path, as opposed to driving on the edges, which is a much bumpier ride. Rocky Road is an acquired taste, and yes, you're supposed to pass on the left. But who decides if this is a "good" or a "bad" thing?

It's your say; anything anyone else tells you is a judgment call. Neil Young, when discussing his record, *Harvest*, said he found himself heading squarely down the middle of the road with this album. He saw that he was being very successful at it, but that it wasn't where he really wanted to be traveling. Yet, he returns to this genre time and again. What's the road map here, then?

"I feel like I'm more in the middle of the road," Ali Douglass muses. "The 'average guy' appreciates my work, but a 'hip chick' may look at a piece and possibly laugh—it's too 'happy and cute.' But I'm excited about it. So what if it's not 'hip' enough?"

That's correct; you heard her right. No tattoos and piercings; no women in compromising positions, nothing sexual. It's not depressing or dark.

People see Douglass's work and enjoy it *because* it is fun and upbeat. "And I like that," Douglass states. "That's a great thing. I think it is fine to bring out that particular emotion. This maybe puts me in the 'normal' category; more the middle of the road rather than the avant-garde. But it's all good."

Yes, sometimes Douglass feels pressured to be do art that is "cool," more for "her generation," gallery-type work, edgier stuff. But as a wise mentor once reminded her, she realizes that she doesn't *need* to. It is what it is: amusing and entertaining; fun, happy, and downright silly is more than okay.

VICTORY

Competition. Is this a "good" or "bad" thing? Is this all about motivation and drive? How do *you* handle the competition? Who—or what—is *your* competition? Is it actually a grudge match between fact and fiction—*real* competition and *imagined* competition?

"We're all competitors," Sealock says, "sometimes with others and always with themselves. We compete with every design we have created and the ones we want to create.

"We compete with our skill level and technical ability. We compete with our pre-existing concepts, our notions, and our expected approaches. We compete against labels and definitions, fears and security. We compete."

INTEGRITY

"Is this the devil's advocate part of the book?" Sealock asks. Could be, because maybe you don't really think about it all that much. And without a doubt, there is no one who does the job quite like you, right? But, if you disregard the competition (or choose not to compete), what does that mean for you, as a designer, as a businessperson?

"It's more the business of creating than selling for me," Sealock considers. "The creativity portion is separate from the price tag. I create because I love and need to. It's a bonus that someone wants and will pay for my work."

Again, to each their own. If you judge the creative level of your design by its dollar value, that's your call; so be it. But that's certainly not Sealock's mindset. He maintains that selling doesn't mean giving up artistic control. On the contrary, not only can you keep artistic control, but you can work to build on it, maintain the integrity of your art, and further its creative merit and development.

And selling it does *not* mean you are selling out and losing your artistic integrity, either. "Giving it away is losing your integrity," Sealock emphasizes. "Besides, you *can* sell out or have no artistic integrity and still be very successful. It's whatever you think is correct for you.

"Personally, money comes and goes," Sealock comments, "but your integrity has to remain intact, defended to the end. It's difficult to do at times, as we're only human, but you must try and that is the key.

"Yes, giving it away for free *would* be a compromise," Sealock sums up. "If you feel your work is worth *nothing*, then give it away for that. But if you feel it is worth *something*, then get something for it."

GREAT TALENT/BIG HEART

Chris Haughton has, amongst other things, written, designed, and illustrated children's books. He's created toys connected to those book projects, commercial animation, murals for hotels, and packaging design for chocolates. He is justifiably proud of the work he has done for the fair trade company, People Tree, an amazing group of folks who support schools and orphanages around the world. "They work with eighty producer groups in fifteen different developing countries," he says. "They produce ranges of clothing and gifts with womens' shelters and disabled groups. I have been helping out with the designs of some of those products: bags, T-shirts, stationery, and repeated patterns for clothing and dresses." One of the ideas Haughton is most excited about here is making rugs from digital designs.

Fees? The profits here all go to building schools and training workers. Staying busy? That's an understatement. "The best thing to do is to work, even in your spare time," says Haughton. The "success"? "Find a way of working that you like and enjoy," Haughton tells you. "Don't force style. If your content is unique, you definitely will land better and more interesting work. Produce a body of your own work—work you feel comfortable with."

And, as Haughton points out, probably the most important thing to do is to get your stuff out there. "If you're shy about 'showing off,' you won't get half as much work as you should be getting.

"But I think design has a potential for greater things," Haughton says after a pause. "It can make our world and communication clearer and more beautiful. It can help communicate things that are unable to be communicated by language. Sadly, perhaps because of its power in communication, it really has been totally hijacked by advertising and corporate communication. The word *design* has kind of become synonymous with branding; I want to counter that."

Haughton thinks ethical considerations are crucial to good design, and tries to design "from every angle," always figuring out how the thing can be done better. And this is a challenge that, for Haughton, all comes back to ethical considerations. "I became a bit disillusioned in my own design when I was doing advertising and branding for large companies," he tells us, "so I wanted to do something that was more rewarding. I think design has a great potential for positive change and I would love to be involved in that aspect of it—*that's* the exciting part!"

THE NEIGHBORHOOD

Chris Spollen makes this statement, "Your passion is what will define you." This is just *so* true. This zeal for art, the gusto for your design (and hopefully, the lust for life) should be a no-brainer. But why go it alone? Passion can be absolutely infectious. And if social skills are your challenge, *then meet the challenge.* "Create a *community* around you," PJ Loughran advises. "Get out. Socialize."

It's safe to say that networking is how *most* people get most, if not *all*, of their work. As Shaun Tan says earlier in the book, it's what you know *and* whom you know (emphasizing the *what* over the *who*).

But that "who you know"—folks branching off and reaching out—is critical. It is referrals and repeat customers, promos that follow art directors jumping from job to job. I've said this repeatedly, but it's solid advice: network at *every* opportunity.

The Internet and email were science fiction when I started out, so you had to do the leg work. Sure, modern marketing and promo gambits, new portfolio strategies, plus all the shiny digital toys are indeed game changers. However, smashing interpersonal communications (writing, phone calls, one-on-one contact, attending conferences and art shows, joining art organizations, etc.) are still part of the playbook.

Along those lines, I understand that wearing a club jacket (metaphorically) is not for everyone, but art organizations I've mentioned previously (the Guild, AIGA, your local design club, for instance) all have a common charge:

the preservation and advance of the profession for the good of the membership. The fellowship is invaluable.

Of course, the global forums of the Internet, the cornucopia of professional and personal networks, discussion groups and message boards, all of these mean you can network electronically 24/7, without even getting out of your pajamas. No jacket required.

So, make the rounds, stop by, and stay in touch. Spend some time; be there; pay it forward. "We're all together in this thing," says Dan Yaccarino, "and we all have to support each other."

IF YOU SUCCEED, I SUCCEED

There are a lot of designers out there. It seems that somebody couldn't keep a secret and it went viral: this is one of those coveted "good jobs." Whoa . . . at times, it feels like it's "Everybody in the pool!" So, is diving into that pool like swimming with sharks and piranhas?

Yo, dawg, it doesn't *have* to be dog-eat-dog. Spollen is one who feels exactly the same. "I *love* keeping in touch with fellow artists, " he says. "And if work comes my way and I feel it's more up someone else's alley than mine, I will pass it on. I'm always looking out for my friends and I believe they do the same for me."

Know, also, that it's more than okay to seek feedback from sources within and outside the creative neighborhood. In addition to advice and critique from other designers, input from family and friends, even fans, when appropriate, can be invaluable.

"I can't 'see' my work that well," Melia candidly says here. "But my wife can. When I work on a job, I'm too close to it to see it *objectively*. She hates to criticize me, though. She feels she's hurting me. But she's actually doing me a favor by telling me what's wrong with something so I can correct it. That's a helpful process."

LONERS

Isolation can crowd your style. I say that with a bit of tongue in a lot of cheek. You *love* the peace and comfort of house and home. You feel truly *alive* in your studio. But the fortress of solitude has a front and back door for a reason. Sometimes, you just gotta get out. It may be trite to say, but the play is to be a highly functional "people person." Ilene Winn-Lederer feels that being a loner is rarely a choice one makes consciously. "Usually the individual's personal, physical, and financial circumstances contribute to this status more so than the choice of profession," she comments.

"As much as we might wish to be on an island left alone to do the work we love," Winn-Lederer continues, "such a dream is ironic." She knows that without balance, the work can become monotonous, even mediocre. She understands that in an industry where staying fresh remains the ingredient for success, the personal and professional cost of leading a one-dimensional life is an expense few can afford.

Jenny Kostecki-Shaw also realized early that if you just hole up in the studio, you could lose your real world skills. "You must make the effort to go to town, socialize," she says. "*Be a part of something else.* Don't isolate yourself.

"It *is* a balancing act between solitude and community," Kostecki-Shaw sums up. "Whatever you do away from the drawing board may be small scale, but it can be a big thing for the quality of your life. For me, it is about letting go of judgments and expectations and being open to things different and all that has to teach me."

WRAPPING UP

It is fitting in this final chapter to talk about *connections*. Erin Brady Worsham says it well. Worsham feels that, as artists, we can't know where we're going until we've seen where we've been. To that, let's add that you don't know who you are until you recognize and interact with your community.

Let's *not* lament or grouse about the state of the *business*. There's plenty of opportunity to do that, but certainly, if we pay attention to the aforementioned connections, there's the manpower, time, and commitment to do something about it, too. "An optimist suggests that for every door that closes, one opens," Tom Graham says.

To keep opening doors, you'll need to consider where you've been, where you are, and where you're going and *growing*. To do that, you must keep those vital connections.

And you may want to leave some kind of legacy, to make your mark, to have made a difference. Sealock suggests that it might be more reasonable to ask what *not* to be remembered for. "Don't be boring, don't be safe, don't be a sell out, don't be a suck on society, and don't proliferate 'bad' aesthetics," he admonishes. Here, Paul Dallas picks up the thread. "Yes," he says. "Be mindful of what you don't want to do, perhaps more than what you want to do. Allow yourself to gravitate to, rather than aim specifically at, something. You will crash-land otherwise."

As Federico Jordan says, "Communication is the essence. Communication—that's really the ability to look through another's eyes." Or, as Sealock once told me: "It's all in the I's ... you strive to be innovative, interesting, and introspective."

Reiterating earlier sentiments, this communication is now truly global. More than ever, you can broaden one's focus into a panoramic worldview. And as Ward Schumaker sums it up for us, "The world is really just one big conversation; [go help] pass ideas around."

GET A MOVE ON

"Experience. Opportunity. This is the key to succeeding in anything," says Mike Salisbury. Five-year goals? Salisbury makes the excellent point that even the best, most comprehensive plot lines mean nothing without opportunity.

And education? Self-taught, Salisbury just may ring in as the most qualified educator you'll ever meet (check out his résumé if you think I'm over exaggerating), but he chooses not to teach. (1) It's a personal decision, and (2) he easily epitomizes that shop-worn scenario of being overqualified for the job (not from Salisbury's perspective, mind you, but from the "vantage point" of HR).

He's also a classic multi-tasking design entrepreneur. "Design is not a stand-alone business anymore, if it ever was," he comments. "It is but one ingredient in a marketing plan . . . so the more one understands that design is *part* of marketing—and not *art*—the more one can contribute. Designers and marketers have to get some experience in selling."

Salisbury tells us that the world of print has greatly diminished. "One has to learn *motion*," he states. "A current complaint is that magazine and newspaper grids are stifling. But the trick is to keep the packaging of that information uniform, readable, and creative within those formats; to keep it fresh and educated."

"There is hope," Salisbury says. "I am seeing a great leap forward in print now."

RIGHT ON POINT
(PROFESSIONAL VIEWPOINTS IN 50 WORDS OR LESS)

I work almost entirely digitally now and am very grateful to the computer as a tool. Digital images are almost endlessly malleable and I am very interested in the possibilities of digital tools. It's exciting to think that when the technology is so new, its makers can't foresee exactly how it will be used.

—Chris Haughton

I've made my peace with the fact that, while I'm trying to do something interesting, or different, or challenging, I'm doing this stuff for money. [This should not be] a smack in the face with a dead fish when you get out there; [don't be] disappointed or horrified.

—Dan Yaccarino

© Chris Haughton 2014

The word "good" should be replaced with "effective." I feel that design today is neither good nor bad—it's only effective or ineffective.

—Gerald D. Vinci

I have a really big neighborhood. Whenever someone I know moves away to a new town, I always figure the neighborhood just got bigger. This cast of characters is a great source of creative energy for me.

—Lori Osiecki

You can work to live, or you can live to work. I prefer the former.

—Darren Booth

I didn't exactly know where I was heading. But, frankly, even when we think we are sure, we never actually know, do we?

—Antonio Rodrigues

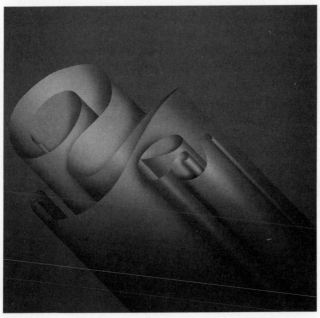

CHAPTER 21

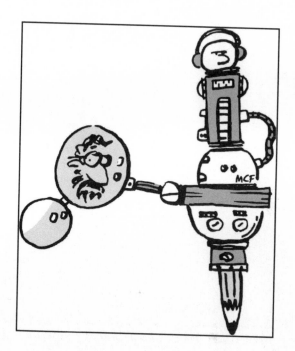

FORMS, CHARTS, TEMPLATES

For more charts, forms, and templates go to
www.michaelfleishman.com

START-UP COSTS

MONTHLY	ESTIMATE	ACTUAL
RENT OR MORTGAGE		
LEGAL		
ADVERTISING/PROMOTION		
SUPPLIES AND MATERIALS		
ACCT/BOOKKEEPING		
OTHER PROF. FEES		
INSURANCE		
OWNER'S DRAW		
SHIPPING/DELIVERY		
TELEPHONE		
INTERNET		
CABLE		
UTILITIES		
LOAN AND INTEREST		
MAINTENANCE/CLEANING		
AUTO		
TRAVEL		
OTHER		
SUBTOTAL		

ONE-TIME ONLY	ESTIMATE	ACTUAL
OPERATING CASH		
LICENSES/PERMITS		
UTILITIES DEPOSIT		
DECORATING/REMODEL		
FIXTURES/EQUIPMENT		
INSTALLATION OF EQUIPT.		
RENT DEPOSIT		
LEGAL CONSULTANT		
ACCOUNTANT CONSULT		
INITIAL ADV./PROMO		
MISCELLANEOUS		
SUBTOTAL		
TOTAL CASH NEEDED		

This start-up worksheet will help you figure out such initial expenses as deposits for utilities as well as ongoing expenses, such as supplies and materials and telephone bills.

BUDGET WORKSHEET

YEAR:	MONTH:		MONTH:	
BUDGET	ESTIMATE	ACTUAL	ESTIMATE	ACTUAL
INCOME: CASH ON HAND, FIRST OF THE MONTH				
RECEIPTS				
LOANS				
SAVINGS				
A. TOTAL CASH AVAILABLE				
EXPENSES: RENT/MORTGAGE				
HEALTH/LIFE/BUSINESS INSURANCE				
SUPPLIES AND MATERIALS				
SHIPPING				
UTILITIES				
TELEPHONE AND RELATED				
REPAIRS AND MAINTENANCE				
LEGAL				
TRAVEL AND TRANSPORTATION				
MEALS AND ENTERTAINMENT				
ADVERTISING AND PROMOTION				
EQUIPMENT				
CLEANING				
DUES AND PUBLICATIONS				
ACCOUNTING AND BOOKKEEPING				
OTHER				
SUBTOTAL				
LOAN PAYMENT WITH INTEREST				
OWNER'S DRAW				
CAPITAL PURCHASED (DEPRECIATED ITEMS)				
B. TOTAL CASH PAID OUT				
SUBTRACT TOTAL B FROM TOTAL A (+ OR -)				

This budget worksheet will help you see how much money you must make to cover your expenses—or how little you can afford to spend. First, estimate how much actual cash you have on hand each month (when in doubt, go low). Then list what you'll need to cover expenses. If you can't make ends meet on paper, you won't in real life either. Keep refiguring your expenses until you get a workable result. Once you're up and running, track your actual expenses and see how your budget is working out. How we doin'?

Proposal Form

Date _____

By _____

CLIENT INFORMATION

Name _____

Address _____

Phone _____

Address (Billing) _____

Phone _____

Cell _____

Fax _____

Other Contact Information _____

PROJECT

Name _____

Location _____

FEE INFORMATION

Fee _____

Hourly Rates _____

Expenses—Billable (with markup) _____

Expenses—Billable (without markup) _____

Expenses—Travel _____

SCOPE OF WORK

WORK PLAN

	START-END DATES	BUDGET	DURATION
Concept Development		$	
Design Development			
Production			
Project Implementation			
Total			

CLEVELAND DESIGN

date	October 21, 2010	*estimate*
to	Bob Marketer	
from	Jonathan Cleveland	

Project **Advertising for Tech Solutions**

Three concepts presented

Design	$2100
Copywriting	$1500
Meetings	$ 700
total estimate	$4300

Stock photo $500   (price to be determined)

Multiple insertion orders for various sizes will be charged for production at $150 per hour.

Timeline
Creative Briefing Conference Call – Technology Corp. and Cleveland Design
Concepts presented by Cleveland Design – 8 to 10 business days
Review and feedback from Technology Corp. – 3 business days
Changes presented by Cleveland Design – 3 business days
Final Approval from Technology Corp. – 3 business days

20 McKenna Terrace
Boston, MA 02132
617.469.4641 TEL
617.469.0040 FAX
www.clevelanddesign.com

© Cleveland Design 2014

A proposal, like the example here, and the alternate proposals following, should clearly define the design services to be provided, describing them in enough detail for the client to know easily what will be done and when.

As you can see, proposals can vary in length and content, depending on the client and the nature of the project. In any scenario, certain key features are common, such as expenses itemized in the billing schedule established.

Your document should spell out how client changes will be handled (and do include a request for the client's signature to acknowledge agreement with these costs for work to commence). It should be clear that work not described in the proposal—such as extra presentations—would be billed in addition to the expenses listed in the proposal.

STARTING YOUR CAREER AS A GRAPHIC DESIGNER

E S T I M A T E

CLIENT _____ DATE _____

CONTACT_____ JOB NUMBER _____

PROJECT_____

DEVELOPMENT   DESIGN _____

                    COPYWRITING _____

                    EDITING/TYPEMARKING _____

                    PROOFREADING _____

                    _____

                    _____

PREPARATION   ORIGINAL ILLUSTRATION _____

                    ORIGINAL PHOTOGRAPHY _____

                    STOCK ILLUSTRATION _____

                    STOCK PHOTOGRAPHY _____

                    COMPOSITION _____

                    PAGING _____

                    REVISIONS _____

                    _____

                    _____

PRODUCTION   FINAL FILE PREPARATION _____

                    PROOFS _____

                    PRINTING _____

                    _____

                    _____

TOTALS   SUBTOTAL, NONTAXABLE _____

                    SUBTOTAL, TAXABLE _____

                    SALES TAX _____

                    SHIPPING _____

                    TOTAL ESTIMATE _____

ACCEPTED _____ DATE _____

Vandeventer Graphic Design. 273 Clay Street, Monterey, California 93940   408/372-6851

Project Confirmation Agreement

AGREEMENT as of the _____ day of _____, 20 _____, between _____,
located at _____
and _____ (hereinafter referred to as the "Client")
(hereinafter referred to as the "Designer") with respect to the creation of a certain design or designs (hereinafter
referred to as the "Designs").

WHEREAS, Designer is a professional designer of good standing;

WHEREAS, Client wishes the Designer to create certain Designs described more fully herein; and

WHEREAS, Designer wishes to create such Designs;

NOW, THEREFORE, in consideration of the foregoing premises and the mutual covenants hereinafter set forth and
other valuable considerations, the parties hereto agree as follows:

1. **Description.** The Designer agrees to create the Designs in accordance with the following specifications:
   Project description_____
   Number of finished designs_____
   Other specifications_____
   The Designs shall be delivered in the form of one set of finished ❑ camera-ready mechanicals ❑ electronic
   mechanicals, more fully described as_____
   Other services to be rendered by Designer_____
   _____
   Client purchase order number_____Job number_____

2. **Due Date.** The Designer agrees to deliver sketches within _____ days after the later of the signing of this Agreement
   or, if the Client is to provide reference, layouts, or specifications, after the Client has provided same to the Designer.
   The Designs shall be delivered _____ days after the approval of sketches by the Client.

3. **Grant of Rights.** Upon receipt of full payment, Designer grants to the Client the following rights in the Designs:
   For use as_____
   For the product or publication named_____
   In the following territory_____
   For the following time period_____
   Other limitations_____
   With respect to the usage shown above, the Client shall have ❑ exclusive ❑ nonexclusive rights.
   This grant of rights does not include electronic rights, unless specified to the contrary here _____
   _____, in which event the usage restrictions shown above shall be applicable. For
   purposes of this agreement, electronic rights are defined as rights in the digitized form of works that can be encod-
   ed, stored, and retrieved from such media as computer disks, CD-ROM, computer databases, and network servers.

4. **Reservation of Rights.** All rights not expressly granted hereunder are reserved to the Designer, including but not
   limited to all rights in sketches, comps, or other preliminary materials created by the Designer.

5. **Fee.** Client agrees to pay the following purchase price: $_____ for the usage rights granted. Client agrees to pay
   sales tax, if required.

6. **Additional Usage.** If Client wishes to make any additional uses of the Designs, Client agrees to seek permission
   from the Designer and make such payments as are agreed to between the parties at that time.

7. **Expenses.** Client agrees to reimburse the Designer for all expenses of production as well as related expenses
   including but not limited to illustration, photography, travel, models, props, messengers, and telephone. These
   expenses shall be marked up _____ percent by the Designer when billed to the Client. At the time of signing this
   Agreement, Client shall pay Designer $_____ as a nonrefundable advance against expenses. If the advance
   exceeds expenses incurred, the credit balance shall be used to reduce the fee payable or, if the fee has been fully
   paid, shall be reimbursed to Client.

8. **Payment.** Client agrees to pay the Designer within thirty days of the date of Designer's billing, which shall be dated
   as of the date of delivery of the Designs. In the event that work is postponed at the request of the Client, the Designer
   shall have the right to bill pro rata for work completed through the date of that request, while reserving all other rights
   under this Agreement. Overdue payments shall be subject to interest charges of _____ percent monthly.

It may suffice to send long-time clients a simple working agreement. But with all first-time clients, or when taking on big projects, you'll need something more formal and detailed like the contract sample provided by Optimum Design and Consulting, and this Confirmation of Assignment from Business and Legal Forms for Designers. Look for other pertinent business documents in this great resource from Allworth Press. Ms. Kisielewska offers great business tips throughout this book.

C O N T R A C T

CLIENT _____   DATE _____

CONTACT _____   JOB NUMBER _____

PROJECT _____

SERVICES

SCHEDULE

FEES

ACCEPTED _____   DATE _____

ACCEPTED _____   DATE _____

Victoria A. Vandeventer Graphic Design. 273 Clay Street, Monterey, California 93940. 408/372-6851

© Victoria Vandeventer 2014

When working with a client you know well, you could send a short-and-sweet, simple working agreement (maybe even incorporating this as part of the proposal) like this contract provided by Vicki Vandeventer. This may be all the documentation you need.

To easily keep track of project details, deadlines, and expenses, Vandeventer created business forms when she started her freelance career. "This was years before there were spreadsheets and apps for everything," she smiles. These forms (along with other documents you'll see in this chapter) were also useful as self-promotion pieces as they show an inexpensive, creative treatment of routine information. The forms won an award from Print, *appearing in the magazine's regional design annual.*

All Estimates/Proposals Are Subject to the Following Terms of Service
!!! IMPORTANT - PLEASE READ IN ENTIRETY !!!

It is the desire of Paragon Moon™ to delight the Client. One way is to make clear our understandings with each other. Following are the Terms of our agreement to work together:

1. Authorization. Client named herein is engaging Paragon Moon™, a sole proprietor, as ship, an independent contractor for one or more graphic designs, web and/or printing projects. The Client represents to Paragon Moon™ and unconditionally guarantees that the person named herein is the stated Company's representative and has been authorized by said Client to authorize project commencement, approve artwork, request revisions and authorize payment. .

2. Client Cooperation. The Client understands that the Paragon Moon's™ ability to meet a specified deadline is dependent entirely upon timely submittal by Client of all information necessary for Paragon Moon™ to perform contracted Work (such as photos, copy, logo, etc.). In the event that Client does not provide the required information within the timeframe as is specified per project, Paragon Moon™ retains the right to cancel said project with five (5) days written notice to the Client.

3. Basic License. Paragon Moon™ hereby grants to Client a perpetual, non-exclusive, non-transferable license to use the Project, or any part thereof, for the permitted use of that discrete project *only*. This means you cannot use the design or any part of the design, for any other purpose besides the project it was specifically created for. All other rights in and to the project including, without limitation, all copyright and other intellectual property rights relating to the Project, are retained by Paragon Moon™ or the supplier of design elements Paragon Moon™ has used in the said project (i.e. stock images). Extended license or a copyright release for a design project or any part of a design project is optional and may be purchased by Client from Paragon Moon™, for a fair and reasonable cost, which will be determined on a per-project basis.

4. Estimates. All Estimates are based on the Client's description of the Project. Estimates include concept, design, layout and print cost (unless stated otherwise) and are based on a standard design turnaround time frame of three weeks from project commencement (unless stated and agreed to by both parties otherwise). All projects are described in the Estimate provided to the client and all project estimates incorporate the terms of this document.

CLIENT INITIALS_____   CONTRACTOR INITIALS_____

Here's the first page of Kristine Putt's "boilerplate" contract. Drafted by an attorney, the document, as the designer puts it, "Cost me a fortune—but it's legit and water-tight." Notice the prominent disclaimer at the top of the page and the slots for both client's and contractor's initials. Like Barbara Jordan, Putt requires clients to initial all pages, a practical confirmation that the client signs off on and—at least on paper—understands the agreement.

CYNDA MEDIA LAB
Web Design Agreement

DUE DATES: CML will make every effort to meet agreed upon due dates. The Client should be aware that failure to submit required information or materials may cause subsequent delays in the production. Client delays could result in significant delays in delivery of finished work:
1. CML agrees to deliver three visual design options five working days after the Client provide reference, content (images and texts), and branding guidelines and graphics.
2. The Client will provide feedbacks and suggestions for up to two rounds of adjustments in three working days.
3. Finished work shall be delivered five working days after the Client's approval of the visual design.
4. CML will continue to monitor the site for the purpose of troubleshooting and debuging for two days after the deployment of the site.

PAYMENT SCHEDULE: Payment shall be advanced to CML in phases as follows. At the time of signing this Agreement, Client shall pay $XXXX, which is roughly one third of the total fee. Upon approval of visual design, Client shall pay $XXXX, a further third of the total fee. On the date of CML delivery of the final Work, Client shall pay $XXXX, the final third of the total fee. Late fees past thirty days will be charged at 1.5% per month.

GRANT OF RIGHTS: Upon receipt of full payment, CML grants to the Client the right for use the finished design on the Internet. The Client will maintain full access and ownership to the domain name, hosting server space, and the source codes for the entire completed site.

RESERVATION OF RIGHTS: All rights not expressly granted hereunder are reserved to CML, including but not limited to all rights in sketches, comps, or other preliminary materials.

ADDITIONAL USAGE: If Client wishes to make any additional uses of the work, Client agrees to seek permission from CML and make such payments as are agreed to between the parties at that time.

PERMISSIONS AND RELEASES: The Client agrees to indemnify and hold harmless CML against any and all claims, costs, and expenses, including attorney's fees, due to materials included in the Work at the request of the Client for which no copyright permission or previous release was requested or uses which exceed the uses allowed pursuant to a permission or release.

EXCESSIVE CHANGES: Changes in client input or direction or excessive changes will be charged at $90 per hour.

ᴄynᴅᵄ://   102 Woodbury Rd., Edison, NJ 08820 | hello@cyndamedia.com | http://cyndamedia.com

C. J. Yeh's design firm is called Cynda Media Lab. This is one page from his company's "boilerplate" contract. Yeh states that Cynda makes minor adjustments for each client or project, but that the basic document covers "most of the things that we need."

Business Income and Expenses

3

☐ Taxpayer ☐ Spouse	Your Name		State		☐ NJ-SE/IC ☐ Y-203 ☐ NYC-202-UBT ☐ MTA LEAVE BLANK

A Business/ Professional Activity

B Business Code LEAVE BLANK

C Business Name

D Employer Identification No.

E Business Address ☐ SAME AS HOME

City   State   Zip

I Did you make any payments in 2012 that would require you to file 1099 forms? ☐ Yes* ☐ No *Did you/will you file the required 1099s? ☐ Yes ☐ No ☐ **Estimated**

H Is this the first year or final year of your business? ☐ YES ☐ NO If yes, starting date: / / 12 or ending date: / / 12 ☐ **Health Ins.**

PART I – GROSS INCOME FROM 1099-MISCs AND YOUR RECORDS

DO NOT INCLUDE INT. INCOME, OR W-2 AMOUNTS!	Amount Recvd by 12/31
1a. Total received with credit cards, PayPal 1099-K	
Total received with 1099-Misc	
1b. Other payments received without 1099-Misc	
6a. Reimburse. Exp. Income included above	(LEAVE BLANK)
6b. Reimburseable Expense Income not included	
6c. Sales Tax from Customers included above	(LEAVE BLANK)
6d. Sales Tax from Customers not included above	
Total	(LEAVE BLANK)

PART III - COST OF GOODS SOLD

COMPLETE ONLY IF YOU SELL MERCHANDISE OR HAVE HIGH DIRECT COSTS

35 Inventory at beginning of year	
36 Purchases	
37 Cost of labor	
38 Materials / supplies	
39 Other costs (Include sales tax paid directly to your state)	
Reimburseable Expenses	
41 Inventory at end of year	( )
42 Cost of Goods Sold	

PART II - BUSINESS EXPENSES

8 Advertising	
9 Car / Truck Expenses	(SEE OTHER SIDE)
10 Commissions / Agents Fees	
11 Contract Labor working on your premises (See note F other side)	
12 Depletion	
13 Depreciation + Equip. / Furn. (More than $500 each)	(SEE SECOND PAGE)
14 Employee Benefit	(LEAVE BLANK)
15 Business Insurance (Not Medical + Disability)	
16a Interest – (Mortgage on Business Property)	
16b Interest – Credit Card (Business Portion)	
17 Accounting / Paychex / BizPlan	
18 Office Expenses	
19 Pension / Profit Sharing (Only for Employees)	(LEAVE BLANK)
20a Rent – Auto / Machinery / Equipment	
20b Rent – Studio / Office (Not in Your Home)	
21 Repairs (Not to Your Home)	
22 Supplies	
23 NYC UBT Tax 2011 EXT UBT	
23 NYS MTA Tax 2011 EXT EST	
24a Travel / Lodging (Out of Town for Business)	
24b Meals / Entertainment (Enter 100%)	
25 Utilities / Phone (Not in Your Home) See back	
26 Wages (Only if you issued W-2)	(LEAVE BLANK)
27-01 Appliances / Small Tools	
-02 Bank Charges – (Business Portion Only)	

-03 Books / Publications	
-04 Business Gift / Gratuities (See note D other side)	
-05 Cell Phone (Business Portion Only)	
-06 Cleaning – Office / Studio (Not in Your Home)	
-07 Computer Supplies / Services / Software	
-08 Dues – Professional Associations	
-09 Exhibits/Trade Shows/Conventions/Museums	
-10 Freelancers (See note F other side)	
-11 Internet / Website	
-12 Job Site Catering	
-13 Local Transportation	
-14 Messengers / Postage / FedEx / UPS	
-15 Moving / Storage (Business Portion Only)	
-16 Parking and Tolls / Interest on Auto Loan	(SEE SECOND PAGE)
-17 Payroll Taxes	(LEAVE BLANK)
-18 Performing Artist's Expenses (attach list)	
-19 Photography / Labs / Props	
-20 Portfolio Expense	
-21 Printing / Copying	
-22 Professional Education / Seminars	
-23 Research / Reference Material	
-24 Equip. / Furn. (Less than $500 each)	
-25 Miscellaneous	
Other expenses, please attach list:	

©2013 JUDA KALLUS / MARY ANN NICHOLS   ☐ NO BACK

Total Expenses	COS	H/O	Net

Please Initial

Designer MaryAnn Nichols created this Business Income and Expenses *form with her husband, accountant Juda Kallus. The sheet is a fairly detailed list of items that can be deducted as business expenses, as well as "office-in-home" items on the second page. This sheet and the following forms, plus others, can be found at www.judakallus.com.*

TIME CARD	Client Consult	Travel	Supervision	Writing	Roughs	Comps/Layout	Production	Revisions	Illustration	Photo	File Transfer	Communications	Hours	
													Billable Hours	Non-Billable
Date 4/29/51														
Designer														
MAX														

Billable Hours	
Non-Billable Hours	
Total Hours	

You will find templates online (for instance, at www.judakallus.com). You can buy or download apps and/or software to automate any or all of your accounting responsibilities. But maybe you're a bit of a do-it-yourself designer. Regardless of origin, daily time cards, as suggested by the late Read Viemeister, can be an integral part of efficient record keeping. I mocked this one up in Adobe Illustrator.

For accounting purposes, record the job number plus activities and time spent. Transfer the time records to a master card for each job.

Career path	Description	Positive	Negative	Salary
Print Designer	Designs printed materials (i.e. brochures, books, magazines, signage, etc.)	• Work is pretty easy • Work has a defined deadline • Technology doesn't change much/fast	• Can get stale after doing it for years. • Late evenings and weekend due to pending deadlines	In Houston, most print designers peak around $65k/year
Web Designer	Designs web projects (i.e. web pages, email graphics, electronic newsletters and ads)	• Field is constantly changing, always something new and changing to learn or grow into. • Deadlines are incremental. Most web projects never completely die they turn into maintenance work or later updates.	• Things are constantly changing • Projects are generally longer and can seem to drag on forever when compared to print. • Have to test everything (different browsers, mobile devices, etc. technology can be frustrating)	In Houston web designers can make as much at 100k/year...maybe more if they are really good or share some skills from another titles like if they know a fair amount about web development and can do that too.
Web Developer	Not that different from the web designer. As anyone who has done a website knows, websites are part design and part development. The developer does the coding, scripting, programing...that most designers don't like to do or just cannot handle.	• Very similar to the web designer but I don't think it is as competitive as web design to get into.	• Much more technical... very left brain, but I know designer that can do it. • Very intense and tedious work. • Lots of testing and tweaking. • Technology and browsers are constantly changing and well as the coding.	Very much the same as web designers... can make quite a bit more if you are really good.
Animation or Multimedia	This is a very diverse field. You have pure animation, animation with interactivity and video and all of these are very specific and different. All are creative but each has there own set of tools and skills although there is some overlap	• Projects can be and tend to be very high end and very cool or high profile • Budgets can be small to extremely large depending on scope. • Type of work can vary dramatically from project to project.	• Very technical field (like web development) the difference is the software is more hardware intensive do to large files and heavy computer processing loads. • Projects can be very long term...months to years depending.	Salary depending on company and clients vary widely. It ranges from print designer salary to above web designer salary.
3D Modeling/ 3D Artist	The newest and probably fasting growing job in this field. Web design and developer might be close. This is becoming ever more present in today's world with movies and video games and corporations wanting to virtually show something without having to actually build it. Most of the time you are working on either a video, an application, or something that will eventually be printed or placed on the web.	• Very competitive • Fast moving • Constantly growing and changing. • Projects are or can be very cool. • This is an extremely technical field. • Software has probably the steepest learning curve of all.	• Has the longest work cycle of all. • Work can be tedious and difficult. • Deadlines due to hardware and software can be difficult and tight. • Software and hardware are expensive...much more so than any of the other software for the previously mentioned jobs.	This probably has the most potential for future money and job growth with Hollywood (entertainment) and the software industry driving most of that. This industry can be very small, depend ing on which direction you go. If you decide you want to go down this road pick your job market well, i.e. there aren't a lot of 3d modelers, animators or artists in the middle of nowhere most of them are around major cities.

© Ken Bullock 2014

Ken Bullock says your career path is paved both geographically and economically. Larger cities—like Bullock's Houston base—may offer freelance or full-time circumstances a more economically depressed location might not. His informative table addresses a number of career specifics and looks at some choices and their unique advantage/ disadvantages.

	Pro	Con
College or University, Vocational School	• "Classroom" model will be familiar to most students who came up through a public or private school system. • Professor/instructor is present to answer questions or offer help. • If professor/instructor is a working artist or designer, students will benefit from his/her experience. • Collaborative environment between students in classroom can enhance learning and understanding.	• Expensive. Depending on the tuition, R.O.I. could take decades. • Vocational school Usually issues a diploma. Lack of a degree could be a problem when applying for certain jobs such as corporate creative services department positions.
Internet College Degree Program	• Reduced expense • Collaboration between students can be achieved through online groups, forums or image-sharing sites.	• Professor/instructor only available by email. Getting questions answered can take time.
Art Guild Classes	• Some local art guilds offer non-college credit classes taught by local working artists and designers • Reduced expense • Professor/instructor is present to answer questions or offer help. • If professor/instructor is a working artist or designer, students will benefit from his/her experience.	• Lack of college credits or a degree could be a problem when applying for certain jobs such as corporate creative services department positions.
Self Study	• Reduced expense • Collaboration between students can be achieved through online groups, forums or image sharing sites. • Learning can be at student's own pace. • Lots of online learning resources and tutorials available online for free or minimal expense.	• Requires tremendous focus, discipline and dedication. • Few opportunities for many individuals to work on an assignment from the same brief and compare and crit results. • Lack of college credits or a degree could be a problem when applying for certain jobs such as corporate creative services department positions.

We cover different educational options in chapter 2. Here, Mark Hannon expands that dialogue to create this simple chart to help break down which options are a good fit for your circumstances. While everyone's situation is different, this easy pros and cons format offers a fruitful "at-a-glance" comparison to evaluate your apples and oranges.

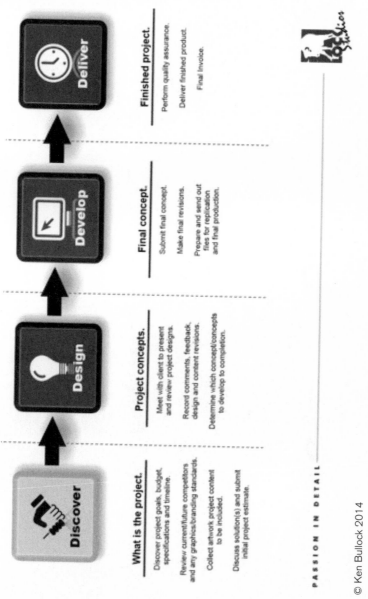

As Ken Bullock will tell you, some guidelines are good. Here are Bullock's four "D"s of design: discover, design, develop, and deliver. This is Bullock's design project overview; used to explain the process to clients "who usually don't get what we do or how we do it." It works for most any gig (high level or simplified) and provides an understanding of the usual steps involved in delivering a logo, brochure, website, animation, video—whatever Bullock is producing for that customer. ©Ken Bullock 2014

INDEX

Note: References to sidebars are in *italics*.

Books from Allworth Press

Allworth Press is an imprint of Skyhorse Publishing, Inc. Selected titles are listed below.

AIGA Professional Practices in Graphic Design
by Tad Crawford (6 x 9, 336 pages, paperback, $24.95)

The Art of Digital Branding, Revised Edition
by Ian Cocoran (6 x 9, 272 pages, paperback, $19.95)

Building Design Strategy
by Thomas Lockwood (6 x 9, 272 pages, paperback, $24.95)

Brand Thinking
by Debbie Millman (6 x 9, 320 pages, paperback, $19.95)

Business and Legal Forms for Graphic Designers, Fourth Edition
by Tad Crawford and Eva Doman Bruck (8 ½ x 11, 256 pages, paperback, $29.95)

Design Firms Open for Business
by Steven Heller and Lita Talarico (7 ⅜ x 9 ¼, 256 pages, paperback, $24.95)

Design Literacy, Third Edition
by Steven Heller (6 x 9, 304 pages, paperback, $22.50)

Design Thinking
by Thomas Lockwood (6 x 9, 304 pages, paperback, $24.95)

Designers Don't Have Influences
by Austin Howe (5 ½ x 8 ¼, 192 pages, paperback, $19.95)

The Elements of Graphic Design, Second Edition
by Alex W. White (8 x 10, 224 pages, paperback, $29.95)

Emotional Branding, Revised Edition
by Marc Gobé (6 x 9, 352 pages, paperback, $19.95)

Graphic Designer's Guide to Clients, Second Edition
by Ellen Shapiro (6 x 9, 256 pages, paperback, $19.95)

How to Think Like a Great Graphic Designer
by Debbie Millman (6 x 9, 248 pages, paperback, $24.95)

Starting Your Career as a Freelance Web Designer
by Neil Tortorella (6 x 9, 256 pages, paperback, $19.95)

To see our complete catalog or to order online, please visit *www.allworth.com*.